KILLING THE ELITES

KILLING THE ELITES

Haiti, 1964

JEAN-PHILIPPE BELLEAU

Columbia University Press

New York

Columbia University Press
Publishers Since 1893
New York   Chichester, West Sussex
cup.columbia.edu

Library of Congress Cataloging-in-Publication Data
Names: Belleau, Jean-Philippe, 1966– author.
Title: Killing the elites : Haiti, 1964 / Jean-Philippe Belleau.
Description: New York : Columbia University Press, [2024] | Includes bibliographical
    references and index. Identifiers: LCCN 2024006973 | ISBN 9780231213783 (hardback) |
    ISBN 9780231213790 (trade paperback) | ISBN 9780231560023 (ebook)
Subjects: LCSH: Jérémie Vespers Massacre, Jérémie, Haiti, 1964. |
    State-sponsored terrorism—Haiti—History—20th century. | Duvalier, François,
    1907–1971. | Political atrocities—Haiti—History—20th century. | Haiti—Politics and
    government—1971–1986. | Haiti—Social conditions—20th century. |
    Jérémie (Grand'Anse, Haiti)—History—20th century.
Classification: LCC F1928 .B45 2024 | DDC 972.9407/2—dc23/
eng/20240305 LC record available at https://lccn.loc.gov/2024006973
Cover design: Noah Arlow

To my mother Monique in memoriam

To my beloved father-in-law Nandalal Bhowmik, in memoriam

To my friend Kaka Iralu, 1956–2020, in memoriam

To Jean Reghem, 1926–1944, in memoriam

And to all the innocent victims of the Duvalier regime.

Contents

PART V: THE RELATIONAL DESPOT

Acknowledgements

I t is customary for ethnographers to start their books by thanking their interlocutors, since the latter are crucial to the gathering of information. It has of course been the case for this book; for reasons examined in the introduction, testimonies were essential to establish and verify events. However, as my research progressed, it became clear that my interlocutors were providing more than just information and hospitality. They resisted the role of interlocutor and its formality, and instead transformed a mere transactional relation with a stranger into a meaningful, permanent bond. The warmth and tolerance that my Jeremian interlocutors, particularly Eddy Cavé and Guiton Dorimain manifested toward my research and me quickly became an anthropological *question*. Their affection contradicted the violence I was trying to understand, and oriented my research toward sociality. As Claude Lévi-Strauss understood, anthropologists borrow their theories from the people they study. I am therefore grateful not just for the set of data my interlocutors provided, but also for helping me understand through their behavior the centrality of social bonds in all aspects of life in Haiti. These interlocutors are Eddy Cavé, Guiton Dorimain, Jean-Claude Fignolé[†], Alix Cédras, Roger Chassagne, and Jean-Claude "Tiga" Garoute[†], all Jeremians; and in Port-au-Prince, Jacmel, and Miami, they are Ralph Allen, Elliot Roy, Hervé Denis, and Frantz Desvarieux.

I could not have written this book without Devoir de Mémoire-Haïti, the organization dedicated to the memory of the victims of the Duvalier regime. I met its founders, Guylène Sales and Marguerite Clérié, for the first time in 2016 and have since communicated with them almost on a daily basis. They understood my project and I felt I understood them. To a large extent, I wrote this book for them. Their dignity and fortitude influenced my gaze the same way the abovementioned sociality did: by helping me to understand how people deal with oppression and trauma. Sadly, the way in which Devoir de Mémoire-Haïti has been treated by all governments, all presidents, the justice system, and some sectors of civil society since 1986 shows that Duvalierism and noirism are structural phenomena.

Many individuals contributed pointed, yet crucial knowledge and family archives that little by little brought to light the general picture of the events and its actors. Vincent Royan (Father Barthélémy Péron's grand-nephew), Michael Margolies (Jacques Wadestrandt's roommate at Harvard), Dominique Blain (Captain Kesner Blain's daughter), Hervé Denis (Lorimer Denis's nephew), Kenzo Jacques (Gracia Jacques's grandson), and Anariol (Jean Dimanche's cousin). Francis Charles, an officer in Duvalier's Presidential Guard; Daniel Supplice, a student of the Duvalier regime who possesses personal archives; and Fritz Cinéas, a member of Duvalier's inner circle generously shared knowledge and sometimes documents. Jean Alcide†, William Régala†, and Abel Jérôme accepted to testify about their respective roles in the Jérémie massacre. Four more interlocutors who wished to remain anonymous also provided key information.

Having the support, knowledge, networks, friendship, and sheer intelligence of Haiti's foremost sociologist, Michèle Oriol, my *soeur d'âme*, was an extraordinary asset and experience. Michèle helped me at every step of the research and of the writing. Often we agree on nothing, and yet she demonstrates a tolerance for intellectual disagreements that has become all too rare elsewhere. She opened doors, facilitated all types of connections, convinced inconvincible individuals to testify, and shared her unsurpassed knowledge of Haitian history. I am also grateful to all the friends, colleagues, and scholars who helped me in spite of the anarchy into which Port-au-Prince has fallen, a place where accomplishing basic professional tasks has become nearly impossible. I thank in particular my *compère* Rolphe Papillon. The extraordinary friendship of Joël, Love, and Joeden Lochard allowed me to access and navigate the most secluded social networks.

My fellow scholar and Haitianist Anne Fuller has been incredibly supportive. Her ongoing research and exemplary methods on the Thiotte massacre, where peasants and rural elites were massacred in June 1964, will further highlight the reality of the Duvalier regime. To have a fellow researcher working on mass violence by the same regime was a formidable asset.

Alex Dupuy, Robert Fatton, and Henry "Chip" Carey are probably unaware that their company, conversations, and mentoring at HSA (Haitian Studies

Association) conferences over the past two decades have been fundamental: I thank them here. I am also indebted to fellow scholars and friends for advice and comments: Silvia Montenegro, Leslie Péan, Serge Sabalat, Fidèle Ingiyimbere, Rodrigo Bulamah, Philippe-Richard Marius, Chelsea Stieber, Vlado Petrovic, Lorenzo Macagno, Omar Ribeiro, Marc Saint-Joie, Mario Ranaletti, Patrick Tardieu, Sinisa Malesevic, Ruhul Abid, Nir Eisikovitz, Julianne Prade-Weiss, João de Pina-Cabral, Leslie Manigat dagger symbol, Christian Gros, Thierry Pécout, Eric Gasparini, Marco Zappone, Carlos Guérard, Sebastião Nascimento, Béatrice Collosio and Daniel Soupper, and Jean-Pierre Bartoli. I thank Christian Winting and Marcella Munson for their judicious comments. I am particularly grateful to Marie-France Forbin, Alix Cédras, and the Genealogical Association of Haiti. Chiara Torrini, John Steinberg, and the Fiske Center realized the map of the massacre: I thank them here. My former deans, David Terkla[†] and Emily McDermott, gave me the academic support I needed to write this book: I am immensely grateful to them.

Finally, the idea for this book came from Jean-Claude Fignolé. Although I do not remember when we first met, I started to gather notes from him on the massacre by the early 2000s as we developed a father-son relationship. After the 2010 earthquake, his publications and manuscripts were transferred to my home institution, UMass Boston, which created the Fignolé Library. I explain his crucial contribution in the book's introduction.

As do most people who write on violence, I felt an obligation to the victims—a mandate that grew stronger as I noted the endemic victim-blaming. I started this book when my daughter was the same age as Marie-Catherine Sansaricq, and finished it when she was Lyssa Villedrouin's age. The Jérémie massacre had become such an obsession that when I closed my eyes, it was not the image of my children that I saw but that of the Sansaricq children as they appear in the sole picture that remain of them, together with their mother Graziela. This book is for them.

Victims and Local Protagonists

THE VICTIMS

AUGUST 11

1. Louis Drouin, baker
2. Guy Villedrouin, bank director
3. Roseline Villedrouin, née Drouin (Guy's wife and Louis's daughter)
4. Gérard Guilbaud, shop owner
5. Alice Guilbaud, née Drouin (Gérard's wife), cashier
6. Victor Villedrouin, (trading house supervisor)
7. Guy Drouin (son of Louis and Louise Drouin), photographer

SEPTEMBER 19

8. Adeline Villedrouin (Victor's wife), librarian; and their children:
9. Lyssa Villedrouin, 17
10. Frantz Villedrouin, 15
11. Louise Sansaricq, née Laforest (Pierre's wife); and six of her children:
12. Fred Sansaricq, 23 or 24
13. Pierre-Richard Sansaricq, 19
14. Hubert Sansaricq, 18
15. Reynold Sansaricq, 13
16. Marie-Catherine Sansaricq, 11
17. Jean-Claude Sansaricq, 32, shopkeeper (son of Pierre and Louise Sansaricq).

18. Graziela Sansaricq, née Sansaricq, 28 (Jean-Claude's wife); and their children:
19. Jean-Pierre Sansaricq, 6
20. Stéphane, 4
21. Régine, 2
22. Edith Laforest (Louise Sansaricq's sister), store owner
23. Lily Sansaricq (Pierre Sansaricq's sister).

SEPTEMBER 25

24. Pierre Sansaricq, 61, shop and gas station owner (Louise's husband)

OCTOBER 16

25. Louise Drouin, née Degraff (Louis Drouin's wife)
26. Corinne Villedrouin, née Sansaricq, 83 (Guy and Victor's mother); and her daughter:
27. Fernande Villedrouin (mentally handicapped)

MILITARY OFFICERS

Second Lieutenant Abel Jérôme, '59—Jérémie's military commander
Second Lieutenant Jean Dimanche, '59—firing squad leader
Lieutenant Colonel Jean-Baptiste Hilaire '54—member of the Presidential Commission
Major Mercius Rivière, '54—member of the Presidential Commission
Major René Prosper, '56—member of the Presidential Commission

JÉRÉMIE'S DUVALIERIST PATRICIANS

François Cajoux—prefect; public notary
Raoul Cédras—mayor; store owner

Louinès Degraff—Member of Parliament (Jérémie)

Antoine Jean Charles—Commissaire du gouvernement; hardliner; anti-mulatto

Joseph René—deputy to Commissaire du gouvernement

Saintange Bontemps—surveyor; college graduate; Member of Parliament (Tiburon)

Dalvanor Etienne—Member of Parliament (Roseaux)

André Jabouin—executive at Water Department

Willy Verrier—doctor; director of the local hospital

DUVALIERISTS (NON-VSN, NON PATRICIAN)

Gérard Léonidas—hospital administrator

Antoine Apollon—cabinetmaker; head of state tobacco agency in Jérémie

Jean Alcide—teacher at a vocational school

Lunford Joseph—teacher

Antoine Désyr—customs clerk

VSNS IN JÉRÉMIE

Luc Desroche—vocational school teacher

Villefranche "Bido" Desroche—teacher, scout chief who later worked for the regime in Port-au-Prince

Sanette Balmir—small business owner; direct relation of Duvalier's

Robert Nauze—mayor of small commune

Antoine Désir—customs clerk

Luc Jeune (Jr.)—clerk at the Ministry of Agriculture; amateur photographer

Lucien Jeune (Sr.)—government clerk

Fritz Balmir—Member of Parliament

Kersuzan Bélizaire—shoemaker

Mérès Bélizaire—shoemaker

Willy Bourdeau—suspected of arson at Jérémie's high school in 1957

Max Frédérique—driver, Ministry of Public Works; anti-mulatto

Tony Frédérique—driver; present at Numéro 2 on August 11

Marcel Myrtil—unknown; semiliterate

Gérard Brunache—post office clerk; amateur musician and perfume-maker

Séraphin Rémy—plumber, Water Department

Massillon Thélus—small shop owner; nickname "*La pouvoir*" (*sic*); semiliterate

Choby—Performed odd jobs; musician during carnival

Magesse—Performed odd jobs; semiliterate

Benoît Gély—Performed odd jobs; semiliterate

Thiafisgirl—Performed odd jobs; semiliterate

KILLING THE ELITES

MAP OF JEREMIE IN 1964

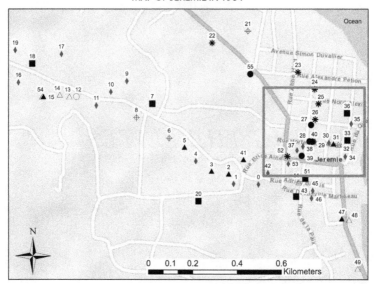

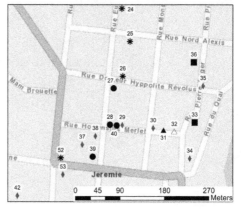

Legend

Houses

- ♦ Neighbors and Sites
- ○ Duvalierist Hardliner
- ● Duvalierists Neighbors
- ■ Government Officials (Duvalierists)
- ⊕ Military
- ✳ VSN
- ▲ Victim
- △ Arrested but not killed

1. Nicole Stoodley
2. Col. Roger Villedrouin
3. Victor & Adeline Villedrouin
4. Roger Chassagne
5. Gérard & Aline Guilbaud
6. Abel Jérôme (rented)
7. Elie Legagneur
8. Kesnér Blain, rented in 1957 (rented)
9. Michel Desquiron, writer
10. Carl Nicolas
11. Judge Roger Hilaire
12. Villefranche "Bido" Desroches (rented)
13. George Jérôme
14. Alain Rocourt
15. Fred Sansaricq & Mona Ambroise
16. Antoine Roumer
17. Gal. Lavaud (ex-president, in exile)
18. Raoul Cédras
19. Fritz Allen
20. Antoine Jean-Charles

21. Military Base
22. Luc Desroches
23. Sanette Balmir
24. Gérard Brunache
25. Antoine Désir
26. Max Frédérique
27. Jean Alcide
28. Gérard Léonidas
29. Sansaricq store
30. Zette Vincent
31. Pierre Sansaricq & family
32. Frantz Perrault
33. Dalvanor Etienne
34. Simerine Ogé
35. Prison
36. Lunès Degraff
37. Saint-Louis Cathedral (ex-church)
38. Gérard Guilbaud's general
    store, Guy Drouin's studio
39. Louis Jabouin

40. Willy Verrier
41. Brière house
42. Emile Roumer, writer
43. Joseph René
44. Ary Balmir
45. Eddy Cavé
46. Excelsior & City Hall
47. Louis & Louise Drouin
48. Sicot Gardère
49. Numa house
50. Marcel Myrtil
51. François Cajoux
52. "Fort Réfléchi"
53. Guiton Dorimain
54. Mona Ambroise (15)
55. Antoine Apollon

Introduction

On September 28, 1964, at noon, the United States Embassy in Port-au-Prince sent a cable marked "urgent" to the State Department in Washington:

Reports circulating widely [of] arrest and execution of Sansaricq family in Jérémie plus other mulattoes there, including Mrs. Victor Villedrouin and her two daughters . . . persistence of reports [of] widespread arrests in Jérémie indicate new waves of reprisals against mulattoes there has probably occurred.[1]

This document is the oldest primary source available on a massacre that occurred in slow motion from August to October 1964 in Jérémie, a coastal town in southwestern Haiti. The cable's language betrays the difficulties the embassy staff experienced in sorting out rumors from facts, yet it correctly identifies previous violence: there had been an earlier wave of executions. This was the second wave; there would be two more later. The diplomatic cable also stated the victims' racial identity—"mulatto," a term its author, Ambassador Benson E. L. Timmons, had avoided in his communications since he had assumed his post in 1963. Over the course of the following year, the François "Papa Doc" Duvalier regime (1957–1971) would increasingly target this sector of the population, and Timmons understood that reality. Finally, that Timmons found it important to let the State Department know about the death of these particular families (Sansaricq and Villedrouin), taking care to spell out their names, indicates their social status. In earlier communications about repression, the embassy provided such details only when victims were socially important.

These four waves of execution did not receive the unifying and apocryphal name of "Jérémie Vespers" (*Vêpres de Jérémie*), as the massacre is known in oral history today, until much later. The first wave occurred on August 11 when seven civilians, including two couples from the same family, were executed in the context of a small, isolated, ill-fated insurgency known as Jeune Haïti. The second took place on September 19, weeks after this insurgency had been defeated. Sixteen people were killed on that day, eight of whom were children. The family patriarch, Pierre Sansaricq, was executed alone on September 25. Finally, on October 16, three older women were slaughtered. All twenty-seven victims were from the town's upper class and from three of its oldest families, one of which (Sansaricq), was allegedly the richest.[2] Each time, the victims were arrested at night in their homes, taken to a remote landing strip, and led into a ditch about six feet deep. The soldiers shot them from above and at point-blank range. It was the first time since 1812 in Haiti that entire families were executed in cold blood by soldiers following a methodical process that started with a presidential order. This was a state crime. Yet this is not how the event has been represented in historiography and much of oral history.

In the literature, this massacre is known, yet remains shrouded in mystery. At least twenty books describe or mention it, although typically in no more than a few lines.[3] A memorial to the victims was built on the execution ground in 1986 and restored in 2016. Questions about the identity of perpetrators and causality remain largely unanswered. The unintelligibility of the last three waves of executions, not to mention their pitilessness, inspired apocryphal explanations that attempt to rationalize a massacre that seems without motive. Legends and rumors have framed this mass killing as an act of popular violence, eviscerating from it the role played by the country's ruler and the military. It became what mass violence scholars today call a "massacre of neighbors."[4]

The poor, entirely absent from the Jérémie massacre, ended up at the center of its apocryphal narrative. In this version, victims were killed (1) in spectacular fashion (2) by a mob. As the first published accounts on the massacre stated, "Men, women, and children were tortured and executed, their homes looted and burned. Estimates placed the victims at more than one hundred. . . . The Sansaricq, a mulatto family is paraded naked through the streets, triggering the laughter of the Duvalierist mob. . . . The children are then killed with knifes in their mothers' arms, then the adults are executed."[5] In another account, "in one single night, about eighty people were slaughtered, among whom the Drouin and Ville-drouin families."[6] A thirty-two-page pamphlet on the massacre authored by a Jérémie native mentioned rapes and torture and vehemently placed the blame on the local population, including a priest, the militia, and other townspeople for their role in the tragedy.[7] For Robert and Nancy Heinl, "Duvalier simply gave *mulâtre* Jérémie to the *noir Milice*. Whole families were slaughtered—Villedrouins, Drouins, Guilbauds, Laforests, Sansaricqs, and others. The Drouin and Sansaricq families were stripped naked and herded through the town to execution. . . . At least a hundred prominent Jeremians died," adding that children were sadisti-cally tortured by National Security Volunteers (Volontaires de la Sécurité Natio-nale or VSN).[8]

While these alleged atrocities committed by locals had found their way into mainstream historiography, much of the event's oral history is similarly framed by a narrative of social revenge, as exemplified by historian Daniel Supplice's candid statement that the Jérémie Vespers were "an anti-apartheid movement."[9] This "massacre of neighbors" narrative consists of two interdependent parts: (1) the local population and not just the VSN perpetrated the massacre; and (2) these locals acted out of social revenge, triggered by the victims' personalities and behavior. The level of atrocities was commensurate with, and proof of, the population's ire; violence received became evidence of culpability.

As an epistemological hopeful, my goal throughout the research that preceded the writing of this book was to reconstitute what actually took place. Memories, their problematic use, their editorial industry, and postmodern truth-relativism all have their merits. Yet, to understand a massacre, one has to first posit that mass murder is not a social construction and can therefore be reconstituted. I am not refuting advances made in historical studies since the 1960s, or by Edward Carr on subjectivity in historiographic writing; but before having the luxury of relativizing historical truth, it is worth figuring out what actually happened during the Duvalier regime. The scarcity of primary sources does not change that. It is crucial to deconstruct the narratives, put aside sensationalist accounts, and question the widespread victim-blaming before reconstructing the course of events and identifying responsibilities. As such, the ethnographic research for this book was daunting work: it required finding credible witnesses, sorting out rumors from facts, and breaking down the event day by day, sometimes hour by hour. When information was uncertain, when responsibilities could not be verified, when the sequence of events was unclear, I say so. The results of this research are, in many ways, less voyeuristic but more terrifying than intimate mass violence.

Over the past three decades, the analytical study of genocides, massacres, and ethnic cleansing has drawn from disciplines in the social sciences and the humanities, with anthropology being a relative latecomer.[10] *Killing the Elites* focuses on three aspects of mass violence that have been overlooked: (1) the victimization of the elite; (2) the role of social ties in determining behaviors and decisions within, against, and outside of the repressive state; and (3) why some regimes choose to target entire families rather than specific individuals. It also examines the functioning of an idiosyncratic, sociocentric authoritarianism. For each of these threads, the book moves back and forth between the Duvalier regime and episodes of mass violence in other spaces and times, engaging in what Marshall Sahlins, via Frazer, wittingly called "uncontrolled comparison[s]".[11] Through this movement, the book offers examples to refine explanations of a particular aspect of repression or point at larger phenomena beyond Haiti.[12] Briefly comparing, say, the targeting of kin in Haiti under Duvalier to the Great Terror in the Soviet Union does not infer similarities between Haiti and Russia, but attempts to refine explanations of a particular aspect of repression or to point to larger phenomena that are not limited to Haiti.

Anti-elite violence is hardly unique to Haiti. To a large extent, elites have been the main victims of genocides, massacres, and ethnic cleansing in the twentieth century. The largest episodes of mass violence of the past century, including the so-called "canon" of mass violence (the Holocaust; and the Armenian, Cambodian, and Rwandan genocides) all had a strong anti-elite dimension. During these events, all of the targeted social sectors were, without exception, constructed as society's elite or as an elite.[13] The same is true of the Holodomor in the Ukraine (1932–1933); the Anti-Rightist Campaign and the Cultural Revolution in Mao's China, which may have caused over thirty million deaths; the mass executions of Katyn (1941); the execution of the Bengali elite during the Bangladesh genocide (1971); the killings of Americo-Liberians in the 1980s; the Hamidian massacres (1894–1897); and the urban victims during genocides in the former Yugoslavia, events for which the term "eliticide" was coined.[14]

In all these instances, writers, doctors, lawyers, university professors, journalists, businesspeople, traders, store owners, former government officials, military officers, prominent patricians, and religious leaders took on the form of the enemy. Sometimes, the targeted groups had none of these socioeconomic profiles but were nonetheless constructed as powerful and as elite by the perpetrating regime, as during the mass famines in the Ukraine and China. The notion of "class enemies," used by communist regimes, epitomizes elite stigmatization.[15] Elite sectors under various names (aristocracy, bourgeoisie, class enemies, and so forth) could suddenly fall victim to ideologies and events and be obliterated from their country's history.[16]

Two other dimensions of anti-elite violence in Haiti call for comparisons. The first is the centrality of the state. Elites in Haiti were never killed by an angry mob of disenfranchised civilians but always by the state—that is, by *other* elites. Anti-elite mass violence, as with any genocide or ethnic cleansing, is a state crime and therefore, above all, a political fact whose decision makers and executioners are located within the state's repression apparatus. The second is the othering of the dominant class as foreign and illegitimate members of the nation. Such was the case in Haiti, where the victimized elite were often constructed as an antagonist ethnic group, an "Other," or foreign in origin.[17]

What may be unique to Haiti however, is the recurrent, almost persistent character of such political violence. In 1812, 1848, 1869, 1882, 1883, 1908, 1915, and throughout the Duvalier regime, entire sectors of the social, intellectual, and economic elite were decimated. Three times in Haitian history, the most celebrated writer of the era was arrested and executed by government soldiers. In 1848, hundreds, possibly even thousands of men of the social elite of the capital and several southern towns were executed. In 1883, the capital's merchant class was destroyed. In 1915, hundreds of young men from the urban elites and middle classes were executed in a few hours. In Jérémie alone, city leaders were arrested and executed in 1848, 1867, 1884, and 1911. The fate of one elite family exemplifies this repetition: Louise and Edith Laforest, two of the victims of the 1964 Jérémie massacre, were the granddaughters of Pétion Laforest who was executed under President Salomon in 1884. They were also relatives of Andrée Roumer whose husband, the internationally renowned novelist Jacques-Stephen Alexis (1922–1961), was tortured to death in 1961 under Duvalier. Alexis's own grandfather, Mesmin Alexis (1820–1882), a senator, had been executed in 1882; and his great-grandfather, Jean-Jacques Dessalines, the founder of the Haitian Republic, had been assassinated in 1806. Louise Laforest's eight children would be executed during the Duvalier regime.

This pattern of political violence against the country's elite over the *longue durée* is paradoxically both widely documented and strangely overlooked—the historiography has recorded the facts, but scholars have not drawn conclusions. These killings are overlooked not because the elite are socially invisible but because they are too visible, their victimization in dissonance with their dominant position. An anti-elite bias among progressive scholars might not be the main cause. A dominant focus on ethnic and ethnoreligious identities and differences, as Dirk Moses has pointed out, frames the scholarly gaze.[18] There is no entry for the elite in our contemporary taxonomies of victimization.

Social ties and repression form the book's second thread, with three areas of focus: social ties between perpetrators and victims, among regime members, and within society at large. Co-optation of regime members, including the recruitment of henchmen by Duvalier, almost always followed webs of close personal relationships and kinship ties rather than ideological conformity, merit, or other considerations. Rather than contributing to or contradicting the political science literature on regime classifications, I have stayed within anthropology's boundaries. I have done so because the cultural coordinates that framed behaviors were not restricted to the regime itself: the intertwining of ties and repression betray a sociocentric logic that permeated all aspects of social life, not just the regime's modus operandi. The identification of targets by regime members (or, often, by Duvalier himself) was also sociocentric, as it followed webs of interpersonal relationships. It is impossible to understand how the Duvalier regime functioned, whom it targeted, and whom it spared without considering social ties—within the regime, between regime members and regular citizens, and within the rest of the population. Relationships, rather than institutional functions or ideological concordance, framed behaviors.

Over the past two decades, a growing literature has focused on "neighbors killing neighbors," particularly on high-profile historical events including pogroms in the European borderlands during WWII, genocides in Rwanda and in the former Yugoslavia, and the 1572 Saint Bartholomew's Day massacre. This body of scholarship has coined such concepts as "intimate mass violence" and "massacres of neighbors."[19] This "neighborly turn" in mass violence studies contends that social ties across antagonist communities break down under pressure and neighbors can turn into perpetrators. This historiography has undoubtedly increased our understanding of mass violence at the microlevel. However, in continuation with the groundwork laid by two recent research pieces, I will argue against its use here.[20]

The arch-dominant pattern is that social bonds did not rupture during the Duvalier regime. Hanna Arendt famously argued that, to obtain obedience, totalitarianism relies on the *atomization* of the social body; it must break social ties and social institutions. Once isolated, she believed, individuals can no longer offer resistance and fall into obedience.[21] There was no social atomization in the Caribbean island. Neighbors, relatives, friends, colleagues, and acquaintances of victims may have been subdued and turned into paralyzed bystanders, but almost never into accomplices, and even more rarely into perpetrators. I did not find a single documented instance where ordinary people violated social bonds to actively assist the regime in its repressive endeavors. In Jérémie, even individuals with strong sentiments against the town's upper class avoided becoming perpetrators—bystanders, yes; accomplices, never. Rather, evasion characterized behaviors during the Duvalier regime.

There are of course many reasons why individuals avoid harming people in the context of extreme political tensions. Values, morality, and ethical consciousness are the most obvious. I argue here that aversion to harm was also triggered by preexisting social ties even when these inhibitions contradicted group loyalty (Duvalierism), ideology (resentment against the elite), or institutional functions. I call this phenomenon *relational exceptionalism*.[22]

During the Duvalier regime, most individuals avoided being implicated in harming people with whom they shared bonds. This was true for civilians in general, followers of the regime, even members of the military. Social bonds have properties, one of which is to produce inhibitions against harming a party to the relationship, including in violent liminality. Unbridled political violence among neighbors, as in the abovementioned instances of genocides and massacres, typically concerned neighbors from antagonist ethnic groups between whom social ties were weak, fraught, or altogether absent.[23] In Jérémie, a small town of less than 5,000 people *intramuros*, nearness was conducive to a thick social fabric which cohabited with, yet contradicted the socioeconomic hierarchy.

Yet, nearness also unveiled one's socioeconomic conditions, wealth, tastes, political affiliations, and personal and family history. Social ties between people of different social, racial, and political sectors produced contradictory sentiments such as cooperation and envy, amity and resentment; it also triggered, at the moment of truth, powerful ethical inhibitions. Contrary to the image "that presents Haiti as a peculiar site of grotesque cruelty in the Americas," as J. Michael Dash put it, the resilience of the social fabric most likely limited the regime's repression.[24] Duvalier was cognizant of this phenomenon and had to rely on two dozen henchmen he had a dyadic relationship with rather than on institutions, as chapters 10 and 11 show; these henchmen were responsible for the killing of a majority of the regime's victims. Killing great numbers of people requires large numbers of people willing to kill. This did not happen in Haiti.

A major motivator of mass violence examined in this book concerns the intellectual edifice behind it. Ideas and representations, often referred to as "ideologies of hatred," may not be the only motivators of perpetrators and regime members, but they certainly constitute an indispensable one, as Jacques Sémelin and Siniša Malešević have argued.[25] Later on in this introduction I will further develop what this ideology entailed in the particular case of the Duvalier regime—"noirisme." But one finding can be noticed across different ideologies of hatred: the attribution of hatred to the victims.

It may sound contradictory that haters attribute hatred, but for a group to be stigmatized, the anti-value of the moment must be attributed to them—it is an essential piece of their demonization. As examined in chapters 2 and 8, if violence poses as counterviolence as a means of self-legitimization, the perpetrators unconsciously conceive hatred as counterhatred. For anti-elite violence to be framed as social revenge and retribution for prior harm, elites must not only first be diagnosed as the source of society's ills, but must also be seen through psychological portrayal as conceited and superior. This combination of sociology and psychology is perhaps what differentiates recent ideologies of hatred from earlier ones—a sense of illegitimacy or the pressure to be more scientific. To a large extent, with modernity, ideologies of hatred have become more academic. The fact that anti-elite violence is typically implemented coldly by the state rather than by an uncontrollable mob of *misérables* à la Gustave Le Bon gives the lie to social revenge and socioeconomic deterministic explanations.[26] The notion that violence is predetermined by larger social forces overlooks individual agencies and exculpates the government that made the choices and the military that pulled the trigger.

The targeting of entire families for the alleged crime of one of their members is another pattern found across space and time, from Stalinist Russia to ancient Greece to China's Cultural Revolution, to Haiti under Duvalier. This book articulates *mutuality of guilt* as the increase in scale of guilt through a logic of kinship. In the twentieth century it has been an antithetical mix of modernity and reaction, the reproduction of traditional family ideology by states that professed the most progressive agendas. Although well-known, this phenomenon has seldom been studied in a comparative fashion. Yet its manifestation in states without shared political ideology calls for an exploration of such similarities. The practice of punishing kin relies on a non-individual conception of the person, one that coincides with a group, usually defined through kinship. Kinship provides such perpetrators with a grammar to understand the scale of the enemy.

"YOU MADE US COME HERE FOR TWENTY-SEVEN PEOPLE?"

I often felt the need to apologize twice over to my fellow scholars for this research. First, for the number of victims. A few years ago, during the first talk I gave on the Jérémie massacre at the National Museum of Rio de Janeiro, an anthropologist and former professor of mine whom I admired interrupted me after a few minutes with a perplexed expression: "You made us come here for twenty-seven people?" As I mumbled to justify my presence, I had to recognize that, by twentieth-century standards of mass violence, twenty-seven was perhaps not a number capable of striking horror and reflection. There is little doubt that the academic mind of today is haunted by the specter of genocide. Massacres too small in scale stand in a scholarly no man's land, with little theoretical framework to borrow from, not to mention a lower trigger for indignation.[27] Of course, the historical significance of a violent event is not necessarily commensurate with the number of victims—the 1770 "Boston Massacre" had three immediate victims. The significance of the Jérémie massacre is not found in the number of its victims, nor does this number explain its haunting presence in Haitian memory. Nor is it my intention to compare "genocides" and "massacres" or to propose a theoretical framework for the study of massacres. However, a heuristic of massacres can only benefit from the larger corpus of genocide studies. What justifies the borrowing of key notions and cases from genocide studies throughout this book is that both massacres and genocides depend on three central elements: (1) the key role of ideologies, beliefs and representations in constructing a social sector as the enemy; (2) a chain of events that precipitate the killings and turn killings into a political solution, a notion developed by Christopher Browning; (3) the role of key individuals who orient actions and reactions toward repression and mass murder.[28]

The second source of discomfort among fellow scholars concerned the victims' backgrounds. Positing the elite as victims, I was warned, would be the kiss of death. Elites are often, if not systematically, blamed for oppression, exploitation, and inequalities—and all the more so in a country ravaged by poverty. I heard "they deserve it" more than once. How, then, can one write about the victimization of people often suspected of being victimizers themselves? How does one write critically of anti-elite sentiments and violence in a country plagued by exclusion and injustice?

There is no recipe for walking on eggshells, although our unrestricted scope of inquiry should allow us to reify the eggs. Anti-elite violence is indeed hard to posit as a social fact and an object of study: the sector that was racialized, essentialized, and victimized was not an impoverished and discriminated minority, but instead a privileged one. And yet, deterministic explanations of violence (such as the idea that physical violence is determined by culture, race, identity, or socioeconomic positions), notions that symbolic violence could compare with physical violence, and the view that political violence is social justice all work to shift the scholarly focus of causality back onto the victim if the latter is elite. In other contexts, this would be called "victim-blaming."

In the post-facto narrative of the Jérémie massacre, political oppression and economic exploitation by insufferable elites supposedly drove their neighbors to commit murder or approve of it. While no serious student of anti-Semitism would focus on Jews as an epistemology, explanations for anti-mulatto violence are fixated on mulattoes. Anti-elite violence does not trigger visceral moral reaction because, before considering the actuality of physical violence, we almost instinctively look at the victims' socioeconomic identity and privileges. Scholars' moral anxiety about relating elites to victimhood may also suggest something about the ideologies that target elites in the first place. The apocryphal transformation of a state crime into an act of popular violence, and the brushing-off of the kind of empirical details that relativize socioeconomic determinism, required a set of ideas and representations that motivated the regime in the first place and later provided intellectuals with a set of causalities.

Why talk about a "massacre of elites" and not a "massacre of mulattoes"?[29] First, the Duvalier regime victimized elites regardless of their supposed racial identity. Lawyers, scholars, doctors, writers, teachers, businessmen, sport stars, journalists, and military officers were killed regardless of their phenotype and complexion. Second, in the regime's mind, "elite" and "mulatto" identities were to a large extent coterminous and conspired to create a third one: opponents. Yet at the same time, ideas constructing the "mulatto" elite as illegitimate were framed by socioeconomic notions, and more precisely by egalitarian values, not just racialist views. Anti-elite language is egalitarian. It is ontologically, normatively, consciously egalitarian; it is egalitarian in ideology, in values, in taking hierarchy as illegitimate and racial hierarchy as absolutely illegitimate. Anti-elite hatred and violence are fundamentally triggered by egalitarian ideas and representations. The fundamental intellectual error would, then, be to assume that one condemns equality because they point at the crimes committed in its name.

To a large extent, the "elite" has been an almost emic category in Haiti's intellectual production, and probably as essentialized as "mulattoes," since the nineteenth century. Here I will make the same distinction that Manuela Carneiro da Cunha made between culture and "culture": the former is within the scholars' realm, the latter within the public's after a semantic spin-off. In the case under study, the elite concept does not explain as much as its semantic spin-off "elite." "Elite" corresponds, I believe, to the definition or perception used by much of the literature examined in this book, first among them noirist intellectuals. I define "elite" as people who are perceived to avoid intimacy with "non-elites."

This rather Maussian definition does not follow traditional socioeconomic-centered ascriptions. It is nonetheless justified by the local conditions. In Jérémie's relational world (and this is likely true for Haiti as a whole at that time as well), where hierarchy and sociality cohabited, where the elite's lifestyle could not be concealed, some type of sociality was expected of people from different social sectors. When it was denied, powerful sentiments of victimization and injustice ensued. "Denied intimacy," a key concept of this book, is a trigger of resentment and violence, yet only in social settings where people of varied socioeconomic backgrounds and symbolic capitals live side by side, certainly not in apartheid-like societies as a certain historiography would have it. As chapters 5 and 6 explain, denied intimacy (or the perception thereof) is a better predictor of resentment and even hatred than the absence of any intimacy in the first place.

"Elite" is also an acid bath of sociological undifferentiation that dissolves subtler contents. I define elites (without quotations) in the most heuristic manner as the highest segment of a specific hierarchy with relative and moving borders; and without ascribing any qualities, moral or otherwise, to its members.

Philippe-Richard Marius relies on a more neutral vocabulary: "formation" rather than "class" or "race"; "privileged" rather than "elite."[30] I will seldom use the vast sociological literature on the elite. Since Pareto, Ortega y Gasset, and Mosca, the elite has typically referred to a minority that holds power and exercises it over a majority: if "elites" are killed by the state, then the mulatto elite hardly fits that definition.[31] Yet, again, the subject is not the elite but the violence against it. When comparing Duvalier's Haiti with other instances of mass violence where elites were targeted, elite is not used as a meta-identity but as an umbrella term that covers various appellations such as bourgeoisie, aristocracy, class enemies, the upper class, etc.

I mean to clarify the use of racial categories for a non-Haitian audience. The families killed in 1964 were identified in racial terms, and this was one of the main reasons for their executions. By "mulatto" and "Black," I simply mean people who are, or were, identified as such. The book does not address the question "what is a mulatto?" but rather "what did the regime believe about and project via the term mulatto?" This book is therefore not about race or the "color" question in Haiti, and its economy does not rely on any epistemic solution to this question. These subjects, as well as the combination of race and class for quotidian cognitive classifications, have been amply treated elsewhere.[32]

We must also assert the obvious: "mulatto," as with any racial category, is a notion with no anthropological or sociological merit. Neither race nor any other identity for that matter predicts or explains behavior, and for that reason I chose (contrary to the unfortunate habit of a small part of the historiography) not to add a racial label to each subject identified by name in this book. Racial identities will be mentioned only insofar as they indicate how subjects were *seen*, not how they *acted*. Rather, as many Haitian authors have argued against a persistent background of racial essentializations, class trumps race.[33] I also endorse in its entirety Philippe Marius's groundbreaking anthropology of the upper classes in Haiti, which demonstrates that "it is class, and not color or race, that primarily produces distinctive Haitian socioeconomic formations."[34]

NOIRISM

The intellectual context of the events analyzed in this book was dominated by an inchoate ideology and set of representations: *noirism*.[35] Its epistemic presence precedes its neologization in the mid-twentieth century—Robert Fatton uses the term for the entirety of Haiti's postcolonial history.[36] In the context of the U.S. occupation (1915–1934), noirism, at first glance, argued for the rediscovery of Haiti's African roots, advancement of the culture of the masses, and control of the presidency. To a large extent, noirism hopped onto a larger, humanist bandwagon that included other intellectual and cultural movements—that it would, in the end, annihilate. Noirism was also, if not mainly, a political ideology that inferred a classification system indexed on skin complexion and class. The "mulatto," not the whites, gave noirism its sui generis character. Half-baked, *bricolée*, and maybe even half-sincere, noirism constructed "mulattoes" as illegitimate members of the nation. This double delegitimization (race and class) is characteristic of genocidal ideologies, as Ben Kiernan has shown, and as I further explore in chapters 2 and 3.[37]

Noirism intensified a long literary stigmatization of "mulattoes," as Marlene Daut shows.[38] In the tradition of Foucault, Daut's scholarship on the archaeology of literary representations of "mulattoes" highlights the resilience of a fossilized construct that cannot not hide its entirely subjective basis. The construction of the "mulatto" as a social problem and a figure located outside of Haitian-ness significantly hardened with Louis Joseph Janvier, a nineteenth-century intellectual who articulated a racialized definition of national identity based on exclusion. Then, in the twentieth century, noiriste literature dipped in and weaponized biology, sociology, and history to construct the "mulatto" as the figure of the enemy. Framed as the biological and cultural child of the slave owner, uprooted and anti-Black, the "mulatto" is not Haitian. Noirism would become state ideology under Duvalier, with devastating consequences. What made it powerful, as Péan noticed, was noirisme's "corruption of language."[39]

Prominent Haitian intellectuals were lucid about it. A dejected Jean Price-Mars (1876–1969), arguably Haiti's most important twentieth-century intellectual, called noiristes "upturned racists" (*racistes à rebours*).[40] For René Depestre, noirisme's belief in the racial division of humanity could only lead to political catastrophe.[41] The famed Senegalese poet Léopold Cédar Senghor, who had once seen in Duvalier a hope for negritude, bluntly called noirisme "racism."[42] Leslie Péan compared it to Nazism,[43] an analogy also made by historian Dantès Bellegarde.[44] Communist intellectuals anticipated what noirisme had in stock for them: Léon Laleau (1892–1979) famously called it "reverse gobinism" (*gobinisme à rebours*) while Gérard Pierre-Charles derided noirisme's belief in biological determinism.[45] Many communists, starting with Jacques Roumain, the founder of the first Haitian communist party, were mulattoes. To a large extent, communism was mulattoes' response to noirisme, a doubling-down on Haitian-ness and on sympathy for the masses.[46]

THE DUVALIER REGIME

The lack of available archives from the regime has limited the development of a scholarly literature on the Duvalier regime. However, during the regime itself and immediately after its fall in 1986, there had been a dynamic production, with two works, by David Nicholls and Michel-Rolph Trouillot, towering over the literature in English.[47] Although they focused primarily on intellectual history, class struggle, and economic determinism rather than on the working of the regime itself, these two books provided the first problematization of Duvalierism. Over the past thirty years, however, this regime has inspired remarkably little literature.[48] One exception is Weibert Arthus, who has contributed a thorough examination of Duvalier's foreign policy.[49] Journalist Bernard Diederich, an informed observer of Haiti for six decades, has also provided important contributions on both resistance and repression under the entire Duvalier regime (1957–1986).[50] In addition, several important works have approached modern Haitian politics in the *longue durée* and have touched upon the Duvalier regime.[51]

Killing the Elites examines the regime at the micro level. I steer away from an exclusive focus on Duvalier himself and on the pathological, opting instead to approach the Jérémie massacre through an anthropology of the Duvalierist state. Duvalier had an inner circle, followers, and a state apparatus behind him. Between his decision to execute civilians and the killings themselves, there were many intermediaries. The Jérémie massacre must be explored through this wider lens. The Duvalierist state was also a regime where neither the military nor the VSNs could decide on their own to eliminate prominent individuals or large numbers of people. Of course, there were elements, particularly in the VSNs, in both the capital and rural areas, who killed individuals on a whim without referring to Duvalier, often for material or temperamental reasons. But to assume that the military could have taken up the execution of twenty-seven family members without having received a formal order from the head of state ignores both how the Haitian military functioned throughout the twentieth century and how the regime itself operated. Even if Duvalier's orders were often vague, which gave considerable freedom of interpretation to local enforcers, no individual on the ground acted with the type of zeal that dramatically increased the magnitude and nature of atrocities. Duvalier himself was responsible for the scale.

Pathologizing Duvalier and making him as all-powerful, omniscient, and cunning as he wanted the public to believe he was, or pronouncing his political crimes as simply insane, is lazy epistemology. To try to enter the mind of a dead dictator, examine his sanity, then render authoritative judgments is also a risky exercise in general. It becomes even riskier when orality informs collective memory. Duvalier functioned well socially, which fueled his social and political ascent. It is within this context that we must explore his decision to execute entire families without any political activities, and to brutalize Haitian society more generally.

PRIMARY SOURCES AND ACCURACY

Duvalier's presidential archives, known as "the Duvalier Library," were transferred after his death in 1971 from the Presidential Palace to an officers' mess in a house appropriated from an opponent in the Pacot neighborhood. In 1986, these archives were either destroyed, dispersed, or, according to a rumor, bought in entirety by a collector in New York. I was therefore unable to find a copy of the orders sent by François Duvalier to execute civilians in Jérémie, nor any government document pertaining to these events. The archives of the Haitian Armed Forces (Forces Armées d'Haïti—FAD'H) are unclassified and therefore unusable. They are literally decomposing, as I discovered, in hundreds of jute bags in the scorching attic of Haiti's National Archives in Bel Air.[52] Several of the available state documents were "privatized" by military officers. Another question concerns the VSN archives: even former members of this organization do not seem to know if they ever existed. The absence of state archives is probably the main reason for the striking paucity of scholarly research on François Duvalier, his regime, the Haitian military, and twentieth century Haitian political history in general.

The most important primary source on the massacre is a two-page document written in 1964 by a Québécois friar, Bruno Laroche (1926–2022), who was teaching and living in Jérémie at that time. I found it in in the archives of the Brothers of Christian Instruction (*Frères de l'Instruction Chrétienne*) in Pétionville, managed by a younger Québécois friar, Gilles Morin (1934-), who was also in Jérémie in 1964. Unreferenced by the historiography, this document confirmed the names of the victims and the chronology of the massacre as given by key witnesses. Fifty-five years after the events, I corresponded by email and by phone with Fr. Laroche, who became one of my interlocutors. He remembered the events vividly and provided key information about the victims' life in Jérémie. Incredibly, he had been, earlier, Second Lieutenant Abel Jérôme's own schoolteacher in Jacmel, and officiated at his wedding in 1965—Jérôme was Jérémie's military commander in 1964.

Since accuracy is of the essence, I asked Laroche and Morin separately how they were learning of the events *in medias res*. Laroche could no longer remember, but Morin recalled learning about them in two stages. First, the morning after each wave of executions, a Haitian priest accompanied by the French priest Barthélémy Péron, visited the Brothers of Christian Instruction's home and narrated the arrests and executions "in an emotional state." Morin confirmed that the Haitian priest was "in communication" (*avec ses entrées*) with the authorities. The Québécois friars learned others details about the executions from other parishioners later. Neither Morin nor Laroche disclosed who these "parishioners" were. Suspecting that they had received more information through confessions, I did not pursue the conversation. In any case, the friars learned almost immediately of all executions, including the secretive killing of Pierre Sansaricq on April 25.

Diplomatic cables are another key source. In the summer and early fall of 1964, the U.S. Embassy sent a cable almost every day, sometimes twice a day, usually signed by Ambassador Timmons. Reading these documents at the College Park location of the U.S. National Archives, I felt I learned as much about Timmons as about the events he documented.[53] Declassified CIA documents show an organization predictably more focused on insurgencies and exiled groups, whether communist or not, than on the fate of civilians. Two CIA papers authored in Haiti confirmed the actuality of repression in Jérémie. On August 21, 1964, an Office of Counter-Intelligence Weekly Summary stated on page 18: "President Duvalier continues his repressive measures. He has, for example, order[ed] the arrest of entire families in the Jérémie area as hostages for relatives alleged to be among the rebel invaders. Such punitive actions cow the populace and help deter any possible impulse to rise against the government." On February 5, 1965, a two-page "Central Intelligence Briefing to the House Appropriation Committee" on the failed Jeune Haïti guerrilla stated on page 1 that "Entire mulatto families were put to death by the regime."

Foreign correspondents of U.S. newspapers, usually operating from outside the country, relied on intermediaries and struggled to verify facts and details.[54] Haitian newspapers, notably *Le Nouvelliste*, which I went through at the library of Collège Saint-Martial in Port-au-Prince, did not, and could not, cover the events, except when reporting Duvalier's presidential decree stripping the victims of their citizenship and legal persona.[55] Two residents of Jérémie, local personalities who had been arrested during the events under study and later released, later wrote an account of their ordeal. This completes the set of available primary sources.[56]

TESTIMONIES AND ACCURACY

I collected testimonies from sixty-three individuals, about two-thirds of them in several sequences.[57] This large number is explained by the fact that I looked for evidence on three distinct, albeit related, subjects: the massacre itself; life and social structures in Jérémie; and the Duvalier regime. Unless otherwise specified, they were all interviewed in person at their homes. I base reconstitutions primarily on accounts by individuals who were actors, direct witnesses, or secondary witnesses. By direct witnesses, I mean eyewitnesses to the executions, to the decision process, or to the arrests. By secondary witness, I meant individuals who received information directly from actors and protagonists of whom they were relatives or close friends. Communications were received in French, Kreyol, or a mix of both. When the original version of a term matters, I wrote it in parenthesis. All goverment written communications transcribed in this book were originally in French.

I met Abel Jérôme, '59, presented in the literature as the primary individual responsible for the massacre, at his home on three different occasions and recorded over six hours of testimony.[58] Jean Alcide, a visual witness of the first wave of executions, courageously provided a self-incriminating account. His testimony is key. Guiton Dorimain's topological hypermnesia allowed me to verify key locations. Another native witness, Eddy Cavé, today a memoirist and a historian, was a friend of several victims. His three consecutive memoirs on Jérémie, as well as his selfless willingness to continuously testify, gave a meticulous picture of mid-twentieth-century social ties in Jérémie. Cecil Philanthrope's chronological hypermnesia allowed me to verify key sequences and key dates. Pierre Chérubin, a candid former army general, was a member of a commission that investigated the Jérémie massacre in 1986.[59] Although the commission was quickly dismantled by the military junta at the time, Chérubin nonetheless had time to interview several of the protagonists and developed an intimate knowledge of the massacre. His testimony is also critical for establishing responsibilities. Three other key interlocutors wished to remain anonymous.

The most important witness and interlocutor for this research was a poor, unknown twenty-three-year-old man in 1964. He would later become an internationally renowned novelist with works translated into several languages. He is at the origin of this book. He encouraged me to write the story of the Jérémie massacre and had wished to remain an anonymous source for it. Unbeknownst to his friends, family, and social milieu, in 1964 he was an official of the People's Party of National Liberation (Parti Populaire de Libération Nationale—PPLN), the underground Communist Party, collecting information on the regime and actively recruiting for the party. He was a close friend of one the victims, Fred Sansaricq, and also of the military commander, Abel Jérôme, from whom he extracted key information he then transmitted to PPLN headquarters. He followed the events in Jérémie as closely as he could, until he himself was arrested in mid-August 1964. He immediately understood their historical significance and in October 1964 wrote a long report for his hierarchy in Port-au-Prince.[60] Jean-Claude Fignolé (1941–2017) was this person. After his premature death, and with the agreement of his widow, Fulvie, I decided to lift his anonymity. That an intellectual of his stature and integrity was a witness to the events under study, and able to provide extensive testimony, was a considerable asset.

Data on governance and decision-making in the Presidential Palace were collected principally from about two dozen individuals. Key among them were Fritz Cinéas, Duvalier's personal secretary from 1962 to July 1964; Francis Charles, Elliott Roy, William Régala, and Prospère Avril, former members of the Presidential Guard and all close to Duvalier; Duvalier's daughter Simone; and children of key members of Duvalier's inner circle. Finally, this book's analysis, particularly on genealogy and sociality, is informed by my own experience. Between 1995 and 2010, I lived a total of four years in Haiti, in three different cities—Les Cayes, Cap Haitien, and Port-au-Prince—with short spells in two villages—Barradères and Monbin Crochu. Giving night classes at Port-au-Prince's Faculté d'ethnologie from 1998 to 2000 allowed me to build a network of colleagues, friends, and interlocutors which later enabled most of the fruitful encounters this research is based on. Although I could not focus fully on this research until 2016 because of earlier commitments, I continuously collected data on the Jérémie massacre for almost two decades.

THE LAYOUT OF THE BOOK

The first chapter reconstitutes the massacre day by day, sometimes hour by hour. Readers can go back to it while reading other chapters to better grasp roles and responsibilities during the course of events. The ideological causes of anti-elite violence, particularly during the Duvalier regime, is covered in chapters 2 and 3. Readers interested in the massacre itself can go directly to chapter 4. Political normativity came from prior episodes of anti-elite violence, which were later referenced by Duvalier; chapter 4 reports the most important ones. This pattern refutes the widespread notion that mass state repression and anti-mulatto sentiments both emerged as a reaction either to the successive "mulatto"-led governments imposed by the U.S. Occupation (1915–1934), or to the founding of a modern military in the 1930s.

When a state crime is committed in a small town, the behaviors of the victims' neighbors—supporters of the dictatorship, silent opponents, and all the others— is a matter of interest for scholars. Over the past two decades, mass violence studies have intensely focused on such behaviors. What did these neighbors do during the Jérémie massacre in particular, and the Duvalier regime in general? Did they try to rescue, did they fear being targeted as well, did they stand idle? These questions are addressed in chapter 7. Yet, to understand how social ties were tested, one has to grasp how life was organized and lived before repression started. Chapters 5 and 6 sketch this ethnography and refute stereotypes of "rich people" standing aloof. The elite did not live separate lives; socioeconomic hierarchies coexisted with sociality. Jérémie had a strikingly thick social fabric. Yet, as a result of nearness, the elite's intimacy was in full view, generating envy and resentment, particularly in a society with strong egalitarian ideologies. Chapter 6 examines in particular the one institution that was exclusive: a local social club, the Excelsior. In Jérémie's relational culture, the Excelsior, where the local elite threw parties, was an exclusive place in full view—a slap in the face. Social fantasies about the Excelsior and elite balls were actually about gender and the place of elite women in the imagination—beautiful, inaccessible, scornful. The chapter's second section transitions to a related topic: the fate of women during the Duvalier regime. Because of traditional cultural coordinates that sacralize the mother, the brutalization of women was not a mere aspect of repression but arguably the most crucial piece in establishing a regime of terror.

The military carried out the order to kill the victims of the Jérémie massacre; during the massacre, the VSNs remained the subalterns they were in everyday life. Chapter 8 examines the military's role in mass violence during the Duvalier era, and more particularly the role of the town's military commander, Abel Jérôme.

Social ties are treated throughout the book but are theorized in chapter 9. Choices, hesitations, behaviors, and risks taken at the most local level and within the government were often framed by preexisting social and kinship ties, and not just by institutional functions, ideological views, or moral stances. This phenomenon is key to understanding how a highly relational society brutalized by a lethal dictatorship functioned.

The book's last two chapters focus on the dictator, his inner circle, and the government's decision-making process. Chapter 10 links Duvalier's decision to execute the Sansaricq family, the most prominent family in Jérémie—and for that matter one without any noticeable political involvement—to one main consideration informed by one preexisting sentiment: his anxiety as a ruler and his hatred and visceral distrust of the mulatto elite. Chapter 11 examines the particular twist on authoritarianism provided by the prevalence of social bonds. Duvalier was not a socially isolated despot, but instead surrounded at all times by people, friends, and family. He made decisions in a highly social environment; before ordering the execution of the Sansaricqs, he consulted widely. Duvalier was also highly cognizant of the effects of interpersonal relationships, and complained about the lack of zeal among his followers and regime members. Repression therefore relied predominantly on a very small group of henchmen, each of whom had a personal relationship to Duvalier.

PART I

The Massacre

CHAPTER 1

Chronology of the Massacre

AUGUST 6, 1964

Before dawn, thirteen insurgents of the Jeune Haiti organization land by boat in the Lesson area of Dame-Marie, a commune thirty miles southwest of the city of Jérémie.[1] All are Haitian exiles from New York. Their original plan was to land in Jérémie's harbor at night, take over the city, and create a guerrilla stronghold for other opposition fighters to join. For unknown reasons, the boat did not reach Jérémie. The insurgents spent the next three months moving around the mountainous southwestern peninsula, engaging in sporadic fighting with the military. They never approached Jérémie, nor did they communicate with anyone there during this period. Isolated, demoralized, and lacking food and ammunition, they fell one by one. The last two, Louis Drouin, 31, and Marcel Numa, 22, were captured separately in late October and executed in Port-au-Prince on November 12.

This small insurgency constitutes the immediate context of the Jérémie Vespers. Unaware at first of the group's size and origin, Haiti's regime was destabilized for several days. Four of the fighters were Jeremians: Louis "Milou" Drouin, its leader; Guslé Villedrouin, the second in command; Marcel Numa; and Gérard Marie "Géto" Brierre. Jacques Wadestrandt, a Harvard graduate from Cap-Haitien was a close friend of the Jeremians of Jeune Haiti.[2] The other eight were Yvan Laraque, Mirko Chandler, Jean Gerdès, Roland Rigaud, Réginald Jourdan, Charles Forbin, and two brothers, Max and Jacques Armand.

Their motivations were both political—to overthrow a despotic regime—and personal, even intimate. Seven had close relatives killed earlier by the regime. The respective fathers of Guslé Villedrouin, Yvan Laraque, and Max and Jacques Armand, all retired officers of the Haitian armed forces

(Force armée d'Haïti, FAD'H), were executed in April 1963.[3] Geto Brierre's seventeen-year-old brother, Eric, was arrested for no known reason and tortured to death by the head of the National Security Volunteers (Volontaires de la Sécurité Nationale, VSN) in the presidential palace in early 1961.[4] Roland Rigaud's father, a physician named George, was kidnapped and killed in 1962. Charles Forbin's father, Alfred, and his second cousin, Edouard Roy, were killed in April 1963. The remaining five members—Jourdan, Drouin, Numa, Chandler, Gerdès, and Wadestrandt—were either close friends or distant relatives of the abovementioned victims. Intimacy and attachment therefore underlie both the motivations and composition of this group.

As the sun rises on August 6, the insurgents move from the beach where they landed to the nearby hamlet. They are weighted down with supplies, including machine guns, radios, medical supplies, and cash. Their intention is to take the only car in the area. It belongs to the local priest, Raoul Lefèvre, whom Géto Brière had known since the 1950s when they attended Catholic seminary in Les Cayes together.[5] Once at the presbytery, however, they learn that the priest is in Les Cayes—with his car. The insurgents would therefore never reach Jérémie. They have several interactions with the local population in the first hours of the day. Local peasants immediately informed the *chef de section*, the highest authority in rural areas, of the presence of armed men. Following the administrative chain of command, the presidential palace is quickly informed, most likely by phone. At this early point, the government is unaware of the insurgency's size or of the presence of Jeremians in it. It would learn these details only by the evening of August 10.

The regime believed this landing was related to a different insurgency that had taken place in the country's southeast in June, the Fred Baptiste guerilla.[6] It was not. The two groups were unrelated, and each was likely entirely unaware of the other. Nevertheless, their quasi-simultaneous activity led the regime to believe it was under siege. Its reaction now was substantially different from its response to Fred Baptiste's insurgency two months earlier: then, the regime had procrastinated, taken uncoordinated measures, and brought large numbers of VSNs from other regions to carry out indiscriminate massacres against the rural population.[7] This time, Duvalier put together a four-man presidential commission tasked with overseeing the military counterinsurgency operations from Jérémie. The commission's president was Pierre Biamby, a civilian and Duvalier's new private executive secretary, one of the most trusted individuals of the president's inner circle.[8] The three other members were military officers:

Lieutenant-Colonel Jean-Baptiste Hilaire, '54, its vice president; Major Mercius Rivière, '54; and Major René Prospère, '56.[9]

AUGUST 7

Between 6:00 A.M. and 10:00 A.M., the Commission arrives in Jérémie by plane.[10] It stays until the third week of August and then relocates to Les Cayes, on the southern coast, to continue overseeing counterinsurgency operations. In Jérémie, the Commission is now de facto the highest government authority in town; Second Lieutenant Abel Jérôme, '57, the District Commander, is informally demoted. Biamby's personal connection to Duvalier, and not just his formal title—President of the Presidential Commission—makes him the most powerful man in Jérémie. The Commission's members are housed on the second floor of the military base, work in Jérôme's own office, and sleep on camp beds in the room adjacent to it. A local lady, Laurence Mombeleur, is tasked with cooking meals every day, three times a day, for the Commission, which are then brought to the base by a military jeep.[11] Incredibly, none of the Commission members ever ventured in town and were therefore never seen in public—this is probably why they seldom appear in oral history. This was certainly a decision on their part. Biamby, whose wife was a Jeremian, and René Prospère, whose uncle, Antoine Prospère, had been a priest and a teacher there for eight years, had deep social connections with locals.

The military operations start on August 7 when two planes airlift seventy-seven soldiers from Caserne Dessalines, the main military base in Port-au-Prince. They are led by Second Lieutenant Achille Léon, '59, assisted by Second Lieutenant Prosper Avril, '61. The troops are immediately dispatched to the Chambellan area, about 25 miles from Jérémie.[12]

In the late morning of August 7, the Commission takes its first decision: a curfew is imposed; from 7:00 P.M. to 5:00 A.M. people are forbidden to leave their homes. Biamby informs first the mayor, Raoul Cédras, and Abel Jérôme of his decision. There are two versions about the curfew: in one, it was bugled every day by trumpet, usually by Corporal Bonnet, from a jeep driven throughout the town; in another, an ambulance's siren was used for the curfew. The actual time of curfew varied greatly—anywhere from 6:00 P.M. to 8:00 P.M.—and at least once, Bonnet forgot to sound the bugle. To enforce the curfew, Abel Jérôme, the only military officer with transportation, shut off the town's electric plant (which ran on oil) every evening at 9:00 P.M. The Commission also prohibited anyone from leaving Jérémie, with the exception of priests, pastors, and members of the military. Only Biamby (then Jérôme after the Commission's departure) could issue a travel pass. Therefore, very little information would filter out of town and reach the capital during this period.

The U.S. Embassy in Port-au-Prince sends its first cable about the insurgency to the U.S. Department of State on August 7 at 12:30 P.M., after having been both briefed and interrogated that morning by the Haitian government, which was trying to obtain intelligence about the landing: "Theard also said at present GOH [Government of Haiti] has only peasant reports and does not know identity of people nor numbers (although Theard at first spoke in terms of exiles). He also said that group now lodged in building of catholic school located at village of Lesson."[13] Since this incident takes place in the context of the Cold War, the State Department forwards the embassy cable to the White House, where it arrives at 2:55 P.M. The U.S. Ambassador to Haiti, Benson Timmons, writes a second telegram at 5:00 P.M.:

> Story of new landing has spread rapidly in Port-au-Prince today until it now [is] common knowledge and, despite lack of details, first reports appear unhesitatingly as true. . . . One source with good connection inside GOH states Duvalier called TTMS (VSNs) and militia to palace at 10 P.M. last night [August 6] for two-hour session during which he told them 36 men had landed at Dame-Marie. Same source reports GOH extremely nervous yesterday and today.[14]

SATURDAY, AUGUST 8

Morning

Two peasants from Dame-Marie arrive at the military base.[15] They are seasonal coffee workers who are familiar with Jérémie. One of them goes by the nickname "Dola" and works on the docks in the summer. They first meet with Corporal Clerc, who makes them wait in the guardroom on the base's ground floor. They are then led to the second floor where they meet with Biamby and the Commission. The peasants report having seen armed men the day before. Biamby asks if the armed men are foreigners (*blan*). Dola answers they are Haitians and several are "mulattoes." He adds that he recognized one of them from when he worked at the wharf in Jérémie's Grande Rue.[16] From then on, the Commission suspects that at least one of the insurgents is a Jeremian and a "mulatto."

In the afternoon, Astrel "Casamayor" Benjamin, the VSN Chief in Les Cayes, arrives in Jérémie in a military pickup truck. Casamayor became one of the most infamous VSNs and had a reputation of brutality. He is accompanied by half a dozen VSNs. A native of Fond Rouge near Jérémie, Benjamin has a personal relationship with Duvalier. Once at the military base, he meets with Biamby and shows him a telegram from Duvalier ordering him to go to Jérémie, meet with the Commission, and then go fight the rebels. Biamby shows him the rebels' position on a map and orders him to proceed to Les Irois, on the southwesternmost tip of the peninsula. However, one to two hours later, Casamayor and his VSNs are back at the base with three civilians they have arrested: George Jérôme, Georges Clérié, and Alain Rocourt, a Methodist pastor and important local figure. All are "mulattoes" and members of the town's elite. The three men are kept in a cell at the base.[17]

Dr. Jacques Fourcand, the president of the Haitian Red Cross, Duvalier's personal physician, and a native of Jérémie, arrives in a plane piloted by Antoine Fénélon.[18] Fourcand stays in Jérémie for two to five days before heading back to Port-au-Prince. He remains at the Saint-Antoine hospital for the entirety of his stay.[19]

After Curfew

Soldiers, or a combination of soldiers and VSNs, go to the homes of seven men and arrest them: Louis Drouin, his son Guy Drouin, Frantz Perrault, "Sicot" Gardère, Dr. Louis Laurent, Wesley Clérié, Harry Balmir, and Marcel Duval. They are taken to the guardroom at the military base where they are forced to undress.[20] Pierre Sansaricq is likely arrested with them. (The Friar's diary does not indicate his date of arrest.) Only the Drouins have a family member in the guerrilla.

AUGUST 9

Morning

News of the previous day's arrests spreads through town and creates a climate of terror.

Afternoon

A Beechcraft lands in Jérémie bringing Second Lieutenant Jean Dimanche, '59, and a platoon of soldiers. They are sent by the FAD'H General Headquarters. A native of Jérémie, Dimanche is tasked with securing the landing strip, called Numéro 2 and located about six miles east of Jérémie.

The plane returns to Port-au-Prince the same day with the bodies of the first casualties of the military operations: one insurgent named Yvon Laraque and one unidentified soldier.

AUGUST 10

Captain José "Sony" Borges, '54, (1933–1967) arrives in Jérémie in a plane piloted by Antonio Fénélon. A member of the presidential guard, Borges has a personal relationship with Duvalier and a reputation as a henchman.[21] He played a major role in the brutal repression of the rural population of Thiotte in June of that year.[22]

Second Lieutenant William Régala, '59, a young officer in the presidential guard, is also sent to Jérémie by Duvalier.[23] There are now four different envoys in Jérémie who respond directly and separately to Duvalier: Pierre Biamby as head of the presidential commission, Jacques Fourcand, Sony Borges, and Lt. Régala. Others who also have personal relationships with Duvalier will be central actors in the days to come: Abel Jérôme; Sanette Balmir, a VSN; and Saintange Bontemps, a member of the parliament.

A first public altercation erupts between Jean Dimanche and Abel Jérôme.[24] Dimanche refuses to take orders from Jérôme, arguing that they are of the same rank and from the same cohort at the military academy; and that because of this, he will take his orders only from military headquarters, not from Jérôme.[25] Jérôme has already anticipated that civilians will be executed, and is taking measures to ensure that executions do not take place under his command.[26]

Cpl. Clerc is seen running up and down the stairs bringing messages between Biamby's "office" on the second floor and the decoding room on the first floor. Biamby and Duvalier communicate only through coded military messages.[27]

By the late afternoon or the evening, Duvalier makes the decision, based on information provided by Pierre Biamby, to execute relatives of Jérémie's insurgents. They decide on ten people.

There is a crucial question: When did the government learn the insurgents' names and their connection to Jérémie? An old fighter plane from the Haitian air force machine-gunned the insurgents' camp at Prévilé, outside Moron, forcing the insurgents to abandon some of their gear.[28] Two large, heavy bags were retrieved by government soldiers and brought to Jérémie where they were immediately examined by Jérôme, then by the Commission.[29] Inside were passports, Jeune Haiti insignia, and an address book. This might have been the first time the government got wind of Jeune Haiti. The address book linked Jeune Haiti to Jeremian families.[30] The bags were brought by plane directly to the presidential palace:

> [Embassy secretary] Curtis and I saw Am Theard off for Wash via Panam this morning. Theard produced a copy of memo to Duvalier dated Aug 7 purporting to list arms and equipment abandoned by Dame-Marie invaders "under pressure from Haitian army." List contained about 20 items including browning machine gun . . . 3 "Jeune Haiti" insignia . . . Theard, who interrupted talk with me to take phone call from Duvalier, said group led by one Villedrouin, son of former FAD'H colonel, and that GOH has names of some of gang involved in landing, who are all members of Jeune Haiti.[31]

The "memo to Duvalier" was also mentioned by Abel Jérôme, who said it had been written by Jean-Baptiste Hilaire after the Commission examined the two bags. Louis and Guy Drouin were arrested on August 8 either because the Commission knew the guerrillas' identities, or because it had deliberately cast a wide net, as the arrest of other men (Dr. Laurent, Sicot Gardère, etc.) with no relationship to Jeune Haiti suggested.

TUESDAY, AUGUST 11

6:00 A.M.– 9:00 A.M.

Early in the morning, Biamby summons Jérôme and, in the presence of the other Commission members, hands him a written order to arrest and execute civilians. The order contains ten names. Jérôme does not object. Biamby most likely left it to Jérôme to pick a place of execution and burial. Circumstantial evidence further suggests that Jérôme chose the place of execution in order to not be held responsible. Jérôme proposes Numéro 2, the only place accessible on foot from Jérémie that is not under his direct military authority at that moment, although Biamby might not have been aware of this detail.

Biamby and Jérôme discuss the details of the execution. They decide to have common-law inmates walk from the city prison to Numéro 2 under a non-commissioned officer's command and dig two ditches (although in the end, only one ditch would be dug).[32] Biamby hands Jérôme cash to purchase picks and shovels, which suggests a lack of basic tools at the military base. Then, while still in the presence of the three military officers of the Commission, Biamby orders Jérôme to provide ten black blindfolds to place over the prisoners' eyes before the execution.

9:00 A.M.–11:00 A.M.

In the morning, the seamstress Sémérine Bossuet (née Ogé) sees Abel Jérôme enter her shop for the first time. He places an order for ten black blindfolds. She asks what they will be used for, but Jérôme remains evasive. He gives her specific measurements and insists they be ready in the afternoon.[33]

That afternoon, Jean-Baptiste Saint-Cyr, the sergeant in charge of police (and also a native of Jérémie), is ordered to make the arrests later that night and have the prisoners brought directly to the town's prison. (They would be brought to the military base instead.)

Abel Jérôme gives orders to dig one ditch of twelve by twelve feet at Numéro 2.

Later, a second, public fight erupts between Jean Dimanche and Abel Jérôme when Jérôme hands him the order to execute the civilians. Dimanche likely understood at that moment that he had been outmaneuvered and outsmarted, and at first refuses to obey. Jérôme argues that he had merely decided on the location of the execution and was not placing Dimanche under his authority. He then allegedly threatens to report Dimanche to Biamby.[34]

The elderly Louis Drouin, already in custody since the roundup of August 8, is brought from the guardroom or from a cell to the Commission's office on the second floor by Clerc. There, he is interrogated solely by the Commission's four members—Clerc is not present.[35] At this point, they believe that his son Milou is either the head of the insurgents or the second in command. Before evening, he is brought back unconscious to the guardroom, where he is laid on the floor. He would soon die of his wounds, the first victim of the Jérémie Vespers.[36]

Rumors spread among the town's Duvalierists that upper-class "mulattoes" are about to be arrested. This suggests that the authorities failed to keep their actions secret, at least for the first wave of executions.

3:00 P.M.–4:00 P.M.

In the late afternoon, Sgt. Saint-Cyr enters Sémérine Bossuet's shop and asks her for the ten black blindfolds ordered earlier by Jérôme. She said she needs more time, and Saint-Cyr leaves without them. Since a task as basic as cutting ten uniformly square pieces of cloth would require less than an hour for an experienced seamstress, this can be interpreted as an act of resistance, or at least a way of avoiding direct involvement, by Bossuet.

5:00 P.M.

Jérôme returns personally to Bossuet's shop to ask for the blindfolds. She tells him they are not ready.

7:00 P.M.–8:00 P.M.

Army soldiers and VSNs arrest five individuals at their homes: Louis Drouin's daughters, Alice and Roseline, together with their respective husbands, Gérard "Bibeau" Guilbaud and Guy Villedrouin; and Victor Villedrouin. They are brought to the military base. According to Elliott Roy, '59, who had been an officer at the same base two years earlier and is a very reliable interlocutor, the prisoners could have been scattered in several cells, not just the guardroom.[37] Jérôme and Jean Alcide, on the other hand, recall that all of the prisoners were in the guardroom. Dr. Louis Laurent's account on his ordeal is inconclusive on this point. All five prisoners, including the two women, are ordered to undress. According to Elizabeth Abbott and Abel Jérôme, the victims are eventually allowed to put their clothes back on; this is refuted by Jean Alcide's account of that evening.[38]

8:00 P.M.–9:00 P.M.

Twenty to thirty of the town's Duvalierists, all civilians, gather at the base after curfew. (Civilians are usually barred from entering the base). The rumor had spread through town earlier in the day that "mulattoes were going to be arrested." Among those Duvalierist visitors are Antoine Apollon, Jean Alcide, Gérard Léonidas, André Jabouin, Gérard Brunache, Max Frédérique, Marcel Myrtil, Luc Desroche, Kersuzan and Mérès Bélizaire, Robert Nauze, and Willy Thiafisgirl. Jean Alcide walked to the base with a flashlight since it was past curfew. Raoul Cédras, the town's mayor, is also there, although his motivations are likely different from the rest—among those arrested are some of his kin. He is on the second floor with the presidential commission. On the ground floor, some peek into the guardroom.

What can be described as chaotic negotiations take place between some of the civilians and the Commission. Abel Jérôme is seen going up and down the stairs, serving as a link between the two groups, for most of the evening. Only Raoul Cédras is allowed in the Commission's office.

9:00 P.M.–11:00 P.M.

Biamby agrees to transfer Gardère, Balmir, Dr. Laurent, and Perrault from the military base to the town's prison, hence sparing their lives.

The two couples and Victor Villedrouin remain in the guardroom. Around 10:00 P.M., a VSN enters. He binds their hands in handcuff knots using one single rope to create a prisoner chain. The five prisoners, still naked, are then forced to leave the guardroom, walk to the courtyard, and get into the back of a small coffee truck driven by Tony Frédérique.[39] They climb into the truck with great difficulty. Thiasfisgirl, a VSN, gets into the passenger seat next to the driver. The truck then departs for Numéro 2 followed by at least two cars. The one immediately behind the truck is driven by Antoine Apollon with Jean Alcide to his right. In the headlights, they see the five victims. In a second car are Gérard Léonidas and Gérard Brunache. Army soldiers and officers do not follow the convoy: either they did not want to be seen as playing a major role in the execution itself, or they simply trusted the Duvalierists and VSNs to accompany the prisoners to Numéro 2.

The convoy must have arrived at Numéro 2 twenty to twenty-five minutes later—the road was unpaved at that time. Awaiting them was a platoon of army soldiers commanded by Lt. Jean Dimanche. Off to one side, almost hidden, was a small group of common-law prisoners. Importantly, the place chosen for the execution was about 200 yards north of the landing strip, on a small hill that was uninhabited. The closest farms, at that time, were at least one mile away.

Upon arrival, the prisoners are forced to climb out of the truck. At that moment, Gérard Brunache makes a lewd comment about the two naked women. Jean Dimanche explodes in anger, in effect silencing Brunache and the civilians. By ordering the VSNs to remain silent, Dimanche demonstrates that the army is in charge of the execution.

The prisoners are barefoot and walk with great difficulty to the place of execution.[40] They are led by the soldiers and followed by the VSN and Duvalierists. After 200 yards, the group arrives at the ditch that had been dug earlier. The victims are ordered to climb down into it. Once there, they stand in the ditch, facing the soldiers. They do not wear blindfolds. Jean Dimanche orders his men to make a line, move to the edge of the ditch, and aim. Because the ditch was five to six -feet deep, the soldiers most likely aimed at them from above and close range.

After the first burst of gunfire, Dimanche asks Jean Alcide to turn on his flashlight to shine light on the victims. Alcide obeys. Soldiers and civilians can see that all of the prisoners are dead, except for Gérard Guilbaud, who is only wounded. Dimanche asks a soldier, whom I could not identify, to "finish" him off ("*éliminez-le*"), which he does with his rifle.

Dimanche orders the common-law prisoners to pick their shovels, advance, and fill the ditch.

Jean Alcide stated that the victims remained silent during the entirety of their ordeal, both at the military base and at Numéro 2. Secondary witnesses (individuals to whom direct eyewitnesses described what they saw that evening) believe that if the victims had spoken, the eyewitnesses would have reported it, adding that the victims were probably terrified.

When, where, and how Guy Drouin was killed remains unclear. Alcide is certain that only five individuals were brought to Numéro 2 and executed that night. Secondary witnesses agree that Louis Drouin died of his wounds in the guardroom. Guy Drouin must have been interrogated for the same reasons his father had been, and possibly died while undergoing torture—but in a separate cell, not in the guardroom.

If Biamby and the Commission listed ten names on their execution order but only seven were killed, who were the other three named? Victor Villedrouin's wife, Adeline, and their two children, Lyssa and Frantz, were the most likely individuals. Perhaps logistic disorganization was responsible for this, or perhaps one or more individuals in the chain of command took it upon themselves to make sure these three were not arrested that night.[41] Regardless, they would be killed five weeks later, after Jérôme received an execution order that did not contain their names.

AUGUST 12

In Jérémie, news of the executions immediately spreads. The Duvalierist witnesses to the execution talk about it with their respective spouses and share it with their social networks. In late afternoon, Gérard Léonidas gives a full account of the execution to Jean-Claude Fignolé, who would then write it down in his diary.

AUGUST 13, PORT-AU-PRINCE

In Port-au-Prince, the corpse of Yvan Laraque, the first of the Jeune Haiti insurgents to be killed in action, is put on display at a major Port-au-Prince intersection with a sign around his neck stating "Chief of the Stateless (*apatrides*) killed in Grand'Anse."

AUGUST 14

The U.S. Embassy reports the arrests of "Villedrouin, Drouin, Laurent, and Giraud (*sic*)" and uses the term "terrorism" to qualify the ongoing wave of repression.[42]

AUGUST 19

A Jeremian informant of the U.S. Embassy confirms the execution: "Following persons reported executed at Jérémie last week (Source states this info is "certain" but request it be carefully guarded in order avoid pinpointing source recently arrived from Jérémie): Guy and Victor Villedrouin, wife (née Drouin) of former, FNU Guilbaud and wife also née Drouin. The aged father of these two women also slated for execution but died of heart attack."[43]

According to Bruno Laroche's diary, Pierre Sansaricq, allegedly the town's richest person, is arrested "in the middle of August." At this point, the Haitian government is aware that none of the insurgents bears the name Sansaricq, and gives Ambassador Timmons a list of thirty-four Jeune Haiti supporters living in the United States.[44] No one by the name of Sansaricq appears on this list either.

Saintange Bontemps, probably emboldened by the first execution, "requisitioned" (his word) Carl Nicolas's car.[45] Nicolas is an employee of the Weiner coffee import-export house. George Clérié's and Alain Rocourt's respective cars are also requisitioned by the military.

AUGUST 20–22, PORT-AU-PRINCE

Joseph Bajeux, a prominent light-skinned businessman without known political activities, is arrested at his Port-au-Prince home together with his wife and three of their children. All of them are imprisoned in Fort Dimanche and executed a few weeks later.[46]

AUGUST 17–21

The presidential commission in charge of counterinsurgency operations leaves Jérémie and moves to Les Cayes. The government is aware that the now-depleted Jeune Haiti guerrilla poses no significant threat. In Jérémie, the curfew is lifted and the town's movie theatre reopens, a symbol of a return to normality for the population. Many assume that the worst is over, although there is ongoing intimidation by some VSNs.

FRIDAY, SEPTEMBER 18

Around 4:00 P.M.

In the late afternoon, Gérard Léonidas, 32, is chatting on his veranda with Jean-Claude Fignolé, 23. Around 4:00 P.M., Abel Jérôme joins them, as he does most afternoons—he holds Léonidas in high esteem and is friends with both men. A few minutes later, a soldier, sure that he will be able to find Jérôme at Léonidas' home at that time of the day, runs up to him with what looks to be a telegram.

Jérôme asks the soldier matter-of-factly if the message is now decoded. Possibly to impress the two men, Jérôme announces, before opening it, that the message is from François Duvalier himself. Jérôme reads it aloud, and then sits back down in silence. The two other men then took the message from his hand and read it:

> *Dès réception de la présente, disparaissez famille Sansaricq.*
>
>   (Upon receipt [of this message], disappear [*sic*] Sansaricq family).

The two civilians notice the error of syntax immediately: the nonstandard use of the verb *disparaître* in a simple transitive form (*disparaissez quelqu'un*; to disappear someone) instead of its correct causal form (*faire disparaître quelqu'un*; to make someone disappear). This linguistic deviance may have helped Léonidas and Fignolé memorize the sentence. The order is signed by Duvalier himself, "*Président à vie, Chef exécutif des Forces Armées*" (President for Life, Chief Executive of the Armed Forces).[47]

After 8:00 P.M.

Abel Jérôme has still not executed the order. The town's Duvalierist patricians meet at André Jabouin's home to discuss Duvalier's order, probably at the initiative of Raoul Cédras and Abel Jérôme. The dozen or so men who are present consider the possibility of asking Duvalier to reconsider his order, but eventually decide against it.[48]

SATURDAY, SEPTEMBER 19

If the arrests and executions of August 11 were "public" and chaotic, this time Abel Jérôme and the military controlled and hid the entire process. Consequently, less information was publicly known and there were fewer witnesses whose testimony could be collected.

7:20 P.M.

The curfew bugle rings out for the first time since the third week of August. It terrifies the population who associates the sound and curfew with the earlier arrests. The theater owner immediately interrupts the projection of *The Hunchback of Rome* (1960), an Italian film. Moviegoers leave immediately and rush back to their homes. By 7:45 P.M., the town is deserted.

8:00 P.M.–9:00 P.M.

Two military vehicles leave the base to make the arrests: a truck carrying one corporal, one sergeant, and several soldiers; and a jeep carrying Maj. Sony Borges and Saintange Bontemps, the only civilian involved in the arrests. No VSN is involved. Thirteen members of the Sansaricq family are arrested. Edith Laforest, who lives in the Sansaricq home but is not a Sansaricq herself, is also arrested.

The names of Adeline Villedrouin and her two children, Lyssa, 17, and Frantz, 15, did not originally figure on Duvalier's execution order, but they too are arrested. The maid and her mother, who live in the Villedrouin's home, witness the arrest but wait until the morning after to alert the neighbors. (Adeline's husband, Victor Villedrouin, had been executed on August 11.) Adeline, Lyssa, and Frantz may have been the three individuals completing the list of ten names given to Jérôme by Pierre Biamby on August 11. Either they were "added" later by Duvalier himself on September 19, via a communication channel I could not pinpoint with precision (Jérôme or Borges), or one of these two men took it upon himself to add the last of the Villedrouin family to the list—which is unlikely.

Another twist occurs as the convoy makes its way from Rochasse to Bordes, probably before the arrest of Adeline Villedrouin and her children. A military jeep driven by a military officer blocks the street. Mona Ambroise, 21, Fred Sansaricq's wife, is removed from the truck and therefore saved—the only survivor of the entire massacre.[49] Ambroise, who was not from Jérémie, was the daughter of a Duvalierist patrician in Port-au-Prince. More than likely, this was the reason she was removed from the truck.[50]

The victims are transported directly to Numéro 2 by a route that bypassed the military base. Again, a firing squad commanded by Lt. Jean Dimanche is waiting. The victims are taken to two trenches dug earlier that day by inmates, immediately to the side of the one used on August 11. They are ordered into the pits and summarily executed by Dimanche's soldiers.

SEPTEMBER 20

News of the execution spread rapidly around Jérémie. VSNs understand that they were bypassed by Jérôme and the military for these executions. Gérard Brunache is witnessed washing a knife in the street and heard boasting that he killed children with a knife.

The killing of eight children stupefies the population. Rumors of the rape and torture of children and women begin to circulate, increasing the climate of terror. With the only road in and out of the city blocked by the military, "mulatto" families are unable to flee and fear they will be arrested next.

May Clérié, née Sansaricq, Graziela's sister and Pierre Sansaricq's third-degree cousin, the only surviving Sansaricq in Jérémie, is hidden by relatives and friends. She is secretly exfiltrated by boat to Port-au-Prince. Other "mulatto" families leave in the weeks after the massacre. Under threat from VSNs, Jérémie's main priest, Father Barthélémy Péron, who has officiated in Jérémie since 1939, flees not only the town but Haiti itself, accompanied by the Pratts, a "mulatto" family.

The killing of a prominent elite family emboldens several VSNs who now openly express anti-mulatto sentiments in public and intimidate the surviving families.

SEPTEMBER 25

According to Bruno Laroche's account, Pierre Sansaricq is taken out of the prison in the evening, brought to Numéro 2, and executed. He had been in the town's prison since early August.[51]

SEPTEMBER 26

Marcel Numa's father and brother, Louis and Liénard, are arrested and held at the city prison.[52] The family store in Moron is looted after the arrests. This is the first time that the kin of an opponent who are not mulattoes themselves are arrested. Marcel Numa was a member of Jeune Haiti. His family had been spared until then. The Numa were openly pro-Duvalier during the 1957 campaign.

Numa's brother-in-law, Pierre Chavenet, married to Numa's sister Nélande, was Duvalier's ambassador.[53] Numa's other sister Denise was married to Villefranche "Bido" Desroche, a local VSN.

SEPTEMBER 28

The U.S. Embassy finally learns about the killing of the Sansaricq family as well as of the two Villedrouin teenagers and their mother.[54] It took nine days for U.S. diplomats to learn of this event, a sign of the secrecy with which the operation was conducted. On Oct. 6, another U.S. Embassy cable states:

> Nobody in Jérémie seems to know what has happened to the people who were arrested. This, of course, has become a familiar pattern in the Duvalierist technique of getting maximum effect out of terror as an instrument of control. The lack of information following an individual's disappearance feeds speculation and rumors as to his fate and tends to create an atmosphere of greater apprehension and uncertainty than might be warranted by the facts were they known.[55]

AUGUST 12–OCTOBER 18

Since her husband's and son's arrests on August 8, Louise Drouin (mother of Milou and Guy Drouin, and wife of Louis Drouin) remains unaware (or unconvinced) that they have been killed, in spite of the public rumors. She has been cooking and packing meals, which she brings to the prison for them. The Cédras children, all adolescents, and their mother, Gabrielle Rocourt (the mayor's wife), who grew up with Louise Drouin—bring her cooked food several times a week.

OCTOBER 18

Louise Drouin and Corinne and Fernande Villedrouin are killed at night. They are the last victims of the Jérémie Vespers. The circumstances are not established.[56] They were most likely taken from their houses by soldiers, or VSNs, or a mix of the two, and executed at Numéro 2. In the terms of social and symbolic coordinates, killing an elderly woman constitutes a major social violation. For the first time in over 160 years, nobody bearing the name Drouin or Villedrouin lives in Jérémie.

At night, a group of locals break down the front doors of the Villedrouin and Drouin homes to steal valuables. That same night, they proceed to homes of the other victims. The home of Pierre Sansaricq may have been broken into earlier than October 18, according to several accounts, including that of the immediate neighbors. According to interlocutors and circumstantial evidence, this group of locals includes Saintange Bontemps, Sanette Balmir, and other Duvalierists.[57] The spoils were divided. This group did not target the stores owned by the victims, only their homes, where valuables such as money and jewelry would have been located.

The robbers, once done, leave the homes standing wide open.

OCTOBER 19, BEFORE SUNRISE

The new vicar, Willy Romélus, who is new to Grand'Anse, hears *rara* music coming from the town's outskirts, apparently calling the population to gather.[58] He finds it incongruous enough to record in his diary. Such music is usually played on religious holidays or during festivals; there are no such events happening that night. The music stops before sunrise.

8:00 A.M.

Around 8:00 A.M., crowds form and move out from Jérémie's periphery toward the city center, accompanied by *rara* bands. They then proceed to loot and dismantle the homes and stores owned by the victims of the massacre. The mass looting was engineered to cover the robberies of the night before and to implicate the population in the execution. Since it takes place in broad daylight, the entire town is witness to it. Bruno Laroche wrote:

> On [Monday], October 19, a day nobody will ever forget: looting and demolition (the roofs, slats, rafters, window frames) of the following houses: private home of Pierre Sansaricq, of his store and its carpentry wood, zinc sheets,

pipes, drums of kerosene, ice maker, etc.; of Edith Laforest's store, located at the crossroads of the customs' office; Gérard Guilbaud's private home and store; Louis Drouin's private home and bakery; private home of Victor Ville-drouin and that of his brother, Colonel Villedrouin; looting of Gérard (*sic*) Sansaricq's home; looting of the house inhabited by Fred and Jean-Claude Sansaricq; car of Gérard Dégraft (*sic*) reduced to its frame.[59]

Fifty-four years later, the other Québécois friar, Gilles Morin, vividly recalled the looting, which he had witnessed alongside Laroche:

> We (friars and local priests) watched from the bishopric windows. The homes were taken apart methodically, starting with the roofs, one floor after another, all pieces were carried away, windows, doors, nails, hinges, everything disap-peared, then were taken away. We saw people in the street carrying mattresses, doors . . . No, we did not see the police, usually the soldiers and the *macoutes*, they were always everywhere, but that morning, we saw none of them.[60]

The event, another step toward the breakdown of the rule of law, was notewor-thy for the U.S. Embassy:

> Houses belonging to Gérard Guilbaud, Chenier Villedrouin, Louis Drouin and Pierre Sansaricq at Jérémie destroyed about Oct 20, plus house of former Col. Villedrouin at nearby village of Bordes. Stores belonging to Guilbaud and Hilaire clinic were sacked, plus store owned by Gérard Desgraff. Mme Chenier Villedrouin (92-year-old blind invalid) reportedly arrested and killed with Mme Louis Drouin (74-year-old). We assume latter is mother or grand-mother of Louis Drouin . . . and that his capture set off this latest wave of terrorism against mulattoes of Jérémie.[61]

The breakdown of the rule of law and social ethics adds to the climate of terror. Many families conclude that neither life nor property are safe any longer. There were no precedents of this magnitude earlier in the regime. Not since September 23, 1883, when the Salomon government engineered the mass looting of Port-au-Prince's business district had a mob weaponized by the authorities loot stores and houses on such a wide scale. In both cases, it was not spontaneous; sectors of the underclass were incited and led by government agents to create terror.

OCTOBER 19, PORT-AU-PRINCE

Milou Drouin, leader of Jeune Haiti, is captured near Miragoâne. He had been shot in the leg on October 16, could barely walk, and had run out of ammunition. His arrest confirms his identity. He is brought to Port-au-Prince, where he is interrogated in the presidential palace by Duvalier.[62] He will be executed with Marcel Numa on November 12.

OCTOBER 22

Duvalierist patricians meet at night at André Jabouin's home to discuss the fate of Marcel Numa's father and brother, Louis and Liénard, arrested on September 26. This time, they sign a letter to Duvalier asking him to free the Numas and the remaining prisoners, arguing that none of them is a *camoquin* (guerrilla).

OCTOBER 23

The day after, Jérôme travels to Port-au-Prince by plane and immediately goes to the presidential palace to meet with Duvalier in his office. There, he allegedly hands the letter to Duvalier.

The U.S. Embassy learns about the killing of Corinne Villedrouin and Louise Drouin, "the latest wave of terrorism against mulattoes at Jérémie."[63]

OCTOBER 23 OR 24, AT NIGHT

Perrault, Rocourt, and Dr. Laurent are freed from Jérémie's prison, at night.

OCTOBER 26, PORT-AU-PRINCE

A piece of artillery is brought to the crossroads of rue Capois and ruelle Roy, and pointed toward mulatto residential districts higher up [in the] hills and [with the] threat uttered that if [the] Duvalier regime [is] threatened [a] gun would be brought back and used to destroy [the] mulatto opposition. . . . On [the] evening of October 22, Duvalier gave [the] order to his close associates that mulattoes and their properties [are] to be destroyed if [the] situation becomes critical.[64]

Le Moniteur publishes a presidential decree on its front page, announcing that "Roger Villedrouin, Mrs. Chenier Villedrouin, Fernande Villedrouin, Gérard Guilbaud and his wife (Alice), Pierre Sansaricq and his wife (Louise), Jean-Claude Sansaric and his wife (Graziela), Fred Sansaricq, Guy Villedrouin and his wife (Roseline), and Edith Laforest" have had their Haitian citizenship removed and their legal rights stripped away (*mort civile*). Their properties are confiscated. These are thirteen victims of the Jérémie massacre, in addition to Roger Ville-drouin, killed a year earlier. This decree does not specify that they are dead, far less that they were executed.

Jeune Haiti's last three fighters—Roland Rigaud, Réginald Jourdan, and Guslé Villedrouin—are killed in combat at Ravine Roche, near l'Asile. At this point, only its leader, Milou Drouin, and Marcel Numa, both captured earlier, are still alive.

OCTOBER 29

Louis and Liénard Numa are freed from prison late in the morning. As they walk from the military base to their home, townspeople follow them and turn this liberation into a festive event.

OCTOBER 31

Ambassador Timmons writes a lengthy memo on the massacre titled "Retaliation Against the Jérémie Mulattoes." Timmons also states that an informer within Duvalier's inner circle said that Duvalier has explicitly warned in a government meeting that, if a new insurgency were to occur, he would destroy mulattoes and their properties.[65]

PART II

Illegitimate Members of the Nation

CHAPTER 2

Constructing the Enemy

. . . eternal enemies of the masses

François Duvalier[1]

FORT RÉFLÉCHI

At the corner of Brice Aîné and Abbé Huet streets in Jérémie's center stood a carpenter workshop run by two brothers, Kersuzan and Mérès Bélizaire. It had two large inviting doors opening onto Brice Aîné street. The workshop opened at sunrise every day and was busy all day long with social visits and, occasionally, customers. Friends and acquaintances stopped by, talked, gossiped. It was a social place. Most of the visitors belonged to a socioeconomic segment composed of artisans and employees. Most were males and many were "characters." The Bélizaire brothers were National Security Volunteers (Volontaires de la Sécurité Nationale, or VSNs). During the Duvalier regime, their workshop was the meeting place of Jérémie's VSNs and other Duvalierists. It was nicknamed, and is still remembered in oral history, as Fort Réfléchi.

The original Fort Réfléchi stood in Miragoâne,[2] about a hundred kilometers to the east, where in 1883 a civil war pitted President Lysius Salomon's forces against a small insurgency of the Liberal Party led by Jean-Pierre Boyer-Bazelais.[3] Fort Réfléchi was held, with the rest of the town, by the besieged Liberals against surrounding government forces. In the noirist view, Boyer-Bazelais's insurgency symbolized mulattoes' unwillingness to accept a Black man as president and mulatto supremacy. However, Fort Réfléchi was held by the Liberals, first under the command of William Rigaud,[4] a direct descendant of André Rigaud (1761–1811), a mulatto leader during the Haitian Revolution. Why, then, did the Jérémie VSNs in the 1960s pick a historical reference of mulatto armed resistance? Most likely, they were unaware of the details of the 1883 siege.[5] This unfamiliarity is relevant. In the historical context of a civil war seen as the essence of the Black-mulatto opposition, a besieged "fort" is a symbol of defiance, and this is the symbol that Jérémie's VSNs appropriated. They saw themselves as the continuation of Salomon's army. To nickname a mere meeting place Fort Réfléchi reveals the Jérémie Duvalierists's politicized, polarized, and racialized reading of Haitian history.

The 1883 siege of Miragoâne appears in another document. In 1982, while conducting field research on the peasantry in the Moron area of Grand'Anse, sociologist Michèle Oriol made a singular discovery.[6] While she was gathering data on agricultural production, an old landowner and community leader expressed his fear that "mulattoes" would take over his land. Oriol took note of the farmer's concerns when he substantiated his fear by referencing a text's title: *The Testament of the Liberals* (*Le testament des Libéraux*). This was a text she had heard of but never read or physically encountered; the farmer had never read it either, but knew of its content. Several of my Jérémie interlocutors also referenced it during the research for this book when talking about the mentality of "mulattoes." The nephew of a witness to the first wave of executions on August 11 encouraged me to read it, and eventually sent me a copy by email.

The *Testament of the Liberals* is a 1,170-word proclamation written "in Miragôane on April 16, 1883 by a group of mulattoes besieged by President Salomon's army."[7] It is an odious text. Black men are called "half-men" who "should accept their inferiority." Dessalines, the father of the Haitian nation, is called a cannibal. Several heroic figures of Haitian history are debased in crude language. It calls for the recolonization of Haiti, which would enable "mulattoes" to freely dominate the Black majority.

The *Testament* is a literary forgery. Its language and categories point to the second half of the twentieth century. It was never mentioned by Duvalier, noirist writers, or the twentieth-century classics of Haitian history authored by Justin Chrysostome Dorsainvil and Dantès Bellegarde. In addition, its use of the word *autochthone* echoes twentieth-century debates rather than nineteenth-century language. We have authentic samples of the categories, writing style, and vocabulary used by Boyer-Bazelais and his officers in letters, orders, and various notes they exchanged during the siege. They are reproduced in Jean Price-Mars's book on this civil war.[8] These documents bear little resemblance to the *Testament*. In them, forces loyal to President Salomon are named "the enemy" but are neither vilified nor racialized. Boyer-Bazelais praised their gallantry on several occasions and expressed his pride that the enemy (Salomon's forces) "deployed the usual courage of the Haitian."[9] He and his generals avoided racial references altogether. The only derogative expression I found in these primary sources was written at the very end of the siege in a recommendation by one officer, S. Bigailles, to another, Mathurin Legros, possibly written under the stress of defeat and when facing certain death (since captured insurgents were systematically executed by government soldiers): "Ignore the barbarism of these people [the surrounding government soldiers]."[10]

Two other sources open a window onto the categories and writing style of Boyer-Bazelais's fighters. The first one, *Notes de l'exilé*, is a personal diary authored by Charles Desroches, a Cap-Haitien native and poet executed by a firing squad after the insurgency had surrendered.[11] Desroches also praised the enemy's bravery. The other source, Gustave Vigoureux's memoir, includes letters, orders, and other texts by insurgents in Jérémie, the only town besides Jacmel that had joined the rebellion. It reproduces nineteenth-century clichés about liberty, glory, and the motherland, and do not vilify or racialize the enemy.[12]

Another element argues against *Le Testament*'s authenticity: the explicit, raw use of race and colors. Throughout the past two centuries, references to skin color were typically cryptic or metaphoric *in good company*, as many observers and scholars have noted.[13] Roger Gaillard was more nuanced: "people do not dare to approach the color question when in polite company and during peacetime."[14] And this was not peacetime. Yet, making such a statement at a time when the Liberal Party was urgently trying to rally the population to their cause would have been political suicide, although history is full of groups making counter-productive statements. To my knowledge, the only manifesto produced by the 1883 Liberal insurgency was a three-page document written in, and very likely circumscribed to, Jérémie.[15] It is a vociferous, nationalistic text that focuses on Salomon and accuses him of being the source of divisions in the country. It contains no racialized language, whether explicit, implicit, or cryptic; it instead calls for national unity.

The *Testament of the Liberals* obviously recalls the *Protocols of the Elders of Zion*, the anti-Semite forgery authored by the Tzarist police in 1903.[16] Specific techniques of demonization offer constructive points of comparison. Both forgeries attribute a set of negative characteristics to a specific group in order to project dangerousness upon it: chief among them, hatred and the entitlement to rule. A forgery evidences a lack of evidence, the awareness of this void, and the will to counter it, a homage of "epistemic anxiety" to scientific virtue.[17] As Nils Bubandt put it, the point of forgery is to craft "the enemy's point of view": "The forged documents, because they traverse the divide between legitimate and illegitimate forms of writing, form archival evidence of a political imagination in which authenticity is always a problem."[18]

The two forgeries, however, diverge on one point. While the *Protocol* is rather ahistorical, the entirety of the *Testament* is a history of Haiti. This is a central characteristic of noirism. To substantiate its arguments about inequalities, it systematically resorts to history rather than to sociology or socioeconomic data. Almost all the essays referenced in this chapter and the next are historiographic in nature even though their subject is the question of color. They attempt to locate evidence of today's racial inequalities and racial discriminations in the past. In this sense, history has been in Haiti a political science.

Gérard Barthélémy noted, in a book that pays homage to Haiti, that history is everywhere, a form of collective hypermnesia of past events that permeate worldviews and conversations.[19] It is actually not history that is omnipresent in Haiti; it is historiography. Historical references are ubiquitous in discourses, conversations, and books about politics, education, literature, society, the economy, or the "color question"—especially (but not only) in those produced by noirist writers. Yet these references do not simply point to clichéd "uses of history" or even to the production of history. If the place of anthropology in Haitian intellectual history, and particularly in such twentieth-century cultural movements as the *indigéniste* and *authentique* movements, has been amply explored, the use of historical figures and events as evidence for arguments that are sociological and economical in intent not only turns history into a fetish but also erases changes and agency.[20] Hoffmann, who cautioned that his argument is not an explanation but a contribution to the study of Haiti's many crises, offered another angle on this relation to history: "Haiti cannot digest its history. The antagonisms, tensions, distrusts, even the hatred that ruled in the time of the revolution perpetuated themselves until today. To admire Christophe or Dessalines still means to hate Rigaud, Pétion, Boyer and the ethnic and social group they represented. . . . History in Haiti stagnates, and so do its political ideologies."[21] Duvalier's use of the adjective "eternal," in the epigraph at the beginning of this chapter, betrays the belief that history simply repeats itself. As Jean-François Sénéchal showed, Duvalierism's invocation of history was mythical in nature, providing an explanation for the nation's origins.[22] In the conclusion to this chapter I will return to the question of how the historiography became a battleground for noirist intellectuals, chief among them François Duvalier.

FRENCH THEORY

The first extensive essentialization of Haitian "mulattoes" in writing may have been authored by Victor Schoelcher (1804–1893), a French politician and prolific writer remembered today primarily as the main legislator of the final abolition of slavery in the French colonies in 1848. He traveled to Haiti in 1841 and authored a book two years later, one-half of which is dedicated to the country.[23] The book gives a rare ethnographic account of Haitian life in both the countryside and the capital at a time when few foreigners were interested in Haiti. It is also an incendiary book that was used as an anti-mulatto vade mecum by such writers as Louis Joseph Janvier (1855–1911), Alcius Charmant (1856–1936), and François Duvalier (1907–1971) who freely and uncritically dipped into Schoelcher's list of mulatto "flaws." His essentialist and deeply negative stereotypes would not be critiqued until the twenty-first century with the publication of Marlene Daut's precise assessment of his work. Daut underscores Schoelcher's foundational contribution to a racialist ("colored") history of Haiti, replacing it in the debates and epistemologies of the time.[24] I will therefore not add to her work but only highlight each of the major stereotypes that would eventually essentialize "the mulatto" in the noirist imagination of which the Duvalier regime and its massacres are the conclusion.

Schoelcher depicts "mulattoes" as depraved, domineering, brutal, selfish, and foreign. Although the term *mulâtrisme* (mulattoism, "mulatto" political supremacy) would not be coined until a century later, its semantics appeared in their entirety in Schoelcher's work. If Schoelcher's negative essentialization of mixed-race people was widespread in the mid-nineteenth century, it has to be understood in the context of his individual agenda.[25] Schoelcher was so resolute to demonstrate that the Black race (*la race noire*) was in no way inferior to whites, that Blacks were equals in intelligence and morality, and that there was no innate brutality in the African race that he identified these ills in "mulattoes," the most "European" part of the population. To prove that achievements by Blacks were not due to a dilution of African blood, he denied "mulattoes" any accomplishment. Schoelcher's Faustian choice is reminiscent of Bartolomé de Las Casas's advocacy of African slavery in order to spare the indigenous population of the Americas. The result was a book that was both pro-African and anti-"mulatto."

In Schoelcher's work, all revolutionary and post-independence "mulatto" leaders are, without exception, portrayed negatively. He contrasts the marital and private behavior of Toussaint Louverture, Jean-Jacques Dessalines, and Henri Christophe, three historical Black leaders who all formally married within the Catholic Church and thus within French bourgeois norms, to Pétion and Boyer who were not only unmarried but depraved enough to share the same concubine. However, the most salient aspect of "mulattoes" is their tendency to political hegemony. To demonstrate it, Schoelcher uses history. "Mulattoes," he argues, were opposed to abolition: "Far from being the friends of the blacks, they were instead their fiercest enemies."[26] The War of the South in 1799–1800, which pitted Rigaud against Toussaint, provides Schoelcher with yet more evidence. According to Schoelcher, Rigaud hated and despised Blacks; Rigaud was the "sole source" of this war and is responsible for dividing Blacks and "mulattoes."[27] The South's rebellion explains and justifies, still for Schoelcher, Toussaint's subsequent massacre of "mulattoes" at the end of the war, a statement he reiterates later in the book: "[Toussaint] was forced to crack down (*sévir*) on them (the mulattoes) because they stupidly rebelled against the authority of an old negro."[28]

Schoelcher may have been the first to accuse "mulattoes" in writing of having assassinated King Henri Christophe, another assertion that would have a long career in the subsequent historiography: "Mulattoes achieved what they wanted."[29] "Mulattoes" are considered illegitimate to rule the country. For instance, "[Pétion] was wrong to accept power, a yellow man ("mulatto") in the middle of a Black nation."[30] Schoelcher then exhorts "mulattoes": "Yellow men, have the courage to abandon power . . . any action you will undertake to lift the oppressed blacks will be considered an act of oppression by the mulatto aristocracy."[31] Because it is in the hand of *jaunes*, the government prevents "the black masses" from having access to school, while in the North Christophe was "blanketing his kingdom" with schools; "poverty, ignorance, and laziness are tools of (mulatto) government."[32] Finally, "mulattoes" as a group held all responsibility (*culpabilité*) for the racial division of society.

Schoelcher's book and indictment of an entire group were seminal.[33] Louis Joseph Janvier, Duvalier's *maître à penser*, repeatedly referenced Schoelcher in his books, and urged his countrymen to study him. Duvalier found in Schoelcher an authoritative source on mulattoes' greed, disloyalty, and discriminatory behavior.[34] He also referenced Schoelcher's racialized version of the revolution.[35] Schoelcher's belief that a "mulatto" could not legitimately rule the country would become a cornerstone of noirist literature. Hannibal Price blamed Schoelcher—"his immense responsibility"—for producing a "catechism" of anti-mulatto Haitian history.[36]

THE SOCIAL LIFE OF APOCRYPHAL WRITINGS

Alcius Charmant differs from most of the other authors of his time, notably Janvier, in that he explicitly used racial identities when explaining "*mulatto*" interests, "*mulatto*" wrongdoings, "*mulatto*" politicians, "*mulatto*" balls. His book, one of the few referenced by Duvalier, is a long indictment of "mulattoes" as a group and warns Haitians not to be duped by "the Machiavellian calculations, the criminal endeavors of these aristocrats of the skin."[37] The book's title—*Will Haiti Survive?*—is less a question than an accusation. It is illustrated by a drawing that shows a dignified woman representing Haiti, lying in agony in her bed.[38] "Can Haiti survive mulattoes?" seems to be the real title. Although the subtitle, *Study on the Prejudice of Race: Black Race, Yellow Race, White Race*, seems to prefigure an essay on race, what we have instead is another history book.

Literary deceptions and apocryphal attributions are common in this literature. The book's first chapter, "The Color Prejudice," starts with an epigraph by Jean-Paul Boyer (1776–1850), former president of Haiti (1818–1843): "Let us always think about it, never talk about it."[39] The quote is a series of double entendres—what is "it," who is "us," who is talking to whom and about what? Since Boyer is the president most associated with "mulatto" hegemony and since the first chapter is about "mulatto" supremacy, the reader can easily fill in the gap: Boyer is talking to other "mulattoes" about power (to which they are entitled); they are destined to rule. Boyer's axiom explains why there is no written evidence of what would later be called *mulâtrisme*: if "mulattoes" are advised *never* to talk about it, but to *always* act and think accordingly, then we have the perfect racial and intellectual crime. By framing his chapter about racist prejudices with a cryptic "mulatto" obsession and policy, Charmant turns suspicion into an epistemology. Because prejudice and discrimination by "mulattoes" are not overt, they must be uncovered. The epigraph's plural pronoun, "let *us*," is also relevant. Boyer is supposedly talking to a group. This group is not named—nothing in the quote is. Yet, the reader understands who the "we" refers to: "mulattoes." The belief that "mulattoes" act as a group, a unified whole, and in service to this unified whole was central to anti-"mulatto" rhetoric. The usual "they" of ethnic stereotypes assigns a "we" to the group it stigmatizes.[40]

Charmant does not provide a reference, only an attribution, for Boyer's epigraph. I could not find any source documenting Boyer's injunction. This quote is actually from Léon Gambetta, a nineteenth-century French politician.[41] Gambetta was referring to two regions annexed by imperial Prussia in 1870, a territorial loss that framed French political and cultural insecurities over the following decades, with the First World War as its tragic outcome. Reconquering Alsace-Lorraine became a national project and Gambetta wanted this project to be obsessive for every French citizen. Charmant, who lived in exile for several years in Paris, where his book was published, probably assumed that a Haitian public would not notice this rhetorical palimpsest. Yet, while Gambetta was directing nationalistic anger at a foreign power, Charmant was pointing to an internal enemy.

Double entendres are markers of conspiracy theories in which the thinker and his readers are supposed to understand one another.[42] To understand the double entendre between Boyer and the other "mulattos" (the conspiracy), one has to integrate the double entendres between Charmant and his own readers (the theory). If someone *always* thought about *it*, it was Charmant who reread a sentence created within the Franco-Prussian context as a Haitian one. Another of Charmant's arguments will later inspire Duvalier: the belief that Haiti's destiny could be realized only through a savior. The belief that Haiti was destined to lead the entire Black race to liberation was widespread at the time—Hannibal Price also made this argument.[43] However, for Charmant, this manifest destiny was betrayed by "mulattoes," and what was truly needed to restore Haiti's rightful place and wellbeing was a Black savior:

Predestined race that the universe contemplates
. . . .
Slave again, you carry the chains

More humiliating and heavier than ever,

Because 'the Hydra has reappeared' and is showing its power

....

To defeat it, a Hercules is needed.

Overall, Charmant provides a diagnosis (who is responsible for Haiti's ills:): the mulattoes; and the prognosis (the hero). Only a hero can destroy the Hydra (the mulattoes) and restore Haiti's wellbeing and manifest destiny.[44]

ATTRIBUTING HATRED

On June 15, 1882, Hannibal Price (1843–1903) wrote an incendiary letter to Louis Marcelin, a celebrated poet and novelist who was serving in Salomon's government, in which Price accused Marcelin of betraying his race. The newspaper *L'Avant-Garde* later obtained a copy of it and published it: "Mulatto like me, I am sure that you hold blacks in horror, as much as I do. You are a scoundrel for serving this government of [n-word]s. You flatter [n-word]s, and you are of the same stuff as Thomas Madiou."[45] Hannibal Price, the celebrated author of an eight-hundred-page manifesto for the defense (*réhabilitation*) of the Black race, was credited by historian Leslie Manigat for initiating a "cultural revolution" on the subject.[46] In homage to a man he considered an intellectual father, Jean Price-Mars added "Price" to his family name, Mars. In 1979, an international Congress against the apartheid system organized in Kingston, Jamaica declared Hannibal Price "a benefactor of humanity and of the Black race."[47] How could such a man write a letter replete with racist language?

According to Léon-François Hoffmann, he did not.[48] *L'Avant-Garde* published propaganda pieces for the authoritarian Salomon government and regularly fabricated self-incriminating letters "authored" by opponents. Hannibal Price, at the time living in exile in Jamaica, was the most famous of them.[49] It did the trick: the celebrated Haitianist David Nicholls uncritically took these letters at face value, and found in it evidence of mulattoes' superiority complex.[50] The *Testament of the Liberals* was not the only forgery fabricated to discredit "mulattoes."

The strategy to discredit Salomon's most famous opponent was to attribute hatred to him. (*L'Avant-Garde* could have fabricated many other allegations against Hannibal Price—corruption, incompetence, or dishonesty—yet it chose hatred.) In a society that defined itself as Black, the attribution of anti-Black prejudices delegitimized anyone accused or suspected of such beliefs.[51] This attribution was also central to other ideologies of hatred. Tutsis were not only dehumanized by Hutu supremacists, but were also constructed as holding a racial superiority complex against Hutus. Nazi antisemitism attributed the hate of Germans to German Jews.[52] Antisemitism constructed Jews as both uprooted and hateful of the rooted. As an empirical point of discursive comparison, here is what the French anti-Semite, Pierre Gaxotte, said of the French (and Jewish) prime minister Léon Blum in 1936: "How he hates us! He reproaches us everything, our sky, which is blue, our air, which is sweet, he hates the peasant for walking on the French soil and for not having had ancestors who rode camels, wandering around the Syrian desert with his buddies from Palestine."[53] Louis Joseph Janvier, in an incendiary book, had earlier depicted "mulattoes" as people imbued with a sense of racial superiority toward the Black majority.[54] The two stereotypes most associated with the figure of the "mulatto"—hatred and the will to dominate—were then evoked to explain why they could kill with impunity. The inevitable consequence of this racism (by mulattoes) and control of the government (by mulattoes) would be the killing of their Black countrymen. Thus, Duvalier depicts the rule of President Boyer in the most incendiary terms: Boyer "poisoned, deported and executed all the blacks of some intellectual value," an unsubstantiated claim that is absent from the historiography.[55]

A group can be stigmatized only by attributing to it the anti-value of the era—otherwise it does not stick. Attributing hatred turns stigmatization into counter-hatred, subjectivity into objectivity. It moralizes and legitimizes stigmatization. If, as Sartre put it, "violence poses as a counter-violence,"[56] an ideology of hatred has to present itself as counter-hatred.[57] Hatred is first constructed as counter-hatred, then violence is constructed as counter-violence, and finally denialists will both refute the crime's actuality and construct it as popular vengeance. It is the missing epistemic linkage between (noirist) ideology and the belief that perpetrators are mere avengers. While the cognitive mechanism of denial is usually a post-violence intellectual construction refuting that the crime actually took place, denial first appears before and in order for the violence to happen. What is powerfully denied at the ex ante stage are the notions that hatred is projected and that delegitimization is subjective. Immersed in subjectivity, this intellectual structure can turn children into the figure of the enemy.

During both the ex ante and post facto stages, essentialization, totalization, collective responsibility, and vilification structure the entire intellectual edifice. "Denial is the condition for evil," as Reiner Schürmann put it. Noirism appears first as sociology to construct, then returns later as memory to justify.

CONSPIRATORS

The narrative of mulattoes' will to rule crystalized around recurring historical themes. A major one is the assassination in 1806 of Dessalines, the country's founder, by "mulattoes." Charmant argues that Dessalines was killed because of "the color prejudice" by "a military conspiracy of 'mulatto' politicians, particularly Pétion, Gérin and Guérard, his own lieutenants."[58] Roger Dorsinville (1911–1992), a celebrated mid-twentieth-century author, made the same point: "It was the sons of former colonizers who, to appropriate the land . . . assassinated the great Dessalines."[59] It is also a recurring theme in Duvalier's own works.[60] The essayist André Juste took it for granted that the former *affranchis* (free mulattoes) wanted Dessalines dead because they were opposed to emancipation.[61] Recent scholarship shows that Dessalines' assassination had little to do with color.[62]

As Schoelcher had six decades earlier, Charmant asserted that "mulattoes" are moved by a will to control and monopolize political power. Charmant published this book in 1905. Nord Alexis, the anti-Liberal president of the National Party, was the country's president. Charmant was a supporter of the opposition leader, Anténor Firmin, the Liberal Party's champion. For Charmant and Firmin's supporters, there was no doubt that Nord Alexis was a puppet in the hand of the "mulatto" elite. The same accusation was leveled at Firmin by Alexis and his supporters.[63] The notion, apparently shared by the entire political spectrum, that "mulattoes" are illegitimate, manipulative, and control the opposing side highlights a paranoid world.

The belief that "mulattoes" feel entitled to rule, and yet rule only from the shadows, is exemplified by the expression *politique de doublure* ("understudy politics")—a term coined by Hénock Trouillot who, along with Windsor Kléber Lafférières and René Piquion, would later become one of the early ideologues of the Duvalier regime.[64] The term vividly describes the manipulation of a Black president by a mulatto elite acting behind the scenes. In this narrative, a Black president would always be suspected of being a potential puppet of "mulattoes" who hold real power. *Politique de doublure* became a ubiquitous expression that appeared frequently both in common parlance and in noirist discourse. The term is also reflected in modern scholarship on Haiti; even a scholar such as Nicholls endorsed it uncritically.[65] Other contemporary scholars, notably Leslie Péan and Michèle Oriol, have rejected it altogether as representing a biased view of history.[66]

Hénock Trouillot believed it was Céligny Ardouin (1806–1849) who initiated this practice. In early 1847, Ardouin allegedly conspired to place a Black officer, Soulouque, in power.[67] Ardouin, in Trouillot's narrative, became an individual paradoxically devoid of agency, since his actions were determined by race. Duvalier's own interpretation of Haitian history was also that of a long confiscation of the state by "mulattoes." This comes to light in his work *Psycho-sociologie mentalité historique: grandeur et misère d'une classe* (*Psycho-Sociology Historical Mentality: Greatness and Miseries of a Class*).[68] As he explained: "Since 1804, a class of men perpetuated itself in power. When this preponderance (*sic*) led to a feeling of legitimate rebellion among the masses, they resorted to a technique worthy of Machiavelli: *the politique de doublure*."[69]

The scientific affect of this literature stops at empirical evidence—the reader fails to identify proofs, especially beyond the 1840s, that "mulattoes" gathered, organized, planned, and succeeded in placing a Black man they controlled in the presidential palace. There is no smoking gun there. The fact that intent replaces substantiation and that a group is totalized suggests a conspiracy theory. A conspiracy theory presents itself not as belief but as critical thinking: it is able to "see through" and refuses to be duped by appearances—elections in particular.[70] As Taguieff shows, a conspiracy theory presents itself as social science. The *politique de doublure* narrative presents itself as social science *and* historiography. Interpretation replaces demonstration and intentions are attributed—what Taguieff calls "the intentionality bias."[71] Compromises, calculations, negotiations, competing constituencies, individual ambitions—in short, *politics*—are flushed out in favor of a clean, perfectly executed action that competently and graciously put in place a docile Black president ready to betray his race. Taguieff again: "[a] conspiracy theory postulates that an action's final result constitutes the perfect realization of the actor's intent."[72] The *politique de doublure* also represents both a diagnosis and a prognosis: an explanation of Haitian history and a call for action. It is determined to raise the ire of those whose government has been "confiscated." However, if the *politique de doublure* is taken at face value, why did mulattoes need to conspire and hide in the first place to control the presidency? What forces worked to keep mulattoes from openly defending their own interests?

ETHNOGRAPHIC THINNESS

Coined after the Revolution of 1946, the term *mulâtrisme* (mulattoism) names mulattoes' alleged political hegemony and an attendant ideology of racial supremacy.[73] But if noirism is a noirist self-denomination, mulattoism is also noirist in origin. It enables noirism to stand epistemologically and survive morally by constructing a larger binary opposition. Put differently, noirism is a social invention and mulattoism a social construction. Many historical figures, from Boyer-Bazelais to Hannibal Price to Jeune Haiti, were suspected of harboring a hidden agenda of "mulatto" power. Recent scholarship tends to avoid the term and its semantics. Yet, in common parlance and editorials, the term retains considerable currency and remains what Lévi-Strauss called "a floating signifier": a ubiquitous term that functions more as a slogan than a reflexive and critical one, continuing its epistemic career even when the historical conditions that birthed it have long since fossilized.[74]

One would assume that such incendiary semantics would deserve considerable substantiation. It has not been the case. There is no "mulatto" equivalent to the analytical and programmatic texts that the noirist worldview has produced for over a century. I could not identify any document advocating for "mulatto" rule, except as forgery. Even the highly critical Leslie Péan, who courageously equated noirism with racism, also takes mulattoism as an empirical reality; yet, to prove the latter's actuality, Péan turned to a novel by Lilia Desquiron—fiction is indeed full of arrogant, spiteful, and immoral "mulattoes."[75] Roger Dorsinville's famously accusatory *Lettre aux hommes clairs* (*Letter to Fair-Skinned People*), to which I will return later, mainly emphasizes "gestures, words, and looks" and did not substantialize further.[76] Trouillot bypassed empirical thinness: hard evidence cannot be found because it is mulattoism's nature to hide from view.[77] Michèle Labelle argued that mulattoes' prejudices are confined to private space and the family, although she provided no example of it.[78] The notion that individuals would hold prejudices, and that these prejudices would be passed down from one generation to the next privately for over a hundred years, without it ever spilling out into public view or finding its way into a written text in a nation of writers, would require remarkable competency and control but is still within the realm of the possible. However, the notion that a given phenomenon produces no empirical evidence by virtue of its very nature—and consequently, that critiques of mulattoism are simply to be trusted—is a rather unusual epistemology. An ideology of racial supremacy wandering in the catacombs, vying for hegemony but scared, requires forgeries and magical interpretations.

OPPRESSORS

Le problème des classes à travers l'histoire d'Haïti (*Class Struggles in Haitian History*), co-written with Lorimer Denis and first published in 1948, is the most political of Duvalier's early works.[79] In it, the terms "elites" and "mulattoes" are interchangeable; so are *les noirs* and *la masse*, with descendants of slaves understood as today's masses. Without substantializing his claims, Duvalier states four times that mulatto slave owners were crueler, more hateful, and more likely to execute their Black slaves than white owners.[80] Mulattoes did not want to abolish slavery and intended to maintain it. The group solidarity of mulattoes was fueled "by their racial prejudices and their interests."[81] These incendiary pages explicitly make mulattoes, not whites, the enemy of the Black majority. The conditions of oppression are such that "after 144 years of independence, should we be surprised that the descendants of the slaves are integrally maintained in the condition of pariahs?"[82]

In this work, suspicion frames the entire view. Consequently, mulattoes are constructed as traitors or traitors-in-waiting. To sustain his assertions, Duvalier attributes this warning to the French revolutionary envoy Sonthonax: "as long as you will have men of color [mulattoes] among your men, you will not be free. It was then [a] question for a while, according to Madiou, to cut the throats of the mulattos in the hills."[83] After listing crimes committed by mulattoes against Blacks during the Haitian Revolution, Duvalier "conclude[s]: 1) the tendency of the elites to dissociate themselves (*se désolidariser*) from the masses, which has also led to failure. 2) the First of the Blacks (Toussaint Louverture) teaches us that any Revolution, to be deep and sustainable, must aim at the redemption of the masses."[84] For Duvalier, as for Alcius Charmant earlier, this salvation can only come from a Black hero.

In midcentury literary production, the mulatto is depicted as oppressive in both the political and the private space. Jacques Roumain's first novel, *Les fantoches* (*The Puppets*) exemplifies this trend while addressing inequalities entirely in a racialized manner. The Tiballes, a wealthy mulatto family from Bois-Verna, martyrizes a young Black domestic, Charmantine, who is a *restavek*: literally, a child from the countryside who has been placed into domestic servitude. Uneducated, powerless, unpaid, Charmantine is entirely at the family's mercy. They abuse her and randomly beat her. The family's sons rape her repeatedly. Despicable, depraved, utterly selfish, corrupt, the mulatto is pitted against the innocent, noble peasant. It is probably not so much the figure of the mulatto that Roumain had in mind as a rich family he wanted to depict as emblematic. Yet, not one single mulatto character in the novel appears capable of empathy.

Literary production around the time of the 1946 Revolution further crystalized representations of the mulatto. In January, Roger Dorsinville made a seminal set of accusations against mulattoes.[85] The political and intellectual history of this revolution is fully analyzed by Matthew Smith and Frantz Voltaire, who show how racial tensions reached their climax that year.[86] The U.S. occupation of Haiti (1915–1934) favored so-called mulatto-filled governments and institutions, triggering resentment in the Black middle-class. Yet the accusatory ideas and views on mulattoes expressed in Dorsinville's text existed well before the U.S. Occupation.

Dorsinville was a multifaceted individual. First trained at the military academy, he became a teacher, then an evangelist, then President Dumarsais Estimé's Chief of Staff from May 1946 to March 1948. Dorsinville was a prominent figure and ideologue of the post-1946 noirist movement.[87] He was also Duvalier's right hand during the 1957 campaign.[88] Duvalier then sent him on a diplomatic mission, a tactic he often followed to get rid of undesirable members of his inner-circle. Dorsinville's diplomatic career lasted until 1965 when he settled in Africa (Liberia, then Sénégal). He returned to Haiti in 1976. He was also a prolific writer, journalist, novelist, poet, and playwright. Most of his works betray a deeply racialized worldview. Nevertheless, Dorsinville's life should not be "pigeonholed" into one political category; the humanist dimension of many of his works is undeniable. He also influenced many scholars, such as Roger Gaillard and Claude Moïse, fiction writers such as Félix Morisseau-Leroy, and countless students.

Dorsinville opens his *Letter* by stating that he holds no racial prejudices whatsoever. He then accuses mulattoes (as a group) of tribalism and of leading a shadow war (*guerre sourde*) against Blacks. Mulattoes have "an instinct" for it and "boldly lead this war through humiliations; [this war] manifests itself through gestures, words and looks; it is visible in the way family circles narrow, in the flexible play of alliances, in the way people get together."[89] Discriminations are the *Letter*'s main motive: "[Y]ou have mistreated us, despised us, humiliated us."[90] Dorsinville used damning metaphors, such as untouchability, Blacks feeling like pariahs in their own country, Haiti being a colonial system (sic) run by mulattoes; the treatment of Blacks by mulattos being worse (*sic*) than Algeria under the French or India under the British.[91] Another salient aspect of the *Letter* is not simply its hyper-essentialization of mulattoes, but its wide totalization of this group. The letter is not portraying *some* mulattoes or *many* mulattoes, but *all* mulattoes. In many respects, the *Letter* exemplifies the worldview of noirism since the second half of the nineteenth century: the egalitarian (and not just racial) ideologies at work; the programmatic focus on government jobs (rather than, say, the condition of the peasantry); the attribution of a visceral hatred to mulattoes; and, more generally, the depiction of the mulatto as venal, lacking empathy, and a traitor to his country.

Dorsinville's *Letter* also exemplifies the makeshift sociology embedded in noirism. It recognizes only two social classes in Haitian society: the elites and the masses. The masses are exclusively Black; the elites are composed of both mulattoes and educated Blacks. Yet the latter group is so discriminated against by the former that they do not have access to professional careers and end up being relegated to "the masses." There is no intermediate sector, no differentiation, no social mobility—only "a caste" and "a class."[92] Egalitarian ideologies are implicit. Mulattoes are systematically depicted as wealthy, and their wealth was gained through unjust means:

> Meanwhile, the privileged ones, sheltered from any need, developed their quarters in luxury, the luxury of Bourdon, the luxury of Pétionville, the luxury of Kenscoff, the luxury of Furcy. . . . While the masses were being trimmed down, everything was granted to the bourgeois' s sons because of their wealth, so they could have it easy and become the leading and thinking elite. . . . Because there were among us some who were thinking, some who "knew" and guessed that one day we would no longer bend over. . . . Meanwhile, [you] imported white teachers, because we could not understand education and management problems, creating among us an inferiority complex that made us accept as masters those who looked like them. This was done. This was the crime that was committed.[93]

The *Letter* exposes Dorsinville's—and noirism's—contradictions. On one hand, Dorsinville repeatedly accuses mulattoes of segregation; yet, as part of his justification, he states that Blacks are well aware of how "mulattoes" behave because they sit "side by side in the schools" with them, share friendships with them, and sometimes are even part of the same family.

Decades later, Dorsinville offered a self-criticism of sorts in two separate interviews. By the 1980s, defending the regime had become socially unacceptable. The crimes Dorsinville condemned, however, were of another type: "I resigned [from the diplomatic service] in 1965. Duvalier had just committed one of his first crimes. He ha[d] voted in Punta del Este for the eviction of Cuba from the Organization of American States. This announced Haiti's total subjection to U.S. foreign policy."[94] Dorsinville even put the blame for the rise of noirism and the now-discredited Duvalier regime on mulattoes.[95]

NOIRIST "MULATTOES"

Dorsinville's *Lettre aux hommes clairs* triggered several responses reflective of the wider anxieties generated by noirism in the delegitimized mulatto population.[96] Milo Rigaud's self-referential response, *Lettre aux hommes de toutes couleurs* (*Letter to people of all colors*), goes further than Dorsinville's text in its stigmatization of mulattoes. In words that evoke anti-Semitic literature, Rigaud had earlier depicted mulattoes foaming at the mouth with hatred: "If I ask a mulatto where his [Black] brother is, he will answer *la bave aux lèvres:* he is an enemy."[97] In his own response, Simon Desvarieux clumsily justifies himself by stating that even though he is a mulatto, he personally holds no bias against Blacks—an exemption he extends to his family, given that several members of it have married Blacks, but not to other mulattoes, who are not like him.[98] He also accuses mulattoes of having "indecently mulattoized Haiti." The argument being presented is that mulattos are indeed prejudiced, *but not me.*

By attacking mulattoes as a singular racial group rather than targeting specific individuals who happened to be mulattoes, and by assuming that all mulattoes have shared characteristics that determine their thinking and behavior, Rigaud and Desvarieux did as much damage as Dorsinville. The only way to escape delegitimization from mulattoes' group stigmatization would be through an individual strategy. As sociologist David Smith shows, some Jews in the nineteenth century vilified fellow Jews by invoking some of the most clichéd stereotypes associated with Jewish identity, assuming they could escape stigmatization by stigmatizing others or by displaying a set of behaviors that was not coded as Jewish.[99] Publicly deprecating mulattoes as a group allowed for the acquisition of symbolic capital. Some were also moved by belief. Journalist Jean Dominique repeatedly used the expression *mulâtraille* in his career.[100] This neologism, derogative to the extreme, echoes linguistic inventions of twentieth-century racist movements. The term blends *mulâtre* (mulatto) and *racaille* (scum), the suffix *-aille* typically referring to material rather than living entities.[101]

MULATTOLOGY

Haitian historiography was in the mid-twentieth century a racialized battleground.[102] If the only set of evidence that noirism offered to substantiate its political, sociological, and racial views was located in the past, historiography had to be "racially" cleansed of "mulatto" production. In the nineteenth- and twentieth-century works examined in this chapter, mulattoes are driven by in-group solidarity—mulattoes help mulattoes, promote mulattoes, hire mulattoes, conspire with mulattoes, socialize with mulattoes, and marry mulattoes, always to the detriment of others. In this view, historians identified as mulattoes are inherently biased. Noirist authors, including François Duvalier, offered both a biological critique of Haitian historiography to delegitimize the scholarly production of intellectuals identified as mulattoes—and a biologized history to replace it.

L'intellectuel de couleur et les problèmes de la discrimination raciale (*The Mulatto Intellectual and the Issues of Racial Discrimination*), published at the dawn of the 1957 presidential campaign by Hénock Trouillot, entirely delegitimizes mulatto scholars. The mulatto scholar can not articulate individual thoughts.[103] Instead, he is "the writer of his race."[104] Uprooted, alienated from his countrymen, using a foreign tongue, a foreign worldview, and a religion that is not African, the mulatto historian is excluded from Haitianness.[105] Marlene Daut's recent revolutionary research counters this view, providing clear evidence that so-called "mulatto historians" in the early nineteenth century, such as Beaubrun Ardouin and Thomas Madiou, did not produce a "mulatto version" of Haitian history but, to the contrary, betrayed an early Black consciousness and undaunted patriotic convictions.[106]

The stigmatization of early Haitian historians participates in a larger social construction of the mulatto as illegitimate, foreign, and untrustworthy. Yet, Hénock Trouillot also accused contemporary historians; his long, ad hominem critiques of Dantès Bellegarde, a prominent historian and intellectual, exemplified this.[107] René Piquion authored a long indictment of mulatto historians on the same grounds, denouncing "[t]he repeated lie of the descendants of the freed slaves." Historiography, if it is authored by mulattoes, contributes to the oppression of the Black masses.[108] In the real-time context of the Duvalier regime, Piquion made an ad hominem attack against a mulatto historian, Louis Elie.[109] The Duvalierist parliament then forfeited Elie's citizenship in August 1963 by decree. Fearing for his life, Elie fled abroad; he only returned to Haiti in 1986.[110]

CHAPTER 3

Othering the Elite

In the light of science, we must reveal the irritating question of color.

François Duvalier[1]

HATRED BY BIOLOGY

On the morning of August 14, 1964, U.S. Ambassador Benson Timmons received a request from René Chalmers, Haiti's foreign minister, to meet with him and Duvalier. Once in the presidential office, he found the two men carefully examining pictures of a dead body. The corpse on the pictures was that of the first Jeune Haiti rebel killed in action in the southwestern mountains and brought to Port-au-Prince by plane the day before.[2] Timmons realized that Duvalier and Chalmers, their eyes riveted on the pictures, were assessing the dead person's race. Because the face was made unrecognizable by bullet impacts, the two men focused on the body's shape and color. A mystified Timmons registered Duvalier's "ethno-physiological observations." Duvalier eventually and authoritatively diagnosed that it could not be the body of a Haitian man. Rather, Duvalier learnedly explained, the body is quite similar to "Latin American' types such as being Cuban, Dominican, Venezuelan and perhaps Colombian."[3] Timmons was so taken aback by the scene that the two cables he wrote and sent the same day omitted to explain why he was requested at the Presidential Palace in the first place.[4]

There might have been some theatrics from Duvalier and Chalmers, who could have been trying to obtain information from Timmons about the origin of the rebellion, but Duvalier's racialism and performance as a scientist were not affected. Duvalier's relation to the color question has been characterized as obsessive by those who worked with him.[5] Race was the "ontology" of Duvalier's entire thought system.[6] Racialism was so omnipresent in Haiti's intellectual production in the first half of the twentieth century that the celebrated Haitianist David Nicholls dedicated a comprehensive study of its indigenization (my word) and trajectory in Haiti.[7] Chelsea Stieber, who masterfully documents and explores how entire sectors of the Haitian intelligentsia in the 1920s and 1930s were immersed in ideas first articulated by the French far right, links "integral nationalism," the far-right ideology that would propel Duvalier to the presidency, to an indigenous, well-developed, nineteenth-century critique of the Enlightenment.[8]

Duvalier had been immersed in racialist thinking since his childhood. A rather delicate poem he published at the age of 27, "Les sanglots d'un exilé" (An Exile's Sobs), announces the race-based resentment and views he developed later in his books.[9] In it, Duvalier paints himself as a sort of Camusian stranger, at odds with the world, ostracized by society in general and women in particular, solely because of his black skin. From his anthropological publications in the 1930s to his late speeches as Haiti's president, race was a leitmotif and an explanatory principle. His belief in "a genius of the race" and in common ancestry was inspired by Gobineau, the nineteenth-century theoretician of scientific racism. He was also convinced, as Jean-François Sénéchal has shown, that miscegenation was a curse, and that each race has an essence. In this logic, the behavior of Blacks and of mulattoes are determined by their hereditary genes:

> In truth, [even] if stabilized (acculturated) Blacks are influenced by the anarchic and violent impulses of Bakambas, Bakalai, Pahouins, Ba-Soundo, Ba-Binda of equatorial Africa, [while] the mulatto, under the appearance of nice manners hides of [a] psychology of (white) pirates and buccaneers, all cynical and adventurous, who at the beginning of the eighteenth century spread terror on the coastline of the Americas by their looting, pillaging and depredation . . . the Race entity appears in the first place as the moral value of the Haitian nation.[10]

Anténor Firmin, a canonic intellectual who debunked scientific racism as unscientific, is symptomatically absent from Duvalier's work, in which the most referenced authors are, in order, Louis-Joseph Janvier, Alcius Charmant, J.-C.

Dorsainvil, Emmanuel Édouard, and Victor Schoelcher. With the exception of Édouard, all were authors with a deeply racialist worldview. Charles Maurras (1868–1952), the French far-right and anti-parliamentarian theoretician, is mentioned only twice in Duvalier's work but his influence exceeds a mere count. Bob Nérée argues that Maurras was Duvalier's real *maître-à-penser*.[11] Gobineau's and Maurras' presence among Duvalier's references may appear astonishing in the work and thought of a noirist who, once in power, proclaimed himself to be "a Third-World leader."[12]

Duvalier's intellectual appropriations, however, were as half-baked as his theories. From Gobineau, he took racial determinism, not the demeaning of Africans; from Maurras, the repudiation of liberal democracy and the defense of extreme nationalism based on a homogeneous society. Fascist seduction also explains not only Duvalier's creation of an extralegal, armed militia at the beginning of his presidential campaign—the only candidate who did so—but also the name he gave to it: *Cagoulards*. The name was appropriated from a French secret paramilitary organization in the 1930s, la Cagoule (the Hood), whose members were nicknamed Cagoulards and who carried out terrorist actions, as would their eponymous Haitian counterparts led by Clément Barbot.[13] Duvalier would institutionalize and legalize the Cagoulards as the VSNs (Volontaires de la Sécurité Nationale, or National Security Volunteers) only in 1962.[14] The militia's official name was probably appropriated from another fascist organization: Mussolini's Militia for National Security (Milizia Volontaria per la Sicurezza Nazionale).

BIOLOGICAL DETERMINISM

Duvalier and his noirist contemporaries developed ideas immersed in set representations. One nineteenth-century author in particular, Louis-Joseph Janvier, was immensely influential, idealizing the peasantry and representing it as the elite's nemesis in an oversimplified binary opposition that would have a long career. In Janvier's novels and incendiary essays, the figure of the "peasant" was constructed as a racially pure figure of Haitian authenticity, whereas the mulatto was constructed as foreign. Both the peasantry and the mulatto elite were essentialized and racialized in languages that borrowed from both biology and sociology.

In *Le vieux piquet*, first published in 1884, the main character is a peasant leader and an exemplary father, husband, and citizen.[15] He is fundamentally peaceful, yet he courageously takes up arms against the elite, whom he defeats. In victory, he is chivalrous and magnanimous: when the *piquets* (insurgent peasants) who are under his command and support the Salomon government defeat the "bourgeois [town of] Jérémie" in December 1883, they enter and take the town "without anger" in spite of eight months of hardship caused by the mulattoes.[16] The *Vieux piquet*'s Roman-like stoicism yields to German-like romanticism only when a sunset of overwhelming beauty moves him to tears. Not only does Janvier project quintessential nineteenth-century male European bourgeois values onto a character fighting, well, the bourgeois, but he seems to borrow the type of cutting-edge racialism that only his colonial contemporaries in Paris had concocted. Janvier biologized authenticity to portray his own ancestry:

> From both sides, I am made of the nation's marrow. One hundred years ago, my paternal grandmother lived in Morne-à-Tuf; [so did] my paternal great-grandfather.[17] All this can be proven with authentic deeds [of property]. . . . I have cousins . . . in Boucassin and in the Plaine du Cul-de-sac. . . . [Hannibal] Price cannot produce such quarters of Haitianism, or even, I was about to say, of nobility, because in Haiti the peasant, whether indigenous or aboriginal, is the true noble, the patriot par excellence.[18]

Janvier's own Haitianness is made of peasant blood; Hannibal Price, a "mulatto" and, as importantly, an opponent of President Salomon is not.[19] In most of Janvier's works, the mulattoes, or *jaunes*, are treated either as traitors to their nation or, at best, as disloyal, receiving long patriotic lectures. In *Les antinationaux (actes et principes)* and *Les affaires d'Haïti*, Janvier's incendiary tone repeatedly refers to blood while accusing mulattoes of colluding with foreign powers.[20] Leslie Péan astutely observes that it was Janvier's "harsh" writing style, and not just his noirism, that made his writings (as opposed to those of his contemporary Anténor Firmin) particularly attractive to Duvalier.[21] Sociologist Laennec Hurbon argues that "a blood mystique" has been a constant element of Haitian political discourses of legitimacy.[22] For the anthropologist Louis Marcellin, blood is at the center of political and social discourse; it is used as a metaphor to legitimize and delegitimize actors, including opponents at both the local and national levels.[23] Such representations did not construct a racial hierarchy with one group occupying the bottom rung; they excluded the group entirely from it.

The idealization of the peasantry is a common feature of genocidal ideologies and regimes, as Ben Kiernan has shown.[24] Even the destruction of Carthage in 146 BC, "the first genocide," was predicated by the orator Cato in correlation with his idealization of the Roman farmer, in a language that eerily anticipates Janvier's: "[I]t is from the farming class that the bravest men and the sturdiest soldiers come, their calling is most highly respected, their livelihood is most assured and is looked on with the least hostility, and those who are engaged in that pursuit are least inclined to be disaffected."[25] Turkish militarists, Nazis, Soviets, Maoists, the Khmer Rouge, anti-Communist Indonesian authorities, and Hutu supremacists also glorified the figure of the peasant. The historical and comparative perspective provided by Kiernan is astonishing, as it shows the presence of this ideological component, the "fetish of cultivation," across spaces and time, and often in similar rhetoric.[26] Yet this romanticization of the peasant is inherently analogous: it can stand epistemologically only in contrast to a counterexample, an opposite "class": traders for Cato, the bourgeoisie for the Communists, cattle-raising pastoralists for the Hutu supremacists, rootless cosmopolitans, feudalists, and so on—in a word, the elite. These scorned socioeconomic categories justify, explain, and legitimize the idealization of indigenous cultivators—and all the more so when a racial or religious difference is used as a driving wedge between cultivators and city dwellers.[27]

HATRED BY SOCIOLOGY

Biologized as heir of the French colonizer, the mulatto becomes the living link to, and reminder of, the most oppressive past. Biology alone, however, did not suffice to construct the mulatto as illegitimate. The mulatto slot is defined through both race and class, and via analysis borrowed from biology and sociology. Since the early twentieth century, the term "elite" has been a ubiquitous, almost emic category in Haitian intellectual production.[28] Jean Price-Mars set the genre's canon.[29] One of the first authors to make it a central subject, Price-Mars attempted to understand what had made the U.S. occupation of Haiti (1915–1934) possible in a country so viscerally attached to its sovereignty. His conclusions were damning: the elite—its behavior, its views, and, importantly, the education it receives—was to blame. Price-Mars was also the first one to otherize the elite, comparing it to a "foreign organism" that feeds on the nation like "a parasite."[30] The topic soon became routine for intellectuals, would-be intellectuals, and revolutionaries, all reflecting on the elite within larger discourses on injustice, independence, poverty, and, latter, underdevelopment. Invariably, the same sociological diagnosis was made: the elite was a problem. The identification of one culprit for society's ills seems designed to replace another. As is known, nineteenth-century thinkers under the influence of European racist ideologies often blamed Haiti's African heritage for its problems.[31] A similar process occurred in other contemporary societies where intellectuals influenced by positivist ideologies pinpointed an entire social sector as the culprit for society's ills.[32]

In these works, the elite is always external to their authors, no matter their own social position, level of education, or access to power.[33] What, then, do these authors mean by "the elite"? The term is rarely, if ever, defined.[34] Arguments are rarely, if ever, substantiated, an ethnographic thinness that points at preconceptions. (Price-Mars's work does include a study (*enquête*) which focuses exclusively on assigned readings in schools attended by the elite's children; yet the rest of his book is unrelated to this study.) As a consequence the elite depicted in these works is both ahistorical and as totalized as the figure of the mulatto. Further, there are rarely any distinctions made between various possible types of elites: economic, educated, political, etc. We end up with the paradox of an elite that is totalized as an undifferentiated *mass*. There is one exception: Jean-Jacques Honorat, who inferred that the elite is unified and should not be conceptually or sociologically divided between the intellectual elite and the professional classes: "the élite owns both the have and the know-how."[35]

Duvalier examined the elite principally in *Grandeur and Miseries of a Class* (1944), *The Problem of Classes in Haitian History* (with Lorimer Denis in 1948), and *The Elite's Mission* (1949).[36] His argument is built on a classic binary opposition: the elite versus the masses. Yet the figure he constructs conflates three types of enemies of the masses: elite, mulatto, and opponents of a Black government, for Duvalier always returns to the question of the presidency and who controls it. The presence of *la classe*, the Black middle class that emerged as a key political, social, and cultural actor during the U.S. occupation, and of which Duvalier attempted to be the champion, should have invalidated this binary but did not.[37] As Duvalier himself wrote, "the Haitian social question derives from the racial question. . . . There is a struggle between two classes for primacy in the country."[38]

He reiterated this point in *La mission de l'élite* (*The Elite's Mission*): "the bourgeois élite have repelled the middle class or the blacks who represent the majority class with such Machiavellian force that the former ended up refusing its pariah status."[39] The elite, Duvalier asserted, is also anarchical and treacherous. For Lucien Daumec, taking at face value the reflections made about the Haitian upper class by John H. Russell, a Marine brigade commander during the U.S. Occupation, the elite has the mentality of a seven-year-old child.[40]

This intellectual tradition corresponds to a "makeshift" sociology structured around dualisms that pulverize nuance and complexity. It divides Haitian society into two meta-entities, the masses and the elite, essentializing both, romanticizing one, and demonizing the other. Duvalier and Denis's dualist view had been noted by Michel-Rolph Trouillot.[41] Yet this dualist sociology was already implicit in the works of Janvier, Emmanuel Edouard, and Charmant before being fully developed by Price-Mars, the first intellectual who argued that society is divided into two totalized social classes: the poor masses and the elite, without any group in between. In this view, the masses are poor, oppressed, and largely incapable of agency (they instead await a savior), while the elite is homogeneous, all-powerful, and reproduces the oppression of the colonial era.

Foreign scholars of Haiti in the mid-twentieth century also based their sociologies on this binary opposition. John Lobb, a sociologist from Mount Holyoke College who conducted ethnographic research in South Africa before traveling to Haiti in 1937, depicts a society "composed of two clearly delineated classes, the *Elite* and the *Noirs*."[42] For Lobb, this situation had been established two hundred years ago at the time of independence and had not changed since. A similar view inspired James Leyburn's *The Haitian People*, a work whose leitmotif rests on the division of society into "two castes," the elite and the masses, with the former oppressing the latter in all areas of society.[43] (The use of the term "caste" to name race, class, or both in Haiti preceded Leyburn.) Then a scholar at Yale University, Leyburn gave a rather sympathetic account of Haiti devoid of the usual spite. Yet he totalized the elite and the masses and turned the two categories into sociological absolutes. Although he was careful to note that the elite was not entirely composed of mulattoes, he meant the term "caste" quite literally, comparing Haitian society to India's caste system and insisting that birth determines fate and that castes are both socially impermeable and eternally reproducible.

By denying Haitian social mobility and social change (since Haiti's two "castes" have perpetuated themselves since the country's independence), Leyburn posited Haitians as *a people without (social) history.* Viewing Haitian history as a two-hundred-year block unaffected by social change and continuing to perfectly reproduce itself fits rather well in the scholarly tradition that denies history to non-Western peoples, and that Eric Wolf and Marshall Sahlins have magisterially critiqued.[44] Leyburn's unsupported steel theory exoticizes Haiti by pathologizing its elite with assertions that would sound populist if made about Western societies: "The élite do not work with their hands. This is the cardinal rule of society."[45] (Is there a modern society in which the elite does?) Leyburn's view of Haiti as an abnormal exception also extends to marriage: "The elite [in Haiti] are endogamous in that they would not consider marriage into the masses."[46] Even though they works were vastly unsubstantiated, Lobb's and Leyburn's works gave an academic veneer and legitimacy to a binary opposition that was seductive enough to be used by Duvalier.[47]

This sociological affect turns the entire ideology of noirism into a scientific system that not only legitimizes, but also rationalizes hatred. By explaining how society is formed, by providing a diagnosis, and by assigning blame, this sociology coherently offers a Goffmanian frame to its followers.[48] Yet, the blaming of the elite is co-substantial to a larger, enrooted ideology: egalitarianism.

A HAITIAN PASSION

Egalitarianism has existed as a more diffuse and sometimes inchoate set of ideas and representations in Haiti before the more overt, structured, and well documented twentieth-century intellectual currents, including indigenism, communism, and noirism.[49] Yet egalitarianism can also be a way to approach these currents from a different angle, and with a more surgical intent, to highlight the anti-elitist, populist, sometimes plebeian, and anti-mulatto dimensions that permeated Haitian politics, intellectual history, and sources of political and social legitimacy during this period.

How can a society known for its socioeconomic inequalities have egalitarianism among its core ideologies? As André Béteille shows in a survey of egalitarian theories, most thinkers of socioeconomic equality had identified "the deep and pervasive disjunction between the [widely endorsed] ideal of equality and the reality of [socioeconomic] inequality."[50] For Haiti, this disjunction was addressed by Gérard Barthélémy, who believed that "the passion for equality" inspires laws, customs, and social practices and is not limited to racial equality.[51] The latter had been forcefully asserted earlier by intellectuals such as Anténor Firmin, Emmanuel Édouard, and Hannibal Price. For Barthélémy, equality as practice coexists with socioeconomic inequality in all spheres of Haitian society. The existence of familiarity and informality between neighbors of very different socioeconomic positions, as the short historical ethnography of Jérémie sketched in chapters 5 and 6 shows, adds a twist to this contradiction. Yet it was cause and consequence of social relationships within inequalities.

The historian Jean Alix René meticulously documented and analyzed this in his study *Le culte de l'égalité* (The Cult of Equality), in which he identifies equality in both national identity and social values over the *longue durée*.[52] State power founded its legitimacy, at least in the nineteenth century, in the realization of two distinct domains: the social contract found in Haiti's laws and Constitution, and the ethical obligation to protect all lives and provide dignity for all. Earlier, Schoelcher had already noticed the force of egalitarian ideologies when, during his visit to Haiti, he observed the underclass attempting to "crash" dancing parties [*bals*] given by the elite: "[A] citizen who gives a ball must have guards at the door to prevent the underclass (*la canaille*) from entering, because *the underclass always wants to get in*.[53] It understands things without nuances (*en bloc*) and since it has been told about equality, it brutally wants complete equality."[54] We can guess that Schoelcher had not witnessed members of the underclass literally knocking at the door of elite parties in Paris. As chapter 6 will explore, the ball occupies a central place in the Haitian imagination and its intellectual history, including in Duvalier's writings, serving as a symbol of inacceptable social inequality and of inequality's illegitimacy.

The genealogy of such ideas is well-studied, with the Enlightenment usually believed to be the main source of egalitarianism in its modern version.[55] Tocqueville in *Democracy in America* made "the insatiable thirst for equality" a corollary to all democratic nations.[56] The influence of the Enlightenment and of the French Revolution on dominant ideas and historical developments in Haiti have been well documented.[57] Equality is for André Béteille an idea with no return, akin to "a djinn which, once released from the bottle, cannot be put back into it again."[58] The strong egalitarian ideologies over the past three centuries in France, which remained an influential source for many Haitian intellectuals after independence and well into the twentieth century, are documented by Michel Forsé in a book whose title, *L'égalité, une passion française?* (Equality, a French passion?), echoes René's.[59] On the other hand, Barthélémy located the origin of egalitarianism—again, for Barthélémy, not just a set of conscious ideas but empirical social practices—in the African origins of Haitian culture; a case of cultural reproduction (my term). What is the link, however, between egalitarianism and anti-elite violence?

KILLING FOR EQUALITY?

People do not start killing people they identify as elites, or construct them as the enemy, simply because equality has become a dominant belief. It is usually inequality that is associated with violence. Nevertheless, linking dominant, positive, progressive societal value to violence is neither new nor absurd. In the mid-nineteenth century, the socialist and abolitionist poet Alphonse de Lamartine argued that the belief in freedom led to crimes during the French Revolution. In one of his novels, the historical figure of Madame Roland stoically, apocryphally, and philosophically remarks, seconds before being decapitated on the guillotine in 1793: "O Liberty, how many crimes are committed in your name!"[60] Rather than a contradiction, Lamartine raised the specter of causality: mass crimes are committed in the name of a higher cause. The notion that mass violence is moralized may seem counterintuitive, yet it is well documented.[61] To convince large numbers of people to commit massive violations of social norms, hatred must be wrapped into a moral system, and violence be seen as necessary for achieving a greater good.

Historian François Furet's pioneering works documented the link between ideologies advocating for liberty (the greater good) and lethal actions and genocide (evil).[62] For Furet, intolerance and political violence were inherent to French Revolutionary ideas. The contradiction, or "bipolarism," between high ideals (virtue) and terror is the question Timothy Tackett addresses in a nuanced book on the French Revolution.[63] Is it a contradiction, or a logic? In Haiti, the French revolutionary envoys did not just spread ideas but modes of governance and practices.[64] Bernard Gainot attributes the repeated massacres of the Haitian Revolution not only to slavery and the colonial heritage, but to the political norms established by these envoys who reproduced in Saint-Domingue the politics of massacres carried out by the Jacobins in France.[65] More largely, the link between Enlightenment values and mass violence was famously made by Max Horkheimer and Theodor Adorno, while Zygmunt Bauman later associated dehumanization with modernity—although the unpredictable social life of egalitarian values was perhaps most magisterially illustrated by Dostoyevsky's *Demons*.[66]

In Haiti, two concomitant intellectual constructions conspired to erect a frame from which violence would emerge. One was the valorization of equality, "a value to which we [moderns] are so deeply attached that it determines legitimacy."[67] Equality is formally part of the Haitian Republic's motto, enshrined in every one of its constitutions since 1804: *Liberté, Égalité, Fraternité* (Liberty, Equality, Fraternity). The second was the construction of the elite as either "a problem" or "the enemy." Social classification systems (both implied and explicit) of the Enlightenment, and subsequent equalitarian ideologies, constructed a slot for the elite using various names over the following two centuries: aristocrats, bourgeoisie, class enemies, etc. Another parallel can be made between the representation of the French aristocracy in the eighteenth and nineteenth centuries and the figure of the "mulatto" in Haiti. The French aristocrat was not only constructed as the figure of the enemy, but was also ethnicized.[68] The othering of the French aristocracy—as being of Frankish origin and not of Gallic stock (unlike, supposedly, the rest of the French population)—adds a racial element to a social diagnosis that echoes the construction of mulattoes as simultaneously elite and foreign.

Without the egalitarian ideological matrix, anti-elite sentiments across the last two centuries do not make sense. For the revolutionary historian Ran Halévi, whose research focuses on hatred and equality as phenomenologies, "the hatred of the aristocracy is the byproduct of the process of equality."[69] This link was understood in real-time by the Jacobins themselves, as shown by their bellicose cry: "in the name of equality, we will cut the aristocrats' heads."[70] Yet, in Halévi's thesis, anti-elite hatred is a specific type of hatred, produced in specific intellectual and political conditions, an outcome of the French revolution, not of the Enlightenment. The anti-bourgeois hatred, which would emerge in the nineteenth century, is also the byproduct of the same "passion for equality," as Halévi shows.[71] In the twentieth century, socialist totalitarian regimes (another "child of the French Revolution," as François Furet put it) explicitly justified mass repression against "class enemies" in the name of equality.[72] Anti-elite violence cannot exist without overarching egalitarian ideologies.

Egalitarian and anti-elite ideologies rarely spring out of a vacuum; they are instead often formed in the context of hierarchical social systems—ancien régime, feudalism, etc. Yet not all unequal systems produce such ideals, even though anti-elite sentiments present themselves as an objective response to a dire reality. Not all hierarchical societies in the modern era have produced anti-elite ideologies.[73] If hostility against the elite is not necessarily the objective consequence of inequality, what, then, triggers it? For Tocqueville, the French aristocracy acquired more and more privileges over the course of the eighteenth century while governing less and less. This contradiction triggered resentment, then hatred from other social sectors, according to Halévy—a point that echoes Hannah Arendt's analysis of the social and cultural contradictions that nurtured anti-Semitism, which emerges when cultural influence does not match political power.[74] Groups that wield the former without possessing the latter can become, in the right circumstances, the object of envy, resentment, hatred.

The differential between cultural and political elites, between social status and political power, even between status and wealth, brings us back to the victims of the Jérémie massacre. What made the mulatto elite in Jérémie vulnerable was a sharp contradiction between their social status, which was high, if not the highest—resented yet undoubtedly romanticized and envied—and their political power, which was nil. Combined with strong egalitarian ideologies, this contradiction contributed to, if not triggered, notions about their illegitimacy, and eventually led to hostility against them. If, in the traditional sense, elite refers to a minority that occupies power and exercises it over a majority, as Vilfredo Pareto, José Ortega y Gasset, and Gaetano Mosca all famously argued, then the "Jérémie mulattoes" in general (and the Jérémie massacre's victims in particular) did not fit that definition. They did not hold any office and therefore did not qualify as elites. From the perspective of the social sectors who perceived themselves as being in power—the middle class, the Duvalierists, the noirists—mulattoes became insufferable.

Since independence, mulattoes had set Jérémie's norms of propriety, elegance, culture, good marriage, education, and even phenotype. These norms were magnified by nearness and intimacy, as explained in chapters 5 and 6. Their social status was sustained not by wealth, but by habits. For most readers, the Jérémie massacre's first victim, Louis Drouin, a baker who made dough at four o'clock in the morning every day, even in his old age, hardly fits the figure of an upper-class man.[75] His elite status was independent of his income, and he had no political power. None of the Jérémie victims was extravagantly rich. Yet they ruled over social norms, uninhibitedly, with their social club, their fair skin, and (supposedly) French language. This gap (between symbolic capital and political power) was best perceived, and resented, at the local level. The anti-elite violence of the Duvalier regime did not emerge when mulattoes were perceived to "have power"; on the contrary, it emerged when they had none, during the *"pouvoir noir,"* as Frantz Voltaire (2019) put it.[76]

State violence against the elite solves the contradiction between egalitarianism (ideology) and inequalities (dire facts on the ground), especially when a regime such as Duvalier's failed to produce tangible results against poverty and disenfranchisement. We can even hypothesize that, as social justice became more and more elusive, the mere existence of the elite was increasingly posited as irreconcilable with social justice. Before concluding this chapter, I will quickly mention two more aspects of anti-elite sentiments: first, that such sentiments mainly came from relatively privileged socioeconomic sectors; and second, that they were related to the job insecurity affecting these sectors.

THEY SPOKE IN FRENCH

The testimonies I collected show that the mulatto elite was resented more viscerally by people from socioeconomic sectors situated right below it. Individuals from "lower" social sectors, such as the farmers I interviewed on the outskirts of Jérémie in 2016 and in the Moron area the following year, demonstrated a range of views and sentiments that reflected a sense of indifference toward elites they rarely saw.[77] Entirely missing was the visceral anti-mulatto discourse I had heard many times, sometimes uninhibitedly, from former Duvalierists and middle-class members, and which was exemplified in 2017 by the nephew of a Duvalierist witness to the first phase of the Jérémie massacre in August 1964: "To have peace, every twenty years we should execute two hundred mulattoes."[78] Farmers in the Numéro 2 area knew about the massacre from the various commemorations that had taken place in 2014 and 2016, and expressed shock that children had been killed. I was initially surprised by this visceral, genuinely heartfelt reaction to the cold-blooded execution of children because it had often been missing from Duvalierist interlocutors, whether from Jérémie or not. (I would not draw a conclusion on morality and its correlation to class—there are many reasons why people might be inhibited to express horror publicly.) Yet the farmers' reactions suggested that anti-elite views were neither universal across the socioeconomic spectrum, nor the objective outcome of inequalities.

I will give another example. When researching the 1958 brutalization of Yvonne Hakim-Rimpel, one of Haiti's most prominent feminists, by Duvalier's henchmen, I found the violence so far outside the norms (a rape committed for political reasons) that I became interested in the perpetrators.[79] Who could have done this? When I interviewed Hakim-Rimpel's second-oldest daughter, Rose-May, at her home in the Pacot neighborhood not far away from the one her family occupied sixty years earlier, I was intrigued by one detail in her account. This is how she recalled the hooded men who kidnapped, gang-raped, and left her mother for dead in a ditch: "Yes, they spoke in French . . . no, you heard me right, they spoke in French to us, to one another . . . yes, to one another, at least when they talked to one another in front of us, yes, yes . . . They were educated, all of them . . . the one who broke my teeth too [with the butt of his rifle], my 'Duvalier teeth' . . . their voices were young."[80] That the *bombistes* who brutalized Hakkim-Rimpel spoke French to one another does not infer elite status. It nonetheless definitely locates them in a social sector well above that of the disenfranchised poor.

Who were these men? Major Pressoir Pierre gave a detailed, self-incriminating account of the plot.[81] As Duvalier's advisor for military matters inside the Presidential Palace, he personally recommended to Pierre Merceron that he repress the writers who continued to dare publishing anti-Duvalier pieces two months into Duvalier's presidency.[82] Duvalier's inclination for wanton violence and murders had not yet reached its heights but had nevertheless already been clearly demonstrated, inciting public denunciations from courageous writers. Pierre mentioned Yvonne Hakkim-Rimpel to Merceron, who then assembled the group who would perform the deed. They were three officers, Gracia Jacques, Sony Borges, and Franck Romain; and three civilians, Clément Barbot, Luc Désyr, and Eloïs Maître.[83] Barbot was born into a provincial middle-class family from Gonaives, married the daughter of a senator, Crescent Jean-Baptiste, and was a state bureaucrat.[84] His brother was a physician. Sony Borges was from the Bas-peu-de-chose neighborhood, the stronghold of the Black middle class, and a graduate of the military academy. Romain was an engineer and also a graduate of the military academy. The other three—Luc Désyr, Eloïs Maître, and Gracia Jacques—came from social sectors that can be characterized as rural elite or artisan sectors. They had been part of the group of so-called *bombistes* during the 1956–57 presidential campaign, assembling and placing lethal bombs for Duvalier.

Two other known individuals completed the *bombistes* group, although they did not participate in the attack against Hakim-Rimpel: Fritz Cinéas and Windsor Kléber Laferrière. Cinéas was from the middle class and would become a physician. Laferrière was a rare type: a dandy, an ideologue, and a man of action accused of lethal political acts.[85] A prominent writer and public figure throughout the tumultuous 1950s, Laferrière epitomized the populist noirist intellectual who resented not being socially recognized and rewarded with a government position—until he finally obtained one in May 1957 under Daniel Fignolé, and then another in 1958 under Duvalier himself. He was one of the founders and leaders of the Haitian People's Party (*Parti du Peuple Haïtien*), and it was through him that Luc Désyr, another party founder (and future henchman) first met Duvalier. Laferrière owned the party's organ, *Le Souverain*, and was editor-in-chief of another newspaper, *La voix de l'ouvrier* (The Voice of the Worker), in which he published incendiary pieces against the bourgeoisie. Moïse and Diederich describe mobs of Laferrière supporters ransacking government ministries during the volatile months of 1956 and 1957.[86] In February 1957, he was made Undersecretary of State for the National Economy in a provisional government formed to appease noirist aspirations. Duvalier appointed him mayor of Port-au-Prince in January 1958.[87] Five months later, the unpredictable Laferrière was demoted and assigned to a diplomatic post in Argentina.[88]

As a point of comparison, recent scholarship on the Soviet Union's Great terror and the Cultural Revolution under Mao emphasizes the elite background of anti-elite groups. As Darrin McMahon puts it, "in the Soviet Union or Mao's China, with their targeting of class enemies and the bourgeoisie, equality talk has regularly provided a powerful means to bind together dominant groups on the basis of the exclusion of others."[89] Yang Rae's memoir and confession as a former Red Guard makes clear that the most lethal and entitled of the Red Guards, those who persecuted and killed officials, academics, and other members of privileged sectors, themselves came from the most privileged families.[90] The socioeconomic background of Duvalier's followers (not just members of his inner circle) has never, to my knowledge, been studied. Claude Moïse mentioned the following sectors in Duvalier's social base: "A considerable number of [rural] landowners, intellectuals and professionals from the middle classes, [and] many Lebanese and Syrians from the business class."[91] This does not mean that other sectors of society did not support him. In any case, the instrumentalization of egalitarian ideologies by the regime had little to do with an agenda of social progress. Duvalier's own written work included many denunciations but little socioeconomic agendas. What most of the noirist literature of the 1940s and 1950s featured was an obsessive focus on higher offices.

JOBBEURS

A fascination with higher offices of public service appears explicitly in the writings of Janvier, Charmant, Lucien Daumec, Dorsinvil, and Duvalier. Yet, their works also betray an intriguing indifference to socioeconomic debates. They lack any discussion of economic redistribution or, more generally, economic policies that could redress inequalities. Their essays on inequalities and unfairness (*injustices*) mentioned in this chapter and the previous one focus mainly on political offices (especially the presidency) and government jobs. The Duvalier regime was indeed filled, at least at its inception, with writers. Yet I failed to identify a single clear public policy goal in the entirety of the abovementioned works of Lucien Daumec and Roger Dorsainvil, both close to Duvalier before and at the beginning of his presidency.

Absent was any reflection on tax reform, land registry, land distribution, and social justice reform that would address the needs of the peasantry. As Nicholls suggested, Duvalier came to the presidency with a discourse, not a political agenda with concrete projects.[92] It was not wealth that had be redistributed; it was the *jobs*. What was of concern to noirists concerned them personally. There is a telling moment in Duvalier and Denis's *Le problème des classes au travers de l'histoire d'Haïti* when the authors praise Jean-Jacques Acaau, leader of a peasant rebellion in the 1840s in Haiti's southern peninsula.[93] However, instead of lauding Acaau's ambition to give land to those who work it, the only action identified and glorified by Duvalier and Denis was "the fair distribution of public jobs."[94]

The fixation on public jobs betrays the end goal of noirism: public jobs were the holy grail of public policy. This is distinct from embezzlement, kleptocracy, or cronyism, although it overlaps with the latter. From its inception, the regime aimed to acquire such jobs for Duvalier's inner circle (and, to a lesser extent, for Duvalierist supporters) rather than to create mechanisms for true economic redistribution or a new social structure.[95] Contrary to its persistent reputation, the entire Duvalier regime (1957–1986) did not promote Blacks; it mainly promoted Duvalierists and their kin, not all of whom were Blacks. Fritz Cinéas's testimony leaves no ambiguity about this:

> For instance, [every year] the medical school would send us [the Presidential Palace] the names of those who had passed the entrance exam before [the official results] were released. There could not be any mulatto on [the list], but then there were sometimes names [sic] of those who were Black but not Duvalierist; their fathers were Jumelliste or Fignolist. So these four women [staff members] would reassign the seats to Duvalierist families.[96]

Cinéas also confirmed that Pierre Biamby, who would eventually succeed Cinéas as Duvalier's executive secretary, was in charge of selecting cadets at the military academy from 1957 to 1961—on the same Duvalierist, not "racial," basis.

President Salomon used a derogatory neologism (perhaps his own coinage) to depict his opponents and their motivations: "*jobbeurs*."[97] For Salomon, their pursuit of government positions explained their political positioning. The *jobbeurs* were from the urban, educated social sectors, and were not moved, Salomon believed, by any political ideals: those who sought to overthrow his government had simply not yet found a government position. A foreign journalist who visited Port-au-Prince in 1884 expressed his surprise that the dream of young and educated people was to obtain "*un job*" in the government, probably appropriating a prevalent local anglicism.[98] Mulattoes were resented also because they represented fierce competition for such jobs.

For Robert Fatton, the belief that the conquest of state offices is the condition for personal wealth, a phenomenon he calls "politics of the belly," is the paradigm of Haitian politics.[99] For those born outside the merchant class, this path is the only option given the scarcity of resources and jobs. Since the entire postcolonial period was characterized by poverty, politics of the belly became an entrenched habit. Politics, Fatton summarizes, is an entrepreneurial vocation. The politics of the belly paradigm would reveal noirism's nature: instead of being an objective response to injustice, it constitutes a strategy for resource acquisition. The noirist vanguard is then not the legitimate or loyal representative of the masses, but yet another predatory elite. The depiction of noirism as an opportunistic movement concerned with material rewards and social status rather than with social progress, together with the refutation of a grand narrative that frames Black/"mulatto" opposition, is not new. In the late nineteenth century, Justin Bouzon made a strikingly prescient analysis not only of noirism, or in his case of proto-noirism, but more generally of the relation between ideology and politics. His analysis should be quoted in its entirety, for it announces later scholarly analysis of Duvalierism and emphasizes the instrumentalization of racial differences:

> Under the generic term of piquetisme, we must distinguish the *ultra-noir* party from piquetisme. The *ultra-noir* party is a political question [while] piquetisme is a social one. One wants political power and does not want to share it so it can use it as it wants. The other wants prosperity without having to work. These two support each other, but in a very unequal manner. Whenever the ultra-Black party is contested, it puts forward piquetisme; it is its rampart.
>
> The *ultra-noir* party is a kind of oligarchy composed of Blacks and mulattoes, who from time to time pretend to be defenders of the masses; that is its springboard. This oligarchy owns property it certainly does not intend to share with the proletariat, although in its blindness it urges the proletariat to claim the division of properties."
>
> This oligarchy's only program is to exclude those with education from public affairs; Black or yellow (mulatto), all honest people are pushed aside; this oligarchy gets richer with public coffers; without any control over it; and it believes that despotism is the foundation of any government.
>
> But today, since the hatred and prejudices against mulattoes have lost much of their strength, this rather exclusive oligarchy, when it is a little removed from the exercise of political power, attempts again to incite the people to rise up; it speaks in its name; its favorite topic is to make the masses believe it wants their happiness and that mulattoes are opposed to it; which is altogether defamatory and impossible, for how many mulattoes do we not see within this oligarchy pretending to be friends to the people and to democracy?
>
> This democracy is not one that raises the humble and ennobles the small ones, but instead is one that diminishes the good and honest ones in the country. Hasn't this been our history for the past forty years? We saw it under Soulouque, under Salnave, under Salomon. . . . General Salomon remained in power for nine years . . . [and yet] what did he ever do for the people under whose name he claimed power?[100]

The essayist Marcel Gilbert later made a similar argument: from Salomon to Nord Alexis to Duvalier, political power stayed within the same social sector, which Gilbert terms "the historic class of state power" made of both Blacks and mulattoes.[101] Michèle Oriol has even showed that all Haitian rulers from Dessalines to Duvalier fit on only three genealogical trees, racial differences notwithstanding.[102]

JÉRÉMIE'S SPECIAL PLACE IN THE NOIRIST IMAGINATION

From the 1880s to the 1960s Jérémie was represented in the literature as a mulatto and spiteful town. More specifically, it combined three figures: the urban world of the mercantile bourgeoisie; a place of Gallicized, scornful mulattoes; and a hotbed of opposition prone to rebel against Black presidents. If the mulatto was constructed as an illegitimate member of the nation, the mulatto elite of Jérémie was constructed as an enemy.

The representation of Jérémie as a town prone to uprisings against Haiti's centralized government was not built on pure subjectivity. Jérémie did indeed rebel several times. In 1848, it resisted the government's military campaign. In 1869, it rose up against President Salnave, efficiently resisting government forces. It rose up again in 1870, executing two peasant leaders on the government side, Delgriace Jacquet and Siffra Fortuné.[103] It sustained a nine-month siege against President Salomon's forces in 1883 and paid a heavy price for it. It rose up against President Nord Alexis in 1908, and President Antoine Simon in 1911.[104] In the incendiary *Les antinationaux*, Louis-Joseph Janvier equated the town with anti-Haitianism, a term coined by Janvier and that locates Jérémie outside the space of the nation itself: "This is the city that has never wanted to listen to us. If she hears us speak, she pretends to care about what we might think and ask only to better massacre us. For her own sake, she has always had an interest in not admitting our grievances: it is she who, now as always, grows fat through our labor and our sweat."[105] Jérémie is represented in Janvier's entire work as oppressive, domineering, selfish, discriminatory, murderous.[106] In *Les affaires d'Haïti* Janvier openly calls for anti-mulatto violence.

Janvier's work is replete with racial references equating the *jaunes* (mulattoes) to insurgencies, to the Liberal party, and to the opposition to President Salomon: "and how they despise the Haitian people, how they believe they could govern it. . . . Whenever they are not stealing the public treasury, they repudiate us . . . They lick the boots of foreigners and tell them: go, cut Haiti's throat open. . . . The Haitian people must know its duty. If it wants to live, it must get rid of all these renegades who conspire against its independence."[107] Janvier justified repression against Jérémie again in *Le vieux piquet*. Jérémie serves the purpose of magnifying the three figures of the enemy that the noirist literature has constructed: elite, mulatto, ready to attack a government run by noiristes.

Janvier was not the only writer to construct Jérémie as anti-Haitian. Nicholls refers to a debate during the 1946 revolution where Jérémie was denounced as a "bastion du rigaudisme."[108] Roger Dorsinville, Duvalier's closest aide during the 1957 presidential campaign, derogatively evoked "the blue-eyed mulattoes of Jérémie."[109] Duvalier is credited as having said: "There are three types of mulattoes: the national mulattoes, the anti-national mulattoes, and the Jérémie mulattoes." This attribution is probably apocryphal. It nonetheless testifies to the location of Jérémie in the noirist imagination and Duvalier's own classification system.

CHAPTER 4

A Pattern of Anti-Elite Massacres, 1848–1964

Not all silences are created equal.

Michel-Rolph Trouillot[1]

T his chapter lists episodes of anti-elite and anti-mulatto violence that occurred prior to the Duvalier regime. The 1848 and 1883 massacres are the most relevant because François Duvalier would later be inspired by their historiographical treatment.

APRIL 1848: MASSACRE OF ELITE MULATTOES IN PORT-AU-PRINCE

The massacre of civilians that occurred in April 1848, under the rule of President Faustin Soulouque (1782–1867), was one of the largest in nineteenth-century Haiti, although no exact number of casualties was ever provided. It is documented by four primary sources, three of which were written by visual witnesses: a set of reports by Ussher, the British consul; a memoir by the French consul; and a biographic account by a British missionary, Mark Baker Bird.[2] The fourth primary source is by Justin Bouzon, who later gathered court acts and accounts by former ministers of Soulouque to write an exhaustive historical account of these events. The later works by historians Justin Chrysostome Dorsainvil and Dantès Bellegarde are mainly based on these four sources, and possibly on oral history as well. Recent extensive research by the historian Matthew J. Smith using sources located in the National Archives of the United Kingdom has changed our perspective on this event.[3]

Several competing narratives have vied for historical truth on how the violence erupted. There is agreement that the massacre started in the Presidential Palace where, "as if a sign had been given, the soldiers of the [presidential] guard opened fire on the palace gallery, packed with officials and officers ... The killing of mulattos started. . . . Several [of Soulouque's own] aides-de-camp, all mulattoes, were shot (*fusillés*) while they attempted to flee from the palace."[4] Bouzon believed the massacre was an impromptu event. For François Duvalier, who relied on Dorsainvil's account, violence erupted because the arrogant mulatto elite, unwilling to accept a *noir* ruler, was actively plotting an armed insurrection.[5]

Smith's research has disproved this narrative. The massacre of mulattoes had in fact been planned: "Soulouque orchestrated the entire episode." The Jamaican historian, usually rather mild, is blunt for good reason: he found a smoking gun implicating Soulouque in the Foreign Office's archives. The British consul, Ussher, had met with Soulouque before the killing and transcribed that conversation. Soulouque made it plain that violence was going to erupt and reassured Ussher that foreign diplomats and their families would be safe. The goal of the massacre was, according to the British diplomat, to "strike terror into the respectable mulattos whom [Soulouque] has always been thought to consider as his inveterate enemies."[6]

For three days (or five, according to d'Alaux), the Presidential Guard and *zinglins*, an ad hoc paramilitary force loyal to Soulouque, roamed the city executing a large (but indeterminate) number of people. According to Bouzon, the first to be executed were *jeunes gens* (young people): a rather vague, yet gendered, expression which identifies neither class nor race; it could refer to young mulatto officers who were not privy to the plot, or simply to young men. The "butchery" was carried out in the streets by "organized troops."[7] Bouzon further describes the scene: "General Maximilian Augustin, at the head of the Guard, roamed through the capital; and all those who could not find immediate refuge in consulates or foreign-owned houses were killed."[8] Mark Baker Bird stated that on April 16, government forces first fired into the crowd and then began executed unarmed individuals present at the presidential palace, "while others were shot untried."[9] Gustave d'Alaux describes a large-scale massacre during which firing squads rounded people up for summary execution: "[H]igh school teachers, lawyers, merchants, and physicians," including members of "the city's wealthiest families," were hunted down throughout the capital by the presidential guard.[10] Two former government ministers were executed. D'Alaux concluded that the "jaune (mulatto) bourgeoisie [was] exterminated."[11] According to Bellegarde, Soulouque ordered a "horrible killing of mulattoes."[12] As quoted by Bird, a Wesleyan missionary fleeing from his home to the port counted eighteen to twenty dead bodies along his route—all had died either by musket or sword. Yet in the midst of this destruction, Bouzon mentions acts of empathy that occurred, including a government general saving "some of his friends."[13]

Killings continued to take place on April 17 and 18; according to Bouzon, these two days were as murderous as April 16 had been. Mulatto families fled en masse to the French and British consulates, to foreign-owned homes, even to ships in the harbor. In the British legation alone, 700 family members fled.[14] On April 19, the two consuls intervened directly before Soulouque to plead for an end to the massacre. In response, Soulouque wrote down the names of twelve individuals he would not spare.[15] For Hoffman,[16] this massacre signaled the beginning of a reign of terror that, according to Bouzon, would lead directly to the mass migration of the educated elite.[17] All sources point to the state as the main perpetrator, as the zinglins were following direct orders from Soulouque or his generals. The vast majority of victims were adult men, while the families of suspected opponents were generally not threatened.

A few days later, Soulouque embarked on a military campaign in the south. As context, in 1843, a peasant rebellion known as *Piquets* had taken place amid rising social and racial tensions throughout the western part of Haiti's southern peninsula.[18] Throughout the 1840s, the discontent of peasant groups was instrumentalized by a landed Black bourgeoisie that was itself politically sidelined. Amid the political turmoil in Port-au-Prince in 1847 and 1848, various social groups in the provincial towns of the southern peninsula voiced both economic and political claims. According to Bouzon, by 1847 anti-mulatto sentiments were widespread.

Most of the killings of civilians in the summer of 1848 were committed by Piquets, although the term probably covered various social groups.[19] Both primary and secondary sources emphasize that the Piquets (or neo-Piquets) were instrumentalized by Soulouque, who had found a way to disown the violence that he was in fact stoking and exploiting. For Hoffmann, Soulouque "had the reputation of letting the massacres happen before intervening" and encouraged the

Piquets, "to massacre mulattoes in Aquin."[20] Soulouque and his army marched south from Port-au-Prince to Jérémie slowly, and never engaged in any battle. This slow pace allowed killings to take place before the army entered cities. For Bouzon, Soulouque's "tactics were to let crimes be committed then to strike down the murderers."[21] Massacres took place in Aquin, Les Cayes, Jérémie, and several minor towns. Yet Bouzon again exculpated Soulouque, explaining that to appease the Piquets, the president had "offered up the heads of distinguished citizens in the southern cities."[22] Dorsainvil listed some of the names of individuals from the social elite who were executed.[23] For Edgar La Selve, who traveled to Aquin to collect testimonies twenty-five years after the events had taken place, "[t]he mulattos fled into the hills. In Aquin, 189 Blacks from the upper class, who had wrongly assumed they would be spared because of their skin color, were put to death."[24] Bouzon states that massacres took place throughout the southeast in late April and May 1848, but does not specify the victims' racial identity; he does, however, identify the perpetrators as being exclusively Piquets.[25]

Yet executions also took place once Soulouque and the government were in control. "They made a conspirator of every man of color in Les Cayes," wrote Bouzon.[26] He goes on to mention that the senator Edouard Hall was executed by a firing squad, and that Soulouque's army "moves around the south by executing and slaughtering the populations."[27] The number of individuals executed in Jérémie varies—sometimes substantially—from one source to the other, and often with striking specificity: 57 killed according to d'Alaux, 198 according to Hoffmann, who does not give his sources.[28] This episode of terror led to widespread exile of the intellectual elite. As Bouzon put it: "Most of the country's enlightened men fled precisely at that time. Many died in exile, others renounced their Haitian citizenship."[29]

SEPTEMBER 1883: THE DESTRUCTION OF PORT-AU-PRINCE'S BUSINESS ELITE

Lysius Félicité Salomon (1815–1888) had been Haiti's president since 1879. A brilliant, cosmopolitan, highly educated man, Salomon was also an authoritarian ruler so obsessively anti-mulatto that he gained the nickname "*mangeur de mulâtres*" (mulatto-eater).[30] As was true for other rulers in Haitian history, he was nevertheless keen to deny it.[31] Nicholls credits him with having initiated the "black legend" which would later morph into noirisme.[32] Salomon was born into a landed Black family in the southern city of Les Cayes.[33] In 1843, at the age of twenty-eight and within the context of the authoritarian Boyer presidency, Salomon was credited with giving an inflammatory speech against mulattoes.[34] After Soulouque's fall, Salomon spent decades in exile—an experience which, once he became Haiti's ruler, did not make him more inclined to political compromise or more empathetic to the fate of opponents. He finally returned to Haiti in August 1879 and was elected president. His presidency was marked by state violence unseen since Soulouque. On May 5, 1882, fourteen political prisoners, some in their early twenties, all from the local elite, were executed in Saint-Marc on his order. Laroche provides a list of these names.[35] One, Mathurin Lys, was a reformer of Haiti's banking system.[36] Another was the son of an opponent leader in exile, General Desormes Gresseau.[37] Both had been arrested months earlier and held hostage to deter the distribution of anti-Salomon pamphlets.

A low-intensity civil war completes the context of the mass violence that would engulf Port-au-Prince on September 22 and 23, 1883. A group of exiled, armed Liberals (mostly but not all mulattoes) led by Jean-Pierre Boyer-Bazelais had landed in March 1883 in Miragoâne, southwest of the capital, where they were immediately contained and besieged by government forces. In April and May several southern towns, including Jérémie, joined the rebellion; all but Jérémie were quickly defeated by government forces. The two cities of Miragoâne and Jérémie then endured a long siege before finally capitulating at the end of the year.[38] When repression occurred in Port-au-Prince on September 22 and 23, the demoralized insurgency in Miragoâne was already on the brink of defeat. A small party of young Liberals in the capital were alleged to have attempted a Coup. For the historian Roger Gaillard, what followed then was "possibly the most violent repression in [Haiti's] history."[39] The historian Claude Moïse compared it to "a model terrorist operation."[40] An Anglican pastor living in Port-au-Prince, Joseph Robert Love, described the violence as "a deliberate policy of the Haitian government to strike terror in the hearts of Haitians in Port-au-Prince."[41]

Several eyewitnesses gave detailed accounts of these events. A young Salomon supporter, Alfred Jean, wrote an unemotional forty-seven-page book listing the names of insurgents, actors, and victims.[42] It resembles a Stendhalian, Fabrizio-at-Waterloo depiction: fragmented, almost disoriented, highly personal, yet somehow coherent. Crucially, Jean provides the exact locations of the crimes. What was it about Jean's background that enabled him to provide this critical eyewitness account? At the time of the events, Jean was an employee in a government-run pharmacy in the city center. Raised by a single mother in a one-room apartment, he belonged to an intermediary social sector that identified neither with the merchant classes nor with the urban poor or the peasantry (although he mentions that some of his relatives were farmers outside Port-au-Prince). Jean spent part of the first day, September 22, with his cousin Joseph Cassard, looking for weapons so that they could join the government forces and defend the president. He spent most of the second day looking for relatives whose houses were being destroyed by fires. On both days, he was constantly on the move throughout the western part of the capital, and thereby became witness to many key events. Here is a summary of his account, which I have interlaced with specific information provided by other witnesses.

At ten o'clock in the morning on September 22, a group of nine "irresponsible young" individuals between the ages of twenty and twenty-four attacked an arsenal held by general Penor Benjamin and killed him. Jean believes it was a desperate attempt to ease the siege of Miragoâne. When government soldiers left their barracks to confront them, the nine young men fled to the Spanish consulate without putting up a fight. The first wave of the repression was most probably carried out by this first group of soldiers. The first victims of their violence were students who were targeted, Jean believed, because they had avoided the draft by enrolling in universities. As a consequence, resentful soldiers shot them upon first encounter. Both soldiers and civilian officials joined forces for wide-scale implementation of acts of repressive violence. This phase seems to have been planned by the government, with orders given to show no mercy, take no prisoners, and leave no wounded. Indeed, I found no accounts of any prisoners taken during these two days. Jean and his cousin roamed government offices looking for a rifle, but were only able to obtain a sword.

Jean witnessed senseless killings but does not specify if the perpetrators were soldiers or civilians. He does not provide specific numbers, and usually only mentions the dead he knew, leaving us to wonder if most of the anonymous dead were simply left out of his description entirely. According to Bellegarde, only men were targeted on that day.[43] Many fled and hid in the homes of friendly neighbors. These buildings would be set ablaze the following day and those fleeing the flames would be shot. For Hoffmann, the mob hunted "mulattoes with the rallying cry "*aba zoranj yo, viv blacking*" (down with oranges, long live black polish).[44] A pastor noted, "This war is a war of color, blacks against mulattoes—a war of extermination."[45] The alarmed British consul used similar phrasing: "a war of color, the blacks massacring the colored people."[46] Smith, however, believes that this consul overstated the "color" dimension of the attacks, and that people of all colors were victims of violence.[47]

The first act of arson started at noon and on the president's order, according to Alfred Jean; he describes witnessing Salomon proclaim loudly, and with great satisfaction, that his orders to commit arson were being followed.[48] According to Adolphe Cabon, using the testimony of the pro-Salomon archbishop, Mgr. Guilloux, rumors had spread in the early summer in the capital that the Salomon government had planned to set the capital ablaze in case of an attack by Liberals.[49] (On June 2, the government had to issue a formal proclamation denying it had any intention to do so.) Both Jean and Ernest B. Burdel, the pro-Salomon French consul, witnessed arsonists in action.[50] The modus operandi was to first throw kerosene on the houses' front facades before lighting them on fire. Because many houses were made of wood, the fire spread quickly.

By the second day, the fire had moved beyond the bourgeois neighborhoods. Burdel witnessed a military officer among the *pétroleurs*.[51] According to Jean, these arsonists were paid by the government. Looting soon began and would continue all night, with groups of citizens dancing to revolutionary songs (*carmagnoles*). The looting apparently intensified the following day. Cabon mentions a mob rampaging through and setting fire to the *bord-de-mer* neighborhood, where the homes and stores of mulatto merchants were located.[52] Jean also witnessed the looting of Alexandre Bobo's house by people from the outskirts of the city (*peuple des faubourgs*) and describes seeing peasants carrying away looted goods on mules and donkeys.[53] Although the looters were regular people the breakdown of the rule of law was intentional and perpetrated by the state itself. In Gaillard's assessment, the government had deliberately incited nongovernmental *piquets*, "motivated by a blind and primal class hatred, from the countryside outside Port-au-Prince," to action.[54] In 1848, Soulouque had resorted to *zinglins* (thuggish, pro-government urban elements) to exercise terror. In 1883, Salomon would instrumentalize mobs to amplify its effects. After having wandered through the capital together on September 22, the two cousins, Jean Alfred and Joseph Cassard, each went to their separate homes for the night. (This massacre occurred on the 22nd, a number Duvalier would later fetishize.)

The second day, September 23, Jean learned early in the morning that his cousin Joseph was killed. Shocked by the news, he decided to check on his relatives in the midst of the chaos, all while "the fire was spreading with rage, murders multiplied, and looting continued."[55] Once fires engulfed most of the lower part of town, individuals (apparently of all classes) who had sought refuge abandoned their hideouts and fled. Some people died in the fire, burned alive. Known Liberals who were forced to flee their burning hideouts were executed by waiting soldiers. Others were killed while looking for refuge inside the archbishopric. During the night of September 22 and into the early morning hours of September 23, the internationally known poet and parliamentarian Frédéric Marcelin helped Théogène Pouille, his father-in-law, barricade his family into the latter's brick house. Fearing an assault from the mob, they placed iron bars on the main door.[56] Inside, neighbors had found refuge and the house was apparently crowded. According to Gaillard, the brick home was breached with a canon on September 23.[57] The door was destroyed, and looters (or possibly soldiers) entered the home and killed Théogène Pouille. What happened to his daughters is not clear. In his narrative, Jean made a general statement about the *outrage* committed against women, and how some members of the poorest classes helped women to escape. Another house sheltering approximately sixty refugees was bombarded by order of General Deschamps Lambert of the Presidential Guard.[58]

The destruction of a significant portion of Port-au-Prince was a monumental event for contemporary Haitians and foreign observers alike. Nearly all Haitian trading houses were annihilated. Vast swathes of neighborhoods and mercantile areas were destroyed. The obliteration of a significant part of Port-au-Prince's historical heritage added to the trauma. The historian Claude Moïse has emphasized the "social and moral cost" of the repression that "terrorized" the country.[59] On a wide scale, traditional merchant families were killed or ruined; foreign expatriates would later come to fill the void they had left.[60] Cabon concluded: "The indigenous commerce is destroyed."[61] Gaillard later echoed this: "The Haitian mercantile bourgeoisie was annihilated."[62] Hannibal Price regretted the takeover of the economy by Europeans and Syrians. For Jean, "Haitian commerce was being ruined by Haitians! And all this for the benefit of foreigners who stand to benefit handsomely."[63] He could identify only one family, that of Joseph Incident Georges, who was later able to overcome the hardship of having lost everything; all the others were definitively ruined and seemed to have disappeared from the public space.[64] For Péan, "[t]he prejudices that Salomon had accumulated against the hegemonic positions of Haitian merchants, most of them mulattoes, led to the elimination of an entire class of entrepreneurs."[65] The poet Frédéric Marcelin concluded: "From this event we can date the decadence, the irremediable fall of our Haitian families. Impoverished, ruined, decapitated, they were never able to recover and could only languish . . . ."[66] Meanwhile, as the fires raged, refugees sought any available place of shelter: foreign ships in the harbor, foreign legations, expatriates' houses, which are quickly overwhelmed. Panic is palpable in all of the written accounts. As in 1848, the violence ceased when the British consul, Robert Stuart, "persuaded foreign powers to intervene," and led a coalition of diplomats that presented an ultimatum to Salomon. They threatened to send foreign soldiers in the country if Salomon did not relent.[67] By all accounts, the repression and fires ceased immediately.

Four years later, a French journalist on his way back from Panama, Gustave de Molinari, depicted a capital that was still devastated. If he praised the beautiful view of the city from the sea, "the illusion ceases as soon as one lands." The seafront with its commercial establishments is "covered in ruins."[68] None of the state institutions—including the Senate, the Parliament and all of the ministries—had been rebuilt. Employees were still forced to perform their jobs in makeshift structures.[69] This event led to another mass exodus by the elite, as Alfred Jean lamented: "Many Haitians left the country without hope of returning."[70]

December 1883: Execution of Mulatto Leaders in Jérémie

Jérémie was the only town where the insurgency flourished. In Miragoâne, the rebels were not locals; they had merely chosen this port city for its proximity to Port-au-Prince. In Jérémie, by contrast, the local population had freely joined the rebellion and were the last group to surrender; they were finally defeated in December 1883, outnumbered by the government's armed government forces.

Jérémie joined the insurgency in April according to Adolphe Cabon or on May 23 according to Gustave Vigoureux, a local historian who wrote a detailed memoir on the subject.[71] Insurgents immediately arrested four local government officials, including the military commander, and took them to the nearby French consulate. Ludovic Goubault, the French consul in Jérémie and a Black Frenchman, supported the insurgents.[72] The same day, these insurgents issued a three-page manifesto.[73] Addressed to Salomon, the document accuses him of despotism and of imprisoning and executing opponents. It also attacks Salomon personally for dividing the nation, for pitting the Blacks against the *jaunes* and "nationals" against "liberals." The manifesto was signed by the members of a "Revolutionary Committee": Alain Clérié, N. Lataillade, L.P. Acluche, C. Chassagne, A. Lescouflair, Pressoir Jérôme, Maître Lamour, Amiclé Boncy, and Eugène Margron, the insurgency's local president. The local mulatto elite led the rebellion. Two senators (Constant Kerlegand and J. Hippolyte) and four deputies (H. Lestage, C. Robert, L. Bernard, Grandoix jeune, and P.-A. Saint-Cloux) became generals.[74] Jérémie would thus be described both in the historiography and in the collective imagination as the main hotbed of anti-Salomon opposition. After the events of 1848 and 1867, this is the third time Jérémie appears ready to take up arms against a *noir* government.

Before long, the town found itself surrounded by large and well-armed government forces. It was combined with a sporadic maritime blockade, which isolated Jérémie for seven months. Government forces indiscriminately bombarded the town and its civilians. Numéro 2, where mulatto families would be killed in 1964, is mentioned possibly for the first time in the literature, as it becomes the headquarters of the government forces laying siege to the town.[75]

The military power of Haiti's standing army was not the only factor leading to the defeat of the insurgency. The rebellion itself failed to take root among large sectors of the population outside Jérémie, including, but not only, the peasantry. Should we conclude that the insurgents were mostly mulattoes who came mainly from elite sectors? Vigoureux's account falls short in this regard: it gives the names of hundreds of generals, soldiers, officials, and artisans, all from a variety of political sides—but without providing their racial identity. Sometimes, too, Vigoureux fails to provide basic sociological information about military actors. One can suppose that Telisma Cazeau and Louis-Charles are supporting peasant leaders, for they are mentioned as "the first organizers of the uprising in the country."[76] And yet, some armed peasant, called *Piquets*, helped government forces besiege the city, at least by November. Crucially, elite Jeremian families had members on both sides of the front lines.[77] In addition, several actors switched sides during the conflict.

By September, lack of food and near-constant shelling was making life difficult for the town's inhabitants. By mid-September, the French and American consuls left town with their respective families, a sign to the insurgents of their imminent downfall. Then on September 20, boats carried women and children out of Jérémie, likely after reaching an agreement with the besieging forces—this was not a merciless civil war.[78]

Civilians in Jérémie were killed during the siege, although Vigoureux's narrative pays little attention to this fact. For instance, two women were killed in shelling, a fact the reader learns only through a letter from Kerlegand to his officers.[79] The village of Grand-Boucan, that had rallied the insurgents, was razed and burned by Salomon's forces; we do not know what happened to its rural population. In another incident, Arthur Allen, a Jeremian sailor coming from Kingston, was captured at sea and then executed with the entirety of his crew by a firing squad.[80] Although Vigoureux does not mention it, it was possible that their boat was carrying supplies to the besieged population and insurgents, which would explain their execution. Vigoureux also wrote of a "massacre in Corail" without giving further information, leaving the modern reader to wonder if the term is a hyperbolic expression for defeat itself.[81] After the insurgency was defeated and the government soldiers entered town, part of the population and the insurgent soldiers fled by boat. But there is no description of a massacre, other than a brief textual line about it and the mention of another small boat crew that was "summarily executed."[82]

Killings were also committed by Jeremians. On August 19, they attacked a fort held by government forces outside the town, gained entry, and killed forty-six soldiers in "a frightening massacre," although the author does not specify if these government soldiers surrendered before being killed.[83]

On December 18, a peace agreement was signed between Jeremian leaders and government military officers, granting amnesty to all and guaranteeing that no paramilitary troops would enter the city.[84] Jérémie's insurgents surrendered their weapons on December 21.[85] Not trusting the peace agreement, several families embarked on the *Cuban*, a civilian ship, and went into exile in Jamaica, abandoning their properties. On December 23, groups of Piquets entered town, attacked several citizens and looted some properties.[86] However, it seems that the peace agreement was generally respected until Salomon's arrival.

Salomon visited Jérémie on January 25, 1884. He arrived—incidentally or not—on the *Dessalines*, the main ship that shelled the town during the war. A *Te Deum* was celebrated in Saint Louis church as a mass of reconciliation, attended by former insurgent officers and their families, as well as Salomon's officers, all in formal dress (*costumes d'apparat*). As they were about to leave the church at the end of the mass, several insurgent leaders were arrested: Generals

Laforest, Barthélémy, Gachette, A. Moussignac, G. Moussignac, Beau, Dufour, and Colonel Bazile.[87] All but two were tried two days later by a military tribunal and executed; Gen. A. Moussignac and Col. Bazile were sentenced to prison. Several consuls protested against this violation of the peace agreement to no avail. Duvalier would later emulate this form of false clemency and spectacular terror.

APRIL 26, 1963: PORT-AU-PRINCE

Of central importance and yet insufficiently researched, the massacre of April 1963 represents a major event in Caribbean history. The journalist Bernard Diederich, who was a visual witness, characterized it as "one of the worst crimes against humanity committed by Duvalier."[88] Oral history refers to this massacre as "elimination of mulattoes," "purge of officers," "pogrom of mulattoes,"[89] or "liquidation of the mulattoes."[90] It was the first large-scale massacre committed by the Duvalier regime and a departure from the "drop-by-drop" killings that had characterized repression until then. Mulatto officers (both active duty and retired) and mulatto businessmen were its main targets, but not its only victims. The number of victims has never been properly assessed. Diederich and Burt, citing the *Committee to Commemorate April 26, 1963*, put the tally at sixty deaths.[91] Recent research by Devoir de Mémoire-Haïti assesses the death toll to be between 100 and 200. Oral testimonies of visual witnesses recorded by Haiti Inter in 1987, and statements made by other witnesses I interviewed mention killings that are not listed in the above counts. This suggests a higher range of casualties: between 200 and 300, and possibly higher. Most of the killings were committed by members of the Presidential Guard and VSNs stationed at the Presidential Palace.[92]

According to the historiography, the massacre was reactive.[93] However, as the April 1848 and September 1883 massacres, it had almost certainly been planned for weeks by a regime that was seeking a pretext. Clément Barbot, one of Duvalier's many âmes damnées, had turned against his former leader and made a botched attempt to kidnap his children, Simone and Jean-Claude, at their school around 7:25 A.M. on April 26. In the historiography, Duvalier was unaware of Barbot's involvement, which supposedly led the Presidential Guard to suspect young officers. This version was refuted separately by two direct witnesses, both Presidential Guard officers, Elliott Roy and Francis Charles:

> That morning, I was on the ground level [of the Presidential Palace] when a car arrived at high speed. Jean-Claude [Duvalier, then eleven years old] sprang out of the car and ran toward his father while shouting "Onk Kleman! m'te we onk Kleman ak yon zam!" (Uncle Clément! I saw Uncle Clément with a gun!).[94] There was then an immediate meeting with dozens of officers . . . I do not remember if there were VSNs [at that meeting] . . . Immediately, [Captain] Jean Tassy accused [Lieutenant François] Benoît of having helped Barbot.

While the anarchic form of the massacre, which left at least hundreds of bodies in the streets, suggests it was reactive, the systematic elimination of mulatto officers suggests that it had been premeditated. After the impromptu meeting at the Presidential Palace, Presidential Guard officers Harry Tassy and Max Dominique rushed to Lt. François Benoît's home in Bois-Verna, about 800 yards from the Presidential Palace, accompanied by several soldiers and VSNs. They killed all eight occupants, including Benoît's parents and a pregnant woman. (Benoît himself escaped.) Tassy, Dominique and the VSNs then went to the nearby home of the Edeline family—Benoît's in-laws. All six present family members were killed. Killings then spread beyond Bois-Verna to eventually engulf most of the metropolitan area. "Waves of killings began that afternoon."[95] Chaos followed as schools closed and children were sent home. Businesses also closed, paralyzing traffic: "It was panic, everybody was trying to get home, a huge jam all the way from Port-au-Prince to Pétionville, with roadblocks."[96] Sister Dallemand, an adolescent at the time of the event, described the following:

> The [school] bell rang, [and] we had to go home immediately. I walked from Lalue to rue Miot [in the Pacot neighborhood]. I heard shooting [in Lalue] but did not see any [dead] bodies until I arrived in Bois-Verna. At the corner of ruelle Chochotte and [John Paul II], I saw a sixteen-year-old boy I knew laying face up. Then I started to run, and I was crying, I was crying. Ahead there was a group of men. . . . They did not have uniforms, [but] one had a suit, [and] my brother later told me it was Lucien Chauvet. . . . there were bodies at their feet. When I arrived [home], my mother [later] told me, I could not speak for days.[97]

The failed kidnapping allows anger against the elite to be expressed freely, as Diederich remarked: "Militiamen searched people and cars and humiliated those rich enough to own a car."[98]

From inception, there are two modes of killings. Some victims are taken from their homes or arrested at roadblocks by soldiers or VSN, and then brought either to Fort Dimanche or to an open shooting range for noncommissioned officers in Lamentin, where they are executed the same day. Other victims are randomly killed right on the street or in their homes in broad daylight, in the Pacot and Turgeau areas, by roaming VSNs and Presidential Guard officers. Victims include lawyers, businessmen, artisans, a museum curator, and workers—mostly men. Members of the same families are killed together; one example is a branch of the Tippenhauer family in which the father (a businessman) is killed with his two sons. Some of the murdered retired officers were known public figures. Col. Edouard Roy had been Chief of the Presidential House under President Vincent. Col. Roger Villedrouin is also executed. A lawyer witnessed the brutal arrest of Jean Bouchereau, a retired army engineer, in a bookstore, who then pleaded for his life ("I have ten children!") before being taken to the execution site at Fort Dimanche.[99] Of the 120 active duty officers who were killed under Duvalier, almost half were killed on that day.[100]

Yvon Guerrier, a functionary in the Ministry of Transportation who had been "drafted" as an attaché on April 26 to man a roadblock in Lamentin, witnessed Lieutenant Frank Romain stopping, assaulting, and then killing at least eight individuals, including a prominent businessman, Hector Riobé, and two adolescent brothers, Didier (nineteen) and Paul Vieux (sixteen).[101] The bodies, which were later removed from the execution ground, were never found. Guerrier also mentions the murders of two low-ranking VSNs and one artisan on April 27 or 28. Romain had made them work to open the safe at Hector Riobé's home. Guerrier's detailed testimony implicates Duvalier himself in the schemes to steal the victims' belongings.[102]

The massacre convinced many of Haiti's intellectual elites, irrespective of their racial identity, to flee the country. Leslie Manigat, a promising Haitian scholar, fled the country with his entire family. The flight of elites was hardly new in Haitian history, as Matthew Smith shows, but up to that point those who had gone into exile had been predominantly men.[103] On April 26, "state terrorism applied to entire families," causing a massive exodus on a scale not yet seen before in Haiti.[104]

PATTERNS OF ANTI-ELITE VIOLENCE

Several patterns of anti-elite violence emerge. First, the target of repression is rarely the mulatto as such. Rather, it is typically a fluid combination of four categories: elite, opponent, male, mulatto. It must be emphasized also that if "mulatto" is an anthropologically subjective category and if "the elite" is both subjective and relative, so too is "opponent." Such categories are even more volatile in medias res. Not being considered mulatto offers no protection against the wrath of a politically insecure leader. Political opposition was a strong enough motive for execution and even bodily desecration.[105] Since Haiti's independence, intellectual elites, particularly those from the fields of journalism, literature, and education, figured prominently among the urban sectors who publicly voiced their opposition to authoritarian regimes. It made them more likely to be considered dangerous. The political anxiety of successive rulers who believe that their only choices are either to enact brutal repression or accept the risk of being deposed is addressed in chapter 11. Yet, for such rulers, being mulatto was undoubtedly an aggravating circumstance that would dramatically increase suspicions of disloyalty and prejudice.

Second, men overwhelmingly represent the majority of documented victims of political violence. As mass violence scholar Adam Jones has shown, the selective targeting of men is a world-historical feature of mass violence. Episodes of mass violence can thus be categorized in two broad categories: against males; or against all sectors of society.[106] In Haiti, political victimhood has usually coincided with masculinity. That women and children were generally, but not always, spared is also a relevant historical—and conceivably cultural—fact. For this very reason, the targeting of women, and particularly of mothers, by the nascent Duvalier regime would be crucial to establishing a state of terror.

Third, anti-elite and anti-mulatto violence is essentially state violence. It was therefore carried out by other elites. Never were mulattoes or elites killed by a freelance mob acting on his own. Government forces and, occasionally, groups linked to the government were responsible for all killings discussed in this chapter. Governments resorted to mobs, usually for looting and destruction, in the most instrumentalized manner. In 1848, 1883, even 1964, mobs would stop enacting violence and looting and disperse as soon as the government ordered them to.[107]

The personal properties of the 1964 Jérémie victims were looted by a mob that knew where to go and what to spare. This was no Gustave Le Bon's "irrational mob."[108] Finally, in every single instance in which Haitian elites or mulattoes were massacred, the head of state was solely responsible for ordering the killing. As such, the ruler's psychology, the rationale for his political choices, and the obedience required to inflict such harm are fundamental questions that the rest of this book answers.

PART III

Murders Among Persons

CHAPTER 5

Jérémie's World

We knew only the ruins that remain and our memory of its history was ruined as well, by the passage of time, the imperfection of memory, and the falsehoods of those who came after.

Salman Rushdie, *Victory City*.

APARTHEID

The term "apartheid" is widely used in scholarship, lay literature, and oral history to characterize Haitian society, and more particularly Jérémie. Abbott describes Jérémie as an apartheid society: "Jérémie was also Haiti's most color-obsessed city, with a structure akin to apartheid and every aspect of life defined by color/ class lines. . . . Even casual social intermingling was limited."[1] This apartheid, Abbott further explains, was a primary cause of the Jérémie massacre. Historian Daniel Supplice described the Jérémie massacre "an anti-apartheid movement in Jérémie."[2] A Jeremian interlocutor stated that "Jérémie was much, much worse than the apartheid system."[3] A tourist guidebook published in 1999 also used the term to describe Jérémie: "the social segregation between the dominant mulattos and the minority (sic) blacks in the town had been vaguely akin to apartheid."[4] For the essayist Luc Pierre, Haitian society suffers from "cultural apartheid."[5] Sociologist Laënnec Hurbon states: "The Haitian population has lived under a kind of apartheid that was exacerbated under [Presidents] Vincent and Lescot."[6] Leslie Péan also talks about an "Haitian apartheid," while for Michel-Rolph Trouillot, the entirety of Haitian history was a "social apartheid."[7]

An Afrikaner word, "apartheid" means separation and, by extension, separate development.[8] It refers to a total political system that institutionalized a racial hierarchy in all aspects of life in the Republic of South Africa. In this hierarchy, race entirely determined one's position. The Afrikaner preacher Daniel Malan coined the word in the 1940s to advocate for public policies and cultural behavior that would lead to the impossibility of shared public and private institutions and social spaces.

Apartheid made it nearly impossible for common Afrikaners and Africans to meet, socialize, interact. It is explicitly in this sense that Abbot and the other authors cited above described Jérémie: as a place of separateness and institutionalized inequality. In South Africa, and in societies where the term is used metaphorically, such as the American South in the age of Jim Crow, society was separated in at least two distinct groups who lived in separate towns or neighborhoods and whose children were educated separately and raised as two distinct ethnic groups.[9] Such groups tend to be highly endogamous; miscegenation is made nearly impossible by the organization and practice of social life, moral values, and laws.

Jeremian society in the mid-twentieth century was far removed from South Africa's apartheid system. People of different social sectors and backgrounds forged and nurtured social bonds, engaged one other, shared the same social institutions, attended the same public institutions and, crucially, lived side by side. The verticality of the social hierarchy was not commensurate with geographic or social separation. Black and mulatto families attended the same services at the same church (Saint-Louis). The upper class, which was composed of both Black and mulatto families, the middle sectors, and the world of artisans lived side by side.

Networks of friends and informal acquaintances crossed the racial and social divides—more rarely, the gender divide. Black and mulatto children attended the same classes in the same schools. Class pictures from throughout the twentieth century show racially mixed classrooms. Jérémie's entire youth—children, adolescents, and young adults—attended and mixed in two of the most important institutions: scout organizations and sport clubs. People of all social and racial backgrounds played on and rooted for the same soccer teams. This was particularly important since soccer played an important role in Jérémie's identity in the 1950s and early 1960s. Pictures of the official football teams in the decades preceding 1964 show racial mixing. Two Sansaricq brothers, Daniel and Fred, played on the same team as Jean Alcide, who was a Duvalierist. In South Africa, teams did not even need to be segregated since Afrikaners and Africans usually played different sports—rugby for the latter, soccer for the former. The Jeremian testimonies I collected quickly showed me that many friendships developed in childhood and adolescence without regard for racial identities. Friendship loyalty, or friendship ethics, was the rule and lasted for life.

The single most important piece of evidence that invalidates the apartheid analogy is the locations of family homes: people of different social conditions lived side by side, as shown in the Map of Jérémie in 1964. However, that the elite lived in full view affected perceptions. Status and wealth, no matter how relative, could not be hidden. The most evidently contradictory argument, from the very informants who believe in "the existence of an apartheid regime in Jérémie," was that they knew everything about the individuals they accused of being discriminatory and aloof: their ancestry, lineage, habits, personal history, tastes, home location, hobbies, friendships, sociality, spouses, etc. That is, they knew the types of things that people in a small town know about each other—an unthinkable situation in South Africa's apartheid system. In South Africa, places of worships were distinct; that white Afrikaners and Black Africans would attend the same churches and temples was unthinkable. The workplace was also segregated and, most importantly in pre-1992 South Africa, the layouts of towns, neighborhoods and home locations were entirely organized by race, by law, and by practice. Why, then, referring to Jeremian society as an apartheid regime?

RELATIONS[10]

When I started my research on the Jérémie massacre, I was solely focused on repression and the possible involvement of Jeremians in the executions. What made me pivot to the study of sociality in Jérémie was how interlocutors talked about people they knew, including victims and those involved in the killings. The manner with which they recounted their lives in Jérémie revealed a sociocentric world. The attachment and loyalty to friends of any age was visceral and trumped such non-social allegiances as political, religious, or racial beliefs, although this is in no way unique to Jérémie. When an interlocutor was working to recall their memories of a specific person, they typically used a mental route that was entirely relational: they reconstructed the bonds identifying that person through relationships to others and to themselves (the interlocutors). Throughout this process, two patterns struck me.

The first pattern I noticed was that social ties of any kind—kin, friends, schoolmates, colleagues, neighbors, etc.—were used to map the flow of information and, concomitantly, the person's identity. If I asked an open question about, say, Saintange Bontemps to Guiton Dorimain, who did not know the former personally, Dorimain would first identify him by stating how Bontemps was the father of a classmate of his older sister; then would give a personal anecdote involving both; then would expand on what he knew about Bontemps's role during the events. The same epistemic route was taken when trying to recount an event, a date, or a place: tracing how the latter related socially to people.[11] In other words, social relatedness is a mnemonic. The epistemic route taken by my obliging interlocutors to recount the past was almost systematically a social one, echoing Marilyn Strathern's thesis on relations: social relations (kinship, as the basis of all of them) are used cognitively to construct nonsocial, epistemic relations.[12]

The second pattern I noticed was that networks of non-kin intersected closely with those of family. Bonds of friendship were omnipresent, and because they cut across socioeconomic, racial, and political groups, they constituted an essential part of the social fabric—the sum of interconnected interpersonal relationships in a given group. The school of the Brothers of Christian Instruction (École des Frères), the main boys' school serving grades 1 to 9, was one of the main institutions where friendships were formed. To that extent, it played a major role in the town's sociability. The vast majority of its students came from the town's middle classes, so we should regard it as an elite institution. Yet students from poorer sectors and from the villages at the town's periphery also entered the school, although in much smaller numbers. Mulatto children were a small minority at this school according to the class pictures I had access to. For each grade and class level, I counted between two to six fair-skinned students out of about thirty.[13]

And in fact, it was in the context of school that Jean-Claude Fignolé gave a precise account of his friendship with Fred Sansaricq. Since first grade, year after year, Sansaricq and Fignolé had been in the same class together, seated at the same desk.[14] Their bond was built over shared affinities for literature, ideas, sports, and rather innocent views of the town's girls. On Saturdays, they would sometimes meet in town, usually in the main square, opposite the Saint-Louis church. Yet they never visited each other's homes. They would meet up to walk together and talk while circling around the main square, a common pastime for children and adolescents. Sometimes, both would be in town with their respective families: Fred with his parents, Pierre and Louise; and Jean-Claude with his grandmother. The two friends would then acknowledge each other through eye contact and a quick nod of the head, but they would not speak or move toward each other.

They came from two worlds apart, and both were cognizant of it. Of peasant extraction, Fignolé was born in 1947 in Abricots, a village about eight miles east of Jérémie. He was the son of Grand'Anse small farmers and had been raised mainly by his illiterate grandmother. A gifted student, he later became an internationally acclaimed novelist. Fred Sansaricq was a son of the richest man in Jérémie and grew up in a book-filled home in which culture was highly valued. These differences did not prevent them from forging a strong friendship marked by *complicité*.

In Jérémie, bonds of friendship were constituted through dyads and groups of friends. Friendships cut across social sectors and identities, but rarely across gender, at least until the mid-1950s. Groups of boys, sometimes two dozen of them, would often leave the town's perimeter; smaller groups of girls would typically walk on the Place d'Armes. The rare pictures taken during these outings in the 1950s and early 1960s show groups of adolescents, most between eight and fifteen, smiling at the camera.[15] Once outside town and away from their parents, these single-gender groups took advantage of nearby rivers and ponds. Children spent a good deal of time outside and were able to play in nature, given how readily accessible it was.

To a certain degree, these groups also bridged social divides, at least between urban families of different status. The pictures I saw invariably showed young people of different skin color. Dyads and groups of friends bridged the skin color divide, and just as importantly, they also cut across increasing political polarization. As a rule, children whose fathers were on opposing political sides would socialize without much consideration for their parent's beliefs. Adults also had routine social interactions across political divides. One informant stated that by late 1964 Pierre Sansaricq knew and occasionally chatted with Sanette Balmir, a VSN (Volontaires de la Sécurité Nationale, or National Security Volunteers). While this may sound rather incongruous and apocryphal, the fact that this detail was evoked actually reveals that no social relationship was outside the realm of possibility.

The mesh of social relationships extended in all directions and cut across racial, political, generational, and socioeconomic divides—but more rarely the gender line. The Cédras children, whose father was a staunch Duvalierist, played with the Sansaricq children. They continued to bring food to the older Louise Drouin, a close friend of their mother, after it became known that her son Milou was a member of the Jeune Haiti guerrilla. This social mesh was so dense that it seemed to link each family, either directly or through a minimal combination of successive relationships, to almost every other family. Inevitably, that would also be true of perpetrators and victims; Abel Jérôme was friends with Jean-Claude Sansaricq and Guy Drouin; Jean-Claude Fignolé had a friendship with Gérard Léonidas and Fred Sansaricq. What also struck me was the intellectual basis for many of the social relationships my interlocutors evoked. Young and old, they would talk about philosophy and ideas more than anything. The fact that Jean-Claude Sansaricq and Abel Jérôme, neither of whom were particularly intellectual, exchanged books about communism and *tiers-mondisme* is rather telling.

I have mentioned the social importance of schools, sports, scout organizations, and church. None of these institutions was limited to a particular social sector. Other social institutions not only contributed to the thickness and complexity of the social fabric but also impacted dyads. One of them was godparenthood. In Jérémie, godfathers and godmothers were sometimes chosen from outside the extended family, and in a strategic manner. This phenomenon has been well studied in Latin America and has been directly linked to the influence of paternalism inherited from slavery.[16] Such institutions did not prevent social hierarchization or social inequalities, and it has been convincingly argued that godfatherhood may contribute to inequality by turning economic relations into kinship ties. When godparenthood cut across racial lines and brought families of distinct background together, this institutionalized relation often implied a wealthy mulatto godparent and a Black child lower down in the social hierarchy (although not necessarily the economic one). Yet, by enabling families to cut across the color line and by turning a religious institution into a social bond, godparenthood became a powerful vehicle for creating a thicker social fabric and spreading kinship morality beyond kinship ties themselves.

I will give one example. Marcel Numa, the son of Duvalierist small landowners and coffee traders, was Louise Drouin's godson. This godparent-godchild relation cemented ties between the two families, who also lived a few yards from each other. Numa later joined the Jeune Haiti guerrilla because he was a close friend of Milou Drouin since childhood and because they were were living in New York at the same time.[17] The Numas were a relatively wealthy coffee trader family, while Louis Drouin was a baker. Although the families were of approximately equal wealth (with the Numas being perhaps a bit wealthier), Louis Drouin and his wife were invited to the Excelsior, the town's elite social club, and the Numas were not.

A SOCIETY ON FOOT

The size of the town made it possible for its inhabitants to walk almost everywhere: to work, to school, to mass, to run errands, and to social meetings. Distances were short, very short. In 2016, I walked from the former home of the Sansaricq family to the house known as "Fort-Réfléchi," the informal headquarters of the *macoutes*: it took me about three minutes; five to the home of Duvalierist Louis Jabouin; about twelve to Louis Drouin's; less than fifteen to the military base. From any point at the town's immediate periphery to the central Place d'Armes and the Saint-Louis church took a maximum of fifteen minutes. The homes located in Bordes and Rochasses, the hills right above town, were a bit farther away but were not geographically alienated: children leaving there walked to their respective schools. It took me twenty minutes to walk from the Sansaricq home in the center of town to Victor Villedrouin's home in Bordes, barely more to that of Abel Jérôme, and about twenty-five minutes to that of Raoul Cédras. Anonymity in Jérémie was geographically impossible.

When walking to a destination, people would often stop, meet, and talk. To a real extent, to walk was to talk. The route taken on foot could be decided by the social relationships located on the way, with the promise to exchange words. Importantly, many encounters were not transactional but purely relational. People stopped and talked without necessarily having a goal in mind. To walk, stop and meet, to constantly nurture relationships were cause and consequence of a relational society with a dense social fabric. In this social context, one place stands out: the gallery, the open front veranda that most houses had.

An intermediary space between the street and the home, the public and the private, the gallery was a space without a door, open to the street. Anyone could enter if they felt welcomed. Depending on the time of day, people could often be found sitting in their gallery, an informal invitation for walkers to stop and talk at any moment of the day with kin, friends, former teachers, former class-mates, colleagues, acquaintances, godparents, or, more often, a combination of these. This is also how news circulated: from one gallery to the other. Gossip was also a reason for exchange and therefore played an important role in fostering or maintaining relations. As anthropologist Roger Lancaster showed in his study of intimacy, gossip is a form of social exchange intended to strengthen a social bond—to the detriment of a third party.[18]

Importantly, however, the gallery was also the place where familiarity ended: many allowed in the gallery were not invited inside the home itself. Neverthe-less, familiarity cut across class and color lines, the gallery allowing for people of different social spheres to interact. It was precisely the space where, to some extent, hierarchies were contradicted. Finally, it inferred a rather strict separation between two private realms: that of the home, family, and commensality; and that of friends, acquaintances, and neighbors. The gallery was then, to some extent, a place of freedom, outside the more private constraints of family-based social rules.

Words and gestures of affection were the main form of exchange; food was rarer. In Jérémie in the 1950s and 1960s, commensality tended to be restricted to kinship, although exceptions were many. Food was not always served in a gal-lery unless the passing guests would require it. Drinks, especially water or fruit juices, were more common. The gallery created a world that allowed for sociabil-ity but rarely commensality. A relational society is a society founded on *parole*, or speech, and where ties are nurtured by the reciprocity of parole. It does not take commensality for *parole* to nurture the social fabric.

The gallery was not the only measure of intimacy. Physical closeness was, and remains, an expression of social closeness and affinities. Affection was expressed through specific forms of physical touch: giving a shoulder pat, putting an arm around a shoulder, giving a kiss on the cheek. The practice of shaking hands indi-cated a higher level of social distance or affective reserve, more likely to be indexed on the social hierarchy. The use of physical touch to convey social connections var-ied by generations and gender, with kissing on the cheeks a practice more common among women than men, and more likely to be reserved for kin and intimates. Children and adolescents would drape their arms over each other's shoulders.

Goffman's work on interactions and Randall Collins's radical microsociol-ogy "break down" what social lives are made of: myriad face-to-face encounters; and what they result in: fruitful shared emotions and solidarity.[19] Gérard Bar-thélémy noticed the presence in Port-au-Prince of what Collins conceptualized as "interaction chain rituals," the ubiquitous situations where people exchange mutually understood social symbols, creating a social life of astonishing density.[20] Economic precariousness might also increase bond formation as people seek allies within more privileged sectors; and so would the paternalist ethos inherited from the plantation system which incites people to accept ties below their social position. Yet social ties in Jérémie (as well as in Port-au-Prince) were not limited to dyadic ones; they were organized in hypertrophied networks. That is, although Person A and Person C never met, they were aware of each other through Person B, a common friend, and for this reason shared ethical obligations; more on this later.

A LETTERED CITY

There must be very few cities of Jérémie's size anywhere in the world that have produced as many major literary figures: Etzer Villaire (1872–1951), one of the most celebrated Haitian poets, whose *Les dix hommes noirs* is still part of the high school curriculum; Edmond Laforest (1875–1915) whose two daughters would perish in the Jérémie massacre; Thimotée Paret (1887–1942); Emile Roumer (1903–1988); Jean-Fernand Brierre (1909–1992); Serge Legagneur (1937–2017); the poet and essayist Raymond Chassagne (1924–2013); Haiti's most prominent playwriter of the last half century, Syto Cavé (1944–); the memorialist Eddy Cavé (1940–). Jean-Claude Fignolé (1941–2017) and René Philoctète (1932–1995) were, with the Jacmel-born Frankétienne, the founders of Spiralism, the most significant literary movement to come out of Haiti since the 1970s.[21]

This literary ethos was shared by most of the urban population and certainly not limited to a small elite or the middle class. Until the early twentieth century, the town's intellectual elite was small, but it grew larger as formal education became more institutionalized. The Nord Alexis high school was built in 1905, the École des Frères in 1925. The teachers at these schools were highly trained and delivered a classical curriculum. (The first names given to male children from the late nineteenth century to the mid-twentieth century testify to the role of classical influence on Jeremian culture, with many children being given Greek first names.)[22]

Jean-Claude Fignolé believed that the education provided by the Pères Blancs at the École des Frères was a major reason for this cultured culture.[23] However, these friars settled in Jérémie only in 1925; Jérémie's literary tradition preceded their arrival by decades. This literary productivity was clearly an "organic" phenomenon. In addition, classical education and the study of Greek and Latin authors were not new, as shown by the references used by Edmond Laforest and Etzer Villaire in their respective works. My older interlocutors, born in the 1930s and 1940s, were imbued with culture—one was even able to quote a two-page poem by Frédéric Marcelin in its entirety. Rolphe Papillon, whose family were well-off farmers, said that his father and uncles would recite poems at family gatherings.[24] During a Sunday lunch in Port-au-Prince in 2009, a group of older Jeremians emphasized the impact of the international fame encountered by Jérémie's most recognized writers, notably Roumer and later Fignolé, which younger people tried to emulate.

Writing poems and memoirs was widespread. Physical books, rare and expensive, were commonly exchanged. Professionals from all disciplines wrote their own memoirs, published or not. Harry Balmir (no relation to Sanette Balmir), one of the young men arrested at the beginning of the Jérémie Vespers, dedicated his retirement after a career as a lawyer to writing his memoirs. Before becoming Jérémie's most renown memorialist, Eddy Cavé had worked in banking for over forty years. This *Bildung* culture was also a widespread value shared by the population. It was part of social interactions and therefore of the social fabric. The hunger for knowledge and culture was such that the local elite mobilized resources to invite historians. On August 22, 1931 the Cercle de l'Excelsior invited a Port-au-Prince author, Octave Petit, to deliver a talk on the historical figure Défilée-la-Folle. This talk was published the following year by a journal. It notes that the event had been organized by Mrs. Lily Sansaricq, who must have been in her late 20s at that time.[25] She would be executed during the Jérémie massacre.

HOME LOCATION

The city map at the start of this book shows the mulatto families' immersion and dispersion throughout the city. There was no such a thing as a mulatto neighborhood, or a gated community of any kind. Several mulatto families lived in Bordes, a neighborhood located on a wooded plateau immediately west of the city center and that had the reputation of being upscale by local standards. So did the Cédras family, Abel Jérôme, and before him Kern Delince.

The Sansaricq family occupied three different houses: that of Louise and Pierre Sansaricq; that of Graziela and Jean-Claude; and that of Frédéric and Mona Sansaricq. Once a child married, he or she would typically move out. The Villedrouins occupied two: that of Roger Villedrouin, the elder son who occupied the ancestral home, together with his mother Corinne and his handicapped sister, Fernande; and that of Victor and Adeline Villedrouin. Guy Villedrouin worked and lived in Les Cayes with his wife Roseline and would stay with his mother (Corinne) when he visited, which was almost every weekend. Louis and Louise Drouin lived on the city's oldest street, close to the waterfront. Multigenerational households were relatively uncommon. The conjugal household tended to be the rule.

Upper-class families lived in full view of, and were immediate neighbors to, families from other social sectors. For instance, the families to each side of the home of Pierre and Louise Sansaricq were from slightly lower sectors: on one side lived Frantz Perrault, an employee; and on the other was a home headed by a schoolteacher, Mrs. Vincent. The physical proximity between the various social classes and the lack of privacy it implied for the upper classes were considerably more acute than in the much larger Port-au-Prince. The size of the town also allowed people to know most other residents; it also allowed for everyone to see other people's way of life up close. The elite's relative wealth and symbolic capital, as expressed through fashion, conversation, manners, type of entertainment, sometimes cars, and other material possessions, could be seen by all. Because of the town's size, the physical proximity of homes, and the density of social relations, what was "known" about someone extended beyond mere appearances and included family history. The elite's *entre-soi* was therefore in full view. In the context of preexisting egalitarian ideologies, this physical proximity would have dire consequences. Feelings of inequalities could morph into highly personal jealousy and envy. Importantly, the ones who witnessed and resented the mulatto lifestyle tended to be educated and urban. The destitute peasantry lived outside town.

PERSONALISM

Familiarity between people of different social classes is obviously not the same as democracy or equality. It nonetheless invalidates the apartheid regime analogy. It also calls for conceptual clarifications. Anthropology's arsenal offers many heuristic concepts that highlight various dimensions of Jérémie before 1964: "community"; "holism," which, in contrast to the egalitarianism carried by individualism, allows social hierarchy to cohabit with cooperation in a traditional world; "dividuality" and "partibility," where individuals are composed of relationships; Durkheim's classical "mechanical solidarity" or social cohesion resulting from nearness, although in Jérémie it did not necessarily involved a collective consciousness; "world," where nearness and frequency of encounters generally determine the strength of relationships; "relatedness," or the long reach of kinship; "familialism" or favoring one's kin; and the self-explanatory "cultural intimacy."[26]

"Personalism" is particularly operative. The term, coined by Brazilian anthropologist Roberto da Matta via the Indologist Louis Dumont, names a society that is both hierarchical and relational.[27] In such a society, one's identity is defined by one's individual position in society: an identity assigned at *and* by birth. However, position and identity are also defined by one's relationships to others. In other words, relationships are fate in what is, for da Matta, more a sociological model than a strict empirical reality. For instance, social mobility always existed in Jérémie and in Haiti for that matter, in spite of the lack of civil institutions with such a purpose, as proven by the trajectories of the aforementioned Jean-Claude Fignolé or Frankétienne.

For conceptual and theoretical purposes, both Dumont and da Matta contrast a personalistic, or holistic, society with an individualistic society, the latter characterizing Western societies. In a personalistic society, each being is a person rather than an individual. When listening to my interlocutors, it felt as if every person in Jérémie was "a character," known to all, accepted with their idiosyncrasies, a world where nobody is truly foreign to anyone—for to be foreign, one has to come from outside. The Kreyol expression *moun vini* (literally: someone who arrived) names an outsider to a community: someone who cannot be identified through his relationships and kin, someone whose last name does not resonate. Rather than some xenophobic binary that pits "native" against "non-native," *moun vini* is grounded not only in the epistemic and social implications of a small world where neighbors know one another and one another's lineage, but also in the cognitive significance of a finite social world. When discussing home locations, Guiton Dorimain, a Jeremian interlocutor, stated:

When I walked from home in Rochasse to the École des Frères (which is roughly a mile away), I knew the people, more or less, of every single house

I passed, I knew the family names, I knew [who] lived there, more or less, sometimes I knew more details. Sometimes the face but not the names. Now, I barely know anybody, everything has changed.[28]

Every single one of the Jeremians mentioned in this book was immersed daily in sociability. In such a universe, an interpersonal relationship is an asset, albeit not necessarily conceived in utilitarian or strategic terms (although of course it can be). I sketched in another work the sociality of the middle class in the Bas Peu de Choses neighborhood in 1950s Port-au-Prince, a sociocentric world where a social relationship was both an end in itself and a sort of non-utilitarian capital, a world with a bias toward creating and nurturing social bonds.[29] Crucially, endogamic practices, which the next chapter analyzes, must be understood within this highly relational frame rather than as the result of social control or a deterministic structure to perpetuate a group. People marry within existing family circles, within the same milieu, often through siblings of friends, colleagues, or acquaintances. Being close to another family, being friends with a friend's or a colleague's sibling, was highly conducive to mate selection. Multiplied within the same milieu and the same connected networks of families, we obtain what looks like endogamy.

The combination of socioeconomic inequalities and relatively thick social fabric calls for sociometrics: Not only is there an almost infinite gradation of social ties, but also not all social ties are equal in the face of liminality, incitement to hate, or an execution order targeting a particular individual in a social network. Not all social ties carry the same obligations and ethical inhibitions. Social scientists have proposed several typologies of social ties, typically indexed on repetition and trust.[30] Felder's is particularly operative. He distinguishes between four types: (1) absent ties (when ego ignores alter's existence); 2) invisible ties (alter is a familiar stranger); (3) weak ties (alter is an acquaintance); (4) strong ties (intimacy). Whether strong or weak, social ties tend to be inviolable as long as they are not fraught.[31] Importantly, to know another's name, address, or face is not evidence of a social tie but instead the result of interactions. For instance, the fact that "Dola," the coffee hand and seasonal port worker from Dame-Marie, recognized Milou Drouin's face after Jeune Haiti landed in Dame-Marie and yet still denounced him, suggests that mere "invisible ties" connected the two.[32]

Dola, who used to work on Jérémie's wharf located a hundred yards from Milou Drouin's home, must have seen him regularly. Although Dola did not know

Drouin's name or background, he knew his face. They did not share a bond. The probability is that Milou Drouin did not and could not have recognized Dola. When Milou Drouin suddenly appeared in Dame-Marie with his guerrilla group, Dola recognized "a mulatto he had seen in Jérémie," a recognition that would have dire consequences for the local mulattos. An incident of mere facial recognition such as this is unrelated to what Goffman, who emphasized the importance of "every day interactions" in building a social fabric, called "face work," which implies mutuality.[33] Interactions do not consist of what could be called *mutuality of experience* but simply of shared place and time. As David Morgan shows, acquaintanceship within a community is made of knowledge about others without intimacy.[34] In other words, connections are epistemic relations (that we make mentally) without necessarily being social relations (that we have). To identify someone, my interlocutor Guiton Dorimain first constructed a mental social map of his connections before being able to provide information about that person. That is how Dorimain vaguely recalled Second Lieutenant Jean Dimanche, who had grown up in Jérémie and was the illegitimate son of a nightclub owner with a mixed reputation. In spite of that background, Dimanche could be identified by all my Jeremian interlocutors, no matter their own social class. A community is also made of epistemic relations and not exclusively of social relations. (For this reason, there can be no *community* under a real apartheid system, a political creation that seeks precisely to prevent the forging of connections and relationships, and the establishment of a social fabric.)

On the other hand, mutuality of experience characterizes most interpersonal relationships, of any grade, even the most fleeting ones. There can be many indexes to assess ties: trust, repetition, affinities, nearness, etc. But mutuality of experience is, in some ways, the lowest common denominator. As described in memoirs and by interlocutors, the fact that personal social positions were asymmetric, and sometimes deeply asymmetric, did not prevent this mutuality of experience from occurring, "knitting" both a local social fabric and, in some cases, envy. Dalvanor Etienne, a congenial, uneducated Duvalierist mayor of a rural commune, was on a first-name basis with Raoul Cédras, the upper-class owner of one of the town's largest stores. Sanette Balmir, who came from the lowest urban social sector, knew (and was known to) many of the town's elite members before she became a VSN.

Such phenomena do not automatically take place in any given community. Anthropologists Roberto da Matta, McKim Marriott, Louis Dumont, and Anastasia Piliavsky make the counterintuitive argument that not only do inequality and hierarchy not prevent society from being relational (my words), but the relational makes the hierarchy more sustainable.[35] Gérard Barthélémy has even argued that Haiti belongs, contrary to commonplaces, to "societies of the relational and of equality."[36] Equality as a social practice is distinct from equality as ideology and socio-economic equality. For Barthélémy, familiarity amounts to an *engagement in sociality* (my words) that is far from universal. Jérémie's idiosyncratic sociocentrism obviously coexisted with inequalities of all kinds, but it also contradicted them.

Yet, crucially, relationality itself is not bliss. Most ethnographies describe communities struggling with cooperation and envy, amity and entrenched grudges; and Jérémie was no exception. As Maxime Felder shows in his ethnography of neighbors, a tie of any strength can be fraught, even among "equals" (think Cain and Abel).[37] Envy and resentment require and evidence a social fabric in the first place before, sometimes, tearing it apart. Nearness and shared sociality became, in Jérémie, the conditions of envy. Every adult who resented the mulatto elite was able to name and locate the homes of most, if not all, mulatto families. If Jérémie had been an apartheid, a massacre would have been less likely.

SOCIAL INVISIBILITY

Personalism frames the memory of the massacre itself. As chapter 1 explains, the four members of the Presidential Commission—Pierre Biamby, Jean-Baptiste Hilaire, René Prosper, and Mercius Rivière—chose, upon arrival in Jérémie in early August 1964, to stay at the military base. None of them ventured into town during their entire stay in Jérémie (about three weeks), and most townspeople were unaware of their presence. Certainly as a consequence, Biamby and the other Commission members do not appear in oral history and in the historiography although they bear major responsibility for the first wave of executions.

Jacques Fourcand also chose to remain socially invisible. Duvalier's personal physician and confidant, Fourcand was sent to Jérémie two days after the anti-insurgency operation had started. He was supposed to report to the Presidential Commission upon arrival but never did. Instead, having wounded his foot when exiting the plane, he went to the Jérémie hospital where he stayed for several days (I could not determine the exact number) before hopping on the next available plane back to Port-au-Prince. According to Jérôme, Fourcand faked his wound to stay at the hospital. If true, this fake wound would be a remarkable strategy of social and political evasion. Alix Cédras stated: "We learned years later that Jacques Fourcand had been in town." Fourcand, Biamby, and the Presidential Commission's members disappeared. Their invisibility in oral history provides evidence of Jérémie's sociocentric logic.[38] I return to this in chapter 10.

THE SOCIAL LIFE OF COLORS

The social world I describe in this chapter was depicted by my Jeremian inter-locutors who were adults, adolescents, or children in the early 1960s; it is also rendered in the precise memoirs of Eddy Cavé and Jean-Pierre Alcindor. They describe Jeremian life primarily as a relational world, where creating and fos-tering personal relationships were an end in itself. Their primary subjects were either dyads or sometimes larger groups of friends, regardless of social origin, kinship ties, and political beliefs. Possibly for this very reason, racial identi-ties are almost never mentioned in these memoirs. Every time I talked to Eddy Cavé, I had to ask racially explicit questions to identify individuals mentioned in his memoirs. I encountered the same phenomenon with the other Jeremians I interviewed. I realized this fascinating and omnipresent response: one's skin color was an out-of-bounds question when that person was a close friend of the interlocutor. Even older interlocutors who were openly Duvalierist and occa-sionally indulged in anti-mulatto discourse would dismiss the question when talking about a friend or someone they appreciated. Once, an informant who was fifteen at the time of the massacre explained at length to me that "this color thing is overrated," whereas in a prior interview she had compared Jérémie to an apartheid system. Her "overrated" remark came at the end of a recollection of her childhood friendships. Intimacy trumped race. Inversely, if the bond was weak or absent, race could be reified. Racial identifications appeared explicitly in personal accounts only when resentment characterized the speaker's senti-ment toward a particular person, especially when a specific grudge divided the families involved. In other words, race was only used as an element of identifica-tion when social ties were fraught. To add complexity to the matter, resentment from one person toward another (or several) was also framed by intimacy, by knowledge about the other(s). This was even more true when resentment was a by-product of a broken relationship or of scorn. In any case, rancor, jealousy, or resentment were predicated on intimacy for more than one reason. To dislike someone in Jérémie, a social tie was necessary. Both social bonds and their absence were intimate. If one word fails to characterize South Africa's apartheid, it would be intimacy.

Basculement

What happens to a sociocentric world when orders arrive to kill some of its members? Hannah Arendt famously argued that the atomization of society brought about by modernity enables authoritarianism and terror.[39] When isolated, individuals are more prone to obedience; when together, they are more able to resist political power. The social fabric was never destroyed in Jérémie, and Haiti's government under Duvalier (contrary to what Michel-Rolph Trouillot believed) never tried to impose a totalitarian system above and in lieu of the private space. This situation constitutes the core social context of the massacre.

When terror set in in Jérémie, neighbors did not turn again neighbors. Many committed social violations, acted out of cowardice, or refrained from intervening to save friends, kin, or neighbors. Many VSNs also committed social violations, intimidated people they knew and, under order, participated in the arrests of the victims. One noncommissioned officer humiliated the victims on August 11 by forcing them to undress. But nobody from Jérémie participated in the killings. Only two individuals, Sanette Balmir and Saintange Bontemps, as explored in chapter 7, argued in favor of repression. No murderous hysteria suddenly possessed peaceful civilians, as happened during pogroms in the European borderlands, the Rwanda genocide, and the civil war in the former Yugoslavia. Rather, most residents' behavior could be characterized as desistance, precaution, and bystanding.

Jérémie's microsolidarity was challenged by several consecutive moments: the 1957 presidential campaign, which polarized the population;[40] the Duvalier regime itself and its anti-mulatto ideology; and the summer of 1964, an anti-mulatto moment in Haiti's history. During that summer, many (if not most) social bonds were challenged precisely because being associated to someone could bring danger. To what extent was solidarity, to use Durkheim's term, shattered?

Gérard Guilbaud and Jean Alcide were of the same generation and friends. They were not close friends, they were not from the same milieu, but they were more than acquaintances. Their relationship was characterized as a friendship by several informants, although Alcide seemed uneasy with the term when I interviewed him.[41] They played on the same soccer team in their youth, and even on the same wing: Guilbaud as left forward and Alcide as left midfielder. Later, when Guilbaud was a shop owner and Alcide a vocational school teacher, Alcide was seen chatting in Guilbaud's store with him. Their friendship was not intimate. Neither of them invited the other to his house or to his wedding, although Guilbaud attended Alcide's birthday party at least once. Alcide had been a Duvalierist since the 1957 campaign. He was described by informants as a mild-mannered man, and that is how he appeared to me when I interviewed him at his home in Florida in March 2016.[42]

On the evening of August 11, 1964, Guilbaud and his wife stood naked, humiliated, and terrified in the guardroom of the military base. They allegedly did not say a word during the entirety of their ordeal. Together with other Duvalierists, Alcide saw the couple when he peeked in the guardroom, and did not, or felt he could not, intervene. Hours later, a powerless Jean Alcide was witness to Guilbaud's execution: Guilbaud was the only victim to survive the first round of bullets, and Alcide was obliged to use his flashlight to illuminate Guilbaud's wounded body so that a soldier could finish him off with his rifle. Because the social relationship between Alcide and Guilbaud was known in town, a novelistic rumor emerged after Guilbaud's execution. It alleged that Guilbaud was the lone victim in the pit to survive the initial salvo of bullets because they had ricocheted off the silver medallion of the Virgin Mary he was wearing; understanding he would die anyway, Guilbaud theatrically took the medallion off and handed it to his friend Jean Alcide. Alcide refuted the story as ridiculous.

However, Jean Alcide did intervene earlier that evening to save one of the individuals who had also been arrested and was also standing in the guardroom with the others: Harry Balmir. From the information I gathered, the two were not very close but Alcide *knew* Balmir. Two relationships can hardly be equivalent, but the one Alcide had with Balmir seemed to have been of roughly the same nature, if not of lower intensity, as that between Alcide and Gérard Guilbaud. However, when Harry Balmir was standing naked, humiliated, and terrified in the military base's guardroom, Jean Alcide and Gérard Léonidas intervened on his behalf. Why Balmir and not Guilbaud?

I asked Jean Alcide what must have sounded like a blunt question. He was clearly uncomfortable and silent for several seconds, then said: "we believed

Balmir was innocent . . . I told them, 'he is poor, like us.'" I then asked if he believed Guilbaud was guilty and if so, of what. Alcide then moved his arm in the air and whispered "I do not know" several times. Maybe Alcide and Gérard Léonidas "chose" in the moment to save Balmir simply because he was more "salvageable" than Guilbaud, whose brother-in-law Milou Drouin was known by the Presidential Commission to be in the Jeune Haiti insurgency. And maybe, among other factors, the fact that Balmir was of a darker complexion and from a lower social class than Guilbaud, a member of the "mulatto" elite, also made him more "salvageable." The same evening, Jean Alcide and his Duvalierist neighbors behaved as rescuers and as bystanders. In both cases, preexisting social ties framed decisions.

APARTHEIDOLOGY

How could such a world be compared to the apartheid regime? The historiography either grossly underestimated the reality of the apartheid system in South Africa, mistook "apartheid" for socioeconomic inequality, or used a concept to express an anti-value. It expanded the notion of apartheid to encompass unrelated forms of social policy and institutions, stretching the relation between scope and symbol to epistemological rupture. In moral terms, the analogy grossly relativizes the horrors of South Africa's apartheid. One could argue that the term was used hyperbolically. But then, if the core meaning of the original term is "separation"—and separation was indeed enforced in absolutely all aspects of social life in South Africa and constituted the system's core ideology—then the analogy grossly misinterpreted the racial divide in Jérémie in the 1950s and 1960s.

Alongside the concepts of *mulâtrisme* and the "politics of understudy," analyzed in earlier chapters, "apartheid" is another Lévi-Straussian "floating signifier": a buzzword traveling with critical impunity through the historiographic and popular ether whose function is to enable "symbolic thinking to operate."[43] Not every hierarchical society is an apartheid system. This flawed analogy does not aim for sociological or historical accuracy but most likely expresses the egalitarian values of those who use it: in particular, the belief that inequalities and social discriminations are morally inadmissible. This analogy also provides a rational explanation for a massacre constructed ex ante as revenge, for an apartheid system necessarily divides society into a dualistic opposition between perpetrators and victims. Indeed, "apartheid" is one of the most damaging analogies one can use, turning mulattos into Boers—dominating and foreign in origin, the epitome of a group with a supremacist ideology. Yet, in a real apartheid system, the dominant group is not a raft of sitting ducks waiting to be slaughtered.

Jérémie was not a sociological caricature, even if the absence of available socioeconomic indicators forces us to rely on testimonies. Rather than being divided between rich and poor, it had an "elongated" differentiation, with many socioeconomic sectors that did not always coincide with symbolic capital and access to political power. These sectors cut across race, although lighter skin complexion was almost exclusively located toward the top, with some exceptions.[44] However, two institutions were segregated in Jérémie: marriage, and a social club called the Excelsior. They were a magnet for much of the local resentment and racial imagination. Precisely because Jérémie was a personalist and intimate world, segregation was thought of as a social violation. And denied intimacy is a better predictor of resentment than acquired ideology, as I address in the following chapter.

CHAPTER 6

The Excelsior

This chapter aims to understand two distinct facts that share the same underlying intellectual context: (1) the apocryphal narrative that erroneously attributed atrocities against women to "neighbors"; and (2) how the Duvalier regime established a regime of terror by targeting mothers, grandmothers, and children, figures that until then were considered "sacred."

What made the "massacre of neighbors" narrative plausible was not only the empirical existence of social resentments in the non-elite urban population before the massacre, but also the fact that gender was central to perceptions of denied intimacy. Social fantasies were very much focused, unconsciously or not, on elite mulatto women and marriages, as proven by the central place of the Excelsior social club in these representations. Narratives about the Excelsior were not about dancing and partying; they were about the elusiveness of elite women—social fantasies of inclusion and status. Marriage therefore occupied a fundamental place in conceptions of social mobility; hypergamy was conceived almost as a right, a notion implicit in the lay literature. Infra-elite marriages (homogamy) were therefore perceived as a form of denied intimacy and socioeconomic exclusion. And at the same time, the coexistence of personalistic practice with socioeconomic inequalities and egalitarian ideologies fueled resentment. The elite—its habits, its (relative) wealth, its club, its marriages—were almost "touchable" in the small, personalist world of Jérémie; and yet elite women were not.

However, in Haitian history, social fantasies about elite mulatto women almost never materialized into violence against them: not just because they were elite, but because they were women, and women were largely beyond norms of organized violence. Attacking women contradicted a central cultural and moral value in Haitian society: the sacrality of the mother, whatever her skin complexion. This is what Duvalier did to instill terror in the population that he perceived as most likely to question his power: the mulatto elite.

This chapter links these two central facts by focusing on representations of women and the relationship between these representations and Duvalier's use of mass violence. I will begin with an anecdote.

One of the anecdotes I heard most frequently during my research for this book was about a verbal aggression at an elite ball. A Black gentleman attended a ball at the Excelsior club in Jérémie, and when mulatto women noticed his presence, they sarcastically commented: "There is a fly in the bowl of milk." This anecdote was usually recounted as part of a wider set of responses to my general question on the causes of the Jérémie massacre: "Why do you think the Jérémie Vespers happened?"[1]

That something as hateful and belligerent was said publicly to someone who had been invited in the first place to the Excelsior, in the well-mannered, provincial world of mid-twentieth century Haiti, is entirely possible. My point is not to measure the veracity of words spoken (or not) sixty or seventy years ago, nor is it to focus on the implicit victim-blaming nature of the response to an interview question. However, inquiring why people resorted to this anecdote in particular to explain why the massacre took place is relevant. The setting for the anecdote is a social ball. The words could have been uttered in other settings: a professional office, a church, a school, a private home. Instead, mulatto women seemed moved to express a racist sense of sarcasm primarily during balls held at the Excelsior.

The Excelsior was a social club located on the second floor of the city hall. Conferences, marriages, baptisms, and other festivities were organized there, usually for the city's upper classes and only by invitation.[2] It was led by a group of older ladies and housewives, most, but not all, of them mulattos, who followed rigid, unwritten rules with a shared conservative mindset. They would meet days or weeks ahead of social functions, establish a list of invitees, and then send out invitations. Black families were rare; the families of Dr. Louis Laurent, Hannibal Cavé, and Raoul Cédras being among them. Some mulattoes were never invited, such as Roger Chassagne's family. When I asked Chassagne's son why, he answered that people with progressive social views were usually frowned upon and sidelined. When one such person was no longer invited, his or her entire nuclear family would also be omitted from invitation lists. Non-elite mulattoes, such as Serge Picard, a young teacher, could not expect an invitation either.[3]

I had imagined that the Excelsior looked like an aristocratic ball in nineteenth-century Vienna, in the manner of a Hollywood film: a place of refinement and muted elegance where well-dressed men and women displaying ancien regime manners would socialize in a hall with tasteful paintings and glorious lighting. This was my unconscious interpretation after listening to its oral history. Then, one day, one interlocutor showed me an old picture of it: a large, unexceptional room in a wooden house, an unpolished wooden floor, a couple of bulbs hanging from the ceiling, no decoration on the rough boarded walls, some portable chairs. How could such a rudimentary place channel so many social class fantasies and become a leitmotif of anti-mulatto rhetoric?

The Excelsior was an exclusive place in full view: forbidden to most, yet known to all. Those who desired an invitation and never received one would have been acutely aware of every ball organized there. In cities around the world, the upper classes tend to organize events in their own neighborhoods and gated villas. In Jérémie, however, the exclusiveness was public—a slap in the face. The modus operandi of the Excelsior challenged, if not violently transgressed, the town's relational culture depicted in the previous chapter. The unwritten rule that hierarchy did not prevent sociality was violated by the Excelsior; it made hierarchy visible, raw, scandalous. Denied intimacy is a better predictor of resentment, if not violence, than the absence of any intimacy in the first place. Yet denied intimacy alone does not explain the centrality of social balls in the Jeremian collective imagination; vernacular conceptions of marriage powerfully contribute to it.

In Jérémie, visibility and inaccessibility characterized how mulatto women were viewed. In the 1950s and 1960s, the elite could be seen all the time: at school, at church, on the main square, on their galleries and others; yet, mulatto women always seemed inaccessible. With much honesty, Jean-Claude Fignolé and Serge Picard talked about being secretly in love with the young Lyssa Villedrouin, and how they stared at her when she was "walking with her friends on the Place d'Arme, with her long undulating black hair and her shy, Madonna-like face. Everybody was in love with her."[4] But Fignolé was the son of farmers, Picard an illegitimate child, and neither could dream of an invitation to the Excelsior to dance with Lyssa Villedrouin. This club, however, was not a place for matrimonial strategies. Marital decisions in the decades prior to 1964 did not require such a space, and possibly never did. Young people of marriageable age and their families knew each other outside the club. However, for those who were excluded from them, the "balls of the Excelsior" felt like places of encounter attended by eligible young people.

Mulatto balls in Haiti were evoked for the first time in writing, I believe, by Victor Schoelcher. For the anti-mulatto French writer, balls provided evidence of discrimination and mulattoes' prejudices: "I attended dinners, balls, and nowhere did I see any [racial] mingling. I was received in some families, and in none did I see mixed marriages (*mariages de fusion*), or they were really exceptional."[5] Schoelcher's anecdote had a long intertextual life.

A century later, the very first example of racial discrimination provided by Duvalier in his 1948 book on social classes was about balls where "[w]omen of color refuse to dance with men of color."[6] Behind the discourse on mulatto balls lies a critique of "mulatto endogamy," which was not restricted to noirist literature; and a desire for the "mulatto woman."[7] In literary production throughout the nineteenth and twentieth centuries, mulatto endogamy was a fact and an injustice. The mid-century American sociologist James Leyburn, although he provided no substantial quantitative or qualitative evidence for it, also believed the Haitian elite was endogamous, which seemed to evidence some Haitian exceptionality, if not pathology: "The elite [in Haiti] are endogamous in that they would not consider marriage into the masses."[8] If all anthropological writings are analogical, Leyburn surely must have known a place where the elite was not endogamous.

The first marker of racial discrimination given by Michel-Rolph Trouillot in a piece on the subject was also marriage: "Color-cum-social categories . . . operate most vividly in the family alliances typical of certain urban classes."[9] Trouillot had addressed mulatto endogamy earlier.[10] The evidence Trouillot offers is actually a result, not a proof: given the demographic proportions at independence, which are not provided, between a large Black majority and a small mulatto minority, mulattoes should have biologically disappeared; since they have not, they could only do so because of endogamous practices.[11] The Marxist poet Jean-Richard Laforest exemplified the view that endogamy, preventing any socioeconomic and political change, is at the center of racial contentions: "Within relations between blacks and mulattoes, tensions very often crystallize around the question of sexual relations and marriage, sources of underlying tensions. If marriages were enlarged [*sic*], mobility would ensue, whereas in reality the historical will of mulattoes, or of the 'caste' if you wish, led to a kind of immobility, pregnant with their self-interests and socioeconomic efficiency."[12] More recent essays also deplore mulatto infra-marriages and see them as causal to socioeconomic inequalities, exemplifying the endurance of this worldview today.[13] There is no question that color, or race, has often been a determinant of matrimonial strategies since the colonial era.[14] Yet, to pinpoint the cause of a country's socioeconomic inequalities and its lack of social mobility in its elite's matrimonial practices is a rather unusual socioeconomic diagnosis.[15]

HATING AND COVETING

If group hatred is usually coterminous with calls for ethnic purity, the resentment against mulatto endogamy, particularly when coming from noirist authors, appears contradictory. While colonial norms tended to criminalize miscegenation, noirist views vehemently made mulatto endogamy a social violation.[16] How could a racist doctrine, noirism, stigmatize the Other's endogamy? For René Depestre and Leslie Péan, there was no contradiction: noirism never advocated racial purity or its opposite, miscegenation but was instead an articulation of social resentment by mediocre intellectuals.

The figure of the mulatto woman was at the center of contention.[17] Péan put it in raw terms: "the sex of the mulatto woman was a battlefield."[18] For both Depestre and Péan, the young noirists of the "1946 Revolution" were deeply resentful of being scorned by upper-class women, as Depestre put it : "François Duvalier, Lorimel Denis and Louis Diaquoi . . . were frustrated in their social life, and suffered from not being invited into certain *clubs mondains* of the capital where you could see some of the most beautiful girls of Port-au-Prince."[19] Hypergamy was an unfulfilled desire. Having ascended to the middle class through their education and intellect, many still could not integrate into the bourgeoisie. This "matrimonial market," they believed, was closed to them. A certain number, however, did succeed. Péan again: "[b]eing married to a mulatto woman was perceived by the '46ers as evidence that their movement for social reform had succeeded."[20]

It is difficult not to think of the satire authored by Dany Laferrière: *Camarade, où sont les mulâtresses?* (Comrade, where are the mulatto women?)[21] Laferrière imagines a powerful member of the Duvalier regime who, upon arriving at a ball, impatiently asks about mulatto women. Readers aware of the innuendos recognized René Piquion, one of the Duvalier regime's ideologues. Beyond the verbosity of noirism, Laferrière shows, lies mere hypocrisy and deception. The mulatto woman was not the fantasy of some average man but of the urban, politicized, upper-echelon intellectual. For them, the mulatto woman was a civil right. Another, more disturbing anecdote illustrates the combination of fantasies and social resentment. In the immediate aftermath of the Jérémie massacre, the VSN Gérard Brunache fabricated self-incriminating allegations that he had raped the seventeen-year old, upper-class Lyssa Villedrouin on the night of her execution to acquire symbolic capital within the VSNs.[22] The apocryphal rumor spread among a Jeremian population ready to believe the realization of a sordid fantasy dressed up in social vengeance.[23]

DENIED INTIMACY

Why would a group's endogamy, perceived or real, be unbearable to others? Why is the mulatto elite's alleged endogamy typically presented as a moral scandal— an act of "discrimination" in the above-cited words of Trouillot? As Marco van Leeuwen and Ineke Maas show in their *tour du monde* of endogamy, there are few, if any, upper classes in modern societies and beyond that cannot be characterized as endogamous or somehow endogamous.[24] No group, including social classes, can perpetuate itself without some level of endogamy, as the social historian Francis Thompson showed: there is no class reproduction without marriage; and the more unequal and hierarchical a society is, the more endogamous its elite tends to be.[25] To expect any social sector to behave differently seems to reproduce the bias of Haiti as an exception, an abnormality, a freak—a slot.

Conceiving of endogamy as a social violation reveals not only overarching egalitarian values, but also the significance of marriage in a society where the kinship group represents a crucial social resource. The extended family not only occupies a central part in Haitian social and public life; it is also key to providing social relationships beyond the family, as anthropologists have shown.[26] As Guy Dallemand, a professor at Port-au-Prince's Faculté des sciences humaines succinctly put it, "A Haitian confronts life (*affronte la vie*) with his [extended] family."[27] The mid-twentieth-century expression *corps de famille*, or *kod fami* in Kreyol, names more than an extended family; something like a kinship group and its allies. It is this *corps*, and not a political party, that constitutes a candidate's support group during an election campaign.[28] Thorald Burnham perfectly understood the significance of marriage in such a social configuration: to marry someone is to marry into that person's kinship group—and thus possibly, it is perceived, to the detriment of all others, to the detriment of the whole society.[29]

Marriage is therefore a zero-sum game: if I fail to marry that highly eligible person, someone else will benefit from that person's kinship group and its trust, network, and capital. In such a social configuration, marrying tends to be a socially crucial strategic matter and, therefore, a potential motive of anxiety. This is distinct from the customary view of marriage as an "alliance." That a spouse's family provides a wider network, more social capital, and different set of resources is neither new nor limited to Haiti, as Balzac's and Trollope's novels made clear. Vernacular factors, however, come into play: the scarcity of resources, including the limited number of eligible young men and women in the highest segments of urban society; the scarcity of institutions that allow for social mobility; and the particular role of intimacy in an intensely relational world. The elite's endogamy is therefore a source of resentment for ambitious men from lower social strata while the endogamy of other groups, including their own, would be irrelevant. Only the elite's endogamy is therefore conceived as exclusion.

Endogamy, perceived or real, was interpreted in Jérémie by non-elite sectors as denied intimacy. In Jérémie's social fabric and relational culture, interpersonal relationships cutting across groups and status were conceived of not just as social and symbolic capital but as an end in themselves. Intimacy was expected and indeed took place, yet it stopped at marriage and at the door of the Excelsior. Infra-elite matrimonial practices not only denied intimacy and the formation of larger social capital and family alliances, but they denied such formation on hierarchical grounds. The omnipresent egalitarian values (examined in chapter 3) provided a grammar with which to critique the elite's endogamy.[30]

The data I collected from interlocutors for this research show that mulatto endogamy was perceived and resented more viscerally by people from socioeconomic sectors situated right below the elite. Individuals from "lower" social sectors—notably, the farmers I interviewed on the outskirts of Jérémie in 2016 and in the Moron area in 2017—demonstrated a range of views and sentiments closer to indifference toward a mulatto elite they almost never saw. Philippe Marius makes the same argument.[31] Voicing concerns about the "elite" tends to be an elite affair; the underprivileged sectors of society tend to have, for the most part, other concerns.[32]

WERE JÉRÉMIE'S MULATTOES ENDOGAMOUS?[33]

Is the above question even relevant? It is if we assume that how the massacre's victims appeared to others influenced how perpetrators constructed their beliefs. I had taken it for granted that Jérémie's mulattoes were endogamous. Many marriages in the twentieth century had clearly occurred within the thirty or forty families that constituted the mulatto elite there. However, in researching this book, I made a few genealogical sketches both of victims and of the town's Duvalierists. Intrigued by preliminary results, I systematized this effort to include more trees of Haitian personalities at the national level over the past 200 years, using diachronic relatedness. To summarize these findings, yes: Jérémie's mulattoes were relatively endogamous; but everybody was.

These genealogical trees demonstrate relatedness through a diachronic interlacing of people of various racial identities. Class, not skin color, is the most powerful determinant.[34] "Homogamy" is therefore a much more appropriate concept than "endogamy." Philippe Marius demonstrated that much through ethnographic methods.[35] Incidentally, these results also contradict essentialist notions that mulattoes resemble anything like a racial or an ethnic group. These results are not without irony: many prominent members of *la classe*, the middle sector that rose to political and cultural prominence in 1946 against mulatto-dominated politics and culture, have mulattoes among their ascendants or descendants. François Duvalier himself, a man whose forefathers were farmers, is related by marriage (with Simone Ovide) to prominent patrician families. The proto-noirist writer Louis-Joseph Janvier, who boasted that he was made entirely of peasant blood in order to delegitimize Hannibal Price, is linked through his sister Acéphie to the families of Boyer-Bazelais and Louis Borno, symbols in noirist historiography of mulatto hegemony.[36] The intellectual Jean Price-Mars is linked through his descendants to prominent mulatto families such as the Baussan, St. Rémy, and Forbin families, a member of whom would land in Dame-Marie with Jeune Haiti on August 6, 1964.

The interlacing of families identified as Black and mulatto confirms the intuitions of the historian Jean Fouchard, who believed that upper-class families had Black and mulatto branches that kept meeting over several generations.[37] Michèle Oriol compared this successive "branching" of Black and mulatto family trees to "double-helicoidal trees."[38] The genealogical trees of political dynasties presented by Michèle Oriol show that families from the time of Haitian independence to the late twentieth century fluctuate constantly between color lines over several generations, and that mixed marriages were the rule rather than the exception—indeed, all of Haiti's rulers from independence to 1957 are contained in only three genealogical trees.[39]

Michèle Oriol, herself a Black woman, is related to the light-skinned mulatto President Louis Borno (1865–1942), her granduncle, who himself was descended from a Black family two generations above him. In this family tree reconstituted by Oriol, there are ascendant and descendant Black and mulatto branches. Another conclusion is that up until the mid-twentieth century, economic, educated, and political elites can hardly be "separated" and categorized in groups.

Michèle Oriol, drawing on her ethnographic experience in the Grand'Anse peasantry in the 1980s and her wider observations of Haitian society, makes the hyperbolic statement that "endogamy is Haitian"—that this pattern can be found in all social groups, from the peasantry to the urban elites. This would of course require a more systematic study. Yet my own research on Duvalier's inner circle suggests that the matrimonial strategies of the middle class in Port-au-Prince in the first half of the twentieth century, the very social sector that resented mulatto hegemony, tended to be highly homogamous.[40] In Duvalier's inner circle, the kin of ministers, military officers, and other members of the Duvalierist milieu married daughters and sisters of other members.[41] Such practice does not appear to be intentional and organized through family injunctions and group pressure, the kind of social control that anthropologists typically encounter in traditionally endogamous communities. Rather, it is highly linked to non-political patterns of socialization: young people tend to socialize beyond the family only through circles established by kin in the first place.

I would hypothesize, therefore, that endogamy is a result rather than a structure in the British structural-functionalist sense. Because socialization and friendship-formation beyond the family tend to occur within family circles rather than outside of them, homosocial relationships between members of different families are required for their own eligible kin to meet. Rather than social control or group pressure, the condition of knowing a friend's sibling or someone connected to the family appears highly conducive to spouse selection, if not attractiveness. The determination of attractiveness might, therefore, be framed not just through traits related to an individual's good looks, personality, or achievements but also by the emotional security provided by familial circles of trust.

Put differently, and counterintuitively, endogamous mate selection is a result of elective affinities instead of structures of kinship or predetermined pressure to reproduce a group; and yet these elective affinities are determined by a closed form of sociality. When this is multiplied within the same milieu and the same connected networks of families, we obtain what looks like endogamy. This would explain, for instance, why so many members of *la classe* in general and of the Duvalier regime in particular married siblings of other members, and why Jérémie's upper-class families tended to marry within their own.[42]

"I HAVE CHILDREN, PLEASE DO NOT HUMILIATE ME."

If, as argued above, the place of the Excelsior and elite balls in the imaginary points at the centrality of women and matrimonial strategies in representations of equality, then gender played a central role in the creation of a system of fear and the repression of the elite. The brutalization of women was key to establishing a regime of terror. I will use a foundational incident to illustrate this.

Yvonne Hakim-Rimpel (1906–1986) was one of Haiti's most important and influential feminists in the 1950s: a public intellectual, a journalist, and unafraid. In 1934, she and other upper-class women cofounded the Women's League for Social Action (Ligue Féminine d'Action Sociale), the country's first feminist organization, which advocated for women's political rights, particularly suffrage.[43] In 1950, it famously organized Haiti's first mass demonstration by women to pressure the constituent assembly to recognize women's civic rights.[44] Hakim-Rimpel supervised the League's weekly publication *La voix des femmes* (The Voice of Women), before founding her own bi-weekly, *Escale*. This very dynamic intellectual and social life would be greatly diminished by the Duvalier regime. The September 1957 presidential elections were the first time in Haiti's history when women could vote. Hakim-Rimpel supported Louis Déjoie. After Duvalier's victory, she published vitriolic editorials against the military that had helped Duvalier win. In what would be the last issue of *Escale*, in December 1957, she published a front page editorial titled: "A vous Général . . . deux mots," (I have several words . . . to say to you, General) in which she accused Gen. Kébreau of manipulating the elections. (This accusation appears bold, if not suicidal in retrospect, but it actually shows that criticism of this sort was within the accepted norms until Duvalier's election.)

A few days later, shortly before midnight on January 5, 1958, two cars with government license plates stopped in front of her house on rue Babiole.[45] Six *cagoulards* came out, stormed into the house and called out for Hakim-Rimpel. Her two older daughters tried to oppose the men and were beaten—one, Rose-May, lost her front teeth. Hakim-Rimpel was forced into one the cars and taken to a remote area of Delmas where she was raped, beaten, and left for dead.[46] A worker found her in the early morning hours in a ditch, naked and covered in blood. Broken, profoundly traumatized, Hakim-Rimpel never published again. Her twenty-three-year career as a writer and activist was over. In a television interview decades laters, Hakim-Rimpel's elder daughter, Marie-Cécile, repeated her mother's words that night before being taken away: "I have children, please do not humiliate me."[47] Once the cagoulards had started to hit her and she realized what was to come, Hakim-Rimpel tried to reason with her tormentors: as a last resort, she turned to social ethics. Her condition as a mother, she thought, would inhibit them; in the urgency of the moment, she turned to what she thought was the one core value they shared: the mother.

Whether the violation of social ethics was a strategy or logical outcome of Duvalier's brand of terror is a matter of interpretation. It is difficult, however, to imagine that Duvalier was not conscious of his orders, and his henchmen of their actions. In addition, the rumors of Hakim-Rimpel's rape, which spread quickly, could only have come from the cagoulards themselves, as the victim remained silent about it. Marie-Cécile learned it from public rumor and broached the topic with her mother: "Mummy, everybody says you were raped." Her mother ignored the question. Norm-breaking cannot be hidden. The point of terror is not only to break norms but to make the violations be known, while retaining some element of uncertainty. To have the desired political effect, social violations must be spectacular but their true nature somewhat unclear. The rumor, rather than official, trumpeted news, is the public relation of terror. The rumor that Yvonne Hakim-Rimpel, a writer "well-known in the bourgeoisie" and a single-mother of five underaged children had been gangraped, beaten, and left for dead created "a psychosis [and an] *état d'épouvante* (state of terror)" in the upper class, as the very man responsible for this ordeal, Pressoir Pierre, recognized.[48] Importantly this incident targeted a mother but not her children. A change in scale—another shattering of social norms—would occur again during the Jeremian Vespers.

WHAT NORMS WERE TARGETED?

Ethnographers of set communities in Haiti emphasize the centrality of women's presence in family life and the significance of the mother as a personal value and in social representations.[49] The mother figure appears ubiquitous in people's lives and worldviews. She is a central figure in adult men's lives and for their sense of self, as proven by literature, language, and practice.[50] To state that the mother is in Haiti "sacred" might be a clichéd metaphor, but it is certainly an epistemologically operative one. The mother would be targeted by the new regime for the same reason she was traditionally spared from political violence: because she is a revered figure. Historically, the exclusion of women from repression followed their exclusion from public roles.[51]

Hakim-Rimpel was targeted not as the kin of an opponent but instead for her own actions. She had wrongly assumed that her status as a mother would trigger ethical inhibitions in Duvalier and his henchmen. Her ordeal indeed unveils ordinary Haitian ethics, the type that would have to be violated to produce terror. The latter is not necessarily obtained by the volume of repression, but by breaking the norms of organized violence recognized by society's members. William Gamson coined a specific concept, "mode of collective violence," precisely to name eruptions of collective anger that usually follows learned models. Not in this case. Duvalier broke the state's repertoire of organized violence.[52] Fear is instilled when people do not recognize the classificatory category of a particular act of violence. In the 1970s and 1980s, scholarship in the field addressed the question of the historicity of Duvalierist violence. David Nicholls dismissively refuted the notion that this type and degree of violent repression was anything new in Haiti's history.[53] Trouillot believed it was actually uncommon, although, in apophatic fashion, he first stated that Haiti had a long tradition of terrorizing opponents.[54] In real time, however, the answer to this question was for many a certainty.[55]

In the historiography, women rarely appear as targets of organized violence in the nineteenth and twentieth centuries.[56] This includes repressions unleashed by President Faustin Soulouque from 1848 onward: male opponents were targeted but their female relatives were not. Justin Bouzon's account of this episode of terror almost always gives the sex of the victims, whether in the capital or in the Southwest: men.[57] When Salomon peacefully entered Jérémie and had leaders of the Liberal rebellion arrested and executed through deceptive means, their families were spared.[58] In Roger Gaillard's recounting of the 1902 civil war in which the government of Nord Alexis fought against Liberals led by Anténor Firmin, where combatants purposely spared women and even protected the spouses of military adversaries.[59] Female kin of opponents even received protection when their spouses were defeated and fled the battlefield, in scenes that recall chivalrous traditions.

However, women did suffer from political violence in at least three separate historical instances before Duvalier's ascent to power. The first instance was in June 1812, when King Christophe specifically included women when he ordered an extermination campaign of all mulattoes in his northern kingdom.[60] The second instance occurred under President Lysius Salomon's rule. Salomon's brutal repression of elite sectors spared women only on September 22, 1883. The following day, when repression was outsourced to armed supporters during a twelve-hour mayhem on September 23, women from the merchant elite were victimized. The third instance occurred in 1915: a few of the death certificates of the 1915 executions by soldiers faithful to President Jean Vilbrun Guillaume Sam record female forenames, although these account for only a handful among the hundreds of dead.

The societal shock produced by state violence against women under Duvalier "functioned" because past instances of state brutality against women had withered away from collective memory by the time of Duvalier's ascent. Duvalier's scale of repression and choice of targets had to be unrecognizable in people's classification system to produce shock. The repertoire of felt violence did not, or could no longer, predict what was to come. From inception, the assault on social ethics—the ones Hakim-Rimpel invoked in her desperate plea to her aggressors—was a central feature of Duvalier's repression. And the figure of the mother was not the only one targeted. Duvalier repeatedly shattered kinship morality by executing his own family members and by betraying members of his own inner circle, including friends.[61] Nevertheless, Duvalier's transgression did more than serve as an anchoring point for widespread terror: his culturally dissonant behavior was a source of fascination, even of personal charisma.

THREE ELDERLY WOMEN

The nighttime execution of the last three victims of the Jérémie massacre—Louise Drouin (née Degraff), the physically-handicapped Corinne Villedrouin (née

Sansaricq, 1879–1964), and her mentally handicapped daughter Fernande—is the least known part of this historical event. Corinne Villedrouin was the widow of a local judge, Chenier Villedrouin, and the mother of Colonel Roger Villedrouin, executed a year earlier. The other, Louise Drouin, was a *dame patronesse* (in charge of the church's philanthropic works). Although not wealthy and shy, she was a prominent figure of the elite. There were no bystander witnesses to their execution. They were most likely arrested and brought to Numéro 2 by a small cadre of soldiers or VSNs, then executed by the very people who had arrested them.[62] Lieutenant Jean Dimanche and his squad, who had executed the previous victims at Numéro 2, had returned to the Casernes Dessalines in Port-au-Prince by then. If robbery was an additional motive for these murders, then covering up all traces was key. Oral history is less than forthcoming on the subject; Abel Jérôme refused to answer any questions about this last killing.

Where the older ladies were killed (whether at their respective homes or at the execution grounds) matters far less than by whom. Two elements are highly probable. The first is that the deed was carried out by only a handful of individuals, the better to keep it secret. If soldiers were involved, it is unlikely that Jérôme was not aware of it. Since the houses were robbed as soon as the occupants were killed, there is a correlation between killers and robbers. If chiefs and subalterns were involved (as was typically the case in Jérémie and in Duvalier's repression apparatus), the subalterns would have taken the older ladies (or their dead bodies) to Numéro 2, to be executed or buried, while the "chiefs" remained behind to carry out the robberies and keep the spoils. The second is that Duvalier had to have authorized (or even directly ordered) this last killing and the robberies that followed. As Yvon Guerrier's testimony about April 1963 shows, Duvalier could personally oversee robbery schemes involving executions and take his "commission."[63] To some extent, it was a murder of opportunity: high-profile last names (Drouin, Villedrouin, Sansaricq) and objects of value in their homes (jewelry, cash, record players, etc.) conspired to turn them into targets.

The killing of three defenseless, elderly women, including two grandmothers, was a small-scale, local event. It is also unprecedented in Haitian history. The grandmother holds a different place than the mother, perhaps even more sacred, and absolutely beyond politics and repression. The lateness of the event—on October 18, two full months after the execution of their relatives—suggests hesitation, if not inhibition. In the patriarchal world of Jérémie, the killing of two grandmothers precipitated the flight of the remaining elite families.

———◆———

In the mind of many, attacks against elite women and children during the Duvalier regime served as "proof" that the elite had discriminated socially, culturally, economically, and politically against the Haitian population. The unthinkable happened because the arrogance of the elite had reached an untenable level. Such was the logic behind the Duvalierist discourse, its regime of terror, and the "massacre of neighbors" narrative. Victim-blaming certainly turns causality upside down. It also reveals deeper structures and established beliefs: in this case, the illegitimacy of the elite and the inability to conceive of and implement a real social program to enact change.

Violence against women, and more largely against the elite, had no true social or socioeconomic goal—how could it possibly have achieved socioeconomic change? Its purpose was purely political: to achieve submission by instilling terror. The obsessive belief held by many, including Duvalier himself, that marrying into the elite would effect social change betrays the ignorance of, or contempt for larger socioeconomic ideologies—such as, for instance, socialism. It also reveals a very individualist and gendered focus. It was not about Haiti or about change, it was solely about this class of men.

1 Caricature of an elite "mulatto" as a puppeteer manipulating President Nord Alexis. Excerpt from Alcius Charmant's book *Will Haiti Survive?* (p. 17).

2 1964 diary of the Brothers of Christian Instruction in Jérémie, with names of victims and dates of executions (p. 114).

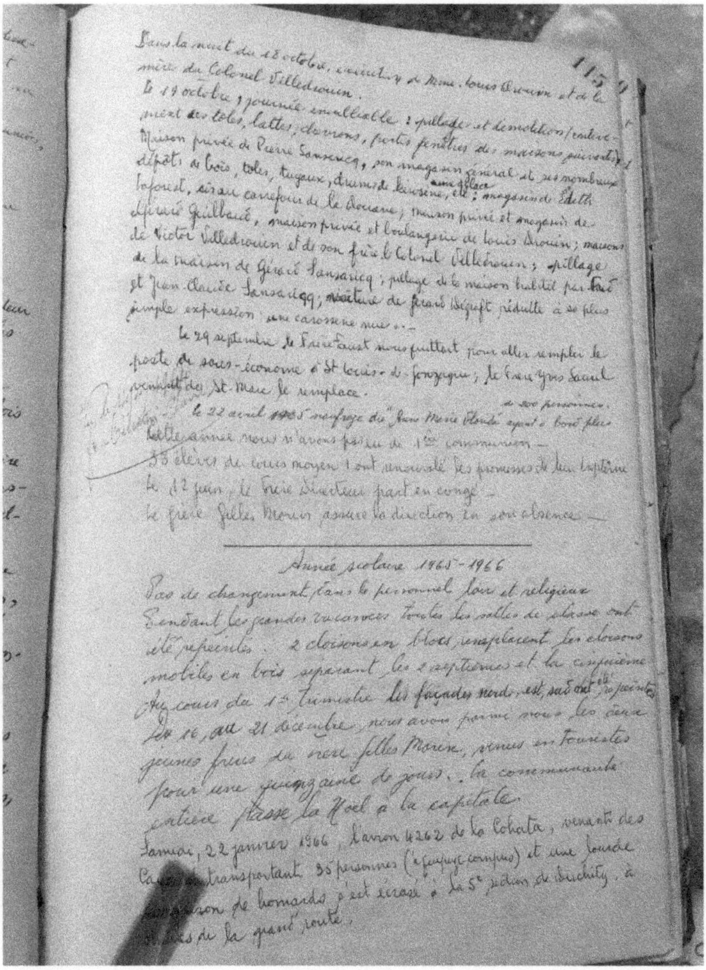

115

Dans la nuit du 18 octobre, incendie [illegible] de Mme. Louis Drouin et de la mère du Colonel Villedrouin.
Le 19 octobre, journée inoubliable : pillage et démolitions (enlèvement des tôles, lattes, chevrons, portes fenêtres des maisons privées) : Maison privée de Pierre Sansaricq, son magasin général et ses nombreux dépôts de bois, tôles, tuyaux, drums de kérosène, etc ; magasin de Edith Laforest, sis au carrefour de la Douane ; maison privée et magasin de Gérard Guilbaud, maison privée et boulangerie de Louis Drouin ; maisons de Victor Villedrouin et de son frère le Colonel Villedrouin ; pillage de la maison de Gérard Sansaricq ; pillage de la maison habitée par [illegible] et Jean-Claude Sansaricq ; voiture de Gérard Wiegeft réduite à sa plus simple expression une carosserie nue...
Le 29 septembre le Frère Faust nous quittait pour aller remplir le poste de sous-économe à St Louis de Gonzague ; le Frère Yves Saül venant de St-Marc le remplace.
Le 22 avril 1965 naufrage du "Jean Marie Plaude" ayant à bord plus de 200 personnes.
Cette année nous n'avons pas eu de 1ère communion –
35 élèves du cours moyen 1 ont renouvelé les promesses de leur baptême
Le 12 juin, le Frère Directeur part en congé –
Le frère Gilles Morin assure la direction en son absence –

Année scolaire 1965–1966
Pas de changement dans le personnel laïc et religieux
Pendant les grandes vacances toutes les salles de classe ont été repeintes. 2 cloisons en blocs remplacent les cloisons mobiles en bois séparant les 2 septièmes et la cinquième
Au cours du 1er trimestre les façades nord, est, sud ont été repeintes
Du 16 au 21 décembre, nous avons parmi nous les deux jeunes frères du [illegible] Gilles Morin, venus en touristes pour une quinzaine de jours. La communauté entière passe la Noël à la capitale
Samedi, 22 janvier 1966, l'avion 4262 de la Cohata, venant des Cayes, transportant 35 personnes (équipage compris) et une lourde cargaison de homards s'est écrasé à la 5e section de Duchity, à [illegible] de la grand'route.

3 Same diary, p. 117.

4 François Duvalier with his military chiefs of staff, circa 1964

Photograph: Unattributed. Collection: May Figaro, Fondation pour la Recherche Iconographique et Documentaire.

5 Pierre Biamby looking at Duvalier, circa 1965

Photograph: Unattributed. Collection: May Figaro, Fondation pour la Recherche Iconographique et Documentaire.

6 From left to right: Lunsford Joseph, Mérès Bélizaire, Saintange Bontemps, Dalvanor Étienne, in Jérémie, circa 1964.

Photograph: Unattributed. @Public domain

7 José "Sony" Borges

Photograph: Unattributed. Collection: May Figaro, Fondation pour la Recherche Iconographique et Documentaire.

8 Sanette Balmir and Luc Desroche in VSN uniform sharing champagne on the veranda of the Sansaricq residence, circa 1965.

Photograph: Unattributed. Collection: Eddy Cavé

9 Inauguration of Jérémie's public library, 1940. Pascal Garoute, third from left (father of Hamilton Garoute, executed in April 1963). Piéril Fourcand, fifth from left, standing (father of Jacques Fourcand, Duvalier's confidant).

Photograph: Unattributed. Collection: Eddy Cavé

10 Group of Jeremian youth during an outing in the countryside, circa 1920. Pierre Sansaricq is kneeling on far right. This picture was found on the sidewalk in front of the Sansaricq home after it was looted on October 19, 1964.

Photograph: Unattributed. Collection: Devoir de Mémoire.

11 *Dames Patronesses* of Jérémie. Louise Sansaricq is standing at right next to Louise Drouin.

Photograph: Guy Drouin. Collection: Devoir de Mémoire.

12 The Pratt family, circa 1957. Graziela Sansaricq is standing second from left.

Photograph: Guy Drouin. Collection: Devoir de Mémoire.

13 Graziela Sansaricq with her three children, Jean-Pierre, Régine, and Stéphane, circa 1963. Photograph: Guy Drouin. Collection: Devoir de Mémoire.

14 Adeline Villedrouin and her two children, Frantz and Lyssa, circa 1953. This picture was found in the street in Bordes after their home was looted in October 1964.

Photograph: probably Victor Villedrouin. Collection: Roger Chassagne.

15 Wedding of Guy Villedrouin (left) and Roseline Drouin (right). Louise Drouin (née Degraff), seated, left; Corinne Villedrouin (née Sansaricq) This picture was found in the street after the Villedrouin home was looted in October 1964.

Photograph: Guy Drouin. Collection: Devoir de Mémoire.

16 Aerial views of Jérémie, 2009.

Photograph and copyrights: Patricia Balandier.

17 Saint-Louis Cathedral, 2009. Gérard Guilbaud's store and Guy Drouin's studio were located in the building to the right of the cathedral; to the left was André Jabouin's home. Photograph and copyrights: Patricia Balandier.

18 Government decree ordering both the revocation of Haitian citizenship and the nationalization of property of the adult victims of the Jérémie massacre and of Roger Villedrouin. *Le Moniteur*, October 26, 1964.

19 Home of Pierre and Louise Sansaricq, center, 1978. To the right is the home of Frantz Perrault, who was also arrested in August 1964; to the left is the home of Mrs. Vincent, a teacher.

Photograph and copyrights: Eddy Cavé.

20 Inside the memorial to the victims of the Jérémie massacre, 2017.

Photograph: Jean-Philippe Belleau

PART IV

Duvalier's Evading Executioners

CHAPTER 7

Kaponaj

This type of leader can achieve such results only because they have first degraded people's souls through a regime of terror.

Beaubrun Ardouin[1]

"Neighbor" has become a category of its own in mass violence studies over the past two decades. The term refers to people living in the same town or region as the victims and signals a scholarly shift toward the microhistory and the microsociology of mass violence.[2] What do neighbors exactly do at the moment of truth, when state violence enter a town and is about to strike? Do they protect, participate, stand by, or do something else not expressed by these categories?

Crucially, the "neighborly turn" in mass violence studies has shown that macro-level approaches based on political outlook and ideology—the ones taken by, for instance, Hanna Arendt and Helen Fein in their analysis of the Holocaust—have omitted to take into account the fine-grained details of civilians' actions and responsibilities. Yet this fine-grain sometimes relies on macro-determinisms: hatred (that is, beliefs generated at a level far above that of a village or town), economic injustices, and ethno-religious identities, to name a few.

The term "neighbor" has also been used liberally to assume that geographic proximity entails sociality, and that sociality is a uniform, homogeneous, repro-duceable mechanism with the same psychological and anthropological expec-tations and results. Of course, "neighbors" in Jérémie were divided: by "race," political belief (noirist, liberal, etc.), social class, social status, and even by function—and these elements did play a role. Yet the most crucial variable when it comes to "neighbor" behavior is the degree of *social* closeness to the victims. This degree can often (albeit not always) explain, determine, and even predict behavior in such situations.

To identify this closeness, we must use sociometrics and look at the fine grain within the fine grain: how the "neighbors" implicated in a massacre were related, or not, to a victim; whether they knew them or not; and if they knew them, how close their relationship was. Neighbors, in the end, very rarely kill neighbors, unless the relationships to the victims are seriously fraught, distant, or absent. In the case of Jérémie, neighbors were indeed both a physical and a social category, as the two previous chapters showed. All the individuals whose behavior is examined in this chapter had a bond with the victims, a social tie of some sort, or knew them (even if superficially). We must understand also that a behavior or action is a result. Before the manifestation of a certain behavior during an episode of mass violence, there is typically a "storm inside a skull," a rapid mental stream of fear and calculations (both petty and moral), and the often-unconscious cognitive mechanism triggered by existing social relationships (to the victims, as well as to Duvalier, Duvalierist actors, and other neighbors). All this happens sometimes within mere seconds before a decision is made and action is taken.

I have developed this reflection in two earlier pieces, the second of which proposes the concept of *relational exceptionalism* to name the cognitive phenomenon that prevents us from harming people we have a bond with.[3] It is a property of interpersonal relationships. Relational exceptionalism does not argue that neighbors cannot violate social norms against neighbors. It argues that ethical inhibitions are commensurate with both the strength of the social tie to the victim *and* with the gravity of perpetration. The most unlikely act is the act of killing a friend. Many other, minor violations can be committed. Moral and social violations cannot be neutralized by social ties when the latter are weak, absent, or distant; indeed, they can even be made more likely, under some circumstances and with some types of individuals, by a certain level of acquaintanceship. Acquaintanceship would allow for a degree of knowledge about the potential victims, people would know about their habits, racial identity, home locations, political beliefs; but there would not be enough intimacy to trigger ethical obligations. In the context of ideologies of hatred, envy, and resentment, this moderate level of intimacy can constitute a lethal cocktail.

I segment neighbors into three categories. The Duvalierist patricians were the closest to the victims—and to Duvalier himself. The remaining Duvalierists were acquaintances or close acquaintances and usually came from the middle urban sectors. Finally, the VSNs (Volontaires de la Sécurité Nationale, or National Security Volunteers) were a peculiar type of "neighbor." They were not drawn from the upper sectors of society, and for that reason had limited social ties to the victims; yet most of them were their acquaintances. They joined the VSN to acquire status and elevate their social standing. Yet they were sidelined during the entire massacre. They did not participate in the killings but instead committed minor violations. They remained subalterns. This would later affect how they behaved publicly in regard to the execution: in the strangest way, some claimed responsibility for perpetration to rescue their status.

The long testimony you are going read is crucial for understanding the Jérémie massacre. It comes from Jean Alcide, an eyewitness to the first execution, whom I interviewed in March 2016. He was a "neighbor." He does not fit in any of the usual behavioral categories (perpetrator, bystander, rescuer), and yet he was a little bit of each, depending primarily on a crowd of circumstances and on whom each victim was to him. The other episodes presented in the chapter also focus on neighbors' behavior during the massacre and their respective closeness to the victims.

Jean Alcide was born in Jérémie in 1934 and grew up on rue Sténio Vincent in a family of artisans. Both of his parents had migrated in their youth from a rural hamlet south of the city. They were of humble means, but not poor. His godfather was a relative of Louinès Degraff, the local member of Parliament. Alcide went to school at the reputable École des Frères, became a teacher at a local vocational school for girls, and migrated to the United States in 1968 with his wife. He had been a Duvalierist since the 1957 presidential elections but was neither a VSN nor a Duvalierist patrician. Instead, he belonged to an intermediary group with ties to most urban sectors. On August 11, 1964, he witnessed the first wave of executions:

The rumor was going around in town that mulattos had been arrested. It was in the afternoon, it was summer vacation, so it was in August or maybe early

September, I don't remember. I forgot who came to fetch me, it was a group, [Antoine] Apollon was there . . . [Because there was a curfew, Alcide leaves his home with his flashlight.] So, we went to the military base. . . . There was a curfew—but anyway, we were allowed in because we were Duvalierists. So, at the entrance to the base, the soldiers, they let us in. I arrived on foot, but some came by car. There were a lot of people . . . Antoine Apollon, Gérard Thémistocle (Léonidas), [André] Jabouin, Thiafisgirl, Marcel Myrtil. . . . Yes, Sony Borges was there, but not in [military] uniform . . . most of the Duvalierists were there . . . no, Saintange Bontemps was not present . . . not [Lieutenant] Régala . . . not Sanette Balmir . . .

The prisoners [*ceux qui avaient été arrétés* (those who had been arrested)] were in the guardroom. . . . It was lit by a single bulb, hanging from the ceiling, like that. . . . Many people were there . . . Gérard Guilbaud, Victor Villedrouin. . . . The women [Alice and Roseline Drouin] were in their nightgowns. . . . No, I did not see [Louis Drouin]. I later learned he had died of injuries in his cell. His son [Guy Drouin], I do not remember seeing him either . . . Sicaud Gardère, Dr. Laurent, Harry Balmir, and Frantz Perraud were all in a cell . . . No, no one was protesting . . . they were forbidden from talking, you know. They did not say anything.

The composition of the group present at the military base that evening reproduced Jérémie's town's political and socioeconomic hierarchy. The Duvalierist civilians who had rushed to the base stayed on the ground level, where the guardroom and prison cells were located. The four members of the Presidential Commission all remained on the second floor. The Duvalierist civilians knew that the people with power were upstairs. Second Lieutenant Abel Jérôme was the informal liaison between the two groups and was seen by multiple witnesses going up and down the stairs that evening. The executions were being negotiated. Several civilians argued that some of the prisoners should be spared. Eventually, Harry Balmir, Dr. Laurent, Sicaud Gardère, and Frantz Perraud were taken out of the guardroom and transferred to the city prison, from which they would be freed a few weeks later. I asked Alcide why he intervened for them:

[Harry] Balmir was poor, like us. Gérard [Léonidas] and myself, we told [Abel] Jérôme that Balmir was not anti-Duvalierist. By that time, there was a lot of people [at the military base]. I saw Jérôme going up and down the stairs. . . . No, I did not know Jérôme well. He was not one of the worst, you know . . .

- Who were the worst?

- Ah . . . There were some . . .

[Then] they made the prisoners come out [of the guardroom] and go to the courtyard. Gérard Guilbaud was there, and his wife [Alice Drouin], [Guy] Villedrouin and Roseline Drouin, and a fifth one. . . . No, it was not a Drouin. I don't remember who it was [Victor Villedrouin]. . . . They were naked, the women also. They walked from the cell to the yard [at the center of the military base]. They were tied with a single rope, men and women together, the rope stretched from one to the other.

- Who tied them?

- It was a VSN. I don't remember who.

- Who gave the order to tie them?

- I don't remember. The prisoners were barefoot, so they were walking slowly, it was difficult for them to climb into the back of the van . . . Well, we helped them. It was a coffee van, used to transport beans, a German-made van. The driver, it was [Max] Frédérique's younger brother [Tony] . . .

- So, by the time the prisoners are taken out of the guardroom, they are entirely naked? And Guy Drouin, he was with them?

- I don't know. There were only five prisoners . . . I am absolutely sure of it, yes, only five . . . I don't know what happened to Guy Drouin . . . Yes, I knew him. Well, not well, but I knew him . . . He was not there. I knew all of them, you know.

- Did you see their faces and bodies? Did any of them bear signs of mistreatment (*coups*) or traces of blood?

- No, no.

We decided to follow with our cars. I was with Apollon. There were only a few of us . . . I don't remember exactly, there was me, Antoine Apollon, Marcel Myrtil (VSN), Thiafisgirl (VSN), Gérard Thémistocle [Léonidas], Gérard Brunache (VSN). I was with Apollon in his car . . . just the two of us. Gérard Thémistocle [Léonidas] drove in his car with someone else. Thiafisgirl was in the coffee van, sitting with the driver . . .

- Did Abel Jérôme go as well [to Numéro 2]?

- No, he stayed at the base . . . Yes, I am sure.

- Sony Borges?

- No . . .

- Saintange Bontemps?

- I told you he had not come to the base.

- Did you see any judges or any lawyers?

- No. No, no, no, it did not work that way.

- Why did you follow the van to Numéro 2?

- We thought it was a *kaponaj*, to punish the mulattoes. Just a kaponaj, you know.

- So, you were driving and you saw the prisoners?

- Yes, they were sitting one behind the other.

- There is a rumor that they were singing canticles during the drive.

- No, they were not . . . We drove to Numéro 2, I could see the prisoners because my car was right behind the van. They were not standing in the back, they were seated, one behind the other. We arrived at Numéro 2, and there was Jean Dimanche waiting with soldiers (*le peloton*).

They made the prisoners climb down from the van, it was difficult because of the rope, it was dark, they had a lot of trouble climbing out of the van. Someone made a joke about the women. Jean Dimanche exploded. He was very upset. He said it was not going to be disorderly. We all froze (*nou sezi*).

- Who made the joke?

- I don't remember, it was dark, it was a VSN, I think. Maybe [Gérard] Brunache. Nobody said anything after that. He (Jean Dimanche) said that the volontaires [VSN] were not going to run the place.

Well, then we walked to the execution grounds, it took time because [the prisoners] were walking barefoot, so they tripped. We arrived at a ditch . . . it was 4 or 5 square meters, it was well made. The inmates had dug it . . . they were still there, they were waiting . . . about 100 yards away. [The soldiers] made [the prisoners] get down into the ditch. It was difficult.

- Did they ever say anything? Did any of the prisoners try to speak to anyone?

- No, they said nothing . . . It was very dark, we could not see much. Once they were in the ditch, Jean Dimanche ordered the soldiers (*le peloton*) to get into position . . . the prisoners were standing in the ditch.

- Did you still think it was a kaponaj, then?

- Ah, I don't know, I don't remember.

They fired like that [from above]. . . . We [the civilians] were standing at a distance (*à l'écart*), behind the soldiers . . . maybe ten meters away. After the salvo, Jean Dimanche ordered me to illuminate the ditch with my flashlight. Guilbaud was wounded, but not dead. All the others were dead. Jean Dimanche pointed at a soldier and said "*Éliminez-le!*" The soldier moved to the edge of the ditch and shot. Guilbaud was the last to die.

- What did you do then?

- We went back home.

Kaponaj is Kreole for "bluff," "intimidation," or "scaring someone for fun." It comes from *kapon*, Kreyol for capon, which stands for coward. Did the civilians who rushed to the military base to observe the scene really believe it was a *kaponaj*? Alcide stated that almost until the last minute he thought it was going to be a mock execution. Even if true, why did Alcide and other civilians choose to form a voyeuristic and heartless convoy that followed the van taking the victims to Numéro 2? If Alcide is sincere, the *kaponaj* version reveals incredulity: the arrest of their upper-class neighbors was an incredible event and their execution *un*-believable. (On the other hand, Abel Jérôme, Jean Dimanche, and the other military officers involved knew very well the fate awaiting the prisoners.) The same logic frames language. Alcide resorted, as some Jeremian interlocutors did, to euphemisms to name and characterize the event: "*fusillade*" (gunshots) for what truly was an execution; "those who had been arrested" for prisoners or victims. Denying the nature of the event—the killing of defenseless civilians; forcing the women to undress and be paraded in front of men—might also suggest a form of dissociation from grave social violations. What happened that evening became, to a large extent, a source of collective shame.

Alcide's general account is also confirmed by secondary witnesses whose kin attended the event. There was nothing orderly about the way the prisoners were held and forced to undress, about the way dozens of civilians were authorized to enter the base and watch for hours their frightened "mulatto" neighbors in a voyeuristic manner, with some laughing, some shouting, some negotiating the liberation of select prisoners. In a fashion typical of the Duvalier regime, confusion reigned while personal relationships superseded institutions, the rule of law, and chains of command. The behavior and interference of civilians at the base and at the execution ground would have consequences for the second wave of repression: on September 19, Abel Jérôme ordered the truck and the jeep transporting the victims from their homes to go directly to the site of execution to avoid any interference by the VSNs and civilians. In this regard, the clash between Jean Dimanche and a VSN making fun of a woman prisoner carries great significance. Dimanche's shouting at Gérard Brunache marked the limits of civilian and VSN interference, if not ambitions. The military would execute defenseless Jeremians in an extralegal manner but would not tolerate civilian interference. The second wave of executions on September 19 would be exclusively a military affair.

THE MEETING AT JABOUIN'S HOME

Over a month later, on the eve of the second wave of executions, another meeting of Duvalierist civilians took place. This time, the attendants were all from the town's upper class. They gathered secretly at around eight o'clock in the evening on September 18, at Dr. André Jabouin's home, located less than 250 yards from Pierre Sansaricq's home. A few hours earlier, Abel Jérôme had received the decoded order to execute the Sansaricqs. He then drove to Raoul Cédras's home to let him know of this order. The two men, who disliked one another, decided to arrange a meeting. At least eight men attended: Raoul Cédras, André Jabouin, Dalvanor Etienne, François Cajoux, Louinès Degraff, Joseph René, Saintange Bontemps, and Abel Jérôme who arrived late. I was not able to identify other participants, although interlocutors universally rejected the possibility that Sanette Balmir attended. No VSN, all of lower social standing, had been convened. Each attendant knew the Sansaricqs personally, notably the family patriarch, Pierre Sansaricq. Several of their own children were friends with the children victims. As soon as the first people arrived, André Jabouin's children were ushered upstairs. From the second floor, they overheard the conversation. The account I give below is based mainly on the testimony provided by Louis Jabouin, then fifteen, and two secondary witnesses.[4]

The meeting was an informal gathering to discuss how they might succeed in negotiating Duvalier's order to execute another group of mulattoes. Its organization betrayed the hesitations and contradictory allegiances of its participants:

to Duvalier and Duvalierism, to social ethics in a small town, and to their own reputations. It concretized their dilemma and relativized Duvalier's order which should have been executed without discussion. It also spread out the responsibility for the action to an ad hoc collective.

The discussion was about the execution order and what to do with it. Only one man argued for blind obedience: Saintange Bontemps. It was enough to sway the group into compliance. None of the others took a clear position. Jérôme remained silent and let the civilians do the talking. The verb used by Jean-Claude Fignolé (who heard about the meeting from several participants) to describe their behavior was "*tergiverser*" (procrastinate). Guiton Dorimain later said that "they tried their best." At some point in the conversation, André Jabouin openly wondered if Graziela and Jean-Claude Sansaricq's three young children could be spared, adding that he could adopt them. (Local oral history would later transform Jabouin's verbal intervention during this conversation into an attempt to save them at Numéro 2 at the moment of execution itself.)

Immediately, Saintange Bontemps accused him: "you're a fake Duvalierist" (*tu es un mauvais Duvaliériste!*); it was the only time someone raised his voice during the meeting. Nobody backed André Jabouin's request and silence followed. Then Jérôme stood up, took from his jacket an unsigned letter that he had apparently drafted earlier, and read it aloud. It was addressed to Duvalier and stated that all the signatories agreed with the execution order. Jérôme then asked all the participants to sign their names to it. It was silent again before someone seemingly expressed their discomfort at signing the letter. Dalvanor Etienne tentatively asked for another solution for the Sansaricq, although his exact words are now lost.[5] In spectacular fashion, Jérôme then took out another letter he had prepared, also addressed to Duvalier. It stated that the Sansaricq were not *camoquins* (rebels) and bore no responsibility for the Jeune Haiti insurgency. The letter did not go as far as asking that the Sansaricqs be spared, but it did withdraw the rationale for their execution.

Jérôme's cunning tactics to avoid being solely responsible for either the execution of the Sansaricqs or for begging Duvalier to spare them had caught the meeting's participants unprepared. By presenting a choice of two letters, Jérôme had outsmarted his camp. The patricians had to choose between sharing responsibility no matter what course of action they took. In other words, Pontius Pilate's position, to use Arendt's self-explanatory category, became explicitly unavailable to them. Eventually, the notables signed the first letter. No one dared contradict

Duvalier. The meeting over, the participants walked back to their respective families. The fate of the Sansaricqs and the two Villedrouin children was sealed.

NO EXIT

Raoul Hilberg famously segmented and typologized behaviors and fates during episodes of mass violence into three categories: perpetrators, victims, and bystanders.[6] Neither victim nor perpetrator or savior, the "bystander" is defined by passive obedience and therefore bears considerable responsibility. Ehrenreich and Cole questioned this categorization as too static to render the complexity and fluidity of behaviors at the local level.[7] As Immaculée Ilibagiza and Lee Ann Fuji showed, behavioral fluidity during the Rwanda genocide meant that the same individual could occupy several positions—perpetrator, bystander, victim, savior—depending on the situation, group pressure, and a crowd of other variables, including ethical inhibitions.[8] Historian Jacques Sémelin, exploring the behavior of people whose action or inaction had the clear purpose of signifying to the perpetrators that they disapproved of their lethal policy, coined the concept of "social reactivity" precisely to name a type of behavior that can curb zealous decision-makers without resorting to resistance or overt opposition.[9] The act of organizing a meeting at Jabouin's home to discuss the dictator's execution orders was a form of social reactivity, even if it failed.[10] (Overall, what restricted Duvalier was both social reactivity and societal passivity—a refusal to engage in zeal, as chapter 9 explores.)

There is something Sartrean about this group of middle-aged Jeremian men cornered in a small room, forced to make a decision without the possibility of evading. As Ehrenreich and Cole showed, bystanders too are tempted to flee, escape, and hide. Not here. The impression that it took only one man, Saintange Bontemps, to tilt the balance in favor of execution may reflect poorly on the dozen other men. Yet the regime of unpredictable terror created by Duvalier applied also to regime members, who were paralyzed by fear, conformism, and possibly personal interests. In addition, in the case of Jérémie, the various possible categories (perpetrators, victims, bystanders, and others) are located within the same community where people knew one another and often shared social ties; this was not the case in the historical examples presented by the aforementioned scholars, including Fein and Sémelin. During the Jérémie massacre, preexisting interpersonal relationships, or the weakness thereof, were the most crucial variable in determining the behaviors (especially social reactivity and desistance) of the non-victim population. The courage to save and ethical inhibitions against harming can be activated by many triggers. It is not simply a question of moral consciousness or decency; an existing interpersonal relationship with a person at risk can also be a powerful trigger.[11] None of the many social ties their family had with others saved the Sansaricqs. The choice created and faced by these men was not about harming or not, but about attempting to save or not; they chose not to.

"MILAT-YO FINI"

September 19 changed the scale of terror in Jérémie. While the inhabitants thought that the crisis was fading away after the departure of the Presidential Commission in late August, the new massacre shocked the population. The first wave of executions, on August 11, had killed seven individuals but no children; the second killed fourteen, including seven children. Jérémie's elite families were terrified.

In the early morning of Sunday, August 20, the maid of the Villedrouin family ran next door to tell Roger Chassagne Sr. and his family that their neighbors and kin were gone. Chassagne immediately told his wife and children to stay inside their home while he went alone to see what had happened. Within hours, he heard rumors that his sister, niece, and nephew had been arrested and executed the previous night.[12] Because it was Sunday, the Chassagnes still went to the Saint Louis church to attend mass at 10, hoping to learn more. As usual, families met in front of the cathedral before mass. Louis Jabouin saw his classmate Roger Chassagne Jr. in tears: "my cousin was arrested." The young Jabouin immediately connected the Friday night meeting at his home to the arrest. Later that day, Roger Chassagne Sr. heard the rumor that his niece, Lyssa Villedrouin, had been raped by VSNs before the execution and believed it. He was convinced that his family would be executed next. In the evening, he barricaded his house, moving furniture behind the front and back doors. He then took his son aside, away from his wife and daughter, and told him to be prepared to kill his mother and sister. Roger Chassagne Jr., today a retired psychologist in Florida, remembers his father's words:

Nobody will touch your mother." Yes, that's the first thing he told me. He pointed his finger, like that. He showed me how to use the gun . . . No, he was very calm. My father was always very calm, you know . . . He had the family gun in his hand, I will never forget, there is no doubt, and he told me how to use it, like that, and what to do when the *macoutes* invade the house . . . Nobody will touch your mother. For weeks or maybe months, every evening, we barricaded the entrance and the back doors [of our home]. The *macoutes* only came at night you know . . . He repeated it, nobody will touch your mother. And nobody should touch your sister. He showed me how to load and use the gun . . . He also told my sister and I to never talk in front of the maid [who would come every morning]. She did not know we barricaded the doors.[13]

As much as he loved his older sister, the young Chassagne was ready to carry out the deed. As he recounted this part of the story, his facial expression constantly vacillated between happiness and sorrow, trying to keep a distance. He still grieves the loss of his cousin and best friend, Frantz Villedrouin. The rumors about the fate of Lyssa Villedrouin haunted him and his father. The elder Chassagne's dramatic choices of fighting to the end was framed by the conviction that, once arrested, the fate of the household's women would be unavoidable and dire. They also had limited options. Since August 7, the road leading out of town had two successive military roadblocks, while the harbor was also heavily controlled by the authorities. Escaping into the surrounding jungle, *marronage*-style, was not part of these families' culture—maybe an adult alone could have done it, but what parents had in mind was their family's safety. Fifty years later, the elder Chassagne was unanimously described by other interlocutors as unafraid, tough, and silent ("*un ténébreux*") as one interlocutor put it. Alix Cédras, then seventeen, the mayor's son described him as such: "Pierre Sansaricq was meek, an intellectual ("*un homme doux et lettré*"). Not Chassagne. Not the type to die without a fight."[14] Chassagne did not fit the stereotype—few did—of the ball-going, frivolous, snobby upper-class man. He was ready to shoot his own wife and daughter rather than leave them defenseless to the *macoutes*. Yet, he was also described by testimonies from within and outside his family as a family man, very close to his wife and affectionate with his children. For such a man to conceive of killing his kin, *jauhar* style, was extreme.

The climate of terror was enforced by the VSNs, who did little else. The most ubiquitous anecdote by witnesses recalls the fear provoked by the threatening sound of the German jeeps used by emboldened VSNs, driven at top speed in the narrow streets of Jérémie, often for no other reason than to instill fear. They did so especially after curfew, when families inside their homes feared being arrested. Fort-Réfléchi, the informal VSN headquarters, became "busier than ever" and, in the population's eye, a new center of power.[15] The few VSNs who held deep anti-mulatto sentiments and had joined the militia for this very reason were emboldened by the new massacre. Two names came up repeatedly in interviews: Max Frédérique and Luc Desroche. According to several interlocutors, Frédérique and Desroche allegedly walked in the city center shouting, "*Milat-yo fini*" (you mulattoes are done with) and "*Nou frekan trop*" (you were too arrogant).

Such outcries would have been a social violation before August 1964. One interlocutor who is still a Duvalierist used this anecdote to substantiate his allegations that mulattoes were indeed insufferable, and that the population was finally liberating itself. The daughter of an upper-class family told the same story to illustrate her family's fear. These intimidations were allegedly made in public by two almost-euphoric VSNs with a reputation for anti-mulatto hatred. They also were performed to acquire status within the VSN and VSN-friendly public. The latter represented what Bourdieu called a field: a relatively autonomous system of people and social positions within a larger system.[16] Inspired by physics, this concept (the field) has many competing actors whose movements and decisions influence the entire system (usually, society). The concept highlights the logic of individual strategies of actors vying for status within a microcosm; outside of it, such strategies and actions may appear futile or incomprehensible. It also underlines the local dimension of the VSN phenomenon. Although the militia was a national organization, the reasons for joining and the behavior of its members were often understandable only at the local level. In Jérémie, this field eventually lost much of its raison d'être with the end of the mulatto presence.

There were other highly symbolic events marking the change in the scale of terror in Jérémie after September 19. One of these was the precipitous ("*en catastrophe*") flight of the parish's priest, Barthélémy Péron (1912–1989), who had been officiating in Jérémie since 1946.[17] A few days after the Sansaricqs were executed, he fled to New York city together with several parishioners, including the entire Pratt family.[18] Other anecdotes reflect the change in the scale of terror. In 2016, Gilles Morin (1935–), a teacher and friar from Québec, provided this edifying one:

> A fourteen-year-old boy, a mulatto, knocked at the down of the bishopric, and asked for asylum. He was afraid. His mother had sent him. He had a bag with him . . . We told him we were priests, we do not offer asylum.

- So you turned him down?

- Yes.

- And what did he say, do you remember his name? He was alone or with his parents?

- He was panicked. He could barely talk. He wanted to stay with us. He had a bag with his belongings. But we turned him down. We could not provide asylum . . . His family lived in front of the bishopric, next to the Cédras's [store] . . . I don't remember their names . . . His mother had sent him to us, to get protection.

- What did he do?

- Well, he went back home.

The intensification of the anti-mulatto terror campaign was worse in Jérémie but was engulfing the entire country.[19] In Port-au-Prince in late October, U.S. Ambassador Benson Timmons reported that a field gun had been brought to the intersection of rue Capois and ruelle Roy, in the center of Port-au-Prince:

> [C]annon was reportedly emplaced for half hour, pointed toward mulatto residential district higher up hill and threat uttered that if Duvalier regime threatened, gun would be brought back and used to destroy mulatto opposition.[20] Another source report[ed] that on evening of Oct 22 Duvalier gave order [at presidential palace] to his close associates that mulattoes and their property to be destroyed if situation becomes critical (comment renewal of this threat coincides with GOH [Government of Haiti] fear that new invasion in offing).[21]

That same week, the government published a rather strange presidential decree announcing that the adult victims of the Jérémie massacre had all been stripped of their Haitian citizenship and legal rights.[22] It made no mention they had been executed or even arrested. It sanctioned the appropriation of all their properties. [See Figure 18]

THE SUBALTERN VSNS

In Jérémie, the VSNs remained in liminality the subalterns they were in everyday life. The entire massacre was a state and elite affair. Their position as subalterns meant that they did not need to evade perpetration, unlike other protagonists located higher up in the socioeconomic hierarchy. Instead, several VSNs exaggerated their participation. To understand this self-incriminating behavior, we should approach the VSNs as a Bourdieusian field instead of focusing solely on the wanton violence they were infamous for at the national level. These crimes are well-described by the literature.[23] Other sources, including an older, precise report authored by the Communist Party, examine the "mentality" of rank-and-file VSNs, emphasizing sadistic tendencies and their quest for status.[24] In one of the rare studies on the sociological background of VSNs, Marvin Chochotte argued that peasants in the countryside enlisted because they had been marginalized for decades, and the Duvalierist project gave them new opportunities.[25] In Jérémie, however, the two dozen VSNs whose background I could identify were city people; at most, the poorest of them came from the immediate periphery of the town. The logic and the functioning were quite different from those described by Chochotte. Importantly, the Jeremian VSNs did not kill.

In Jérémie, they were also a differentiated group that reproduced the socioeconomic verticality that Duvalierism was supposed to address but instead reinforced: the more educated and wealthier VSNs had more informal status and power; they behaved with the lower-ranked VSNs as if their were their own subalterns by giving them orders which the latter carried out. A few VSNs were almost well-off, some were poor, but most were in between; similarly, some were educated, some uneducated, and few were semiliterate. Yet these socioeconomic differences did not seem to have bothered them as much as those between any of them and the mulatto families. Pierre Chérubin provided striking testimony on the matter. In 1986, he was a lieutenant and the secretary of a military commission that briefly investigated the Jérémie massacre.

> We had come to Jérémie to conduct hearings. We wanted to know what people had to say about what had happened [in 1964]. The militias came. Listen, I was astonished: I expected murderers, *j'ai vu des misérables* (I encountered the destitute). Marcel Myrtil showed up barefoot. He was barefoot, looking down, with a pierced straw hat in his hands . . . Can you imagine? That was the face of terror. A guy holding his hat, looking down, barefoot, *pieds poudrés*.[26]
>   - What did he say?
>   - I don't remember. Not much probably. I remember he mumbled. I don't remember what he said, it must have been insignificant. He was insignificant.

Why some individuals joined the VSNs is a legitimate research question. Yet the vast majority of Duvalierists (and of the destitute) did not join. When I asked Jean Alcide why he did not join the militia, he smiled, as if the question betrayed a lack of knowledge or sensitivity on my part: "no, no, no . . . that was not for *us*. These people (*moun-sa yo*) . . . I had friends [who were] VSNs . . . but, well, I was educated (*j'avais de l'éducation*)."

Alcide did not join the VSN for the same reason others joined it: for social status. That most VSNs came from lower socioeconomic sectors was a negative social marker for people situated just above them, as Alcide was. He was highly conscious of social hierarchies. Engaged in a logic of social mobility, Alcide had estimated that being associated with the VSN was detrimental to his ambitions. It was not the only reason. Joining the militia was an uncertain business and involved obedience to orders which, everyone knew, potentially led to unsavory duties. This had a social cost and not joining was also an evading strategy.

Yet, some VSNs in Jérémie, such as the Desroche, Frédérique, Bourdeau, Jeune, and Bélizaire brothers, as well as Gérard Brunache, were far from *misérables*. They belonged to the class of employees and artisans. They did not accomplish physical tasks, which they relegated to the lower-class VSNs such as Thiasfisgirl, Tobysse, and Marcel Myrtil. The quest for social visibility clearly did not motivate only the most destitute; it was a more universal affair. They were also considered lower than the town's Duvalierist patricians. Ideology, noirism in particular, was certainly a key motivation, as shown in chapter 2. Yet, as I examined these individuals closely, I found it hard to generalize from very diverse trajectories, minds, and backgrounds. In addition, the notable number of dyads (brothers, father-son, and friends) in this group hint at social reasons for joining.

THE MOST INFAMOUS NAME IN JÉRÉMIE'S HISTORY

The relegation of the VSNs to a subaltern role during the Jérémie massacre seems to contradict the fact, advanced by the historiography and many observers, that many VSNs were motivated by status. How do people acquire status when they are sidelined? By appropriating perpetration in real time. One of the most intriguing and confusing behaviors during these events was that of Gérard Brunache. In the personalistic world of Jérémie described in chapter

5, Brunache was a "character," known in town, evoked by many, unanimously described as someone eager to be seen and recognized. He was from the world of artisans and sought to move up the socioeconomic ladder. Eddy Cavé once saw him "riding a horse *au galop* with a beautiful blond" on rue Brouette in the middle of a summer day.[27] Cavé added that Brunache was rather unpredictable and liked to boast. Guiton Dorimain, who knew his family, remembers Brunache as a jack-of-all-trades: a musician with his own band, a perfumer with good knowledge of botanics, and a VSN who affected a French accent.[28] Alix Cédras knew Brunache as well, and saw him perform several times with his band *Étincelle* at the Excelsior, the local elite's club.[29] Cédras added that Brunache must have gotten a close-up view of how the elite entertained itself—and of Lyssa Villedrouin. Unlike Saintange Bontemps, however, nobody described Brunache as violent or even difficult.[30]

On September 20, the day after the execution of the Sansaricq family and the Villedrouin children, Brunache was seen by several witnesses in bright daylight cleaning a knife with a bucket of water in the street. Brunache may have repeated the gestures, either at different places or at different times.

To whoever wanted to listen, he shouted that he had been at Numéro 2, the execution ground, the night before and had killed the Sansaricqs with his knife. Frightened witnesses soon repeated the story, and the rumor soon spread about atrocities and Brunache's involvement. The rape of Lyssa Villedrouin may have been added as the rumor spread. The improbability of Jean Dimanche and his soldiers (who executed the victims) patiently waiting for Brunache to be done with his sadistic routine, then with the rape; the fact that Brunache waited for daylight, hours after the executions had taken place, to wash his knife; the ostentatiousness of his behavior the day after the killing; the fact that no other VSNs were alleged to have been present at Numéro 2; the fact that there was no eyewitness account of Brunache, or of any other VSN, at Numéro 2 on September 19: all of this should have made people suspicious of Brunache's self-incriminating narrative. Accounts by Jean Dimanche and his soldiers, which circulated immediately after the execution, also contradict Brunache's.[31] Finally, the conflict between the military officers and the VSNs in Jérémie, described in chapters 1 and 8, further questions the possibility of the military allowing Brunache's behavior. The testimony I collected from a family member of a Jérémie Duvalierist suggests a chronology for Brunache's account. Early that morning, her father had walked to Fort-Réfléchi.[32]

> The day before, they rang the [bell], [therefore] everybody knew that arrests had occurred somewhere. So my dad went to see Mérès [Bélizaire] (a VSN). The executions (*fusillades*), they already knew, from Mérès. Brunache showed up, said nothing (*li rive, pa pale enyien*).

This would suggest that Brunache had learned about the massacre there and realized that (unlike the first wave of the massacre in August) the VSNs had been completely sidelined, possibly sparking some insecurity in him.

Fifteen years later, Albert Chassagne's account of the massacre gave a prominent place to Gérard Brunache, describing him as a sadistic killer who stubbed his cigarette in the eye of one of the Sansaricq children, gutted her with a bayonet in front of her mother, Graziela Sansaricq, then raped another child.[33] This narrative was not invented by Albert Chassagne but by Gérard Brunache himself. Chassagne was exposed to it when he visited Jérémie in the late 1970s.[34] This story was believed all the more easily because Brunache was the one boasting about it. With the execution of entire families by the state, the value of mulatto life had fallen dramatically. The social cost of claiming participation in the execution might have therefore appeared low while, concomitantly, being an actor in it could be perceived as conveying power and providing symbolic capital within the VSN field, especially for people who had, until then, been politically sidelined and socially relatively unimportant—even, or maybe especially, if the action entailed perpetration and atrocities. The deed had to be avowed as loudly as possible. Obviously, to conceive of perpetrating atrocities against neighbors and children as a way to acquire symbolic capital must have required a peculiar individual—but not necessarily a murderer. The rumor of atrocities and rape spread, was believed, repeated, ended up in the historiography and eventually in oral history.[35] As with most *macoutes*, Brunache had found, or thought he had found, a provider of symbolic capital: the VSN. However, even the VSN was a hierarchical place in Jérémie, where status depended on a mix of Duvalierist zeal and traditional socioeconomic status. Brunache was never a prominent VSN; he was far below Max Frédérique, Sanette Balmir, the Desroche brothers, even the Bélizaire brothers. Boasting about his participation in the massacre did not change that. Brunache eventually migrated to the United States and settled in New York in the early 1970s where, according to one interlocutor, he died destitute.

In the end, in spite of blustering behavior from Brunache, Desroche, Frédérique, and other VSNs, I did not collect any testimony of an act of violence committed by Jérémie VSNs before or after 1964. In Port-au-Prince, Gonaives, Cap-Haitien, the Central Plateau, and Les Cayes, stories of temperamental killings, as well as murders motivated by material reasons (notably land appropriation) are many. Not in Jérémie, where assassinations committed with impunity by Duvalierists did not involve the militia, or soldiers for that matter, but instead a Duvalierist patrician, Saintange Bontemps.

SAINTANGE BONTEMPS AND SANETTE BALMIR

The Jérémie massacre was a state crime, ordered by a president and carried out by the military. The Duvalierist civilians discussed in this chapter made choices that are difficult to define neatly but were generally not zealous. There were two exceptions: Saintange Bontemps, as his aforementioned behavior during the September 18 meeting at André Jabouin's home suggests, and Sanette Balmir. Both are widely reported in oral history and the historiography as having conveyed rumors against the Sansaricqs to Duvalier.[36] However, none of these accounts comes from a direct witness, and research has shown that widely-held beliefs about the Duvalier regime can be wrong.[37] Bontemps and Balmir did have direct access to Duvalier, held visceral sentiments against the mulatto elite, were known to have vindictive personalities, and behaved in a zealous manner to gain power locally.[38] This is not enough to wish families dead.

Saintange Bontemps (1927?–1996)[39] was born into a relatively wealthy family with landholdings in the backcountry, and was educated in local private schools. His formal profession was land surveyor (*arpenteur*) but, as were many, he was engaged in many businesses. He was a good father who made sure that all his children went to college in the United States—a costly endeavor, especially at the time. Bontemps was described by my interlocutors as gifted, educated, ambitious, venal, temperamental, violent, friendly, and personable. Pierre Chérubin, who met him in 1986 during the works of the Investigation Commission, bluntly characterized him as "a racist."[40] Two other interlocutors stated that Bontemps's anti-mulatto diatribes did not fade with the end of the mulatto presence in Jérémie and continued until his death. Bontemps's occasional outbursts of physical violence evoke the figure of the feared folk hero. He was said to have committed three murders: two before 1964 (according to two interlocutors), and one in the 1970s (according to one interlocutor). Unable to locate the Jérémie court archives, I could not determine if this was true or not. If it was apocryphal, it identifies him as an unpredictable man outside the locally accepted norms of behavior. Rolphe Papillon, who grew up in Jérémie in the 1980s, told me of one story he heard and one incident he witnessed:[41]

> I heard this story many times when I was young. Saintange is playing cards at night with a group of men in a café—there was no café in Jérémie, you know. One of the players cheats or sneers at Saintange, who tells him to stop, the man continues, then later Saintange calmly stands up, walks to that café's phone, calls the fire station, and quietly explain that a murder has been committed at a location he gives, which happens to be where he is playing cards. Then Saintange returns to the table, sits down, does not say a word, keeps playing, then serenely takes out his gun and kills the man. There was no fire station in Jérémie. I [later] checked, this anecdote was taken from a Hollywood film about the Mafia.

In February 1986, Papillon, then an adolescent in Jérémie, witnessed the *dechoukaj* (turmoil, destructions) that followed the fall of Jean-Claude Duvalier.

> There was a crowd in front of Saintange's home, it was late, sunset. I saw the crowd and went to see. It formed a semicircle, in front of his home, like *this*. Saintange must have been over sixty, I think. When I arrived, he had already come out of his home, with a gun in hand, and started to walk back and forth, talking, almost whispering, very quietly, self-confident, everybody could hear him, but it was almost a whisper, a very, very self-confident whisper: "So who wants to be the first to be killed?" Like that. "You know who I am, you know what I am capable of, I can kill for sure one or two or more before you reach me. So, who wants to die?" [The crowd] was silent, just watching, standing . . . I don't know how long it lasted, they stared at Saintange for a while, and then the crowd dispersed quietly. Saintange, he died in his bed.

According to oral history, Bontemps, already a staunch Duvalierist in the 1950s, was arrested along with several other individuals during the 1957 presidential campaign for having set a local library on fire. The judge, an old local by the name of Catinat Sansaricq, ordered them to be held in prison for a few days before being released.[42] I was told many times that this arrest fueled Bontemps's

resentment against mulattoes, particularly against the Sansaricqs. Whether apocryphal or not, this story turns resentment into an objective reaction and locates
the responsibility of the massacre away from the state and Duvalierism. Other
individuals arrested at that time, such as Hannibal Cavé, did not harbor resentment against mulattoes.[43] Bontemps was elected deputy of Tiburon, a village in
the Grand'Anse, in 1961—under a regime where all elections were rigged and
deputies were in reality appointed.[44] As was true for other local actors, Bontemps
owed his power in Jérémie both to his personal relationship with Duvalier and to
the fact that he knew how to publicly brandish this relationship, although it was
probably a tenuous bond that did not last a full decade.

Bontemps's violent behavior in 1964 in Jérémie was partly captured by a US
embassy cable. Embtel 287 on August 14, 1964 announced that Bontemps had
had a public fight in broad daylight with Abel Jérôme, whom he then killed
(the rumor had made its way into the embassy cable).[45] The repeated conflicts
between two men from August to December 1964 reflected the power vacuum
Duvalier's actions had created at the local level. Relying on dyadic relationships, bypassing institutions, undermining bureaucratic hierarchies, the president had sent three different personal envoys (Fourcand, Borges, and Régala),
in addition to Pierre Biamby, his private secretary; Duvalier also had personal
ties with the local military commander, Abel Jérôme; and with the VSN Sanette
Balmir. Meanwhile, Bontemps pretended to have Duvalier's blessing. All brandished a personal link to Duvalier to obtain compliance from others and to grab
power at the local level. Meanwhile, from August 1964 on, incidents involving
Bontemps multiplied. He went to Carl Nicolas's home one evening, opened the
door, and bluntly ordered the owner that he "was requisitioning" (in fact, stealing) the family's car.[46] Pierre Chérubin characterized Bontemps's behavior in
the summer and fall of 1964 as "unstoppable" (*à plein régime*).[47] Bontemps eventually fell out of grace with Duvalier and after 1965 was never allowed to run
for election.

I collected more data on Sanette Balmir, but not from direct witnesses or
formers acquaintances of hers, making it much harder to distinguish rumors,
many of them sordid, from hard facts. I will therefore not sketch her life. What
seems uncontested is that she was in her late fifties or early sixties in 1964, came
from a lower ring of urban society, and had a strong personal relationship with
Duvalier himself, who appointed her chief of the local militia by mid-August
1964. Abel Jérôme and Fritz Cinéas confirmed that Duvalier called her "my

Marie-Jeanne."[48] *Le Nouvelliste* mentions her as leading the "popular march" in March 1964 from Gonaives to the Presidential Palace that "asked" Duvalier to be president for life. Choosing Balmir for this role must have been decided at the highest level.[49] She only communicated with Duvalier in person in his office, not by phone or military telegrams. This forced her to travel the long distance between Jérémie and Port-au-Prince every time she wanted to report to him.

I had heard many times that Bontemps, together with Abel Jérôme, coveted the victims' wealth after their executions, but was not sure if this part of oral history was apocryphal or not, sensationalist or not. All of the victims' homes had been broken into and robbed immediately after the killing of the last three victims. This took place on the night of October 18, as detailed in chapters 1 and 6. The composition of that group of robbers remains highly uncertain, but had to have included individuals who were privy to the last executions, able to act with some level of impunity, and held relatively high positions in the local power hierarchy. I therefore ruled out all of the VSNs and the non-Duvalierist population. I had discounted most rumors that located Bontemps at these robberies until January 2016 when I witnessed an accidental encounter and conversation in Jérémie between Rolphe Papillon and Dr. Smith François, a local physician. The two men were recalling their time at school together in the early 1980s.

(François)	- Who is that guy? (*ki moun sa* (*sic*) *ye?*)
(Papillon)	- A friend. Doing research on the Vespers . . .
	- Ah . . . yeah, the Vespers, oh! yeah, that reminds me of M., you remember M., Bontemps's daughter?
	- The pretty one?
	- Yes . . . well, both were pretty, no?
	- Yeah, everybody had a crush on them.
	- Well, M., she was in my class . . . One day, she came to school with jewelry. A necklace, with a pendant, big like this. She showed us. Diamonds! It belonged to the Sansaricqs. She had a ring in her pocket, too.
	- No!
	- Yes, she used to come to school to show the Sansaricq's jewelry.
	- She brought that stuff to school?

- She wore it like this. A necklace, with a pendant . . . she brought diamonds. I have not forgotten.
- How did she get it?
- (Twisting and opening his hands) Come on! (*mon cher*) But then, Saintange, he must have told her not to bring that stuff to school any more.

Bontemps's daughter bringing jewelry to school is only circumstantial evidence of his involvement—he could have bought it from someone else, including from one of the robbers. an informant stated that he recognized a 78 rpm record player belonging to Roger Villedrouin—whose house he regularly visited as a child—in Abel Jérôme's own house. Jérôme, who did not advocate for the massacre and even attempted to have the Sansaricqs spared, would then, in the end, have actively profited from it. I do not believe greed was a cause of the massacre, or the reason Bontemps and Balmir may have advocated for killing the Sansaricqs. Rather, the robbery after the massacre was probably a crime of opportunity. However, it highlights yet another social violation committed by the victims' neighbors.

Among all the neighbors, Bontemps is the one who committed the most severe social violation. His vindictive, intimidating refusal to rescue the youngest of the Sansaricq children appears by far as the gravest crime by a civilian during the long Jérémie massacre. Stealing from their homes after their death, although lower on the scale of perpetration, nonetheless remains morally abhorrent. All the other violations by Duvalierist patricians and civilians were of a different order, considerably more "passive": being a bystander, obeying orders, avoiding taking any risk. Bontemps, on the other hand, was vehement, intimidating; and to satisfy his personal ambitions, he was ready to sacrifice an entire family.

This behavior calls for closer examination of the ties Bontemps had with the victims. It is clear from descriptions by interlocutors that he did not have a strong, positive bond with any of the victims. Although interlocutors often described (sometimes exaggerated) dyadic friendships with one of the victims, especially of the same generation, none included Bontemps. Jean-Claude Fignolé, who knew Bontemps, added that none of the adult male victims of Bontemps's generation (Guilbaud, Jean-Claude Sansaricq, Victor Villedrouin, etc.) would have maintained a strong bond with someone as "*caractériel*" (erratic to the point of madness) as Bontemps; it would have been even less likely for victims of a younger or older generation. Still, Bontemps was an acquaintance who knew all of them. It seems to confirm Georg Simmel's definition of acquaintanceship: knowledge (of someone) without the presence of trust and reciprocity.[50]

Bontemps, the VSN, and all those who committed social violations had, as acquaintances of the victims, enough intimacy with them (and with the upper class generally) to know their habits, names, faces, and degree of exclusiveness (for instance if they were members, or not, of the Excelsior). But that intimacy was not deep or strong enough to trigger relational exceptionalism. Relative intimacy, coupled with beliefs that emphasize resentment, maximizes the likelihood of a social violation. In addition, Bontemps and some of the VSNs, especially, but not only, Sanette Balmir, had liminal personalities. The way they were described by Jeremian interlocutors who knew them well, and by Pierre Chérubin who interviewed some of them, leaves little doubt that they were more aggressive and violent than the norm; they were also consumed by resentment and hatred toward the mulatto upper class.

While envy and resentment are often analyzed and theorized by social scientists as ideologies, or as a political opinion formed consciously, these sentiments often emerge in very empirical situations, in reaction to lived experiences, to individuals, and to families who can be observed directly, thus fueling an individual's imagination.[51] Resentment—and this sounds rather obvious—is often personal and social. However, to begin thinking of oneself as victim of symbolic violence and then developing resentment against specific individuals takes more than living in a hierarchical environment: an ideology is also needed. In other contexts, mulatto women marrying mulatto men, or the deployment of upper-class symbolic capital "in your face," would not necessarily appear outrageous. It would, however, with an ideology such as noirism, which instructs people not only to classify information accordingly but also to compare one's own position to that of others. And for that, knowledge about specific individuals is needed. Personalism and social nearness thus increase the possibility of resentment and, under the right circumstances, of social violations.

CHAPTER 8

The Military Commander

I shall strike you without anger
And without hate, like a butcher . . .

Charles Baudelaire

"I KNOW WHAT YOU ARE HERE FOR"

In May 2012, Joel, a former colleague of mine who was then working in a ministry in Port-au-Prince, left me a brief phone message:

"I know where he is."

Years earlier, I had asked Joel to help me locate the whereabouts of retired army colonel Abel Jérôme. Two weeks later, we were driving together on a backroad in the southeastern *département* with Joel reading me directions. We were unannounced, yet I had in my possession what I hoped was an icebreaker, or at least enough that I would not be immediately sent away: a letter from a former friend of Jérôme's from his Jérémie days, someone he had helped free from prison in mid-1964. I was following Joel's instructions closely; we proceeded slowly down a difficult dirt road. The imposing mountain range which started a few hundred yards to the north only allowed visitors to arrive from the south. After a turn, the Grosseline river, until then hidden by high grass, was suddenly in front of us. It was swollen with the previous days' rain, preventing anyone from crossing it. We looked for another, shallower crossing point with no luck; we decided to come back the following day. On our second attempt, the water level had lowered a bit and we crossed the river at slow speed until we saw on the opposite bank a trail going uphill. Obviously, this was not a well-traveled road. All these details are not mere narrative technique: even by Haitian rural standards, Abel Jérôme's place was very difficult to access, his location chosen to deter curious visitors. Only somebody in hiding would be leaving there.

Jérôme was born in 1935 in Lafond, a rural hamlet a few miles north of Jacmel. The only son of two farmers, he went to school in Jacmel where he was educated by Canadian friars at the local Brothers of Christian Instruction school. At the age of nineteen, Jérôme moved to Port-au-Prince for the last two years of high school. In 1957, he applied to the military academy, passed the entrance exam, and joined a group of fifty-three cadets. Among his classmates were six cadets who would later be associated with the town of Jérémie: William Regala, Jean Dimanche, and Léon Achille were posted there during the 1964 massacre; Prosper Maura and Elliott Roy preceded Jérôme as military commanders in Jérémie; and Cecilio Dorcé who in 1986 presided over a short-lived investigation commission on the Jérémie massacre. This cohort graduated in April 1959 after having been "cleansed" of mulattoes by Duvalier, who had been elected eighteen months prior.[1] Twenty-two of the fifty-three graduates, including Jérôme, were posted at the Presidential Guard to serve and protect the new president.

Over the following three years, Duvalier saw Jérôme every day, or almost every day, in the Palace. They developed a bond either at that time or, according to Elliott Roy, during the contentious presidential campaign in 1957, when the military academy was split between supporters of Duvalier and his opponent, Louis Dejoie.[2] Jérôme publicly sided with Duvalier and may have been noticed by him at that time. Another interlocutor stated that, by late 1961, Duvalier suspected that Jérôme was flirting with his elder daughter, Marie-Denise; and that this was possibly the reason why Jérôme was posted to Jérémie for six months in 1962, then to another provincial town, then back to Jérémie in April 1964. He was only at the rank of second lieutenant (*sous-lieutenant*), but since he was the town's highest-ranking officer, he was officially the District Commander (*Commandant de District*).[3] As such, Jérôme had considerable status in town. Testimony from various interlocutors describes him as socializing heavily during the day and often dating at night. He probably did not have much else to do in a town where he had no superior officer to report to. He was also ambitious, as many officers were since the foundation of the Forces Armées d'Haïti (FAd'H) in 1928, to join the ranks of the elite through marriage.[4] The anti-insurgency operations in August 1964 resulted in informally demoting Jérôme: the Presidential Commission brought to town three higher-ranking officers and Duvalier's personal secretary, Pierre Biamby. Jérôme surrendered his own office to them and made arrangements for their room and board as a simple subaltern.[5] In addition, two local civilians with a personal connection to Duvalier would also challenge his authority in a very public manner: Sanette Balmir, a member of the VSNs (Volontaires de la Sécurité Nationale, or National Security Volunteers); and Saintange Bontemps, a member of the Haitian Parliament.

Our car was following the trail uphill at a slow walking pace. Since crossing the river, we had not set eyes on a single farm or living soul. The area seemed devoid of human occupation, although there was a well-tended field on the right and mango trees here and there. I could not see any existing vehicle tracks. Jérôme did not just live as a recluse in a remote place; he seemed bunkered. I had heard from several people who had tried to reach him that, after the fall of the Duvalier regime in 1986 and the repeated public accusations against him, Jérôme had organized his life so that he could go into hiding at a moment's notice in the forested mountains of Haiti's southeast. Then again, maybe he had just chosen to return to the humble ancestral farm where he had been born.

The path then tucked in a ditch while turning left; two thick rows of trees lined both sides, which made it impossible to see beyond the curve. And, as we slowly made the curve, there in the middle of the path stood a tall, thin man with gray hair, hands on hips, looking straight at us. Someone had obviously called him, possibly from the motorbike stand on the asphalted Route 4 an hour earlier, to let him know of an unlikely car heading in his direction.

I stopped the car, went to him, and immediately mentioned the name of the old friend whom he had not seen since 1965. "Jean-Claude sent me," I said, and handed Jérôme the friend's handwritten message. Jérôme's facial expression changed, from hostility to something more accommodating, or maybe perplexity. He paused for a few long seconds, examined me, and finally said his first words: "I know what you are here for. Come back tomorrow morning at seven. You will have breakfast with me."

He then gave me directions to a farm hidden by the vegetation a few yards away. I was back the next day. This was going to be my first interview with the man Albert Chassagne had called "Jérémie's gauleiter," and others simply "the monster."[6]

CRUELTY IS JUSTICE

The first formal interview of a perpetrator of mass violence may have been a conversation initiated by Agrippa d'Aubigné, a Renaissance poet and a Huguenot, with the Baron des Adrets, a warlord.[7] As Europe's Wars of Religion (1562–1598) were fading, d'Aubigné embarked on a research tour around France to collect memories and understand these events, traveling on his horse. One evening in 1573, d'Aubigné knocked at the door of an isolated castle at La Frette, in central France, announced himself, and stated that he wanted to meet its lord. Soon, he was seated with his host by the fireplace, and began to ask questions, the answers to which he wrote down and later published. Des Adrets was not just any warlord. The brutality of his crimes stunned his contemporaries and shocked their imagination. The term "massacre" and the neologism *massacreur* (slaughterer) were used systematically for the first time during these wars whose unprecedented violence shocked European societies.[8]

D'Aubigné's method—meeting in person with a retired military commander to obtain his direct testimony and hear his personal views—seems incredibly modern. Over four centuries later, this has become methodological common sense. In the past few decades, interviewing perpetrators or studying their testimonies has changed the understanding of their mind and behavior.[9] As Peter Browning put it when examining 210 testimonies of "ordinary" soldiers involved in crimes: "Never before had I encountered the issue of choice so dramatically framed by the course of events and so openly discussed by at least some of the perpetrators. Never before had I seen the monstrous deeds of the Holocaust so starkly juxtaposed with the human faces of the killers."[10]

Yet there is something odd about the two men sitting by the fireplace in an old castle, two fellows discussing bloodcurdling atrocities. We understand that des Adrets opened his door because d'Aubigné was from the same side, the Huguenots; he was also a fellow hardliner and former military man. Des Adrets was not living in hiding and had no fear of retaliation. He had changed sides several times during the conflict, always implementing his modus operandi of slaughtering unarmed combatants and cutting children and women to pieces. Des Adrets did not misrepresent actions about which he felt no guilt: he recognized playing a leading role in the killings of soldiers and civilians.

However, as we read about the astonishing encounter between an intellectual (d'Aubigné) and a perpetrator (des Adrets), we expect a higher truth to come out of this investigation into naked brutality. Instead, we are served a concise statement of justification in two sentences:

> [Asked] why he had done cruelties, dishonorable to his great valor . . . He answers . . . that nobody does cruelties by rendering them, [and] That the first are called cruelties, the second are called justices.[11]

In a couple of sentences, des Adrets endows brutality with a circular intellectual structure and self-righteous moralization, legitimizing his crimes as mere counter-crimes.[12] This explicit and succinct articulation in the sixteenth century notwithstanding, positing mass violence as a mere consequence of earlier violence exerted by the victim group is not a product of modernity. It already existed in Julius Caesar's *De Bello Gallico*, which raises the possibility that a moral discourse is inherent to mass violence.[13] To twenty-first-century readers, des Adrets's discourse of counter-violence sounds almost predictable. Awaiting words of contrition or self-reflection, or expecting killers to be repositories of the type of enlightening truths scholars yearn for, may be sheer naivety—intellectual, methodological, moral. Yet how many options for responding does a perpetrator have when facing questioning years after the event? Either recognize facts and take responsibility; lie and deny involvement; or recognize responsibility but deny culpability by assigning it to the victims, as the Baron des Adrets did.

I expected Abel Jérôme to fall neatly into one of these three categories. Given his responsibility in the massacre, I spent the prior night anticipating denials of all kinds and imagining counter-questions. Little did I imagine that Abel Jérôme would serve me a labyrinthic bricolage largely free of *modern* constructions. To center on the moralizing justification of a past massacre implies institutions, tasks, duties, and, above all, a clear binary opposition between us and them, the regime and its opponents, victims and perpetrators. Instead of a world split in two, Jérôme would be solely concerned with persons and how they related to him personally, regardless of "sides," of what they stood for and believed, of class, race, and politics. In this sense, there was something beyond or outside the modern about him. He was everything but "banal" in the sense that his words revealed not the centrality of the state and the anonymization of functionaries, which Arendt believed was the condition for becoming an impersonal cog in a modern death machine; but instead a world where everyone was known and where obedience was conditioned not (or not only) by bureaucratic orders but mainly by personal allegiances and affinities.[14]

———————

When I arrived at seven in the morning at Abel Jérôme's ancestral home, I found an exhausted host. During our brief encounter the day before, he had seemed rather energetic. Now, he looked as though he had not slept. He made me sit on the veranda and brought out juice, bread, and a notebook. Did he spend the night writing in it? I did not see or hear any helper in his home, neither this time nor during my subsequent visits in following years. I knew that his wife, Rose Cadet, had left him with their daughter a few years after their wedding in 1965. At seventy-seven, Jérôme had been living by himself for decades on a remote farm with no immediate neighbor. There was a beat-up four-wheel car in the yard.

By the time I first met Jérôme, I already knew a great deal about him. I had met with former friends of him, including a childhood friend from Jacmel, and had gathered anecdotes from witnesses and acquaintances about the time he had spent in Jérémie, Cap Haitian, and Port-au-Prince. During his two military postings in Jérémie, Jérôme had developed both friendships and animosities; they were enduring and spanned the political spectrum. I knew he had saved at least two individuals from near-certain execution. I was also corresponding with Bruno Laroche, the friar who had been his teacher at the middle school in Jacmel, had officiated at his wedding in 1965 in Jérémie, and, crucially, wrote the primary source of the Jérémie massacre with names of victims and dates of executions in the friar's diary. I also knew that the sensationalist narrative that had made him a sadistic killer was erroneous. There were still plenty of details that remained obscure. I wanted to hear his version of the events and learn about his relationship to Duvalier. Jérôme was the last important actor still alive— Duvalier, Jean Dimanche, and Pierre Biamby had all passed away. Finally, I wanted to know if he had tried to save a victim he was known to have shared a friendship with, Jean-Claude Sansaricq.

THE MILITARY

Oral history and some of the historiography have placed the ruthlessness of the VSNs at the center of the imagination and relegated the military to a second role.[15] The fog of memory, and Prosper Avril's bold argument that the military was a victim of the Duvalier regime rather than its accomplice, increased that perception.[16] In reality, it was the military and not the VSN that constituted the repressive apparatus's steel frame. Temperamental assassinations, blustery intimidation, and petty thievery, allegedly the stuff of VSNs, do not qualify as a steel frame. Only the military offered the competency to provide guaranteed and unquestioned enforcement of all repressive measures taken by the regime over the entirety of the territory. Only a formal, structured institution such as the Haitian Armed Forces, with its own organic elite and sense of discipline, could provide this.

Duvalier placed trusted officers, not VSNs, at the helm of institutions carrying out repression. Several officers became heads of state, ministers, and members of the parliament during the post-Duvalier era; no VSN ever reached such a high-ranking position. The VSN was a chaotic entity with chaotic individuals who, for most, could not carry out complex tasks. In Weberian terms, the VSN barely qualified as a bureaucracy. Yet the FAd'H is a largely under-researched institution, in spite of a few memoirs published by former officers.[17] We know little about the sociology of its officers and soldiers throughout the twentieth century, the ideologies that inspired them during the same period, and how they interacted with other state institutions. Since each army unit outside Port-au-Prince was deeply embedded in a town's social life and politics, relationships with civilians at the local level should also be central to any study of the military.

Seven military officers were involved in the Jérémie massacre: Breton Claude, Jean-Baptiste Hilaire, '54, Mercius Rivière, '54, René Prosper, '56, William Régala, '59, Jean Dimanche, '59, Abel Jérôme, '59, and Prosper Avril, '61.[18] Breton Claude (1908–1980), military commander in Les Cayes in 1964, had a different trajectory. He enlisted as a soldier and rose through the ranks to become a commissioned officer. His family, who was from Jacmel, was acquainted with Jérôme's. His role in Jérémie, however, is not clear. He briefly visited Abel Jérôme, thirty years his junior, in Jérémie in early August 1964. Jérôme confirmed this visit but did not reveal its purpose. Breton Claude became the warden of Fort-Dimanche, the regime's main prison and execution ground, by 1966.[19] Jean-Baptiste Hilaire (1928–) graduated second of his class at the Military Academy in 1954. After Duvalier repeatedly purged the higher ranks of the armed forces, Breton and Hilaire quickly rose through a depleted hierarchy. Duvalier made Hilaire commander of the National Penitentiary in April 1964, a position he held until 1974. Revealingly, Duvalier always placed these two institutions, Fort-Dimanche and the national penitentiary, in the hands of military officers, not VSN. In 1974, Jean-Claude Duvalier chose Hilaire to be commander-in-chief of the FAd'H, a position he held until his retirement in 1978. On August 6, 1964, Hilaire was chosen to be vice-president of the Presidential Commission overseeing the anti-insurgency operations in Jérémie. He was a key actor in the regime's repression apparatus.[20]

BREAKFAST

Immediately after we sat down on the veranda, Jérôme opened a notebook and to my stupefaction, began to read aloud. Had he been writing these lines for years or had he begun merely the night before, as his exhausted look suggested? I tried to interrupt him, but he continued reading at louder volume. Eventually he stopped and started to answer questions, but Jérôme proved very hard to interview. Whereas Jean Alcide immediately laid bare what he had witnessed without calculating the cost for his own reputation; and whereas almost all the other interlocutors and informants were rather relaxed and unguarded when sharing their own views or stating what they knew, Jérôme remained nervous and guarded.[21] He did not claim any responsibility in the massacre. He gave improbable answers about his whereabouts on August 11 and September 19, 1964 when the executions took place at Numéro 2—that he was on the shoreline all night long with a flashlight, watching for an invasion from the sea.[22] Yet his responses were unexpected in other ways. In the weeks prior to meeting Jérôme, I had had lengthy conversations with many former Duvalierists and several former military officers. A diffuse anti-elite and anti-mulatto discourse often ran through these conversations. The victims of the dictatorship were denigrated, occasionally through gratuitously sordid details, accompanied by self-pity for the fate of Duvalierists since the fall of the regime in 1986. When I arrived that morning at Jérôme's farm, I was expecting the same discourse.

Instead, for the first time, I was encountering a Duvalierist who was praising the innocence of the victims: "They did nothing wrong, nothing." (*Ils n'avaient rien fait, rien.*) In none of the interviews I collected from Jérôme did he use anti-mulatto tropes or innuendos. However, his admiration of, if not his attachment to, Duvalier was intact. There was nothing ideological or even political in Jérôme's long discourse. His account was entirely personalistic. There were people he liked: Duvalier, Gérard Léonidas, Jean-Claude Fignolé, various Jeremian families. There were also people he abhorred: Saintange Bontemps, Sanette Balmir, Astrel Benjamin, Sony Borges, and all the VSNs—never for their opinions or actions, but instead, it seems, because they challenged his power in Jérémie.

He talked for about seven hours straight, from half-past seven in the morning to almost three o'clock in the afternoon. I have met him two more times since then, usually for less than half an hour at a time, with pointed questions that emerged in the course of writing this book. Every time, he seemed glad and terribly annoyed to see me —glad to have a visitor; annoyed because he knew what each visit was about.

THE ART OF CONVERSATION

One may imagine a regime of terror to be a silent one, overseen by a rather guarded inner circle. The opposite was true. Inner-circle members were talkative and daily life in that inner circle was peppered with constant conversations, most of them unrelated to politics. Duvalier himself was a conversationalist in a culture of the spoken word. Conversation was largely an art where one could demonstrate erudition, eloquence, and brilliance. This was still a twisted world: this art of conversation, which Norbert Elias took as a marker of civilization, took place within a repression apparatus.

Jérôme narrated two of his personal meetings with Duvalier in his presidential office in the summer and fall of 1964.[23] Instead of merely recalling these meetings, Jérôme reenacted them. He stood up and recreated dialogue by alternating between Duvalier's voice, language, and expressions and then his own, using first-person pronouns, reproducing gestures. The meetings were carried out mainly in Kreyol, the language of intimacy, with some occasional French. In Duvalier's presence, Jérôme depicted himself, unconsciously, as submissive. (The effect was astonishing.) Responding to Duvalier forty-eight years earlier, Jérôme took the voice of a child; Duvalier had the tone of a benevolent father. When Jérôme started to talk, he apparently said: "*Ou se papa'm* (you are my dad)." At another moment in the conversation, Jérôme (still according to his own recollection) launched into his argument by saying: "I have two fathers: my father and you." Duvalier addressed him through diminutives: "*ou se pitit mwen*" (you're my son), a use of metaphoric kinship which was standard in Duvalier's inner circle.[24]

After the reenactment was over, the change on Jérôme's face was astonishing: he sat staring at the horizon for several seconds, silent and serene, as if he were loved, no longer on a godforsaken farm with a researcher staring at him. I was not sure what to make of this. Anthropology's commonplaces about metaphoric kinship do not provide any explanation. To be a metaphoric son obviously means to be loved. It conveys filial love, filial trust, filial obligations; and in return, what a son expects of his father—to be appreciated and trusted. The best proof of paternal love was to obtain the liberation he had sought for the two individuals he knew, not to be called "my son." Jérôme calling Duvalier "dad" was not prompted by habitus alone; it had, of course, a strategic dimension. He tried to convince Duvalier by demonstrating absolute and unconditional loyalty, or submission, or love: that of a son. Half a century later, Jérôme was remembering the contentment he had felt in that office. Even if his mind and memory fabricated it, what it showed about his personality was the same. Minutes before he recalled this meeting, he had seemed authoritarian; now he had just showed a submissive side.

This counterintuitive mix of authoritarianism and submissiveness was, for postwar scholars, the stuff of Nazi personalities.[25] Yet, this neatly defined psychological syndrome hardly applies to Jérôme or to the other military officers in Jérémie during the events. An authoritarian personality does not imply a murderous one. Rather, evasion and deception characterized Jérôme's behavior throughout the events of 1964. His loyalty and attachment to Duvalier were never in question, but Jérôme tried to reconcile these with his social aspirations.[26]

PONTIUS PILATE'S SOCIAL BONDS

Over six feet tall and slender, Jérôme must have cut a dashing figure in his youth. He was often described as a ladies' man. Several interlocutors mentioned that he forged social bonds across the social spectrum, several of them during his first tour of duty there in 1962. (He also alienated a good number of people.) In

Jérémie, a town with a large population inclined to write literature, he sought and found the friendship of young aspiring writers.

This included a friendship with Jean-Claude Sansaricq. I had first learned about their relationship from Jean-Claude Fignolé who was in possession of material evidence of the tie between Sansaricq and Jérôme. Almost the same age (Jérôme was twenty-nine in 1964, Sansaricq thirty-two), they were close enough to exchange books, like *Perspectives de l'homme* by Roger Garaudy.[27] Garaudy, a French Marxist and Communist Party leader with a very dogmatic reputation, was being read in Jérémie by the son of the richest local man and a military officer serving an anti-communist dictator. Beyond the irony of it, this may suggest that an inclination for new ideas or maybe aesthetics were a more productive ingredient in the chemistry of elective affinities than ideology. In any case, Sansaricq had lent the book to Jérôme before being arrested on September 19. Months later, Fignolé received a book from Jérôme who said that it was too difficult for him and that he "could not give it back to its owner." Fignolé took it home, opened it, and on the third page saw that the original owner had written his name: Jean-Claude Sansaricq. He concluded that Jérôme had forgotten or was unaware of the handwritten evidence of ownership.

Social relations with military commanders in provincial towns were coveted by the local elite. Not all these relations were strategic or utilitarian, as proven by the fact that some of these bonds lasted a lifetime.[28] Men of the same generation and with the same relational ethos easily forged bonds. Whatever the motivations of the people to whom he was connected, Jérôme was part of many networks. He enjoyed the importance he had, and not just the friendships. Military commanders and officers in general were immersed in Jérémie's social world, both as officers serving a regime and as socializers. Some married locally, as Jérôme eventually would. This situation also made him the most visible actor during the 1964 events, unlike Biamby, the head of the Presidential Commission, who was never seen in town.

About two hours into the interview, I asked Jérôme, perhaps too abruptly, about his friendship with Jean-Claude Sansaricq. I wanted to explore whether this friendship could have been the decisive factor that had led him to try to obtain a letter on September 18 from the Duvalierist patricians requesting that Duvalier rescind his execution order.[29] Jérôme refused to answer, becoming agitated and raising his voice. The conversation moved on, then I asked again a few minutes later: "Is there anything that could have been done to at least spare his children "No! No! I know nothing about that . . . There is nothing that could have been done." The execution of Jean-Claude Sansaricq and his family signaled to the population that having a friendship with Jérôme offered no guarantee of protection. If being the military commander had made Jérôme a potential protector and given him both political importance and social privileges, the execution of even his friends demoted him twice over: politically within Duvalierist circles, and socially within the town's population.

A PERPETRATOR AND A GOOD SAMARITAN?

Abel Jérôme saved two individuals from possible execution. The first one, chronologically, was Jean-Claude Fignolé, who told me his story and gave me the aforementioned letter to "break the ice" when I first met Jérôme.

In mid-August 1964, Fignolé, then twenty-three, was arrested at his home by two soldiers on foot, brought to the military base, then ushered to the second floor where he was forced to sit on a chair with his hands tied behind his back.[30] In the room was Pierre Biamby, the head of the Presidential Commission, and several other men he did not know. Biamby was holding a sheet of paper and said he had received an anonymous letter accusing Fignolé of being a Communist. Biamby then asked him if he was a member of the PPLN (Parti populaire de libération nationale; Party of National Liberation), the Haitian communist party. Fignolé denied it. In his recollection, Fignolé stated that he was not tortured or beaten, although he was slapped. He could not remember who did it, but believed it was not Biamby. He was then brought to a cell on the first floor.

Jérôme, twenty-eight, and Fignolé, twenty-three, had become friends through Gérard Léonidas (1928–2016), a staunch Duvalierist and a "big brother" figure to many. Léonidas was cultured and interested in the classics—his legal last name was "Léonidas," but he preferred "Thémistocle," a Greek hero he appreciated more. Fignolé came from the same social sector as Jérôme: small farmers (Jérôme from the southwest, Fignolé from Abricots). Léonidas was from an urban family from Jérémie. The three friends often met in the late afternoon on Léonidas's veranda, discussing politics, their respective ambitions, and women. Neither Jérôme nor Léonidas ever suspected that Fignolé was a Communist Party member who reported to the PPLN in Port-au-Prince and was actively recruiting in the Grand'Anse. Fignolé stressed that his friendship with the two men was sincere—that he did not seek their friendship for future political protection.

When Biamby received the anonymous letter denouncing Fignolé, he may have been told that Jérôme knew him personally. In any case, Biamby bypassed Jérôme and asked a sergeant to arrest Fignolé. Jérôme discovered Fignolé in a cell either later that day or the morning after. A day or more later, possibly even a week, Jérôme hopped on the very plane that was carrying soldiers who had been fighting the Jeune Haiti guerrilla back to Port-au-Prince. Once there, he went straight to the Presidential Palace where he was received by François Duvalier. Jérôme pleaded for Fignolé's release, which he obtained.

Fignolé said that, days after his liberation, while on Léonidas's veranda, Jérôme recalled his own meeting with Duvalier almost euphorically, theatrically showing that he knew the President, feared him, but nonetheless went to see him. In the end, it appears that Duvalier trusted Jérôme's account of Fignolé and decided upon his release. In my conversations with him, Fignolé was generally unforgiving of Jérôme, whom he accused of having "done nothing" to save Jean-Claude Sansaricq, and "having enabled" (*permis*) the regime of terror in 1964 in Jérémie. However, he was also unambiguous about Jérôme's role in his release:

"Abel saved my life."

ADORNO IN JÉRÉMIE

Adorno might have characterized Jérôme's personality as authoritarian. It came through quickly during my first interview with him. He could raise his tone abruptly as none of my other interlocutors, military officers included, had. His body and facial language conveyed self-confidence, authority, even domination. Whenever a question was too pointed, he would dismiss it and raise his tone while making a suffering face or moving his left hand in a way that conveyed power and that seemed to come instinctively to him.

For the outsider, interpreting facial language or a fleeting gesture seems like hubris on steroids; for anthropologists, however, it is the methodology of scarcity, deployed when the holder of information is not letting much else out, and even then often half-heartedly. Yet, interpreting ineffability is ethnographic business, as Pierre Clastres and Clifford Geertz made clear.[31] Jérôme conveyed a personality I had rarely encountered during my research. Many anecdotes I was told also depicted a man with an authoritarian bent. His openly hostile relationships with the unsavory Saintange Bontemps and with Sanette Balmir were framed through competition for authority, not political disagreements or moral principles. "He does not let anyone push him over. Except Duvalier," Fignolé had told me.[32] Another anecdote, told by one of Raoul Cédras's children, illustrates a petty and vindictive side. I will add, before presenting his testimony, that Raoul Cédras was Jérémie's Duvalierist mayor and had a personal relationship with Duvalier since the 1940s. I will also add that, during his posting in Jérémie, Jérôme dated extensively and generally pursued eligible, young, upper-class mulatto women—he eventually married one.[33]

> There was this young woman, L. D., her mother had died and she was living by herself. So, one Sunday, after mass, we (the family) went back home [to Bordes] for lunch, so my parents had invited her after mass for lunch with us. So it was us and her. We were already eating. Suddenly, we heard the loud sound of a diesel car, a jeep, enter our property very fast and brake suddenly on the gravel. Mother rushed outside and saw Abel Jérôme [getting out his car]. Oh! she immediately understood why he was there. He expected to be invited inside. She said *"Nous sommes en famille"* (We are having a family gathering), a way to convey an intimacy that was beyond Jérôme's reach. He was not leaving. She pleaded: *"Abel, nous sommes en famille."* The young woman, she was at the table, she was afraid that Abel would enter and sit with us. It lasted a bit, but mother did not invite him in. He [finally] left, making the tires screech on the gravel, very loud, very loud. He felt humiliated. Now, my mother was a mulatto woman, but my father was not and he was close to Duvalier and he was the mayor. You think this would have deterred [Jérôme]? The same day, I was arrested. In the afternoon, I walked [from Bordes to the city center] with mother, and there outside our home, a few meters down, there were two soldiers, they asked for my papers, I did not have any, so they took me to the military base, "for verification" they said. I was let go, but they all knew me, the sergeant also. The day after, as I walked with Mother [a few yards from our home, toward the city center], he drove by very fast in his jeep, drove right on our side of the road, through a mud puddle . . . Mother had to return home to change her clothes.

In theory, Jérôme's personality would make him a strong candidate for perpetration of violence and indifference to causing harm. There is a gap, however, between an authoritarian personality and a murderous one. Jérôme's own inclination for power and control also had the effect of restricting the anti-mulatto hatred of those who challenged his authority. Since he had been appointed Jérémie's new military commander in April 1964, Jérôme thought of himself as the most important man in town and expected to be recognized as such. However, the counterinsurgency operations of 1964 changed the balance of power at the local level, as explained earlier. In addition, Bontemps and Balmir flaunted their personal relationship with Duvalier to intimidate others. They tried to demote Jérôme's to subaltern status, giving him orders in public. Not only did Jérôme viscerally resented being disrespected, but he also believed that his institution (the Armed Forces, of which he was also a product) should not yield to civilians. When I interviewed him almost fifty-five years later, his dislike of Bontemps and Balmir was fascinatingly intact. However, the hostility had no ideological or political basis; it was purely personal, except for Jérôme's belief in his institution. The U.S. diplomatic archives hold evidence of these clashes. On August 14, the U.S. Embassy announced that Abel Jérôme had been murdered by Bontemps:

> Jerome killed in altercation . . . Bontemps, recently elected deputy from Tiburon, arrived in Jeremie few days ago in "special mission" and started throwing his weight around when he tried giv[ing] order to Capt. (sic) Jerome, dispute ensued in which both men pulled guner (sic) and fired. Jerome died at once and Bontemps a few hours later.[34]

The US embassy fell victim to the rumor mill; however, there were at least two actual public brawls between the two men in the summer of 1964. Fignolé once remembered an incensed Jérôme showing up on Gérard Léonidas' gallery in 1964, recounting to his friends a dispute from earlier that day. According to Jérôme, Bontemps once accused him in front of Duvalier of being a *camoquin* (anti-Duvalier guerrilla)—potentially a death sentence. Jérôme said he traveled to Port-au-Prince and the Presidential Palace on October 23 to plead for Gérard Noël's release. Jérôme's presence on that day in Port-au-Prince is confirmed by a U.S. Embassy cable:

Abel Jerome was here (in PAP) as of October 23, according USA RMA source. Jérôme reportedly stated Dame-Marie invaders originally numbered 14, of which 11 are "accounted for . . . Remarks by Jerome also indicated that a wave of retaliation against mulattoes in Jeremie has in fact occurred. [35]

When he entered the Presidential office (still according to Jérôme's version), Jérôme saw Milou Drouin, the leader of the Jeune Haiti guerrilla, who had been arrested a few days earlier. Drouin was tied to a chair. Casually, Duvalier asked Jérôme while pointing at Drouin, "*ou konen moun sa-a?*" (do you know this individual?). Jérôme said he denied it. The sheer fact that Duvalier asked either testifies to his doubt about Jérôme, or to a desire to intimidate him, or both; as well as to the damage done by Bontemps to Jérôme's reputation. Another cable stated that Milou Drouin was indeed interrogated in the Presidential Palace on the same day.[36] In the end, Duvalier ignored Saintange Bontemps' accusations, who later fell out of grace with Duvalier. Bontemps never again held any official position with the regime.

The dispute between Bontemps and Jérôme was both personal and about power. The same can be said of Jérôme's fraught relationship with Sanette Balmir, the powerful local VSN, as she too attempted, albeit more successfully, to relegate the town's military commander to a subaltern role. The two had very distinct personalities. Jérôme had a good formal education, aspired to a higher social class, and socialized with members of the local elite. Sanette Balmir was infamous; all who talked to me about her stated that she had been a prostitute in her youth, but this reputation might have been constructed after the events as a way to dissociate the town from her deeds.

True or apocryphal, the story locates her in local memory at the fringe of society. It was actually difficult to gather dependable information on her. Pierre Chérubin confirmed that Balmir had been an informer of Duvalier's in 1964.[37] To communicate, Balmir traveled to Port-au-Prince by any means achievable—boat or car. Providing information made her powerful and Balmir most likely gave reports on Abel Jérôme's behavior—notably on his unwillingness to cooperate with her. And although no interlocutor stated so or even hinted at its possibility, I also wonder if, to undermine Jérôme, Balmir reported to Duvalier that he very publicly dated young mulatto women. The young lieutenant had alienated the VSNs early on and seems to have despised them, not least because they posed a challenge to the Armed Forces' authority, but also because some came from the lower strata of the town. From a noirist point of view, to socialize with mulattoes, as Jérôme did, was not the best way to acquire symbolic capital. Duvalier replaced Luc Desroche with Balmir as head of the local VSN in late August or early September, although I could not determine the exact date of that appointment. When asked about it, Jérôme corroborated what Régala had first told me: that he had received a written order from Duvalier after the departure of the Presidential Commission in late August to "cooperate with Sanette Balmir, my *Marie-Jeanne*," an injunction that demoted Jérôme and the FAD'H in the power hierarchy. Jérôme's lack of zeal eventually eroded Duvalier's trust in him.

THE FAILED EVADER: JEAN DIMANCHE

As our first meeting was nearing its end, one subject stood out by its absence from the conversation: Jean Dimanche and his platoon. Second Lieutenant Jean Dimanche, member (along with Jérôme) of the 1959 military academy cohort, commanded the firing squad that executed the victims on August 11 and September 19; his soldiers shot the victims. As chapter 1 shows, Jérôme had maneuvered to have Dimanche be the main executioner of the Jérémie Vespers. What did Jérôme have to say about Dimanche, whom he had known since his military academy days, and about his soldiers? What was his version of the very public dispute between him and Dimanche over who would command the execution platoon?

Dimanche was born in Jérémie in 1932, the illegitimate son of Mme Alophène Aleau, who ran a small nightclub, and Antilus Richard, a shoemaker. When Aleau finally married, her son took his stepfather's last name. Dimanche belonged to a socioeconomic sector that is difficult to locate. If everybody knew of Madam Aleau, her nightclub with a mixed reputation, and her successive romantic unions, her son did not grow up poor. He attended the Ecole des frères alongside the children of the local elite. He was at some point in the same class as Jean-Claude Sansaricq. By the time he left Jérémie, Jean Dimanche likely knew of, or knew about, most of the future victims of the massacre. Dimanche moved to Port-au-Prince for *rhétorique*, high school's penultimate grade, at the age of twenty-four. He allegedly entered the military academy on a recommendation from General Antonio Kébreau, who was dating his older sister, Adrienne.[38] Too unremarkable to join the Military House (the Presidential Guard, then), he was posted in Pétionville. At a dance party in the summer of 1963, he was allegedly involved in a brawl with Luckner Cambronne, a member of Duvalier's inner circle, and was discharged from the military before being reintegrated a few months later and eventually posted at Casernes Dessalines, in Port-au-Prince. On August 7 or 8, 1964, he was sent by plane to Jérémie to secure the airstrip as part of the counterinsurgency operations, probably chosen by the leadership of the military headquarters for his Jérémie connection. He and his platoon slept in tents at Numéro 2. When the counterinsurgency operations were officially terminated in mi-October, he returned to Port-au-Prince with his platoon. His career stagnated; he was briefly married, never had children, and died on August 5, 1995. He was unanimously described as depressed and bitter for most of his later life.[39]

Dimanche carried out the execution orders and spared no one. He had tried, poorly, to avoid complying with the execution order.[40] Evasion had been Dimanche's primary reaction to having to kill. He was also described as indifferent to politics and ideologies. If he held strong Duvalierist or noirist beliefs, it did not come across in the interviews of those who knew him. Importantly, he was never named or mentioned in any of the sinister episodes of the regime that appear in the historiography or oral memory, aside from the Jérémie massacre. It seems also that Dimanche did not build the sorts of relationships, or have the level of academic schooling, that were usually necessary to move up through the military hierarchy and become a high-ranking officer.

In the summer of 1964, Dimanche was outsmarted by Jérôme, who successfully schemed to have the execution take place at Numéro 2. This was the only place in Jérémie's environs that was not under Jérôme's direct military command, thus enabling him to avoid having to command a firing squad. From his dealings with the Presidential Commission, Jérôme suspected as early as August 8 or 9 that repression was going to include Jeremian civilians. On August 11, Biamby, the Commission's president, handed Jérôme the order of execution but was probably indifferent about its location. As the town's official military commander, it was up to Jérôme to identify a place for it. Had he chosen the military base, or the usual firing range used by the soldiers, or any more remote location, Jérôme himself would have had to lead the firing squad. Instead, he opted for the only site where another military officer had been posted: the airstrip, about six miles from the town. When he announced this location to Dimanche on August 10 or 11 during an informal meeting, Dimanche vehemently refused. The conversation quickly degenerated. Dimanche argued that he could not receive orders from

Jérôme since they were of the same rank and from the same graduation cohort. When I asked Jérôme about this meeting, the only thing he was willing to say was that Dimanche "did not realize at first that I was the [town's] military commander (*plus haut gradé*)." In the end, according to Anariol Joseph, Dimanche felt compelled to comply with the decision that Jérôme had already made.

Through some strange twist of poetic justice, or perhaps a slice of ghastly irony, Jérôme, in spite of his efforts to evade direct responsibility, ended up in the historiography as the main villain while Dimanche remains absent from the literature. If Jérôme had yearned for social recognition and ascension, the massacre destroyed any hopes of achieving it. He left Jérémie in February 1965 after eleven months there, to be posted in Port-de-Paix. He never returned. He continued his career, never reaching the rank of general. In 1977, the publication of a booklet on the Jérémie massacre made him out to be the main perpetrator, ignoring entirely Biamby, Dimanche, and Duvalier's orders. In 1986, the fall of the Duvalier regime and the newly gained freedom of expression led Port-au-Prince radio channels to address the massacre and named Abel Jérôme in a very public manner. He became a pariah, forever associated with a massacre. Shortly after his retirement, instead of settling in Port-au-Prince as most of his peers had, he went back to the remote farm where he had grown up. He lived there in isolation, as if his parents' ambition to see him go up the social ladder had miserably failed.

I first thought that Jérôme's account was frustrating, with many central questions unanswered. As I later listened to Jérôme's recording, however, I realized his discourse revealed something crucial about culture and about the "issue of choice," as Peter Browning put it when talking about soldiers facing orders to massacre. Browning identified several German soldiers during the Second World War who chose to evade mass killing. Yet their relationship to the victims was not and could not have been a variable in determining their behavior. Jérôme and Dimanche, on the other hand, knew the victims. Social ties certainly were not the only determinant, but they were a major one. Evasion remained a widespread behavior during this event. On the other hand, the soldiers who composed the firing squad that executed the victims of the massacre were all from the Casernes Dessalines in Port-au-Prince, dispatched by plane on August 6 or 7 and posted at Numéro 2 to secure the airport during the anti-insurgency operations.[41] They most likely knew nothing about the victims; they had not even been authorized to visit Jérémie during their posting at Numéro 2. They faced families in a ditch and fired. For the first time since 1812, soldiers executed children in cold blood.

CHAPTER 9

Bonds That Hold and Bonds to Break

The guiltless will pay for the deeds later: either the man's children or his descendants thereafter.

Solon

TERIN SAN

On a late afternoon in June 1964, Second Lieutenant Elliott Roy was on sentry duty in front of the Duvaliers' private apartment on the second floor of the Presidential Palace when he saw François Duvalier arriving from the main stairway.

> I was on sentry duty that evening, it was about 5:00 P.M., something like that. Duvalier arrived, he started to talk to me [rather than immediately enter], he often did that, he started to chat, he liked to chat with us (young officers). But he seemed nervous, not like he was usually. He said 'I am back from Fort-Dimanche.' He complained that too few are willing to participate (*hésitent à s'impliquer*) . . . Me, I just listened. And then he said 'I, for instance, I just executed my own brother-in-law.' He continued and was saying that not enough participated, too many were halfhearted (*tièdes*) . . . "*Fok tout moun met tout bra yo nan terin san*" (everyone should put their whole arm in a *terrine* (*sic*) of blood).
>   - What did he mean?
>   - I did not understand the word, I imagine that's the reason I never forgot it. The meaning was: people relented (*ça suivait pas*), that was clear.[1]

Roy was already aware that Lucien Daumec, Duvalier's own brother-in-law, speechwriter and longtime confidant, had been arrested a few months earlier. He then understood that Daumec had been shot through his cell bars by Duvalier himself and not executed with a semblance of dignity on Fort-Dimanche's execution grounds. Michèle Oriol, using other testimonies she had heard about this event in her childhood, corroborated this version, suggesting that Duvalier lost his self-control in the course of a conversation with Daumec, who refused to apologize to (or possibly even abused) Duvalier, who then grabbed his aide's rifle and shot Daumec.[2]

I had never heard the word *terrine* in this context; Roy had not either. *Terrine* is a cold, country dish of minced meat, usually several inches deep. Did Duvalier's metaphor reflect the casualness of killing? Roy's anecdote reveals several lay dimensions of Duvalier's repression: the arbitrariness of many executions; the fact that the most violent aspects of repression could be openly discussed in the Presidential Palace; how casual personal conversations were mixed with explicit references to violence. Duvalier's almost candid admission of frustration at the lack of zeal among his inner circle and the Presidential Guard highlights a paradoxical dimension of repression. The regime caused the death of thousands of people. Yet many, possibly most, members of the regime, while benefiting from their "membership," still worked to avoid being seen as perpetrators.

The dialogue between a dictator and a young officer thirty-five years his junior also lays bare the relational ethos in which the regime was immersed. Its content shows that Duvalier himself was aware of evasion, to the point of frustration. This chapter focuses on social bonds and is divided in two parts. The first is about evasion and how evasion correlates with sociality. The second examines how the regime targeted entire families. In both cases, social bonds were at the center of motivations and worldviews.

Elliott Roy corresponded to Duvalier's ideal of a Black military officer, once comparing him during a military parade to "a Prussian officer."[3] That he was of peasant extraction was an added value for Duvalier, who became fond of him and called him "son" (*pitit mwen*). Elliott Roy was born in 1936 on a farm in the Southwest. Thereafter, he led an extraordinary life, the stuff of movies. He left the peasantry, became a military officer, a member of the Presidential Guard, then a Communist, barely escaped arrest in Port-au-Prince, studied at the Sorbonne in Paris, became a guerrilla instructor in Cuba, spent decades in exile in France, married three times, and eventually returned to Cayes-Jacmel and a peaceful home by the seaside. In January 2019, he agreed to share his experience in the Presidential Palace in a series of interviews he granted at his home. He gave his dispassionate testimony in a soft-spoken tone that often contrasted with its content. He described life in the Presidential Palace through a string of anecdotes rather than making broad generalizations. Roy realized early that the Palace was a deadly place where alienating anyone could have dire consequences; he refrained from participating in intrigue and gossip, but nonetheless developed an ulcer, as did others in the Presidential Guard.[4] His descriptions were not fundamentally different from those made by others. I found it intriguing, however, that he still felt some attachment to Duvalier, whom he did not demonize. His words and depictions acquired more weight. His recounting of Lucien Daumec's death exemplifies two central aspects of Duvalier's repression: not everyone was ready to kill for Duvalier and he was aware of it; brutality was intertwined with intimacy.

THE EVADERS

Duvalier's frustration about his men avoiding taking part in repression, as recalled by Elliott Roy, evokes a historiographic debate about the motivation of German soldiers during the Second World War: the intentionalist versus functionalist debate. On the intentionalist side, Daniel Goldhagen argues that German society in its entirety was moved by overwhelming hatred and beliefs.[5] Soldiers did not need to be convinced or forced by the state and their military hierarchy. Killing was eagerly supported and eagerly carried out. On the functionalist side of the debate, Peter Browning, makes obedience and microsolidarity, not ideology, the paradigm of troops' behavior.[6] Dirk Moses remarked that this binary opposition evokes another: structure versus agency, to which I return later.[7]

The question about behaviors during the Jérémie massacre, as the two previous chapters show, was as much about "why did the soldiers kill" as "why did most of the protagonists attempt not to be involved in killing?" The main pattern of behavior of Duvalierist civilians and army officers can indeed be characterized by evasion, desistance, or unwillingness.[8] The town's commanding officer, Second Lieutenant Abel Jérôme, schemed to avoid commanding the firing squad and "passed" the act of killing onto Second Lieutenant Jean Dimanche, who resisted this order in vain. The latter ended up in this position after having been outfoxed by Jérôme. Hours before the first wave of executions on August 11, several Duvalierist civilians successfully argued for the release of five prisoners.[9] Before the second wave of executions, on September 18, one Duvalierist patrician, André Jabouin, timidly tried to remove children from the list of victims. Others pondered their allegiance to Duvalier with their social standing and bonds with Jérémie's inhabitants. The VSNs (Volontaires de la Sécurité Nationale, or National Security Volunteers) did not participate in the act of killing and did not harm the victims physically either, although some participated in their arrests.

Evasion and unwillingness do not turn the above protagonists into heroes. Most of them enabled the massacre to some degree. There was no spectacular refusal to carry out orders. No actor actively tried to prevent the massacre. They evaded both perpetration and efforts to rescue. Most of the men and women I categorize here as "evading" were not necessarily moral. Some may even have engaged in thievery and shared the spoils of the massacre; many, if not most, disliked the mulatto elite and supported a brutal regime from the beginning to the end. Yet, to dislike someone is one thing; to want them dead is another; and to kill them, yet another—especially if there is a social tie. Only one individual in Jérémie, the parliamentarian Saintange Bontemps, vocally supported the order to have his neighbors executed, letting his deep hatred of the mulatto elite and his personal ambitions motivate his actions. Yet he also avoided being present at the execution grounds. None of the other civilians amplified the scale of the orders. Unwillingness and evasion are not dissent, nor are they resistance. The wide range of reactions covered by such categories imply disagreement or discomfort with homicidal orders. I would define evasion in terms of time: the moment when ethical inhibitions collide with ideologies, resentment, political beliefs, and obedience.

Efforts to evade perpetration had one consequence that Graham Greene found tragicomic and derided in his novel on Duvalier and his regime: performance.[10] Jean Florival describes scenes where sycophants, ambitious Duvalierists, or simply state functionaries would make a show, exaggerate, perform.[11] Performance is a facial, corporeal, or discursive action whose trigger is located somewhere between uncontrolled anxiety and resilient ambition. Anxiety—not appearing

Duvalierist enough, trying to acquire symbolic capital within the Duvalierist field—is of course the most likely. Performance had to be public—typically, a vociferous demonstration of unconditional loyalty to Duvalier—to be reported to or noticed by Duvalier himself. Jacques Fourcand's grandiloquent speech to erect "a Himalaya of corpses" was a performance; Victor Never Constant, Duvalier's amanuensis who was known as a rather mild, even charming individual in private, would make rabid calls for repression once he was in public; the boastful behavior of Gérard Brunache, described at the end of chapter 7, was also performance, intended to acquire symbolic capital through sordid theatrics. I found no anecdotal information to suggest that the regime's henchmen and killers engaged in performance; they did not need to prove their allegiance.[12] However, Duvalier himself was a performer. He is credited, apocryphally or not, with encouraging his followers to be ready to kill their own children to prove their loyalty to him. If there is one society on earth where family would not come after political allegiance, it is Haiti.[13] Duvalier himself was aware of that.

Haiti has a specific term to characterize evasion: *marronage*, in French, or *mawonaj*, in Kreyol. During slavery, it referred to slaves fleeing from plantations and hiding in the back country. Used metaphorically today in common parlance, *marronage* names an individual's effort to avoid being implicated in public affairs. For Barthélémy, who theorized this behavior, the contemporary "maroon" flees from taking responsibility, from obligations, from the formal world and the public space.[14] The term has had a career beyond the colonial and revolutionary periods to name forms of land occupation or the subsistence economy.[15] Another social institution, the *lakou*, has also been seen as a form of withdrawal. The *lakou* system refers to a form of organization prominent in the countryside in which a cluster of homes allows multigenerational peasant families to be relatively autonomous from state and society. *Marronage* in its contemporary forms would then be some sort of cultural reproduction favored by a culturalist approach.

The opposite appears closer to the truth. A prime concern of actors engaged in evasion during the Duvalier regime was their social standing in the public world. Instead of fleeing from the public space, evaders were concerned with their place in it. Being seen as perpetrators would have affected their status, relationships, and ambitions. Those who grew up in the personalist world of Jérémie were keenly aware that being personally associated with social violations—repression of neighbors would certainly have been a major one—would have affected both their own reputation and relationships with other bystanding neighbors. For individuals on an ascending social trajectory, as many of the military officers were, especially in the Presidential Guard, targeting the upper class, which they sought to join and often succeeded in joining, was rather counterproductive. Some perpetrators even attempted to hide from public view during the entirety of the Jérémie massacre.[16] Jacques Fourcand, Duvalier's envoy, hid at the local hospital for three days before returning to Port-au-Prince. The four members of the Presidential Commission remained at the military base for three weeks and were never seen in town, although its own President, Pierre Biamby, and another member, René Prosper, had deep connections there. Their spectacular absence from public view was a deliberate strategy to avoid incrimination and pay a social cost. Using Bourdieu's concept of distinction in the context of repression might be unexpected.[17] It nonetheless helps to qualify and situate this type of behavior. Evasion in this case is not about acquiring symbolic capital, as in Bourdieu's view, but about not losing it. Social psychologists also argued that avoiding harmful actions can be motivated by "reputational management."[18]

There is another cause of aversion to harm, empirically correlated to the previously mentioned causes but conceptually distinct: preexisting social relationships. I addressed the cognitive impact of social ties on behavior during mass violence through a theory of ethical behavior.[19] What produces the aversion to harm a party to the relationship is a preexisting social tie, not (or not only) ethical reflection or conscious humanist beliefs, even if the act of rescuing vulnerable individuals contradicts personal beliefs, group loyalty, and execution orders. I name this phenomenon *relational exceptionalism*. To trigger relational exceptionalism, a relationship does not necessarily require reciprocity, trust, obligation, affinity, nearness, or repetition of encounters. It does require these three elements, at a minimum: some degree of intimacy, even for a short period; the relationship cannot be fraught; and autonomy from the social environment, or at least the understanding of its possibility. If the unlikelihood of social violations is determined by the level of intimacy, there should be a threshold that would trigger aversion to harm, even if this activation varies in space, time, and personal history. As Max Weber counterintuitively suspected, bonds can be both fleeting and strong.[20] What allows for relational exceptionalism is the possibility of autonomy against group solidarity. It can be present in the most fleeting relationship, in a weak or a strong tie.

This argument goes against the grain. From the classics to psychoanalysis to much contemporary scholarship to the morning paper, intimacy is a place of danger. You can be killed by your brother (Cain), your son (Oedipus), your father (Agamemnon), your mother (Medea), your husband (Louis Althusser), or your best friend (pick any classics). Every single war in the Mahabharata is fratricidal. Fratricidal also, the murders in the Shahnameh. Anthropology's ethnographic archives of set communities reveal neighbors usually dealing with hostility and envy, not just cooperation and microsolidarity.[21] A more recent tradition, spreading "power" wholesale across topics, forcing any situation anywhere at any time into the ironclad theoretical frame of "domination" and "exploitation" invalidates the possibility of noninstrumental social ties. Sherry Ortner, Michael Brown, and Marshall Sahlins have lamented this tendency to focus exclusively on power and instrumentality to the detriment of other motivations.[22] The literature on massacres of neighbors only feeds on these traditions. With such an outlook, interpersonal relationships inevitably become mere power relations or a proxy for structures, instrumentalization, and functions. And the antiquated individual "human nature," as brandished by Hobbes, still occupies front stage. Presented with the intellectual charm and professional usefulness of spectacular counterintuitions, even the most benign social practices such as hospitality are linked to hostility.[23] In this tradition, even friendship, the strongest of bonds, can be depicted in nihilistic terms: the otherwise profound Amazonist anthropologist Carlos Fausto, telling the story of a friend who calmly stated he wanted to kill him, concluded that bonds of friendship in reality cover a "mixture of intimacy and aggression," a final Hobbesian touch which reminds me of Skipper-the-Penguin's philosophy in the movie *Madagascar*, as endlessly repeated by my kids: "A friend is just an enemy who has not attacked yet."[24]

To argue against Aeschylus, Freud, Foucault (and Skipper) is an uphill battle. Yet few of us barricade ourselves every night behind our bedroom door from fear of attacks by family members, and we keep joining friends as often as we can to share laughter and food. Myths may indeed be nothing more than a function, as British structural functionalism and Claude Lévi-Strauss proposed, and not reveal objective past events as nineteenth-century scholars and René Girard believed. In an epistemological break, Randall Collins and Sinisa Malesevic show a contrario that physical violence is incredibly rare, and that if we humans are predisposed to anything, it is to a mental inhibition against physically hurting others.[25] And if it is hard to hurt someone, it is even more the case when we share a bond with them.

Most importantly, for this argument to stand, ties cannot be conceived as an undifferentiated fact. Two epistemological divisions need to be made, both of which render social ties unequal in front of liminality: differences of quality and of healthiness. Acquaintances are not friends or the like. To *know* someone is not only distinct from *having a social bond with* someone; it is of an entirely different social scale, with distinct obligations, forms of reciprocity, and psychological implications. Deleuze recognized it when affirming, "to recognize is the opposite of meeting."[26] By choice, we do not forge bonds with everyone we know, even with people we know well. In dramatic circumstances, social capital may turn out to have "a dark side," as Jérémie Foa perfectly saw in a spectacular book on the St. Bathelemy massacre; with strong ties, this is far less likely.[27] The stronger a bond grows, the less it can be violated. Similarly, nearness or repetition of encounters is no guarantee of a healthy bond. Some of the sharpest antagonisms can occur within the family. For relational exceptionalism to be triggered, the relationship cannot be fraught in the first place. Individuals can harm people they know when social ties are weak or already fraught; when social ties among neighbors are strong, harm is extremely unlikely, even when ideologies of hatred overwhelm the real-time context. The divisions I am making between acquaintances and bonds, and between fraught and healthy relationships, is purely analytical; reality is more diverse (probably infinitely so) than a two-tier typology. Nor is it an irenic theory of interpersonal relations or of human life. Atrocities happen. But they are typically perpetrated by people who do not have a social bond with their victims. Peoples, societies, states have resorted to militaries for a good reason. Civilians are not good at killing, at least not people they know.

The breakdown of the social fabric, not the power of ideologies of hatred over the individual, leads to the collapse of ethical inhibition and to mass violence by neighbors. In Haiti under Duvalier, the social fabric—that is, the sum of social ties—overall held. In Jérémie, the social fabric was battered, damaged by decades of political and racial polarization, notably the 1957 elections, but was not torn apart. Polarization, divergent opinion, and personal resentments were entangled with social relationships cutting across social sectors.[28] All the Jeremians mentioned in this book were indeed neighbors who shared social ties. They were not necessarily friends, but they knew one another. They knew each other's faces, names, and the location of their homes; they occasionally exchanged pleasantries. They may have resented the status and sometimes the wealth of their mulatto neighbors; they may have had grudges; but overall, they shared small but relatively healthy ties. Duvalier resorted to the military to have the victims killed.

There are of course many other causes for aversion to causing harm, and conscious values are usually the most recognized. Helen Fein, the first scholar who addressed the considerable variations of the fate of Jews across Nazi-occupied Europe, stressed, in Durkheimian fashion, the importance of values, solidarity, and empathy to explain the motivations of gentiles who rescued endangered Jews (who were not their neighbors or people they knew).[29] For Hanna Arendt, a central question was: what triggers aversion to harm when the chain of command orders subordinates to hurt or kill people?[30] For Arendt or Fein, ethical concerns can only come from a conscious, Kantian principle, one that is triggered by feelings of guilt or "the voice of consciousness." Arendt, quoting Eichmann (whose own choice of words was not lost on the philosopher), calls the behavior of someone who feels no guilt when participating in a killing machine that of "Pontius Pilate": "At that moment, I sensed a kind of Pontius Pilate feeling, for I felt free of all guilt," said Eichman about his responsibilities in the Holocaust.[31] The Roman governor enabled an execution of an innocent Jew, yet declared he bore no responsibility in it. Arendt later adds: "Eichmann himself adds that no inner voice came to arouse his consciousness."[32] For Arendt, the lack of ethical inhibition (my terms) among members of repression apparatuses makes mass violence possible. As controversial as this may sound to relatives of the victims of the Jérémie massacre, Abel Jérôme, Jean Dimanche, and most of Jérémie's Duvalierists, whether patricians or not, were not free of feelings of guilt during the event and in the decades following the massacre. They were aware in real time of the impact of their actions—and inactions—on both their reputation and their existing relationships. Ethical inhibitions were not strong enough to overcome their allegiance to, belief in, or fear of Duvalier; nevertheless, an examination of the available evidence, including testimonies, shows strong ambivalence in the behaviors and justifications of the actors rather than anything resembling blind obedience. An evader, at first epistemological glance, is therefore one who attempts to move, successfully or not, from the category of perpetrator to that of bystander.[33]

Rather than structure—*marronage*—it is agency that frames evading decisions typically taken at the individual level. However, characterizing a person's unwillingness to be an actor as *agency* may seem rather contradictory; certainly, it points to the limitation of the binary opposition—structure vs. agency—which itself echoes a Haitianist debate about repetitions and ruptures in Haitian history.[34] If concealment is produced by socialization or culture (*marronage*), so is relational exceptionalism. The paradoxes of evasion suggest that structure and agency may be entangled or, as Peter Berger and Thomas Luckmann believed, entertain a dialectic relationship.[35]

EXTERMINATING LINEAGE

The incident Elliott Roy recalled suggests that François Duvalier was both aware of and frustrated by evasion. Duvalier chose to hand over the bulk of repression, especially torture and killings, to no more than a dozen henchmen who each had a dyadic relationship with him. Duvalier's choice was as much a consequence of this awareness as a reproduction of a sociocentric habitus for which the relational trumps the formal. This intensely relational worldview did not just govern social ties; it also provided the regime members with a grammar to understand the logic of opponents and to scale guilt. The execution of Lucien Daumec in June 1964 as reported by Elliott Roy exemplifies this phenomenon. Within a few days, two of Daumec's kin were arrested: his brother and his sixteen-year-old stepson. Both were executed a few days later. The Jérémie massacre too was a massacre of families. The Duvalier regime often, but not systematically, chose to execute not only opponents but also their kin.

Why kill entire families? What intellectual mechanism makes victimizers assign responsibility to others than just the suspected opponent? How can children become the figure of the enemy? There are, at first glance, three distinct possible interpretations: that victimizing the kin of opponents was a mere strategy to produce terror; to preempt vengeance by kin; or that guilt was extended to kinship, a frame that rests on a nonindividual notion of the person. The distinction between the three motivations actually becomes moot after examining the cultural coordinates that inform all of them. Targeting relatives to obtain submission or to deter revenge relies on an "anthropology" (by the regime) that emphasizes, knowingly or not, what social sciences call familialism, an ideology of unmatched allegiance and attachment to family members as a behaviorial and psychological determinism. This "anthropology" concomitantly identifies people's central values. As mentioned earlier, ethnographers emphasize the centrality of the Haitian family in both social organization and ideology.[36] Beyond the private space, one's life, choices, and vision of the world are framed by the attachment to family. For Herns Marcelin, family should be considered the paradigm of both public and private life in Haiti.[37] Families, children, and mothers were therefore targeted by the Duvalier regime for the same reason they had been spared until then: because kin are supremely important.

When I interviewed him, the otherwise cautious William Régala, perhaps in order to shift my attention away from the actions of the military during the Jérémie massacre, shared a fascinating series of anecdotes about Luc Désyr, a henchman and an evangelist pastor. Régala confirmed that Désyr tortured people with a Bible in hand, a detail I had heard and read with skepticism. Once, Régala went inside the police station by the Presidential Palace and saw "an *aéropage* of VSN and officers working on (sic) a suspect." Désyr was the one torturing and pretended to quote the bible, according to Régala: "Désyr was the ideologue of the regime, you know, the ideologue of torture. He said that you had to kill the entire family, he said it, otherwise relatives would come back for vengeance, you know."[38]

Calling Désyr's statement "the regime's ideology" might have been exaggerated, but nonetheless pointed to the regime's understanding of people's allegiances and the regime's own insecurity. Familialist reactions were feared by the regime's enforcers: individuals could become opponents because a relative had been their victim earlier. Vengeance was indeed part of the motivations of seven of the thirteen Jeune Haiti guerrilla members whose fathers or brothers had been executed and, in some cases, tortured.[39] Other kin, such as Hector Riobé who in July 1963 attempted to avenge his father killed a few weeks earlier by Major Franck Romain, took up arms against the regime. Eliminating kin therefore aimed at preventing retaliation. Yet considering the killing of kin to be a tactic intended only to preempt retaliation seems a rather utilitarian explanation. The likelihood that the elderly Louis Drouin, or the mild-mannered Victor and Guy Villedrouin, all victims of the Jérémie massacre, would have retaliated against the regime for the earlier execution of their relatives was remote. The vast majority of most victims' kin did not seek vengeance, and both Désyr and Régala must have been keenly aware of it. Désyr's fear of retaliation, mentioned at the beginning of this section, does not merely identify the family as a challenge to the ruler, but also suggests an understanding of relatedness. To better explicate the practice of punishing kin, I will use two distinct corpora of knowledge: one from history and political science, on the targeting of kin in repressive regimes; the other from anthropology, on notions of the person and kinship.

The practice of punishing kin has been observed in both traditional and modern societies.[40] In ancient Greece, as Renaud Gagné brilliantly shows, guilt was passed on vertically from father to son.[41] In ancient China, during the Qin dynasty, those guilty of political treason saw their entire families executed or enslaved.[42] Collective punishment arrived in Russia from China through the Mongols, according to Horace Dewey.[43] Kin were punished for being kin during the Great Terror (1936–1938) in the Soviet Union, as Golfo Alexopoulos and Cynthia Hooper show with great precision—although children were targeted as early as the Leninist period (1917–1924) by a Bolshevik regime that promoted "the fundamental displacement of biological connections by political ones."[44] Kinship provided a sort of grammar to detect and understand the scale of the enemy for the Stalinist regime.[45] Although from inception Mao Zedong's regime victimized relatives (particularly children) of landowners and those generally categorized as reactionary or "politically deviant," the Cultural Revolution in Mao's China developed an entire theory of "blood lineage" which justified "extreme violence and ruthless massacres."[46] The children of Party officials, on the other hand, "inherited" loyalty to communism and to Mao. In Shin Dong-hyuk's memoir on life in a North Korean camp, families are systematically deported and punished for the alleged fault of one member.[47] Even kin two generations removed from a politically tainted individual can be arrested and deported to camps.[48]

The epistemological route taken by victimizers of entire kin groups is predicated on two main anthropological notions: a nonindividual conception of the person, and the attribution of collective responsibility. In this case, the person is spread over the primary group, which is usually, but not always, the kinship group. The reasoning used to identify and "scale" the enemy resembles the same one used by many "traditional" societies to form social organization, kin representation, and understanding of personhood.

Scholars who have explored non-Western conceptions of the person tend to emphasize that circles of kin are constitutive of the individual. For John Mbiti and Roger Bastide, personhood in African societies is "spread" over an entire group.[49] Whereas for, say, a Western perspective one's person is supposed to coincide with one's body—the view famously exemplified by Descartes's *cogito ergo sum*—, the person in traditional African philosophy would come into "being" only through multiple circles of kin, both alive and dead; a conception summarized by Mbiti with the formula "I am because we are."[50] Explicitly contradicting Descartes has since become a *passage obligé* for many scholars working on traditional societies. McKim Marriott on India and Marilyn Strathern on Melanesia took the "in" out of the individual; the "dividual person," for Marriott, is made of transferable elements that compose this personal substance.[51] These elements can then "travel" from one person to another according to a logic of mutuality, such as caste or family. For Strathern, the "dividual person" entails the incorporation of other persons, who are usually kin: "Far from being regarded as unique entities, Melanesian persons are as dividually as they are individually conceived. They contain generalized sociality within. Indeed, persons are frequently constructed as the plural and composite site of the relationships that produced them."[52] Sahlins, using ethnographies of kinship systems from around the world, coined what is possibly the most operative concept in the matter, "mutuality of being," to name the notion that "kinsmen are persons who belong to one another, who are members of one another, who are co-present in each other, whose lives are joined and interdependent. Ethnography tells repeatedly of such co-presence of kinsmen and the corollaries thereof in the transpersonal unities of bodies, feelings, and experience . . . kinsmen are people who live each other's lives and die each other's deaths."[53] Ties to ancestral figures are generally included in the aforementioned studies and imply an animistic understanding of nonliving entities as being in communication and altering each other's identity, a notion I will return to later.

The notions of personhood held by the Duvalier regime were within the exact same anthropological spectrum as those conceptualized by the aforementioned scholars. The regime *applied* these notions to scale guilt and identify the enemy. Repression does not stop at one individual; it spills over to this person's kin, yet would rarely go further—the enemy stopped where kinship stopped and society started. If the person is spread over her or his kin, so is this person's deeds, identity, and guilt. Yet, guilt is as collective as it is selective. We can call it *mutuality of guilt*, a notion of culpability based on a conception of personhood that coincides with a group, typically kinship; an animistic regime where being supersedes deeds and where substance (guilt) can be transferred. To characterize this practice as animistic, I rely here on a specific aspect of animism based on a rather traditional Tylorian view of it: transfer.[54] Substances can "travel" from one entity to another without the agency of either. Transfers can be immaterial and unspoken, regardless of whether such transfers happen between entities that are living or not. Nurit Bird-David convincingly links the aforementioned "dividual" notions of personhood to animism.[55] Animism, she argues, is above all a relational epistemology. (Mutuality of guilt also involves a relational epistemology—a paranoiac one). Marriott, however, emphasizes movements of particles, not just communication or reasoning.[56] In the case under study (victimizing kin), the one substance that is transferred from one person to another, from one person to her kinship group, is culpability (anti-Duvalierism, anti-Haitian hatred, etc.). Both the scale and rationale of the transfer are kinship, and the mutuality allows for the transfer to take place. We can even hypothesize that all notions of collective responsibility, whether based on ethnicity, race, class, kinship or any other group identity, are predicated on (1) nonindividual notions of the person; and (2) transfer. Without this "belief" (for lack of a better word) in such transfers, we may be stuck with the Cartesian, individualist model of responsibility.

Kinship can be a messy object of study—it is easier to know where it starts (the mother-child relation, the nuclear family) than where it ends.[57] For such, or maybe for all, societies, individuals and relationships on the edges of kinship classification systems do not seem to have a clear slot; they appear stranded in an epistemic no-man's land where the structures of kinship, so to speak here, are not absolutely clear. I am talking particularly about relationships beyond the biological, especially between affines and friends.[58] The victimizer faces the same conundrum: where should mutuality of guilt and, therefore, repression end? If guilt is spread over kin, where does kinship end? Duvalier ordered the extermination of consanguines during the Jérémie massacre. If consanguinity was the logic of repression and the names to exterminate were Drouin, Villedrouin, and Sansaricq, two individuals appear on the margins of kin classification: Edith Laforest (executed on September 19) and Gérard Guilbaud (executed on August 11). The former was Pierre Sansaricq's sister-in-law, and therefore not a consanguine. But she resided with her sister and her brother-in-law. Did residence make her more than an affine? Gérard Guilbaud was Alice Drouin's husband, and therefore also an affine.

Co-residency, an anthropological object of study that intersects with, sometimes complements, and sometimes contradicts allegiance to kin, appears as a factor in the classification system of which mutuality of guilt it the result.[59] Affines of the Jérémie victims, such as Roger Chassagne's family, who lived next door to the Villedrouins, were not arrested—nor were they ever slated for execution. In the understanding of kinship held by the regime's enforcers, the question of what to do with co-residents who are not consanguines but affines (such as Edith Laforest or Guilbaud) was posited in medias res. Domestics and helpers, who were also co-residents of victims, were not arrested; but they were not mulatto or elite either. Co-residency then became an aggravating identity and in the course of events, mutuality of guilt spread to resident affines. The presence of father-son dyads in both repression and rebellion also raises questions. Claude Rosier mentions families of peasants arrested together for alleged opposition to the regime.[60] In these cases, all the kin were men. Once, three brothers were imprisoned and left to die in Fort-Dimanche; another time, it was two brothers; and in a third case, a father and his three sons. (The only exception provided by Rosier concerns the upper-class Bajeux sisters, executed together.) If mutuality of guilt is sanctioned in a partial manner, it occurs most systematically in vertical fashion from father to son, and, to a lesser extent, horizontally among brothers.

Exterminating families of opponents was not a systematic policy. None of the kin of Alix Pasquet, Philippe Dominique, and Henri Perpignan, the authors of the first coup attempt against Duvalier in 1958, were arrested. This absence of systemization illustrates again the deeply erratic character of both the regime and Duvalier himself. Yet, two strong correlations can be made. The first is historical. If targeting families can be observed throughout the regime's existence, it seems to have reached its peak in 1963–1964. A second correlation points at family members and elite status. The Benoît, Edeline, Fandal, Bajeux, Drouin, and Villedrouin families, all of them nearly exterminated between April 1963 and October 1964, were educated and relatively well-off.[61] Belonging to the social elite was an aggravating circumstance. The case of the Fandal family is particularly striking. Educated, living in the Thiotte area, the Fandals were relatives of Emmanuel Fandal, a state cadre and a supporter of Daniel Fignolé's party (one of Duvalier's opponents during the early stages of the 1957 presidential campaign). Emmanuel Fandal was executed in Port-au-Prince, although I could not determine the exact date. The regime, then, seems to have gathered his relatives in the Thiotte area and executed them by firing squad.[62] On April 26, 1963, in the heat of an immediate reaction to an assassination attempt against Duvalier's children, Second Lieutenant François Benoît, a sharp-shooter suspected of the attempt (falsely, it quickly turned out), had his parents and other relatives killed in his house while his infant son, Gérald, was kidnapped and never seen again. The soldiers and the VSN, led by Second Lieutenant Max Dominique, Duvalier's future son-in-law, also killed François Benoît's father-in-law, René Edeline.[63] An unrelated person, Benoît Armand, was killed that day for having the same name, although only as a first name—therefore he was thought to be a kin. A year later, in the summer of 1964, five other adults of the Edeline family—one grandmother, two men, and two young women—were arrested in Port-au-Prince by VSNs and soldiers led by Lt. Harry Tassy and executed at Fort-Dimanche. The young Edeline children were also hunted but were successfully hidden by a neighbor.[64]

Not all families of elite opponents were arrested or brutalized, but mutuality of guilt was most likely to be applied when these two identities—kinship and class—were correlated. Mutuality of guilt operates through ever-larger overlapping circles: family, clan, class, ethnicity, religious identity, race. The Mongols under Genghis Khan would apply scalar collective responsibility according to their anger, with extermination of the family being the lesser one and the eradication of an entire city the greater one.[65] Class warfare coincided with the targeting of kinship groups.[66] Class enemies had their entire families disenfranchised or killed. For instance, destroying the conditions under which the kulaks could survive as a class also implied destroying the family as an entity that could potentially challenge both party and state. In the case of the Drouin, Villedrouin, and Sansaricq families, their mulatto upper-class identity framed the targeting of kin.

LEVERAGING RELATEDNESS

The world in which individuals were socialized and evolved in mid-twentieth century Haiti was highly sociocentric, perhaps more so in Jérémie but in Port-au-Prince as well. More than overlapping social networks, the relatedness of society attempts to render the idiosyncrasy of an immense number of crisscrossing links connecting people and producing social capital. In Port-au-Prince, this relatedness was more likely to create "invisible ties" within the upper half of society.[67] But in the rural areas, where VSNs, VSN chiefs, and other officials lived in villages and often came from the peasantry, relatedness was also a last resort. Families with few ties (whether direct or through networks) to officials in the government, the military, or the VSN were particularly at risk. Social capital is then a resource of the most important type: life or death. That is why the value and place given to social capital varies by location: the more precarious (economically and politically) a society, the more emphasis people will put on social capital, as a safety net of all sorts.

The relatedness of society is a result of three phenomena: the number of social ties; the fact that ties crossed socioeconomic and political divides, therefore going deep into society through invisible networks; and the relative compactness of the society in which ties are formed, whether it be Jérémie or Port-au-Prince in the mid-twentieth century. Chapter 6 showed that people of quite different backgrounds could be related by social ties—not necessarily directly, but through a third or fourth party. Port-au-Prince was a much larger city in the 1950s with a much higher level of social differentiation. Yet, in both places, the conditions were propitious for repeated face-to-face encounters. The sheer number of people *known* to average individuals in this personalistic and relational world seems to have been significant. They knew, *knew of* and knew about people within and outside their milieu. All of these are nonetheless social ties, and they often carry ethical obligations. (The person, or even family, located in position C is not only aware of the person in position A but holds for a moral place for them even if C and A are only connected through B.)

Relatedness under Duvalier could mean an aggravating circumstance or the possibility of survival—or even liberation in case of an arrest. Even before the start of this research, I encountered several accounts of prisoners, some even slated for execution, who were eventually released, and in each case it was because of a kin's or friend's intervention before an official, or Duvalier himself. There may have been cases where people were released after due process, but I admit that I never identified or heard about such a case. If symbolic capital (such as education or elite manners) could put members of the elite in harm's way, social capital was likely the only hope for anyone who was arrested. This is how Andrée Roumer, wife of Jacques-Stephen Alexis, who had been tortured to death in 1961, explains her own release:

> Someone went to tell Duvalier that Emile Roumer's niece had been arrested.[68] And Emile Roumer and Carl Brouard were the ones who had put Duvalier forward in the journal *Les Griots* (in the 1940s).[69]

Claude Rosier owes his own survival in Fort-Dimanche and the National Penitentiary to social ties. One of his relatives from the same Artibonite town was Vernet Valéry, a low-ranking VSN and an acquaintance of the infamous François Delva, a powerful VSN chief who occasionally visited Fort-Dimanche in Port-au-Prince. These ties were not enough to obtain Rosier's release, which was dependent on higher-ups, but Delva made sure that Rosier always had enough to eat and was never added to an execution list. Twice Rosier mentioned talking to Delva in prison.[70]

Louis and Liénard Numa had been arrested because they were father and brother of Marcel Numa, of Jeune Haiti.[71] The Numas belonged to the rural elite: a family of small coffee traders from the rural commune of Moron. Marcel and Liénard's sister, Neylande, was married to Pierre Chavenet (1927–1998). Chavenet, a brilliant man with a multifaceted career, was also a member of Duvalier's inner circle. In 1961, at the age of thirty-three, he was granted ambassador status.[72] The Numa had yet another connection to Duvalier: the third Numa brother, Rodrigue, was close to Windsor Laferrière in the 1950s and became a Duvalierist militant. He also became a diplomat in 1961. He had pleaded, unsuccessfully, from his post at the Haitian embassy in Ivory Coast, for Duvalier to release his brother Marcel.[73] Louis and Liénard Numa were therefore not random prisoners related by kinship to an anti-Duvalier fighter, but individuals linked through only two degrees of separation to Duvalier himself. On October 29, the latter ordered the liberation of Louis and Liénard Numa. Fritz Cinéas offered an insider's account of these negotiations.[74] Duvalier never considered sparing Marcel Numa in spite of his family ties, but he did consider punishing the latter's father and brother until others pleaded for them. Family members typically advocated for their imprisoned kin despite the risk this implied. They also pressured family friends with connections to the regime. When individuals with a connection to Duvalier did not oblige, the families took it as a betrayal.[75] Such examples testify not only to a social organization in the form of relatedness, but also to the social nature of ethical obligations.

PART V

The Relational Despot

CHAPTER 10

The Ruler's Anxiety

He lived in terror of being assassinated. Always, he thought of that, always.

Fritz Cinéas[1]

[François] Duvalier seems [to] have fanatical will to survive and is ruthless in methods. These well-known qualities are major psychological deterrent to both oppositionists and any inside [the] regime who might otherwise be tempted to move against him. Palace-inspired stories of bloodbath in Port-au-Prince if things get really bad are beginning [to] circulate and will presumably have [the] deterrent effect Duvalier intends (as in May 1963). . . . Also, we cannot completely rule out possibility that Duvalier might perpetrate act of terrorism so brutal that revulsion combined with fear could initiate chain reaction.

U.S. Ambassador Benson Timmons[2]

PERFORMANCE AND LACONISM

On Friday, September 18, 1964, in the late afternoon, Second Lieutenant Abel Jérôme parked his jeep in front of Gérard Léonidas's home, in the center of Jérémie.[3] Léonidas and Jean-Claude Fignolé, both friends of Jérôme, were already chatting on the veranda. The executions of the Drouin and Villedrouin families had occurred more than a month earlier. Jérémie seemed to have returned to normalcy. The three young men started to chat as they did almost every late afternoon when Jérôme's aide-de-camp suddenly arrived on foot, carrying a message sent from Port-au-Prince. Jérôme had received the coded message earlier in the afternoon, and had sent it to the base for decoding. The noncommissioned officer handed him the decoded version. The story of this late afternoon was told to me first by Fignolé and then, years later, by Jérôme. Their versions coincide, although the two men neither met nor communicated after 1965. Jérôme opened the envelope, read the message silently, then sat down. The two other men then took the message from his hand and read it: "Upon receipt of this order, disappear Sansaricq family."[4]

Fignolé told me he was embarrassed that what had first caught his attention and that of Léonidas was the error of syntax. This error was the reason, he believed, the words "got printed in [his] memory." Even though Fignolé and Jérôme were certain that the order had been signed by Duvalier himself, I remained open to the possibility that someone else in Duvalier's inner circle had written it, made the syntactic error, and sent it.

The phrasing contains a historiographic reference. In 1848, during a military campaign against the mulatto elite in the country's south,[5] President Faustin Soulouque sent to headquarters an order to execute David Troy, a former member of his government who was already in prison: "Upon receipt of this order, execute David Troy."

The stylistic similarity between the two orders is striking, and suggests that the person who wrote the 1964 execution order knew his country's historiography. As explained earlier, noirist authors, including Duvalier, wrote and read history. By 1964, Soulouque's 1848 execution order had been quoted in two major historical works, one by Justin Chrysostome Dorsainvil, the other by Dantès Bellegarde.[6] It had appeared earlier in a lesser-known work by Justin Bouzon, although neither Dorsainvil nor Bellegarde made mention of this source.[7] Duvalier, in *La mission des élites* (published in 1948 on a different topic), took a quote from the exact page where Dorsainvil mentioned Soulouque's execution order.[8] Then later on in the same book, when talking about the "mulatto and bourgeois animosity," Duvalier quotes another passage from the same page in Dorsainvil's book. The order to execute David Troy appears in a footnote at the bottom of that page, which obviously Duvalier had thoroughly read.[9]

Duvalier had the kind of personality to be inspired by such lethal and cynical laconism. Soulouque's order to have David Troy—a man who had once been his confidant, political ally, and who was already being held defenseless in prison— shot by a firing squad without trial is deeply tragic. To be inspired by such a situation and laconic style betrays a megalomaniac personality for whom murder is an end unto itself. I will return to Duvalier's order at the end of this chapter, but first I will examine the normative role of historiography in Duvalier's thoughts and actions to better understand how he made the decision to have a family of fourteen people killed.

FETISHISM OF HISTORY

If Louis Joseph Janvier and Arthur de Gobineau were Duvalier's *maîtres-à-penser*, as chapter 3 shows, two former rulers, Faustin Soulouque (1782–1867) and Lysius Salomon (1815–1888), were his *maîtres-à-agir*. In both his written works and public speeches, Duvalier referenced a variety of authors and thinkers; but when he elaborated on past policies of interest to him, Soulouque and Salomon were his most ubiquitous references.[10] Duvalier's interpretation of the events of April 1848 (under Soulouque), and of September 1883 (under Salomon), are key to understanding the most repressive actions undertaken by his own regime.[11] Both Soulouque and Salomon unleashed terror against the elite. Both had a visceral distrust of elite and mulatto sectors that they thought could turn against them at any time.[12] Both created precedents of ruthless repression against the elite and mulattoes.[13] Both men reacted to threats—real, perceived, or fabricated—by mulatto opponents; in both cases, the response was brutal. Duvalier believed that mulattoes were racially inclined to dominate, and therefore would seek to terminate a noir presidency.[14] For Duvalier, the threat to his rule was real and proven by history. Duvalier praised Soulouque's use of terror and sound political judgement, which was, he believed, determined by his racial background: "Fortunately, Soulouque, coming from the depth of his Race because of Mandingo origin, this fertile Tribe that gave so many leaders of peoples, responded to the arrogance of the Elites that he was not of the kind to be used. As skillful and astute as his ancestors."[15]

I referred earlier to the conclusion Léon-François Hoffman drew from his study of Haitian history and cultural production: that history reproduces itself and is "relived not in its admirable universalist aspects but, unfortunately through the most lamentable struggles of predatory factions."[16] By referencing Hoffman's judgement here, I do not imply that history in Haiti would be some sort of Freudian eternal recurrence or that structure trumps agency. However, if historiography is consciously taken by cultured actors as a political vade mecum, then actions and policies are more likely to be imitated. Duvalier in fact believed history was circular, a "perpetual return" (*recommencement*).[17] He did not read it as being in the past, but as contemporary sociology, a manual packed with diagnoses about potential enemies and with solutions on how to deal with them—a template. Repetitions, or the impression of historical déjà vu, were more likely to occur with Duvalier's fetishist relationship to historiography—a fetishism that looks like ideology. Salomon in particular represented an appealing model. That a highly educated man such as Salomon considered it legitimate to use terror against the elite must have increased the power and appeal of authoritarianism in Duvalier's mind.

MEGALOMANIA AND THE LIBERALITY OF THREATS

On Sunday, April 23, 1882, President Salomon, while on a political tour in the north, gave a public speech in which he explicitly threatened to burn Cap-Haitien, the country's second-largest city (and its most beautiful), and kill its population if an insurgency against him were to start there. This might be one of the most incendiary speeches given by a head of state in Haiti's history:

> I know all of those who are trying to destabilize my government . . . Woe to (*malheur à*) Cap if a single shot is fired from here. This shot would be the signal of a massacre and a fire. I will add, since I owe you the truth, my friends, that it also will be the start of looting. . . . Cap is a dark stain on the Republic. . . . The only strongman in this country is me and I will prove it by breaking all the horns whatever their length. . . . At the current moment, if a single shot is fired from Cap, none of my generals will be powerful enough to contain the punishment that will be inflicted on the town. All those who would try to oppose it would be whitened (destroyed). . . . Cap is a dark stain on the Republic, an obstacle to the nation's progress. . . . To help me, I have the force of the bayonets and the love of the nation. . . . [District commanders (*commandants d'arrondissements*)], I expect you to march by my side when I punish those perverts. . . . Blood will flow from the explosion of the gunpowder, and this blood is a very intoxicating drink. Once you start drinking it, you feel a consuming thirst. If a single shot is fired in Cap, I would be incapable of stopping evil. . . . What I am saying is not meant to intimidate, but to

warn. . . . If a single shot is fired, none of my military generals, not even the President of Haiti will have the power to oppose the reprisals (*châtiment*) that will be inflicted upon the rebellious city.[18]

This quadruple threat—mass executions, setting a city ablaze, mass looting, outsourcing violence to extralegal forces—would be fulfilled to the letter seventeen months later in the nation's capital. The speech also highlights Salomon's megalomania, a personality trait evidenced by his self-referencing, including praising his own humility and calling himself "father of the motherland."[19]

Historically, the imaginary of fire is grounded in the war of independence, blazes being associated with freedom, fighting, collective unity, and victory. The 1791 slave uprising began when rebels set plantations on fire.[20] It was as much "scorched earth" as "scorched town" policy. On February 6, 1802, Henri Christophe, the northern kingdom's future king, ordered his troops to burn Cap-Haitien "and led by example by setting his own house on fire."[21] Léogane is set on fire on February 9. The same month, Jacques Maurepas, one of Toussaint Louverture's generals, burns Port-de-Paix to the ground. General André Vernet burns Gonaives in February 1802 after having evacuated the city. Saint-Marc and the surrounding towns are burned in 1803, again to prevent the French from using them. Toussaint orders his troops to burn Port-au-Prince if the French expeditionary corps were to occupy it.[22] To lead by example, several officers and leaders set their own houses on fire: not only Christophe, but also Maurepas, Vernet, and Jean-Jacques Dessalines. Finally, the Act of Independence itself makes setting towns on fire a military tactic as well as a patriotic duty: "People should make blood flow, set fire to seven-eighths of the globe; they will be innocent before God who did not create men to see them groan under a shameful yoke."[23] Article 28 of the 1805 Constitution reflects the routinization of setting cities on fire: "At the first cannon shot, cities disappear and the nation stands up."[24] Over a century later, in 1919, this call was normative enough for Charlemagne Péralte, leader of an insurrection against the U.S. Occupation (1915–1934) to brandish it again: "Setting our cities on fire should not matter! At the first cannon shot, cities disappear and the nation stands up."[25] One of Dessalines's famous mottoes, "*Koupe tèt, boule kay*" (cut heads, set houses on fire), is today commodified as a theme of popular culture on T-shirts and in songs. Two interlocutors educated in the 1950s stated that, during high school, the self-destruction of Haitian cities was evoked with pride by history teachers. Eddy Cavé related how professors at the École des hautes études internationales in the 1960s conceived the act of setting fire as part of the national heritage.[26] To a large extent, at least for Duvalier's generation (and probably beyond), the relation to historiography can be characterized as "cultural intimacy," to use Michael Herzfeld's self-explanatory notion. Herzfeld's other key concept, "body impolitic," also comes to mind: cultural heritage as a millstone around the neck.[27]

Threats of fires, mass destruction, and mass murder against the population were articulated throughout the Duvalier regime by Duvalier himself and members of his inner circle. Threats increased or decreased depending on the level of real-time political insecurity—or rather, how insecurity was perceived. Duvalier replicated Salomon's 1882 points to the letter when he was faced in mid-1964 with two insurgencies (the regime thought it was one single movement): he threatened to set Port-au-Prince on fire if he were attacked in the capital.[28] From 1963 onward, Duvalier regularly alluded to mass repression against the civilian population, not to counter the insurgencies themselves but their possible support among the populace. On October 22, 1964, he instructed his advisers that, in the event of an invasion of Port-au-Prince, mulattoes and their properties had to be destroyed.[29] In the middle of the day on October 26, soldiers brought a piece of artillery to a major intersection in Port-au-Prince and pointed it "toward mulatto residential districts."[30] On July 7, 1965, Jacques Fourcand—a medical surgeon, Duvalier's confidant throughout the 1960s, and the president of the National Society of the Haitian Red Cross—made in a public speech what must be one of the crudest calls for mass murder by an official in the annals of twentieth-century history:

> The earth will burn from the north to the south, from east to west, the flames of fire will purify evil, the dead will be buried under a mountain of ashes, blood will flow as it never did before, rivers of blood will (incomprehensible—applause). Haiti will know days of apocalypse, the chaos will be such that nobody will recognize the day from the night, there will be neither dawn nor sunset, one single immense flame. . . . The earth will burn because our cause is just. . . . This day [there] will be a Himalaya of corpses and (incomprehensible) will be the biggest bonfire of all time.[31]

Fourcand's hallucinatory speech reflected a turn in the regime's history wherein evoking mass death and destruction became a legitimate discourse. It points at an unexceptional phenomenon: variation across time. Duvalier did not have one set opinion of the mulatto elite all his life; it varied. Similarly, his anxieties about being challenged varied over the course of his regime. The words uttered by and actions taken under Soulouque, Salomon, Sam, and Duvalier nonetheless reflect the intersection of two phenomena: a deep-seated political insecurity fueled by a siege mentality; and continual mental calculations about how far to go to obtain submission.

MILITARISM, DUVALIER STYLE: THE DESPOT WHO LIVED IN MILITARY BARRACKS

To understand Duvalier's insecurity and how it affected his decisions, including orders to execute families in Jérémie, we first need to focus on the physical and social world in which he lived, worked, and socialized during his entire presidency. This world was the Presidential Palace.

Duvalier's political anxieties as a ruler crystalized nine months after he was sworn in. In July 1958, a ragtag group of three ex-military officers and four foreign adventurers carried out the first of several coup attempts against him. To consider it the most important turn in his fourteen-year presidency would not be an exaggeration. Even if it was short-lived, small, and amateurish—casual, even—it nonetheless shook Duvalier and his supporters enough to trigger major organizational changes.[32] Duvalier reconceived the spatial organization and the human composition of Haiti's massive Presidential Palace. To a large extent, and contrary to a historiography that presents Duvalier as deeply distrustful of the FAd'H [Forces armées d'Haiti] (Haitian Armed Forces), Duvalier increased the visibility and size of the military presence both in his palace and in his regime.[33] On December 15, 1958, he formally abolished the Maison Militaire (Military House), composed of forty-five soldiers and twenty-one officers.[34] In its place, he created the Presidential Guard, formed of one battalion of over 400 men and twenty-five to thirty officers who took their orders directly from the president.[35] The entire first floor was now occupied by soldiers and low-ranking VSNs (Volontaires de Sécurité Nationale, or National Security Volunteers) who, at night, slept on military cots, a routine that lasted until the early 1970s.[36]

The Duvalier family was housed on the second floor of the northern wing.[37] (This had also been the case with previous heads of state.) Day and night, an officer, usually a lieutenant or a second lieutenant, was on duty outside the only door to the Duvalier apartment. Immediately in front was the office of Duvalier's personal secretary. Adjacent to it was Duvalier's own office, whose door was also guarded by a military officer.[38] All of this was on the second floor of the northern wing. The Executive Secretary's office was located in the center of the second floor, its main entrance guarded by two officers who stood at attention in the visitors' waiting room. As for the palace's southern wing, it was the realm of the Presidential Guard's officers. Two large rooms were used during the day by officers carrying out various duties related to governance, while another large room served as dormitories for officers on night duty. Therefore, at night, dozens of officers, soldiers, and VSNs slept on both floors of the Presidential Palace, with officers always only a few yards away from the Duvaliers. During the day, every employee of the Presidential Palace worked surrounded by soldiers and officers. (Persistent oral accounts lamented that having young officers living side by side with Duvalier's daughters created a highly dysfunctional environment.) Every time one of the family members went somewhere in town, even on an errand, one or more officers on duty in the palace accompanied them. I calaculated that at least 75 percent of the space in the Presidential Palace was occupied by the military. To a foreign visitor—and there were only a few during Duvalier's entire rule—it must have looked like informal military barracks adjacent to the official military barracks, the Casernes Dessalines. This reorganization alone testifies to Duvalier's anxieties.

Haiti's well-documented militarism therefore did not end with Duvalier's alleged distrust of that institution.[39] To imagine that a regime as insecure as Duvalier's would discount the military or think of it as a nuisance or a threat ignores how crucial the military was to the regime's survival. Duvalier's entire rule was populated by soldiers, not just his palace. The siege mentality that characterized the regime started early, as mentioned, and engulfed the entire Duvalierist world, but particularly its inner circle. In addition, whether by education or conviction, Duvalier was fascinated by military ethos and affairs, a penchant perhaps overlooked by the historiography. Testimonies collected from his inner circle leave little doubt that he was fascinated by the officers' *prestance* (allure, charisma). Like the rest of the nation, Duvalier associated the Haitian military with sovereignty, history, and glory.

The regime did carry out repeated purges of the military through forced dismissals and executions. Soon after he was sworn in, Duvalier started purging the military hierarchy of the very officers who had helped him rig the 1957 elections, notably General Antonio Kébreau, head of the provisional government then. Pressoir Pierre gave an insider account of these early purges, which he helped organize as the head of the Presidential Palace's "Military Bureau" until he himself became a victim of it and sent to Paris on a diplomatic mission in April 1958.[40] Duvalier also started to purge the military of mulatto officers early.[41] At the military academy, the graduating class of 1959 (which had entered in 1957) was entirely cleansed of mulattoes"—most of its highest-ranked graduates would be assigned to the Presidential Guard and would serve Duvalier directly. After 1961, the targeting of mulatto officers increased; it would culminate on April 26, 1963 with a massacre of hundreds of active and retired officers. Yet there were still a handful of mulatto officers in the military, including General Pierre Merceron, '41, (1916–2001).[42] Merceron had been a devoted Duvalierist since the mid-1950s and highly compromised in the 1957 presidential campaign.[43] He was chosen by Duvalier as the military's Chief of Staff (1958–1959), a position he held until he was purged and sent to France on a diplomatic mission in 1961.[44]

These actions, which decapitated the institution at the beginning of the regime, had their own rationality, even if paranoia played a part in Duvalier's decisions: reassuring an anxious ruler and securing a regime. This phenomenon is not confined to Haiti or Duvalier but typical of a strongman who, upon ascending to power, distrusts existing institutions of organized violence not yet under his control. For this reason, Duvalier also created his own institution, the VSN, entirely devoted to him. All this reveals Duvalier's major preoccupation: contrary to all of its discourse about revolution, the regime was fixated on politics and its own survival—not culture.

TO ENDURE

In 1971, the Haitianist scholar David Nicholls published an in medias res analysis of the regime in which he contrasted totalitarianism and despotism.[45] The Duvalier regime, Nicholls argued, falls largely into the second category. The fact that a refutation of the totalitarian paradigm was articulated so early on suggests that academic and journalistic circles were already trying to capture what type of regime they were dealing with. Leslie Manigat had already characterized Duvalierism as "a [form of] tropical fascism."[46] Gérard Pierre-Charles called it "a third-world version of totalitarianism."[47] Michel-Rolph Trouillot later categorized it straightforwardly as a totalitarian regime.[48] Although he did not provide a theoretical framework for his assertion, nor did he make reference to studies (either recent or foundational) on totalitarianism, Trouillot's argument acquired traction. Nicholls later reviewed Trouillot's argument in order to strongly refute it, while Jean-Germain Gros emphasized that the economy remained almost entirely in private hands.[49] Robert Fatton returned to the question to take apart, gently but firmly, Trouillot's totalitarian paradigm: none of the markers of totalitarianism—the single party, the attempt to control the totality of life, the establishment of a police state—existed in Duvalier's regime.[50] In any case, my analysis here is not about the nature of the regime or its putative slot in a classification system, a question that political science is better equipped to address than anthropology. Yet if the regime was not concerned with changing Haitian culture or implementing preset policies, what were its goals and how do they explain the Jérémie massacre?

At first glance, and unexceptionally, terror was a means to an end; and the end was to endure, not to implement, a program. Duvalier never really conceived or articulated a plan, nor did he seek to create a so-called New Man in the manner of totalitarian regimes. As examined in chapter 3, neither Duvalier nor anyone in the noirist movement had a concrete political agenda. Totalitarianisms want citizens to be engaged; despots want them to be disengaged, argued Nicholls. To state that Duvalier's main objective was to persist in power is nothing new. Contemporary observers of the regime noticed this in real-time, as U.S. Ambassador Timmons noted in this chapter's epigraph. In 1966, Duvalier was asked in an interview with a British journalist who his successor might be. Duvalier answers with a smile: "All my successors, they are now studying at school."[51]

Nevertheless, the notion that Duvalier's sole goal once in power was to keep it has analytical implications that have perhaps been overlooked. In that regard, Nicholls made two counterintuitive points that highlight the regime's governance and repression:

- a despotic regime is less predictable than a totalitarian one; and
- it is solely concerned with its own survival and is indifferent to a society's culture.

Nicholls insisted, as Bernard Diederich would later, that Duvalier attempted to control state and civil institutions—the military, universities, unions, the Church, the business community, the Scouts—solely because they posed or could pose a challenge to his personal authority, not because he sought to reshape Haitian culture.[52] Institution-building, a hallmark of totalitarianism and many dictatorships, is entirely missing in the history of the regime. Trouillot recognized that Duvalier did not really bother to implement policies, without realizing that this would be rather strange for a totalitarian regime. In addition, and crucially, Duvalier did not have relations with institutions but with persons. A hallmark of his regime was, in fact, a *lack* of ideology, with the exception of noirism, (a rather adaptable) nationalism, and (when his interlocuters were Americans) anticommunism. His inner circle was an ideological potpourri to a degree almost certainly unmatched in the annals of twentieth-century regimes anywhere, ranging from communists or former communists (Hervé Boyer, Jacques Oriol, Paul Blanchet) and socialists (such as Frédéric Desvarieux) to Maurassians such as Gérard de Catalogne and Duvalier himself.[53]

If the most efficient strategy for remaining in power is to ensure the political disengagement of the wider public, the most efficient means of achieving this, in Duvalier's calculation, was to exercise terror. The latter was achieved through the unpredictability of (1) its targets, (2) its scale, (3) its timing, and (4) the personalities of unstable henchmen; all of these factors hastened the necessary disengagement of the population. In this configuration, the political innocence of the Sansaricqs—a family without any known political activity—was an added advantage. In addition, for Duvalier and his regime, who saw themselves as the product of the masses, opposition to Black presidents could only emanate from the country's elite. With such a political imaginary, Duvalier and his regime could not conceive of a threat originating from the very sector they themselves came from. It is rather telling that the massacre of mulatto officers on April 26, 1963 was a response to political crisis and intense anxiety generated in the immediate aftermath of an aborted coup organized by four military officers, none of whom was a mulatto.[54]

Nicholls's views on dictatorial rule complements those of the Italian classicist and anti-Fascist Guglielmo Ferrero: the more unsecure a government, the more insecurity it creates.[55] Fear becomes policy when rulers are afraid. The repressive turn of the Duvalier regime in 1963, which saw a dramatic increase in both the extent and the unpredictability of repression, and then the anti-"mulatto" summer of 1964 followed six coup attempts or guerrilla movements, four of which in 1963 and 1964.[56] The other point raised by Ferrero, who compared the rules of

Mussolini, Napoleon, ancient Rome, and the French Revolution, concerns subjectivity: the dangers faced by the ruler are often imaginary. An insecure ruler is not just a subjective one, but one whose subjectivity verges on paranoia. Most of the coup attempts and insurgencies mentioned previously were minor, if not insignificant in size and were marked, for most, by perplexing delusion. Members and observers of the regime nonetheless noted the panic these coups created in the government. How could they have possibly created such panic? Ferrero identifies two reasons that both apply to Duvalier.

For Ferrero, it is precisely this lack of legitimacy that creates political and moral vertigo in the ruler's mind: "Power conquered by a *Coup d'Etat* has the diabolical power to frighten the one who had seized it before frightening others."[57] The coup that created the most insecurity in Duvalier's mind may have been the only one that succeeded during his rule: his own. In June 1964, Duvalier had installed himself as "President-for-Life" after having de facto abolished the Haitian Republic as it was, violated its Constitution, and brutalized all its long-standing state and civil institutions from the Parliament to the Catholic Church. Yet, through a series of historical actions in 1964, most importantly abolishing presidential elections, Duvalier had relinquished any pretense of basing his rule on popular legitimacy.[58] The root source of the ruler's anxiety is thus the awareness of his own illegitimacy. Ferrero's epistemology, based on the notion of societal rules, may seem dated. He was also persecuted by Mussolini's regime, which influenced his views in medias res. Yet Ferrero attempted to explain a contradiction: *why do dictatorial rulers systematically use terror if they already are the masters?* If power originates neither from God, nor the gods, nor the people, but from the ruler himself, insecurity will be inherent to his rule. There is no peaceful autocrat.

Most importantly, anxiety is shared by the ruler's followers and inner circle.[59] And the ruler is aware of it. Duvalier had many dedicated supporters, possibly thousands, although these things are difficult to measure retrospectively. Yet, conviction and belief were not the question. When a ruler is (or feels) besieged, how far is his base willing to go? When the thirteen fighters of Jeune Haiti roamed among the southern peasantry for nearly three months, they were not attacked a single time by locals—even as their numbers quickly dwindled, even when only two were left alive. Anne Fuller makes the same point about the Fred Baptiste insurgency in the southeastern part of Haiti in June 1964.[60] In the twelve documented attempts to overthrow or attack Duvalier over the entire length of his regime, neither the historiography nor oral history offers an example of a spontaneous, collective response where people rallied to help the regime.[61] This was hardly unique. Jean Price-Mars, noting the low numbers of participants in civil wars, perfectly captured this societal evasion at the end of his book on the Boyer-Bazelais uprising: "Where was, where always is the Haitian people during this type of attempts?"[62]

It is difficult, when doing close readings of the available primary sources or listening to oral history, to consider the most emblematic civil wars (such as the ones involving Sylvain Salnave in 1869, Lysius Salomon and Jean-Pierre Boyer-Bazelais in 1883, Nord Alexis in 1902 and 1908, and even those led by Soulouque in 1848 or Vilbrun Guillaume Sam in 1915), as large-scale events.[63] What passes for "civil war" was largely limited to infra-elite conflicts, that did not involve large segments of society, the main exception being rebellions in the immediate decades after the country's independence in the southwest and the resistance to the US occupation led by Charlemagne Péralte in the late 1910s. To a considerable extent, the wider public was detached from the mobilizations and passions that gripped the country's various elite sectors, as the works of Roger Gaillard illustrate. I am not saying nor implying that fear or apathy inhibited the larger population. Rather, forms of indifference, withdrawal, evasion, or the result of calculations involving larger anthropological phenomena in which social structures and immanence, rather than political transcendence, are instantiated, may more accurately capture this phenomenon. The successive waves of panic that shook the Duvalier regime with each of the various attempts against it, reflected an awareness of this phenomenon.[64] The government was on its own, and knew it. Duvalier did not trust his followers, the VSNs, or the military to defend his rule, let alone fight to the death for it. This was probably its main source of anxiety, linked to all the other ones evoked here.

BESIEGED

The inability of the various social sectors that compose Haitian society (and not just the elite, taken here as a vast socioeconomic sector rather than as an emic category) to agree on the basic constitutional principles that determine a government's legitimacy, especially as it concerns principles for the transition of power, has been a feature of Haitian political history since its independence.[65] Political legitimacy remained ancillary to the personalization of power—what seemed to matter most to elite sectors was *who* occupied the presidency. This was a central topic in Duvalier's own work as well, as examined in chapter 3. Diederich, referring to the desires of the entire political field in the 1950s, called the Presidential Palace "the prize."[66] There was only one. And perhaps the most salient consequences of this total lack of consensus on the foundations of political legitimacy have been insecurity and anxiety—a core feature of presidents and governments, as well as a central motivation for repressing opponents. Of the forty-nine rulers of Haiti from its independence in 1804 to Duvalier's election in 1957, forty-nine were overthrown, at least twenty-four left in exile, and three were killed while in power. Not a single one handed over the reins of the presidency in an orderly manner. The entire work of Robert Fatton is dedicated to the ruptures created by an authoritarian political culture.[67] Not until René Préval, whose first presidential mandate ran from 1996 to 2001, did a head of state enter and leave the Haitian presidency according to constitutional rules—in the presence of a highly visible United Nations peacekeeping force, and in the absence of the Haitian military, which had been dismantled.[68]

Political insecurity ran through the real-time experience of every ruler from 1804 to Duvalier. A man who ascended to the presidency could only be aware of the precariousness of his rule. The situation faced by Vilbrun Guillaume Sam in 1915 might be less known than those of Soulouque, Salomon, and Duvalier, but is no less edifying. Educated by the rapid succession of six presidents in four years, facing mounting opposition only five months into his presidency, Sam was facing the same choice as his predecessors: leave the presidency unceremoniously and go into exile, or activate disproportionate repression. He opted for the latter and ordered the execution of hundreds of individuals, the vast majority from urban elite sectors.[69] The actions and words of Soulouque, Salomon, Sam, and Duvalier illustrate this political insecurity and not just their lack of moral inhibitions.[70] There are, of course other larger, more ideological contexts for the fact that a president's political legitimacy has been structurally questioned. Also playing a role are strongly egalitarian ideologies and, possibly, notions of self-worth, themselves distinct from the personalization of power explored by Fatton.[71] Strong egalitarian ideologies render the presidency vulnerable by making it open to all.[72] In Haiti, the idiosyncratic conditions of a small country and a restricted middle class also worked to desacralize the presidency and banalize the figure of the president.

My argument here actually does not differ fundamentally from Fatton's view of Haitian political history as being characterized by an "authoritarian habitus."[73]

Rather, it explores this notion further: what happens to rulers who can only be cognizant of that habitus? What happens to rulers who are aware that their opponents are also governed by this habitus rather than, say, a belief in established constitutional principles? The siege mentality of the Duvalier regime was not just the product of events happening in real-time, but also of an established mindset that classified these facts according to an awareness of the authoritarian habitus. Most rulers were likely aware of it, but to turn that awareness into active state violence requires a particular personality. This would explain why state violence was not a universal occurrence throughout Haitian history; rather, it was restricted to only a handful of these forty-nine rulers. For them, viable threats—opponents—could only arise from among the elite. As a result, they did not turn against the peasantry, which was more exploited and disenfranchised than repressed. This points to one of the structural causes of the recurrent victimization of the elite in Haiti's postcolonial history. For the most ruthless rulers, targeting, intimidating, exiling, or killing the elites were strategies for political control of the entire society; the other social sectors were perceived as less prone to opposition.

THE SIDE OF INSECURITY

How does one govern under such conditions? By either accepting to leave the presidency unceremoniously in the face of virulent opposition and go into exile, possibly forever; or by adjusting repression to a level perceived to be necessary to remain in power. Exile was a fact of Haitian political life, as Matthew Smith recounts.[74] When Duvalier was elected in September 1957, his two predecessors, Daniel Fignolé and Paul Magloire, were in exile. A ruler's response can therefore be located on a spectrum with acceptance on one end, and the "fanatical will to survive," as U.S. Ambassador Timmons called it, on the other. This spectrum of political choice may therefore be coterminous with one of ethical inhibition.

Another possible reason for Duvalier's insecurity was his awareness that few were willing to risk their lives to defend his regime. He might have had widespread support in the peasantry, as Rony Gilot, Pascal-Trouillot and Trouillot, and Duvalier himself argued, but putting one's own body in play is another story and requires having a different type of relationship with the collective.[75] How was it possible that small, almost insignificant insurgencies took the government months to disband? Both the Fred Baptiste and the Jeune Haiti insurgencies, each composed of fewer than fifteen exhausted, demoralized individuals running out of ammunition, managed to survive for months among the peasant population. They surely failed to recruit any peasants; but just as surely, they moved freely among the peasantry, finding food and shelter without any concern. On July 29, 1958 a ragtag group of seven men, four of whom did not speak the country's languages, threatened the palace. Although Duvalier supporters rushed to defend it, they only did so after one o'clock in the afternoon once the number of the coup plotters became known—and not on July 28. This same lack of alacrity was also seen in the military's formal responses to coup attempts: with each attempt, it struggled to produce zeal in its counterinsurgency operations. Not all of this can be blamed on the military's legendary incompetence, but rather on the motivations (or lack thereof) of its members. The lack of engagement on both sides (against the regime, and to defend it) raises questions about evasion, if not the source of transcendence itself, that are beyond the scope of this book but still nevertheless pertain to anthropology.

Several observers have argued (or implied) that Duvalier exercised violence in an irrational manner. Diederich finds no satisfactory explanation for the many arrests and executions ordered by Duvalier, which therefore appear absurd.[76] Trouillot recognized that people could be executed with no shadow of a pretext required without realizing the purpose of such modus operandi, suggesting, rather, some pathological underpinning.[77] As an example, Trouillot states that an entire soccer team was exterminated without sufficient pretext—yet he does not provide key details of the event itself (what team, when, and where), and arrives at the conclusion that there is no satisfactory response to how and why such events occurred. Nicholls takes the opposite perspective: he situates unpredictability at the center of the repression's modus operandi, and through this, identifies the regime's rationality. The more unpredictable the repression, the more effective the terror—an argument that is certainly more banal and, academically, less spectacular. But unpredictability does not mean that the arrests and slaughter were indiscriminate, nor that the violence was limitless, as any comparison with the worst authoritarian regimes in the twentieth century quickly show. Unpredictability is causal to the establishment of terror because it implies and relies on a certain level of indiscriminate killing: some people were victimized *because* they were not political opponents. In addition, Duvalier's empowerment of unpredictable, temperamental henchmen was the condition for this dimension of terror, as the next chapter will analyze.

SECURITY AND IDEOLOGY

The distinction this book makes between ideology (anti-elitism, noirism, etc.) and politics (the regime's political anxieties) is mainly thematic and conceptual. The Duvalier regime illustrates well the dialectic (and certainly not simply "dynamic") relation between ideology, which varied in intensity throughout his rule, and security (politics). The bouncing back and forth between ideology and politics not only affected each of them but made them morph into distinct entities that created a new situation, mass killing. Insecurity alone would make a ruler go after opponents (individuals); a modern ideology makes him go after a group (mulattoes); and a cultural logic makes him go after their families. Political scientist Jonathan Maynard emphasizes the role of security over ideology in understanding mass killing: believers are political opportunists rather than orthodox followers; ideologies lack agency and remain dependent on politics in times of violent liminality: "Mass killing must be understood as a form of ideologically radicalized security politics . . . [they] are strategies to achieve familiar security-centric aims, such as defeating perceived enemies, upholding regimes, policing societies, and winning wars."[78]

General evasion and the need for internal peace can tamp down ideological motivation. When real or perceived threats emerge, political process—or "the event," as post-Annales historians had it—would be the point of convergence between ideology and security politics, with unpredictable results. More precisely, the ideology's classification system (since an ideology, as any belief, is always endowed with one) would move to the center, becoming both a nodal space and nodal moment. Let me explain (and justify this structuralist bias): the classification system is activated through the immediate pressure of political developments. Information received is unconsciously dispatched in medias res to fixed entries established long ago in the classification system. The more immediate and urgent a piece of information is, the less time is available for its political assessment, and the more likely it is to be sent through a cognitive triage system consisting of a preexisting classification system—in other words, to the ideology. Security panic—such as those triggered by an insurgency and the urgent need to respond to it—suddenly gives ideology a leading role.[79] The mulatto elite occupied a preestablished slot, that of visceral, hateful opponent, which left them perpetually at risk. Conversely, this is also the reason why Duvalier praised the peasantry: his classification system allocated them to a no-threat slot.

WHY THE SANSARICQS?

Why did Duvalier execute the Sansaricq family? Although circumstantial evidence presented at the beginning of this chapter identifies Duvalier as the author of the Sansaricq family's execution order, it does not provide a motive. In the case of the Drouin and Villedrouin families, the will to destroy them finds its immediate context in a process with the counterinsurgency at its center. The Sansaricqs, however, are killed over a month later, once the identities of all the insurgents had already become known (without a single Sansaricq among them) and after this insurgency had already been defeated. There is absolutely no direct evidence or witness testimony that suggests the government believed there were Sansaricqs in this (or any other) guerrilla insurgency—or even in the opposition in 1964.[80]

Duvalier made the decision to execute the Sansaricq family in September 1964 with a contradictory mix of impulsion and cold calculation, of subjectivity (insecurity and hatred) and opportunism:

(1) a confluence of identities assigned to the Sansaricqs: mulattoes, upper-class, the richest family in a specific town;

(2) the town most closely associated with mulatto opposition to a noirist ruler;

(3) at a moment when the political cost for this mass murder was deemed to be low, and the feasibility of inflicting terror high;

(4) concomitantly, exercising the tactical power of terror—exterminating a prominent family with no known political involvement—was likely to further violate social norms and produce compliance from elite sectors.

Duvalier's political anxiety and his hatred of mulattoes are key to understanding why he made this decision at this particular moment. In October 1964, Duvalier's decision to spare Louis and Liénard Numa, father and brother of the Jeune Haiti guerrilla Marcel Numa,[81] unambiguously shows the racial standard and logic used by the regime's repression apparatus. One of the very few non-mulatto families that was, to my knowledge, killed by the regime for the supposed action of one its members was François Benoît's family on April 26, 1963. Benoît's relatives were killed and his newborn son was disappeared. Yet this killing happened in medias res; it was not a premeditated decision such as the one involving the Sansaricqs.[82]

I now return to the debate between functionalist and intentionalist approaches in mass violence studies. I first evoked this debate in chapter 10 to analyze motivations of soldiers at the ground level; I do so now to highlight the causal differences for the various phases of the massacre. Functionalists argue that the targeting of civilians is part of a larger and longer political process that turns mass killing into a state's solution at a specific moment. In this context, the chronology of events frames the considerations made by the decision-takers. The intentionalist paradigm, on the other hand, believes in the primacy of ideological causes of mass killings—in the case of the Holocaust, this approach argues that extermination was the plan all along, while German soldiers were moved by visceral hatred against Jews. If this same binary were imported to a study of the Jérémie massacre, the real-time counterinsurgency context since June 1964 would unambiguously point to the functionalist paradigm. The repetition of two insurgencies a few weeks apart, no matter how insignificant they actually were, fed the regime's insecurity and increased a sense of illegitimacy that could only be solved through disproportionate repression. However, the functionalist theory struggles to make sense of Duvalier's *choice* to exterminate the Sansaricqs on September 19. There was no more insurgency or counterinsurgency, then. There indeed were three, or maybe even four, massacres under the apocryphal name of a single one, the Jérémie vespers. Between the first and the second wave, we moved from the functionalist paradigm to another situation with elements from the intentionalist paradigm. Duvalier's successive lethal orders for each of these waves were motivated by a concatenation of multiple elements: a will to power; structural political insecurity; entrenched bias against the mulatto elite in general, and Jérémie's light-skinned mulattoes in particular; information against specific families fed to Duvalier by informers in Jérémie and within the Presidential Palace itself; the breakdown of social and civil institutions that Duvalier had already damaged,; as well as more latent causes, such as desire for revenge and social resentment. Between the first and the second wave of executions in Jérémie, the weight of each of the above elements varied and different intents revealed themselves. State massacres are a means to free governance of political anxieties.

CHAPTER 11

Sociocentric Repression

R epression and sociality were intertwined during the Duvalier regime. Social ties framed the categories we typically use to characterize behavior during mass violence: perpetration, by-standing, recruitment of enforcers, choice of targets, resistance to perpetration, and evasion. The recruitment process of perpetrators and the identification of targets followed webs of personal relationships. Duvalier's decision-making process was also sociocentric as he sought advice from members of the regime. He also had a marked tendency to target opponents he knew or knew of. Orders were executed, evaded, or resisted at the local level in correlation with existing social ties. Horizontal bonds (between people) and vertical bonds (to Duvalier) framed the relation to repression.

Crucially, most of the executions were carried out by a few individuals only. Duvalier had a "knack" for identifying henchmen, individuals with no background in killing or torture but who would nonetheless excel at these tasks. Each of the henchmen, without exception, had a personal relationship with Duvalier. Duvalier, it seems, could not empower someone he did not have a personal, even if deeply asymmetric, bond with. That most of the killings were done by henchmen singularizes this dictatorship. It is fair to say that they were devoted to him. The orders they received were often vague, which left some margin of interpretation to enforcers on the ground. However, objective observers of the regime and of the FAD'H (Forces Armées d'Haïti; or Haitian Armed Forces) in particular agree that neither soldiers nor officers could act on their own without orders, especially when targets included more than one socially visible victim. Whether out of military ethos and discipline, fear of retaliation from the unpredictable Duvalier, or the ambition to ingratiate themselves, high-ranking officers followed orders blindly but did not go beyond. In that respect, zeal, if defined as going beyond strict orders, was expressed verbally rather than through deeds.

This last chapter analyzes the relational dimension of the Duvalier regime. It also aims at understanding how Duvalier made his decisions, including lethal ones. The September 1964 order to execute the Sansaricq family, fourteen individuals in total, could not have been made without consulting widely, as Duvalier typically did.

NEVER ALONE

Robert Rotberg's assessment about how Duvalier exercised his authority exemplifies a widespread opinion about his solitary exercise of power:

> "No one shares Duvalier's power or helps him to exercise it in anything other than a menial way . . . Duvalier operates on his own, not on behalf of a clique, as had his predecessors. He alone (like Haile Selassie in Ethiopia, Kamuza Banda in Malawi, and others) decides whether the funds will be provided for new storm sewers; whether generators will be transported to the Peligre dam via Port-au-Prince or St. Marc; whether foreigners will receive economic concessions, local businessmen special favors, and ordinary Haitians exit permits. He personally examines and decides whether or not to authorize minor research projects, grants university degrees, selects the kind of material to be used for a new highway, and determines the orthography to be used for literacy training in Creole."[1]

Today, testimonies from former inner-circle members say otherwise. Duvalier was everything but aloof and did not make decisions "alone." To a large extent, Duvalier operated almost exclusively within realms of intimacy. He was immersed in sociality for the entirety of his regime and of his life, a relational man in a relational culture. He thought, functioned, and ruled within this cultural repertoire. In this sense, Duvalier was sociocentric. Prior to 1957, Duvalier had many friends and acquaintances, and moved in social circles shaped by shared intellectual views and sociological backgrounds.[2] After 1957, the Presidential Palace was a place of socialization. Even the militarization of the Presidential Palace increased the number of people in Duvalier's lived experience and certainly did not increase his social isolation. The only time Duvalier lived by himself things did not go well. In early 1943, Duvalier had received a fellowship from a U.S. foundation to study in a master's program in public health at the University of Michigan. The archives from the university's School of Public Health show that six to eight months into his program he dropped out suddenly, leaving snowy Ann Harbor without letting his adviser and the administration know.[3] It was also the only time in his life he traveled abroad, although what he exactly saw of and learned from the United States is not clear. He later left no later indication, written or oral, about this stay abroad.[4]

On the other hand, Rotberg's argument perfectly captures Duvalier's actual micromanagement of public affairs. Duvalier did not delegate, except possibly for complex corruption schemes, as Leslie Péan meticulously shows.[5] He strove to oversee and control every single level of government, even the most local, attempting to demonstrate competency in infrastructure, agriculture, irrigation systems, sewage, education, diplomacy, defense, security, and public health. No policy realm was outside his expertise—or interference. Duvalier's micromanagement of public affairs increased the scale of his interpersonal interactions as they involved constant meetings, exchanges, and all types of communications with officials. This modus operandi also considerably undermined state institutions, since Duvalier had a marked tendency not to follow chains of command and established hierarchies. To a large extent, Duvalier did not have relations with institutions, but with the *persons* at their helm.

The sociologist and historian Siniša Malešević elegantly solved the apparent contradiction in the coexistence of sociality (associated in the Durkheimian tradition with irenic situations) and killing (typically linked in the Hobbesian approach to our individual nature):

> "[M]uch of human violence is profoundly social in character. Being social does not automatically imply an innate propensity toward harmony and peace. On the contrary, it is our sociality, not individuality, which makes us both compassionate altruists and enthusiastic killers . . . In contrast to Machiavelli's and Hobbes's diagnosis, a solitary individual is unlikely to fight . . . We fight and slaughter best when in the presence of others—to impress, to please, to conform, to hide fear, to profit, to avoid shame and for many other reasons too . . . ."[6]

Although he primarily focuses on micro-solidarity among soldiers, Malešević relativizes the roles played by beliefs, obedience, and, culture in the collective production of violence. Duvalier's inner circle and his repression apparatus were not soldiers in combat conditions and generally did not risk much, but they were still milieus of intense socialization.

KNOWING THE INFORMERS

Duvalier constantly sought and obtained information from family members, friends, intimates, his inner circle, and his followers—the Duvalierist world. Mostly, he organized his rule and relations so they would have to provide him with intelligence, facts, and opinions. This was a central aspect of his rule, as revealed in every interview with members of the inner circle and their children. Duvalier could summon anyone, at any moment of the day or night, and from anywhere in the country in order to have a conversation and obtain information about a situation or specific individuals. Duvalier would also send individuals from his inner circle to operate in the countryside, in the provinces, or in ministries to keep a watchful eye over local conditions and behaviors. Even individuals with whom he had built personal relationships decades before the start of his political life could be asked to come to the Presidential Palace and talk on a given subject of interest to Duvalier. People close to Duvalier obtained favors, status, resources, power, and other benefits; they also informed his decisions, policies, and actions.

General William Régala, '59, put it best. Known for his role in Haiti's National Council of Government (Conseil National de Gouvernement, or CNG) from 1986 to 1990, of which he was an influential member, Régala had also been Jean-Claude Duvalier's chief of Secret Services in the 1970s. Less known was Régala's time in the Presidential Guard as a young officer throughout the 1960s, during which he had almost daily interactions with Duvalier: an ideal position from which to observe the regime. I interviewed him at his home in 2016. When I brought up the subject of François Duvalier, he immediately stated: "Ah! well, I practiced (*sic*) Duvalier a lot." Even in this context, I found the verb "practice" both unexpected and precise. After one second of hesitation, Régala rectified: "Actually, it was *him* who practiced *me* a lot." The sentence actually highlights how Duvalier functioned. It betrays an asymmetric, yet intimate dyad—"he" and "me"—between the ruler and the subaltern, thirty-five years younger. Régala emphasized something expressed by many: Duvalier studied the people around him, became close to them, and used them. Duvalier had carefully built an aura of psychological prowess and perceptivity. Régala hinted that his relationship with Duvalier was hierarchical but also friendly, although Régala was aware that intimacy did not guarantee security. Régala, as did the other former members of the Presidential Guard I interviewed, made clear that fear was not necessarily instilled in Duvalier's subordinates through the rawness and hard-handedness of power but, to the contrary, through a subtler intimacy. This "psychological" dimension of relationships with Duvalier may tell us about the latter's personality; it also suggests that the relational trumped the institutional.

This was confirmed later when I asked Régala about the summer of 1964. After years of examining the pieces of the Jérémie puzzle, I still could not understand why Duvalier had sent Régala, then a second lieutenant in the Presidential Guard, to Jérémie on August 9, 1964. Régala was a member neither of the Presidential Commission nor of the anti-insurgency operation against Jeune Haiti, nor was he assigned to the town's military base. Régala, therefore, would not respond to any authority in Jérémie and would not participate in the executions of civilians. That, I knew already. Why then did Duvalier send him to Jérémie?

> "[Duvalier] summoned me to his office, I arrive. 'You must go immediately to Jérémie!' he said. He said that I was to report [to him] on the counterinsurgency operations, however, well . . . well, I had to stay in Jérémie (not follow the military in the hills) . . . I eventually understood I actually had to report on the work of the Presidential Commission, I understood later, you know he did not make things always clear-clear, but it was understood."

Régala should have responded to his military hierarchy. Instead, Duvalier bypassed the latter and made Régala report to him directly. Members of the inner circle, of the Presidential Guard, of the military hierarchy, and of the regime also knew about generalized internal spying. It created constant stress and led to caution, if not lack of initiative on the ground; it also decreased the likelihood that members of the repression apparatus would deviate since they were more likely to be denounced.[7] This situation was entirely Duvalier's doing, and further diminished the possibility that the military or the National Security Volunteers (Volontaires de la Sécurité Nationale, or VSN) could have acted on their own without referring to or receiving orders from Duvalier himself. Scholars of the regime such as Michèle Oriol and the former members I interviewed, all dismissed the idea that the military or the VSN could have taken the initiative to commit a massacre at any point in the course of the regime. Duvalier's orders, notoriously vague and open to interpretation, had to be issued and received for the military to act on a large scale.

At the beginning of the counterinsurgency operations in the Southwest in August 1964, Duvalier entertained at least seven dyadic relationships with individuals already in or sent to Jérémie: Pierre Biamby, the head of the Presidential Commission; Second Lieutenant Abel Jérôme; Pierre Fourcand; Sanette Balmir; Second Lieutenant. William Régala, Captain Sony Borge, and Saintange Bontemps. In addition, Duvalier also had a personal relationship (albeit less frequent communication) with four other local individuals: Raoul Cédras, the mayor; Dalvanor Etienne, a member of the Parliament; Antoine Jean-Charles, the government commissioner; and Antoine Apollon, a Duvalierist. These ties, none of which was secret, dispersed power and illustrate Duvalier's inclination to entertain personal rather than institutional relationships.

The regime exemplified the term sycophant twice: in its contemporary sense of someone obsequiously currying favor, and in its original, Greek sense of informer. To be part of his inner circle, one had to be a dedicated informer while members of the regime often had to actually report on other members. Another insightful diplomatic cable signed by U.S. Ambassador Benson Timmons, on August 15, 1964 perceived this aspect of the regime: "Through system of informants and by encouraging officials to tattle on each other, Duvalier [is] in good position to detect and eliminate threats arising in his own ranks. As in past moments of stress tendency of those around him will be to play it safe rather than risk their own and their families' necks."[8] Members of the regime knew one another, often socialized together, and sometimes married within this group. Yet they were also made to distrust and report on one another; some deeply disliked other members and maneuvered to take their positions.[9] Distrust and bonds coexisted. None of Duvalier's governments over his 14-year rule lasted more than 11 months.[10] The constant turnover in government positions led to endless competition, and since appointments were determined by a personal relationship to Duvalier, *coups bas* could be carried out to discredit a competitor.

Denunciations were intimate, and demotions often left their victims wondering what they had done. In 1967, inner-circle members convinced Duvalier that twenty Presidential Guard officers were planning a coup, adding to endemic allegations of inappropriate relationships with Duvalier's daughters. Nineteen of them were executed.[11] Duvalier only found out later that the accusation was specious.

The required internal spying constituted an ethics of distrust, an implicit code of conduct made of fear and malevolence—an anti-ethics. The philosopher Peter Sloterdijk distinguishes between endo-ethics and exo-ethics in the armed apparatus of authoritarian regimes.[12] To be effective, this apparatus needs to follow two totally different codes of ethics: toward the sectors to be suppressed, administrators and soldiers could feel no mercy and had to carry out orders under any circumstances; toward one another, on the other hand, feelings were crucial as they had to be concerned for and show support to fellow members of the apparatus. Between the two ethics, there could be no communication: the border was sealed, even if endo-ethics was the condition for exo-ethics. Endo-ethics is therefore distinct from ideology. While ideology is the larger set of beliefs that concern the existence of the regime itself, endo-ethics is the inner code of conduct expected from perpetrators when dealing with and thinking of each other. Sloterdijk takes as an example a speech given by Heinrich Himmler in October 1943 to the Nazi elite. In this address, Himmler espoused the sub-humanity of Jews and described how to behave and feel toward them (exo-ethics). He also stressed that Nazis should conceive of themselves as a group and behave within it (endo-ethics), emphasizing group cohesion and shared biological and cultural heritage. This binary acknowledges that perpetrators are capable of empathy; only that empathy is reserved for the inner group.

Duvalierism did not have endo-ethics. The figure of Duvalier himself was the ethics, and beyond him endo- and exo-ethics conflated. The only state institution with an established endo-ethics prior to 1957, and thus competing with Duvalierist allegiance, was the military with its inner esprit de corps. Not surprisingly, Duvalier had the military entirely and repeatedly purged.[13] The absence of endo-ethics likely prevented the possibility of a cohesive repression apparatus. If endo-ethics among Nazi troops and officers was necessary to kill unprecedented numbers of people, its absence within Duvalier's repression apparatus (and within Duvalierism in general) may have contributed, along with other factors, to the relatively restricted scale of killing.

THE HENCHMEN AS PERSONS

Closer examination of the regime's perpetrators reveals two closely correlated patterns: (1) their small number; (2) each of them, without exception, had a close, personal relationship with Duvalier.

The literature of mass violence emphasizes that large numbers of participants are necessary to kill vast numbers of people.[14] Yet the number of perpetrators responsible for a large number (possibly even a majority) of the Duvalier regime's victims were astonishingly few: about a dozen (table 11.1).[15] To better understand this phenomenon, I distinguish between four different modes of killing by the regime, as table 11.3 shows.

1. Executions by henchmen;
2. Punctual killings of opportunity by members of the regime, typically for material or temperamental reasons;
3. Natural deaths of prisoners at Fort-Dimanche;
4. Massacres (table 11.2) carried out by the military or an ad hoc mix of soldiers and VSNs.

Massacres were perpetrated by large numbers of people—typically by dozens, possibly hundreds of soldiers (or a mix of soldiers and VSNs)—but they account for a small minority of the victims. The perpetrators I categorize as "henchmen" are responsible for over 5,000 deaths, possibly many more. The idea that all or even most members of the military and the VSN were engaged in killings is vastly inaccurate. In oral history, the historiography of repression, and, importantly, the testimonies I collected from members of the regime, four individuals are consistently named as executioners: Jean Tassy, Franck Romain, Luc Désyr, and Elois Maître. A few other henchmen and one henchwoman were also involved, but to a far lesser extent. These killings were highly localized: most occurred at four locations in Port-au-Prince, with the vast majority of them occurring at Fort-Dimanche and at night; the three others were: the Police station by the Presidential Palace, the Secret Police's station located in the city center, and the National Penitentiary.

The killers were not located at the remote end of a long administrative chain; instead, they were directly under the despot's supervision. Duvalier "entrusted"

TABLE 11.1 The President's henchmen

Henchmen	Years active	Position	Main locations of killings
Jean Tassy	1959–68	Military officer	Station of secret police
Luc Désyr	1956–1971	Head of Secret Police	Fort-Dimanche and station of secret police
Frank Romain	1958–1971	Military officer	Presidential Palace and Port-au-Prince region
Astrel "Casamayor" Benjamin	?–1971	Head of local VSN	Les Cayes region
Eloïs Maître	1956–1971	VSN	Fort-Dimanche and station of secret police.
Rosalie Bousquet		VSN	Fort-Dimanche
Clément Barbot	1956–1960	Founder and national head of VSNs	Presidential Palace and Port-au-Prince region
Zacharie Delva	1957–1971	Head of local VSN	Gonaives and Artibonite region
Lucien Chauvet	1957–1963	Government minister	Fort-Dimanche; Active in April 1963 massacre.
Lionel Wooley	?–1971	VSN	Presidential Palace, Casernes Dessalines, and Port-au-Prince
Jean B. Valmé	1959–1971	Military officer	Port-au-Prince
José "Sony" Borges	1956–1967	Military officer	Port-au-Prince; active in Thiotte massacre

TABLE 11.2 Massacres

Dates of events	Locations	Number killed	Perpetrators
April 26, 1963		150–400	Military + VSN
June 1964	Thiotte/Southeast	> 300	Military + VSN from Artibonite
Summer 1964	Jérémie	27	Military
June 19, 1967	Fort-Dimanche	19 Presidential Guards	Military
April 5–7, 1969	Cazale	105	Military + VSN from Port-au-Prince
April 14, 1969	Fort-Dimanche	30	Military
June 29, 1969	Outside Port-au-Prince	150 prisoners	Unknown
July 22, 1969	Ganthier	80–100	Military and VSN

See Jean-Philippe Belleau, "Massacres Perpetrated in Twentieth-Century Haiti," Mass Violence and Resistance, Research Network, 2008. https://www.sciencespo.fr/mass-violence-war-massacre-resistance/en/document/massacres-perpetrated-20th-century-haiti.html

For the Thiotte massacre, I use information provided by Anne Fuller, personal and email communications with author, Port-au-Prince, 2016–2023.

TABLE 11.3 Number of victims, 1957–1971

	Minimum	Maximum
Massacres	600	1,400
Executions at Fort-Dimanche (mainly by henchmen)	4,160	14,500
Natural deaths at Fort-Dimanche	820	21,900
Executions in other locations (mainly by henchmen)	1,500	2,900
Killings of opportunity and rage by VSNs, officers, soldiers, and regime members	120	8,200

the act of habitual killing to people he knew well. Having a personal relationship with Duvalier was a criterion for becoming a henchman—likely why there were so few of them. They were more than willing to kill; several could probably even be characterized as sadistic. Put slightly differently, to be able to kill "on a regular basis," one "needed" to have a bond with Duvalier himself. The regime's *basses oeuvres* were rarely outsourced beyond this group to more anonymous, institutional killers (the military and the VSN). Indeed, Duvalier's henchmen were not organized under a common umbrella, whether that of an institution or a supporting actor in the regime, but instead reported—with extraordinary frequency—directly and separately to Duvalier himself. This modus operandi distinguishes the Duvalier regime from many, possibly most, other authoritarian regimes. Under Duvalier, repression in general and killings in particular were relational. One possible interpretation, suggested by Duvalier's abovementioned frustration witnessed by Elliott Roy, was that Duvalier did not trust random members of the military and of the VSN to kill.

This personalist configuration offers a very different problematization of repression from that based on functionaries and bureaucracy as offered by Hannah Arendt.[16] For Arendt, bureaucracy was the necessary articulation between personalities and perpetration; ordinary people can be turned into mass murderers *only* if they are first transformed into functionaries. Evil becomes banal through the "grind" of inhibitions and ethics produced by bureaucracy, conformity, and obedience to a chain of command, an essential dimension of which is the anonymization of faces and tasks. There really was not any anonymity within the Duvalier regime, especially within the apparatus of repression. The henchmen were also part of the inner circle and attended social functions, mixing with intellectuals and intimates of Duvalier.

I will offer a detailed biographic sketch to delineate the place of these henchmen in the regime. Jean "Son'n" Tassy was head of the secret police (1962–1966), whose headquarters was close to the Presidential Palace. Tassy was born in 1931 into the urban, lower-middle class of Port-de-Paix, and graduated second of his cohort at the military academy. As did many other officers, he joined the country's elite by becoming a military officer and through marriage. During the 1957 presidential campaign, he sided with Louis Dejoie, the so-called upper-class candidate. A year after Duvalier was sworn in, Tassy was drafted into the Presidential Guard and in 1961 became head of the political police and of criminal investigations.[17] He had a falling-out with Duvalier in 1968 and fled into exile. He therefore committed his crimes between 1961 and 1968.

Tassy was an executioner and a prominent member of Duvalier's inner circle. His marriage to Marie-Anne "Marthe" Guillaume in April 27, 1961 was celebrated with full pomp.[18] His best man (*témoin*) was Aurèle Joseph (1910–1977), a longtime intimate of Duvalier and godfather of Jean-Claude Duvalier.[19] Tassy reported to Duvalier nearly every day, sometimes several times a day, walking the few hundred yards from the secret police station to the palace. Officers on duty would see him coming in and out of Duvalier's office. I could not determine the reason for such frequent encounters, other than telling Duvalier who had been arrested, reporting on their confession, and taking orders.

Beyond the historiography's succinct anecdotes, I learned about Tassy from my interlocutors, especially Francis Charles. After graduating from the military academy, Francis Charles, '59, was assigned to the Presidential Palace where he performed regular duties. He was never posted in the provinces and was never part of the repressive apparatus. When I met Charles, then 80, in January 2019, he appeared incredibly high-strung, giving the impression that he was ready to explode at any moment. The endless political and social chaos of the past thirty years, a subject I was not really interested in but to which he constantly returned, had left him infuriated. Still today a Duvalierist, still distrustful of mulatto officers, Charles came from the lower-middle class of Port-au-Prince and attributed his professional achievements to the promotion of *La Classe* members by Duvalier. He was also incredibly candid about the brutality of the regime, sparing no detail and no individual, including Duvalier himself. Charles eventually erupted during our first interview when I mentioned Jean Tassy: "A murderer!" (*un assassin*), leaning his body forward. He shouted the word perhaps three or four times. Then, for the next half-hour, like a broken pipe, a flow of anecdotes poured forth:

"[Jean Tassy] was boasting (*se vantait*) that he had executed a young groom, [whom he had] arrested on his way to his wedding. He was mocking his mustache. He had arrested him a few hours earlier and had brought him to the [Secret Police] station. He killed him, he was making fun of his mustache, of his tie, how he wore his tie when he was arrested . . . he [had] arrested him like this (snapping his fingers), he said it, like this, [Tassy] just did not like him and arrested him . . . I was on duty [in the Presidential Palace], he arrived, he stopped . . . told me the story . . . He mocked [this man's] fear . . . yes, [Jean Tassy] had tortured him before he executed (*abattu*) him on the station premises."

At another point, Charles had to bring communication from the Presidential Palace to the secret police station and saw Tassy torturing "a young notary" who still had his suit on. The interaction lasted a few seconds; Charles handed Duvalier's message to Tassy, who was unembarrassed, and opened it in front of him. Charles emphasized what others had stated earlier: the regime's henchmen had considerable freedom to execute whomever they wished. I asked Charles who the other executioners were: "Romain. Désir. The other ones, I did not know personally." Charles was not the only interlocutor who testified that perpetration was not a hidden secret confined to a small group, and that torturers and executioners talked openly about it.

I collected another damning account from a rather unlikely source: William Régala, then an officer in the Presidential Guard. Régala shared information about Luc Désyr, at some point head of the Secret Police.[20] This "confession" came as our conversation had finally become friendly and Régala let his guard down momentarily:

"Désyr was the ideologue of the regime, you know, [he] was the ideologue of torture. He said that you had to kill the entire family, he said it, otherwise relatives (*les parents*) would come back for vengeance, you know.

- Was it true that he tortured with a Bible in hand?

- (Smile) I saw it. I saw it myself. I saw it like I see you now. He quoted the Bible while torturing. (Smile). He was a pastor, you know. Evangelical. Quite a fellow.

- You were in the same room when he was torturing?

- I was bringing a message.

- Were there other people with him in that room?
- Yes.
- Who were . . .
- I don't remember."

Franck Romain's behavior during the April 26–27, 1963 massacre in Port-au-Prince exemplifies both the personal control Duvalier exercised over henchmen and the venal dimension of some of the killings. In 1986, a visual witness named Yvon Guerrier gave an interview on Haiti-Inter radio in which he offered a long and detailed description of Romain's actions during these two days.[21] Romain, then a lieutenant, commanded a roadblock in Lamentin, south of Port-au-Prince with a group of soldiers and attachés, including government employees such as Guerrier who had been drafted ad hoc. At least eight individuals were arrested, robbed, and executed on that roadblock. All were from upper-class sectors, none had any known political activities, and three were adolescents. Their fate depended exclusively on Romain's arbitrariness, who alone decided their fates. On the evening of April 26, Guerrier tried to intervene to save a fourteen-year-old boy, William Théodore, whose mother Guerrier knew. As he was timidly trying to find a way to convince Romain and extract Théodore from his grip, Guerrier followed Romain who was driving back and forth between the roadblock and Duvalier's presidential office over these two days. At some point on the morning of April 27, Romain discovered Guerrier's scheming and threatened Guerrier. Shaken and fearing for his life, Guerrier brought the dispute directly to Duvalier himself—Guerrier had managed to obtained immediate and direct access to the ruler through an intermediary (his own boss in the ministry where he was employed). In the presidential office, Guerrier was able to defend himself. Since Duvalier was affable with Guerrier, Romain left him alone. But from the discussion between the three of them, Guerrier was also able reconstruct the entire conversation that had taken place earlier between Romain and Duvalier. Romain was sharing the profits stolen from the individuals arrested and killed at the roadblock directly with Duvalier himself, who had told Romain what to do. Guerrier's stunning account of the dialogue shows that Duvalier felt comfortable openly discussing the sharing of spoils.[22] Among what Romain had looted that day were cars, cash, and jewelry. The fate of their owners, on the other hand, was not discussed in the office. On the second or third day (April 27 or 28), Romain took the safe from the factory belonging to the victim Hector Riobé and recruited two plumbers to open it up that night using a blowtorch; once the safe was opened, he gunned the men down and had their bodies removed.

The regime's main execution ground was located at Fort-Dimanche, a large military compound with several buildings. The main one was a prison. Four written memoirs and two oral testimonies by former prisoners describe survival, torture, and the modus operandi of executions.[23] Many, possibly most of the regime's executions took place there. Victims were either brought directly to the execution grounds, and then killed without being imprisoned; or taken from their cells on site after a period of prison detention that could vary from a few hours to several years. No death certificate was issued; the victims killed on the execution grounds were simply "disappeared," as Diederich put it.[24]

Disease and malnutrition were probably the primary causes of death at Fort-Dimanche. Robert Duval states that seven to eight individuals died every day during the eight months he was at Fort-Dimanche; Patrick Lemoine's memoir gives a much lower estimate. Prisoners were crammed into ten cells three yards by four yards in size; each cell held twelve to forty prisoners. A prisoner received about 300 calories per day, and water only once a day. As Max Bourjolly put it, "you did not send someone to Fort-Dimanche if you wanted him to stay alive."[25] To survive imprisonment at Fort-Dimanche, an exceptional immunity system and extraordinary luck were not enough: protection and support from a guard, who was either paid or related to the prisoner's family or social network, were required. Survival was exceptional under Jean-Claude Duvalier, but almost nonexistent under his father's rule. There is no known survivor of Fort-Dimanche for the François Duvalier years, with perhaps the exception of Claude Rosier, who survived 195 days there before being transferred to the National Penitentiary.

Rosalie Bousquet (1926–1986), a.k.a. Madame Max Adolphe, is remembered as having been Fort-Dimanche's warden since at least 1963 until at least 1971. However, military officers occupied that official function and Bousquet had unformal power, including over the official warden. Bousquet was close to Duvalier. Since her function in the regime was exclusively linked to its repression apparatus, her participation in all manner of festivities organized by the regime (including concerts and other events in which writers and other luminaries participated) shows how socially integrated the henchmen were.[26]

Beyond this group and outside of the few instances of large-scale massacres, killings were rarer. More often, killings by members of the regime (and VSNs in particular) occurred in more mundane contexts, including banditry, competition with a rival, off-the-cuff anger, drunkenness, or what the U.S. ambassador called "rowdy behavior." This is a vastly under-researched topic. These killings are even harder to document since they occurred throughout the national territory and were not ordered by Duvalier himself. Land grabbing was also a motive for the murder of peasants by local VSNs in the countryside.[27] The absence of a land registry since independence has always made the transition of property highly problematic.[28] In addition, when entire families were killed for political reasons, as in the case of the Benoît, Jumelle, Sansaricq, and Villedrouin families, their properties were legally nationalized and then packaged as land redistribution—typically to regime supporters, and certainly not to landless peasants. Importantly, Duvalier almost always created a legal framework for his actions, including land appropriation. Members of the regime also "requisitioned" properties at will. One former Presidential Guard who wishes to remain anonymous on this subject narrated how a combination of a race to wealth and naked impunity encouraged many within Duvalier's inner circle to develop elaborate schemes. He cited the case of Monestime, a lieutenant in the Presidential Guard who killed three brothers because they were the heirs to a large piece of land in Montagne Noire, near Port-au-Prince, that Monestime had been coveting. Monestime acquired the land after the victims' deaths. To the best of this witness's knowledge, this was the only time Monestime was directly responsible for a killing.[29]

KNOWING THE VICTIMS

Duvalier knew, or knew of, many of the victims whose executions he ordered. He had met Colonel Roger Villedrouin at least once in the course of the 1957 presidential campaign, complimented his integrity, and then had him executed in April 1963, even though Villedrouin was living a recluse's life in Jérémie after his retirement with no political activities.[30] The hunt for the other candidates of the 1957 campaign, Louis Dejoie and Clément Jumelle, whom he had also met repeatedly during negotiations, seemed to have been a personal affair.[31] (He had been close to Jumelle and his family since the 1940s, when both families lived in the same neighborhood. Duvalier nonetheless ordered the execution of Jumelle and his brothers.) Duvalier also *knew of* a large number of his regime's victims; among these, the number of victims from the elite, regardless of skin complexion, was disproportionate. He knew of their socioeconomic standing, their skin color, and their position in society. The perception, or understanding, by his aides, henchmen, and members of his inner circle of Duvalier's resentment towards specific people may also have motivated their zeal.

The same might be said of many authoritarian rulers who knew *of* many of their regime's victims simply because they were known public figures with political engagement. The musician Victor Jara and Pablo Neruda, both victims of the Pinochet regime in Chile, come to mind; or Curzio Malaparte in Mussolini's Italy: all were public figures who must have been known to the people who targeted them. In any case, they were not arrested because they were known but because they were communists or antifascist. In Duvalier's case, the victims he knew (or knew of) were not all public figures, or were very minor public figures. And yet, being a public figure increased the chances of being targeted by the regime, even for those without any known political activity. This was the case, for instance, of Joe Gaetjens, a soccer player; Ernest Sabalat, a popular lawyer; and Pierre Sansaricq in Jérémie.

At the time of his arrest, Joe Gaetjens (1924–1964) was one of the most famous Haitians of all time, a soccer player of international fame, and the goal-scorer for the United States in a famous upset at the 1950 World Cup when the U.S. unexpectedly defeated England.[32] For Diederich, "To this day, nobody knows the reason why the President for Life François Duvalier condemned him to death. Actually, many of the 'disappeared' never knew what triggered the dictator's wrath."[33] Joe Gaetjens was arrested on July 8, 1964, imprisoned at Fort-Dimanche, and probably executed the same day. He had no known political activities, although his extended family had supported Louis Dejoie, of whom he was a fifth-degree cousin. (However, the very relatives who openly supported Louis Dejoie were not arrested.) From the outside, the extended Gaetjens family appeared to be the essence of the mulatto family: fair-skinned and Dejoieist, although they were not wealthy and Joe Gaetjens himself was not an opponent. Leslie Gaetjens wonders if his father was accused by an army officer and childhood friend, Daniel Nicolas.[34] Diederich suspects that Gaetjens's fame may have worked against him instead of protecting him, as happened in the case of Jacques Stephen Alexis.[35]

Jacques Stephen Alexis, arguably the most famous Haitian writer at the time of his torture and killing in 1961, was also known to Duvalier.[36] Alexis had written a personal, accusatory letter from exile to the dictator.[37] International fame did not provide any guarantee against execution, especially in the area where

242 The Relational Despot

Duvalier had ambitions, the literary world. To the contrary, it seems to have increased the likelihood of incurring the dictator's wrath, who did not fear the consequences on his image.

Individuals with a high degree of notability were at risk, even if they had no political activity, no political opponent among their relatives, and were not mulatto. Ernest Sabalat was an attorney with a reputation for impassioned, eloquent argumentation during trials. Once, after winning a verdict at a Port-au-Prince court, he was carried on people's shoulders in the street.[38] Days after, VSNs attacked the family home at night. Sabalat, who was armed, defended it with his older son and the VSNs ran away. A few days later, he was disappeared and his two teenage sons, Jean-Robert and Serge, went into exile in West Africa.[39] Was it jealousy on Duvalier's part? Resentment, antipathy, and envy operated with a personalist logic rather than a more ideological one. In any case, the execution of known public figures who had no known political involvement and no close kinship ties to opponents made repression appear absurd and created panic in urban society.

Finally, Duvalier had to have known of Pierre Sansaricq at least since 1957. I did not encounter any evidence or any account that suggested that Duvalier ever met Pierre Sansaricq or any other Sansaricq. Yet it is almost impossible that Duvalier did not know of them, having visited Jérémie several times in the 1940s when he worked as a physician.[40] Duvalier returned in 1957 to campaign there and had lunch at the Cédras family home in Bordes, in a visit organized by Jérémie's military commander at the time, Captain Kesner Blain.[41] That year, a local judge, Catinat Sansaricq (three generations removed from Pierre Sansaricq) had several Duvalier supporters, arrested after they set the local high school on fire.[42] Finally, Pierre Sansaricq was a prominent citizen of Jérémie. Duvalier must therefore have heard of him before 1964. In the summer and fall of that year, he must have heard more.

THE ENCOUNTER BETWEEN THE SANSARICQS AND DUVALIER'S RELATIONAL GOVERNANCE

A despot may hold powers of life and death over his subjects, his prerogatives may be vast, and in the end, he decides alone; but this does not mean he governs alone, even less that he does not listen. Duvalier ordered executions typically after talking and listening to several individuals.[43] Duvalier did not make the decision to kill entire entire elite families in Jérémie, a choice of major magnitude for the country, without having listened to several individuals. Much of the research for this book was spent trying to identify them.

If the decision to execute the Drouins and the Villedrouins in August was agreed upon between Pierre Biamby (who was in Jérémie as head of the Presidential Commission in August 1964) and Duvalier (in Port-au-Prince) via coded military messages, the execution of the Sansaricqs in September was Duvalier's decision. Who said what to him about the Sansaricqs to motivate such a decision? A few negative words about the Sansaricqs were unlikely to have been enough to convince Duvalier to have an entire family exterminated. Yet one or more individuals he trusted made arguments that convinced Duvalier. The study of circumstantial evidence, including location, motivation, personality, belief, resentment against mulattoes, personal interest, relationship, and, most importantly, means of communication, point at four individuals only: Pierre Biamby and Jacques Fourcand, who were in Port-au-Prince at that period; and Sanette Balmir and Saintange Bontemps in Jérémie. In the Presidential Palace, where Duvalier made his decision, the only ones who knew the Sansaricqs were Biamby and Fourcand. In Jérémie, the only ones who resented the Sansaricqs and had access to Duvalier were Balmir and Bontemps.

Pierre Biamby (1917–1984) was Duvalier's private secretary at that time.[44] He was married to a Jeremian, Ketly Ney-Pierre.[45] Jacques Fourcand (1918–1988), Duvalier's personal physician and confidant, was a Jeremian. Duvalier had sent Fourcand as a personal envoy to Jérémie in early August; his speech calling for "a Himalaya of corpses" is analyzed in the previous chapter. Both Biamby and Fourcand knew the three families who were killed. Fourcand likely knew several of the victims personally and was related by kinship to the Sansaricqs.[46] When Duvalier wrote the order to execute the Sansaricqs on September 18, Biamby was working in the Presidential Palace, his office was next to Duvalier's. It was also Biamby who had ordered the arrest of Pierre Sansaricq in August while in Jérémie as head of the Presidential Commission—Sansaricq spent several weeks in prison before his execution. During that fateful week of September 1964, we can only speculate about what Biamby and Fourcand said in the Presidential Palace to Duvalier about the world of Jérémie's and the Sansaricqs.

As for Sanette Balmir and Saintange Bontemps, both were known to have a visceral dislike of mulattoes, behaved in a manner that denoted zeal and ambition, and had a personal relationship with Duvalier, as discussed in chapter 7. Identifying the means of communication between Duvalier and Duvalierists in Jérémie is key to assessing their levels of involvement. Duvalier was known not to communicate by telephone, which was not secure, for sensitive subjects. When in Jérémie in August, Biamby used the coded military telegram system at the base. Duvalier communicated with military officers at the base through the same system. Everybody else, including Bontemps and Balmir, had to take the long arduous trip to Port-au-Prince, either by land (two days) or by sea (one night), to communicate with Duvalier. Neither appears in the U.S. embassy cables among the Jeremians seen in Port-au-Prince, which may only mean that they were not included in the U.S. informants' circles. Abel Jérôme, on the other hand, was reported by the U.S. embassy almost every time he was in Port-au-Prince (three times in the summer and fall of 1964). Jérôme knew that Bontemps had visited Duvalier when he was summoned to the palace in September and then again in October 1964.

Bontemps's behavior in regard to the Sansaricqs should also be understood in light of his own personal agenda. Bontemps attempted to position himself as Duvalier's man in Jérémie and to wield authority over its young military commander, Abel Jérôme. Sanette Balmir, either willingly or instrumentalized by Bontemps, also delegitimized Abel Jérôme before Duvalier. With Bontemps, she formed an alliance of sorts. She became chief of Jérémie's VSNs between late August and early September, taking Max Frédérique's place. Meanwhile, the conflict between Bontemps and Jérôme, evoked in chapter 8, erupted into public view twice, triggering a rumor that found its way into a U.S. embassy cable that stated "Capt. Abel Jérôme was killed in altercations of August 12."[47] Jérôme felt strong enough to resist Bontemps because he, too, had a personal relationship with Duvalier. Power plays were a byproduct of Duvalier's chaotic ways—I have never read nor heard about any such conflict between a military officer and a civilian under previous regimes, with men fighting physically on a sidewalk. In bypassing and delegitimizing institutions, in empowering individuals for the sheer fact that they had a relationship with him, Duvalier created a field where positions were systemically unstable and up for grabs. Jérôme and Bontemps were two personalities that were destined to lock horns as they fought for supremacy; other local Duvalierists, even the most anti-mulatto such as Antoine Jean Charles and Max Frédérique, had the reputation of being more subdued. Yet this modus operandi produced more terror as it led actors to outbid one another, as happened during the meeting at Jabouin's home.[48] Harming the mulatto elite may have also been a way to hurt Jérôme, who had social relations with several of its members, and to show him who wielded power.

What could one or more of these four individuals have said that convinced Duvalier to order the execution of fourteen family members, combined with the motives delineated at the end of the previous chapter (notably the possibility to further terrorize the opposition and the mulatto population)? One should not speculate on the content of what was reported, or expand on today's rumors, apocryphal or not, that place the blame on the victims: that the Sansariqs were arrogant, that Pierre Sansaricq supported Louis Dejoie during the presidential campaign, that Louise Sansaricq was anti-*noir*, that Adrien Sansaricq broadcast from Cuba, or that there were money and jewels to steal from their homes. Whatever the content of those information, repetition was probably a decisive factor. People close to Duvalier repeatedly criticized, belittled, or more likely defamed the name Sansaricq between August 6 and September 18 until Duvalier drafted the execution order: "Upon reception, disappear Sansaricq family."

Conclusion

CHANGING THE PARADIGM ON MASS VIOLENCE

Mass violence and anti-elitism in the twentieth century are correlated, and this correlation should make us change the way we think about mass violence. The intention to either exterminate the elite, decrease its size, force it to leave the country, or fundamentally change it raises a legitimate question: does mass violence exist primarily to brutalize elites?

Instead of being an anomaly, the victimization of the elite constitutes the norm of mass violence in the twentieth century. All twenty-seven communist regimes victimized elites—at first, the traditional elite when the party reached power, then even its own organic elites.[1] The Pol Pot regime in Cambodia started to kill members of the former (Lon Non) government, then continuously enlarged the scope of its targets to include professors, lawyers, teachers, priests, monks, and eventually all those with a formal education.[2] The Holocaust also figures at the forefront of that correlation. Of course, Jews were not killed during the Holocaust because they were the elite, but because they were Jews. Yet German Jews were constructed as rich, educated, and powerful in ways that only an elite can be. This was also true for the figure of the Jew in many, if not most other European societies. The term "elite" has even been used in antisemitic contexts around the world to delegitimize Jews and blame them for a society's ills, notably inequalities.[3] The Ottoman authorities first targeted the Armenian elites before attacking the rest of the Armenian population; Armenians, as well as Pontian Greeks and Assyrians, were largely seen by Turks as richer and higher up the social hierarchy than they were. The same was true for the Tutsis in Rwanda where, since the colonial era, the population was ethnicized and essentialized through a Tutsi-elite/Hutu-peasantry binary. The correlation between mass violence and the targeting of elites also appears in other, less well-known massacres. The regimes of Idi Amin (1972–1979) in Uganda, Jean-Bédel Bokassa (1966–1976) in the Central African Republic, and Francisco Macías Nguema (1968–1979) in Equatorial Guinea victimized educated elites, with Nguema nearly eliminating everybody with a high school education, while Idi Amin also ethnically cleansed the Indian community (the business elite).[4] The Americo-Liberians, who had held positions of power and relative wealth, were "othered" as foreign and systematically targeted during the civil war that started in 1980. In every single one of these episodes, the intellectual elite, the business elite, the political elite, doctors, lawyers, university professors, teachers, businessmen, prominent individuals, government officials, military officers, rich farmers could become the figure of the enemy. Even if they had none of these socioeconomic profiles, they could still be constructed as elite by the perpetrators and thus targeted. The Holodomor, during which millions of kulaks were killed by the Soviets because they were "rich" farmers, reveals the subjectivity of socioeconomic criteria to determine elites: yet for the Soviets, the kulaks were framed as oppressors, selfishly abhorrent and untrustworthy—"class enemies." Whether an ethnic minority is constructed as elite or the elite is "othered" as foreign, the elite remains part of the perpetrator's equation. In Rwanda, as Elizabeth Baisley put it, "over time, Hutu came to refer to the mass of ordinary people as a group, and Tutsi came to refer to the elite as a whole group."[5] Poor Tutsi could be killed because the Tutsi had previously been constructed as elite and elitist.[6]

If these facts are undisputed, the victimization and sometimes outright extermination of groups who occupied, or who were believed to occupy, the top rungs of society is not acknowledged and reified as such, lying in an academic no man's land.[7] This victimization contradicts our dominant epistemological assumptions and political diagnoses of our time. Scholarly taxonomies of victimization do not include an entry for the elite. We can compare this situation (known facts, but no moral "capture") to Adam Jones's counterintuitive work on the gender dimension of mass violence. Jones submitted the gender variable in mass violence to observation and showed that men are by far the main victims of political and mass violence. That most of the victimizers are also men does not change this fact.

Of course, not all episodes of mass violence during the modern era carry the correlation, especially when invasions and conquests are involved. Mass atrocities committed during the many phases of conquests on the American continent do not carry the anti-elite dimension. In particular, the conquest of societies that had little to no social differentiation render this approach inoperative. In Central America during the nineteenth-century coffee expansion, and during the many counterinsurgencies throughout the twentieth century, peasants, especially those of native origin, were the main target of repression.[8] Nor was "elite" a dimension of the 1937 massacre of Haitians in the Dominican Republic, atrocities in the Congo Free State (1885–1908), the colonial massacres in Sétif in 1945 and Madagascar in 1947, and many, if not most, colonial mass killings.[9] Anti-elite mass violence is essentially an "internal" affair. Two exceptions come to mind: the 1971 mass executions of the Bangladeshi elite by the Pakistani military as they were leaving the country; and the Katyn massacre in 1940, when the Soviet People's Commissariat for Internal Affairs (NKVD) executed 22,000 men of the Polish elite.

Yet the largest and most lethal episodes of mass violence in the twentieth century, including the Holocaust; the Armenian, Cambodian, and Rwandan genocides; the Great Leap Forward; and the Holodomor point to a close correlation between mass violence and anti-elitism. The occurrence of anti-elite mass violence across continents and across political regimes, including communist, right-wing, and ethno-nationalist regimes refutes the hypothesis that socialist ideology and governance are solely to blame for it. True, communist regimes almost always massacred vast sectors of the traditional elites. The notion of "class enemies" was at the forefront of this political justification. Yet the French Revolution was not socialist, and not only did it nearly eliminate the aristocracy, but it also undertook the mass killing of members of other elite groups that included commoners such as judges, priests, and members of local parliaments. Duvalier was anti-communist. Hutu supremacy was not socialist either. Therefore, neither the time frame nor the ideological context of these programs of mass violence can be explained by socialism.

Delegitimizing, victimizing, and killing en masse a group of people, not because of their deeds but because they occupy the upper echelons of society is a new phenomenon on the stage of history—a combination of hatred and state policy that appears organic to late modernity. In a traditional world, political elites, small groups, sometimes sultanistic collectives, could be massacred—or another society's elite during a conquest—but not a society's own social elite. The historicity of this construction (the elite as a problem, an enemy, a target) is revealed by its conspicuous absence in classical literature; it appears in none of the classical political inventories, notably by Aristotle, Machiavelli, Montesquieu, and Weber. The recurrence of elite victimization since the French Revolution points at the break opened by the Enlightenment rather than, too easily, to Marxism and socialist ideals. The ideas generated by the Enlightenment, the French Revolution, then Marxist philosophy created a fundamental rupture from a more traditional political and intellectual universe where systems could perhaps be changed and rulers replaced, but no entire class of people was conceived of as deserving annihilation.

For heuristic purposes, a brief mental return to that old binary, modern/traditional, helps determine the historicity of anti-elite mass violence. Mechanical solidarity, hierarchies notwithstanding, contributed to establish and nurture ties (both social ties and shared beliefs) to "make society." From tribal societies to feudal systems, questioning "the elite" was not really imaginable in the moral world and mental safety of heteronomy. The verticality of a traditional society does not affect that situation. Am I asserting that anti-elite mass violence, under most forms, would be nearly impossible in a traditional society? No such example comes to mind. Genocide, massacres, ethnic cleansing can perfectly cohabit with a traditional universe—not anti-elitism. The form of rationality that considers established elites to be an obstacle toward progress, the march of history, or the reach of justice, can only be modern. A metanarrative that includes a before and an after, a historicist dimension that points to elites as an obstacle, is inherently modern. There is no Shigalyev in a traditional world.[10] Modern society is not simply defined by equality; it is anti-elite.[11] With the obsolescence of traditional society and its acquiescence to hierarchy, Pandora's box was opened.

THE HUMAN FORM

There can be no violence explicitly against a society's own elites without overarching egalitarian ideologies, as chapters 2 and 3 have shown. Egalitarianism is certainly not an idea that captured minds and reasons in socialist movements only.[12] Yet egalitarianism is not the only seductive set of values that convinced individuals to adhere to radical ideas. Political emancipation, freeing people from ageless oppression, has long been another powerful one.[13] This is where equality and liberty, often seen as somehow distinct if not antagonist, join to designate a common enemy. Seen from the result (or the victim's side), egali-tarianism and emancipation share "elective affinities," to use Max Weber's idea, via Goethe, of two very distinct entities that, at one historical moment, would happen to share one element that would produce an irresistible, hyper-legitimate intellectual regime.

Equality and inequalities, freedom and oppression, emancipation and dis-criminations, masses and elites: all these remain intellectual notions. Yet an ideo-logical system that identifies ills and injustices can hardly remain within a realm of pure concept and abstractions; designating social ills or obstacles toward improvement, progress, utopia point to people, real people, a group. It would be like talking about the reality of communism, capitalism, or racism without iden-tifying communists, capitalists, and racists. This is even more true of ideologies explicitly designed to fundamentally change people, to create "a New Man," as the communist agenda from the Soviet Union to Cuba would have it. Hatred of priv-ileges, equality as ideology, resentment, liberation constitute or imply social, eco-nomic, political, and cultural diagnoses that designate an enemy. The elite (under any name) is this human figure. There can hardly be an anti-value (oppression, inequalities, or the combination of the two) and not, concomitantly, a human figure attached to it, which can therefore, on these subjects, be construed as the elite. This cognitive step, conscious or unconscious, is the main link between ideology and future implementation of physical violence. With such powerful, emancipatory, generous values and agendas as equality and freedom, what other social sectors could be constructed as an obstacle (at best) or an enemy (at worst) but the very people who hold power—political, economic, cultural power?[14] This "humanization" of an enemy was even more true in a small community such as Jérémie, the small towns of the European borderlands in 1942–43, and the villages of Rwanda, where social nearness combined with hyper-ideologization would make the elite a very concrete figure and enemy.

MOST THREATENING GROUP

Is mass violence produced to solve a problem with the elite? Are elites attacked for what they represent or because they present a threat?

Obviously, people who are educated, well-off, often politically astute, with sometimes self-confident or even entitled personalities, and by definition possessing greater social and symbolic capital could easily be perceived as posing a potential threat to changes—regime change, cultural change, or any other type of change. The potentiality for leadership (political, intellectual, and moral) designates the elite as a security threat, especially when established elites have the most to lose and are resistant to new values and political transformations—even if, as is known, those who lead these changes often come from the elite. Elites of foreign groups are killed first for their leadership potentiality. Anti-elite violence is, to a large extent, a preemption on leadership. For a dictator such as Duvalier, whose sole political ambition was to persist in power, the Haitian elite was a permanent threat.

Yet political reasons should not eclipse other causes. The entanglement of political and material causes, of collective and personal reasons, of pure ideas and social nearness, of ideological and socioeconomic variables characterizes not only the steps leading to anti-elite violence but also the individual calculations of actors. Self-interests are, as we know, entangled in ideologies.[15] In Haiti, it was not so much a fully baked egalitarian project that motivated anti-elite men, but the frustrated desire to become full members of the upper class. When the elite is perceived as closed, secluded, tribalistic—a "club," as the metaphor goes—whose social practices and institutions aim at preserving its privileges and excluding others, frustrations can lead to an explosive situation. This is particularly the case in the context of an impoverished, yet modern (that is, dealing with egalitarian ideas), society. Homogamy, or the perception thereof, is not a side quality here. Elites with hermetic matrimonial borders project an image of themselves as socially alienated and offer a dire diagnosis about their entire society: unlikely mobility, absence of social integration. For men from social sectors below or beside the established elite, this diagnosis is cause for despair. Envy can be triggered by very personal reactions to lived social situations rather than by a general, almost abstract sentiment based on values, as Helmut Schoeck and Marc Angenot believed. When intimacy is expected, yet denied, powerful sentiments of victimization and injustice ensue, especially for up-and-coming, educated men with a high sense of self-worth who feel left outside of strategic alliances and the upper class. This "denied intimacy" can be a trigger of resentment and possibly violence, particularly in social settings where people with different socioeconomic backgrounds and symbolic capitals live side by side. Nearness leads to bond-making but also exposes both inequalities and exclusiveness, as chapters 5, 6, and 7 showed.

In Duvalier's Haiti, as well as in Rwanda, the European borderlands, and the post-colonial East African settings where ethnic cleansing of South Asians took place, people—perpetrators, victims, and the others—lived side by side. Therefore, the elite cannot be considered in a purely intellectual manner, even for the resentful ideologue, but also as a trove of wealth, status, privileges, and jobs to be taken—and, let's face it, women. But the perpetrating groups do not simplistically want to "kill the competition," even if they certainly are the first to help themselves. When victimized elites are cleansed, vast spoils are available, as shown by the immediate post-revolutionary period from Moscow to Havana to Addis Ababa, where not just land but empty homes were distributed; or in Nazi-occupied Europe, where the belongings of Jews were systematically transferred to Germany (and to Germans).[16] The dividends of elite cleansing vastly exceed the repression of any other class, and may increase the legitimacy of the genocidal regime.

ELITE KILLERS

Mass violence against elites is rarely produced by mobs or by the "poor" in search of revenge. As explained throughout this book, elites are victimized by the state; that is, by other elites. The ultimate location of power—the state—is perhaps not exactly synonymous with "elites," but is certainly populated by one.[17] The idea of a furious mob à la Gustave Le Bon going after former oppressors has the advantage of presenting a credible narrative, a thrilling tale in which justice is of this earth and violence works like a litmus test neatly pointing to the guilty. As this book shows, the Jérémie massacre triggered an apocryphal narrative that described the victims' neighbors as their vengeful killers, a coherent, believable, useful, and utterly false explanation that cleansed the historiographic record of the role played by the state. One could counterargue that the state represses elites, or any other group, to please the mob—that the state is compelled by social forces. In Duvalier's Haiti, it was rather Duvalier himself who had to be pleased. Most of society evaded perpetration before being dressed, much later, with the mantle of perpetration. Mass violence, including that committed against elites, is a political endeavor, not a social phenomenon; a state crime, not social justice—except for ideologues.

The victimization of elites should not obscure the fact that elites are also the victimizers. State mass violence is always, and can only be, an elite endeavor. Yet to conclude that mass violence simply comes down to elites killing elites would be syllogistic, even distorting. Yet elites are necessary at every nodal phase of mass violence: the ideologies at work in genocides are first articulated by intellectuals, while policies are later implemented by the elites who control the state at the moment of violence.[18] The state does not protect, oppress, raise taxes, or use them; individuals do. As Thelen Tellers, Vetters, and von Benda-Beckmann show, the state is only made up of individuals.[19] These individuals gain access to government positions because they belong to an elite sector; or they become so (elite) when they obtain these positions. I am talking of course mainly about the higher and middle echelons of the state. That elites would turn against (other) elites raises the question of relations between two groups and of the background, interests, and beliefs of the perpetrating elites. In the case of Haiti, the most resentful and ideologized social sector against the established Haitian elite was constituted of urban, intellectual, well-educated men seeking government positions. They did not do much harm until they controlled the state.

DEFENSELESS

Elites can only be massacred if they are defenseless. Would that not make them less elite? How can the figure of the elite as powerful and shrewd survive in the eyes of the perpetrator and the researcher if they are victimized? This contradiction collapses when observing reality at the ground level and in medias res. We are not just talking about the destruction of civilians who are generally not armed; victimized elites are shut off from political power at the moment of violence. This book did not distinguish between cultural, economic, and political elites because, as Haitian genealogy and sociology show, the same elite families often predominate in all areas of prestige, status, and power. Yet the dissonance between control of political power (essentially government positions) and hegemony in the cultural field appears as a source of group illegitimacy. At the heart of the resentment against, and delegitimization of, the mulatto elite in Haiti, there was a contradiction between having elites that are hegemonic in the cultural field but impotent politically. Their defenselessness does not contradict elite status. The mulatto elite in Jérémie was left exposed by a contradiction between a hystericized social status that catapulted ordinary families with rather average lifestyles into social fantasies triggering sentiments of self-worthlessness in the non-elite population on one hand, and these families' actual access to political power, which was nil during the Duvalier regime, on the other. The fact that elite families in Jérémie constantly attempted to befriend or to "court" (as several interlocutors put it) the military commanders posted there betrays their political impotence right before the massacre.[20] This "courtship" unveiled the fragility of this elite, their lack of effective power, and yet everybody was supposed to abide by their values and imitate their lifestyle. At the national level, the dissonance between real political power and cultural influence and norms solidified hatred against it. Unable to access or convince the decision-makers in power, understanding it was in danger, this elite understood it had to flee the country.

ELITE FLIGHT

Some may celebrate a modern society without an upper class. The current state of Haiti, however, should give us pause. This book is an account of a massacre that occurred in 1964 and the conditions, ideological and historical, that led to it; not a theory of why Haiti is the poorest country in the hemisphere or has become a kakistocracy and fallen into a state of anarchy. Still, the repeated flight throughout history of the economic, political, and intellectual elite, regardless of skin color, raises legitimate questions about its consequences. As Matthew Smith meticulously shows, elite flight happened repeatedly in Haiti's post-independence history.[21] After each episode of violence against the elite, men and sometimes entire families fled the country. There are of course other reasons why the Haitian elite migrated, including the country's general impoverishment and a precarious rule of law. However, the uncanny similarity of written accounts by observers lamenting, decades apart yet in the same terms, the flight of the elite points to a structural phenomenon with structural effects. The government (as Edmond Paul first put it) or the state (in Michel-Rolph Trouillot's slight paraphrase) might have been "against the nation"; it was certainly against its elite as well.[22] The accretion of the flight of an elite already limited in size could only have dire effects on the country's long-term prospects, notably the education system. Rulers such as Faustin Soulouque, Lysius Salomon, Nord Alexis, and François Duvalier went after the most brilliant intellectuals of their time.[23] President Nord Alexis had the most important Haitian poet of his time, Massillon Coicou, executed in 1908 by a firing squad, together with twenty-six other members of the social elite. Anténor Firmin, an intellectual of global importance, the first to refute scientific racism on scholarly grounds, died in exile. Duvalier had one of the greatest and most translated Haitian novelists of all time, Jacques Stephen Alexis, tortured to death in April 1961. The accretion of massacres, purges, mass exile, and migration amounted to a class cleansing of elite sectors. As sociologist Michèle Oriol put it, "Haiti has never been able to capitalize on its elites."[24]

During the Duvalier era, however, the flight of the elite changed scale. According to Philippe Girard, most of Haiti's skilled citizens fled into exile to escape repression, "a brain drain from which Haiti has not yet recovered but that gave Papa Doc a firm grip on the country."[25] Sidney Mintz regretted in 1971 "the attrition by emigration of a sizable portion of Haiti's professional talent. Emigration and exile are old traditions, but for Haiti they may well be an irreversible process—and loss—given the length of the Duvalier regime."[26] For the economic historian Etzer Émile, this "regime made the brains flee. It was a war against science, against intelligence. A war against thinking. They kept those who understood nothing."[27] Popular historian Michel Soukar echoed this view: "If you liked books, you were suspect."[28] Duvalierism not only destroyed civil institutions, underdeveloped the country, and traumatized society, it deprived the country of its teachers.[29] If August Comte is credited with the apocryphal meta-belief that "demography is fate," implying that a community's political future comes down to its demographic vitality or decline vis-à-vis its neighbors, Haiti's historical record toward its elite, notably the ever-shrinking intellectual elite sector, invites a paraphrase of Auguste Comte: Is a country's elite its fate? This paraphrase invites another, of the dilemma offered by Bertold Brecht in *Life of Galileo*: unhappy is the land that breeds no elite, or unhappy the land in need of elite?

Notes

INTRODUCTION

1. U.S. Embassy, Embtel 598, Sept. 28, 1964.
2. The names of the victims and the dates of their executions were recorded as they happened by Bruno Laroche, a Canadian friar in Jérémie, in the official diary of his institution, which I found in the Archives des Frères de l'Instruction Chrétienne, Pétionville. This book is the first, I believe, to use that primary source. Albert Chassagne, using oral history, provided the same number and identities of most of the victims. See Albert Chassagne, *Bain de sang en Haïti. Les macoutes opèrent à Jérémie* (New York: n.p., 1977). The Jérémie memorial, built in 1986 and restored in 2014, "evokes" rather than names the victims. Wives are evoked with their husbands' name: "Mr. and Mrs. Pierre Sansaricq," for instance. The children are evoked under their parents' names: "killed with their children." The memorial's list also includes Roger Villedrouin, who had been executed in a separate incident in 1963 in Port-au-Prince.
3. See Elizabeth Abbott, *Haiti: A Shattered Nation* (New York: Overlook Duckworth, 2011); Jean-Pierre Alcindor, *Jérémie, Haiti . . . il était une fois. Une tranche de la petite histoire d'Haiti* (Port-au-Prince: Média-texte, 2011); Eddy Cavé, *De mémoire de Jérémien: ma vie, ma ville, mon village*, vol. 1 of *De mémoire de Jérémien* (Pétionville, Haiti: Pleine Plage, 2011); Eddy Cavé, *De mémoire de Jérémien: en pensant aux amis disparus*, vol. 2 of *De mémoire de Jérémien* (Montreal: CIDIHCA; Pétionville, Haiti: Pleine Plage, 2016); Albert Chassagne, *Bain de sang*; Frantz Voltaire, *Mourir pour Haïti: la résistance à la dictature en 1964* (Montréal: CIDIHCA, 2015), 28; Bernard Diedrich and Al Burt, *Papa Doc et les Tontons Macoutes: la verité sur Haïti* (Port-au-Prince: Henri Deschamps, 1986); Bernard Diederich, *Le prix du sang* (Port-au-Prince: Henri Deschamps, 2005), 280; Bernard Diederich, *The Price of Blood. History of Repression and Rebellion in Haiti under Dr. François Duvalier, 1962–1971*, 2 vols. (Princeton, NJ: Markus Wiener, 2011); Laurent Dubois, *Haiti: The Aftershocks of History* (New York: Henry Holt, 2012), 341; Robert Fatton, *The Roots of Haitian Despotism* (Boulder, CO: Lynne Rienner, 2007); Robert Debs Heinl, Nancy Gordon Heinl and Michael Heinl, *Written in Blood: the story of the Haitian people, 1492–1995*, 3rd ed. (Lanham, MD: University Press of America, 2005); Gary Klang and Anthony Phelps, *Le massacre de Jérémie— opération vengeance* (Montreal: Dialogue Nord-Sud, 2015); Frantz-Antoine Leconte, ed.,

En grandissant sous Duvalier: l'agonie d'un État-nation (Paris: L'Harmattan, 1999); Leslie Péan, *L'ensauvagement macoute et ses conséquences, 1957–1990. Haïti: économie politique de la corruption*, vol. 4 (Paris: Maisonneuve et Larose, 2007); Gérard Pierre-Charles, *Radiographie d'une dictature. Haïti et Duvalier* (Montreal: Nouvelle Optique, 1973); Ian Thomson, *Bonjour Blanc: A Journey Through Haiti* (New York: Vintage, 2004), 114–15; Michel-Rolph Trouillot, *Haiti, State Against Nation: The Origins and Legacy of Duvalierism* (New York: Monthly Review Press, 1990), 168; Mérès Wèche, *Le songe d'une nuit de carnage* (Port-au-Prince: n.p., 2013).

4. The literature on massacre of neighbors argues that civilians can participate in mass violence and be killers of people they know. On this, see: Jan Gross, *Neighbors: The Destruction of the Jewish Community in Jedwabne, Poland* (New York: Penguin, 2002); Victoria M. Esses and Richard Vernon, eds., *Explaining the Breakdown of Ethnic Relations: Why Neighbors Kill* (Malden, MA: Blackwell, 2006); Lee-Ann Fuji, *Killing Neighbors: Webs of Violence in Rwanda* (Ithaca, NY: Cornell University Press, 2009); Hélène Dumas, *Le génocide au village: le massacre des Tutsi au Rwanda* (Paris: Seuil, 2014); Jeffrey S. Kopstein and Jason Wittenberg, *Intimate Violence: Anti-Jewish Pogroms on the Eve of the Holocaust* (Ithaca, NY: Cornell University Press, 2018); Jérémie Foa, *Tous ceux qui tombent. Visages du massacre de la Saint-Barthélémy* (Paris: La Découverte, 2021). For a survey of this literature, see Jean-Philippe Belleau, " 'Neighbor' is an Empty Concept: How the Neighbourly Turn in Mass Violence Studies Has Overlooked Anthropology and Sociology," *Journal of Genocide Research* (2022).

5. Bernard Diedrich and Al Burt, *Papa Doc: The Truth about Haiti Today* (New York: Avon, 1969), 305.

6. Pierre-Charles, *Radiographie d'une dictature*, 54. Unless otherwise mentioned, all translations and their limitations are mine.

7. Chassagne, *Bain de sang*. A cousin of one of the victims, Chassagne was in exile in New York and returned to Jérémie in 1977. I chose to largely ignore an understandably emotional account. A very affable Chassagne received me at his home in Flushing, New York, in 2004, where he admitted that he had mainly relied on one single informant, Dr. Willy Verrier, the director of the local hospital, who later became minister of health (1976–1980) under Jean-Claude Duvalier. See Daniel Supplice, *Dictionnaire biographique des personnalités politiques de la République d'Haïti, 1804–2014* (Pétionville, Haiti: C3 Éditions, 2014).

8. Heinl, *Written in Blood*, 606. The regime's militia was also known as the *Tonton Macoutes* or simply *macoutes* in French or *makout* in Kreyol. I will use the acronym VSN from now on. VSN units were typically composed of local people—neighbors of victims.

9. Daniel Supplice, personal communication with author, Port-au-Prince, January 2016.

10. Danielle de Lame, "Anthropology and Genocide," *Mass Violence & Resistance*, online, 2007. A pioneering work in the anthropology of mass violence is Alexander Laban Hinton, ed., *Annihilating Differences: The Anthropology of Genocides* (Berkeley: University of California Press, 2002).

11. Marshall Sahlins, "What Kinship Is," *Journal of the Royal Anthropological Institute* 17, no. 1(2011): 2.

12. To be clear, this is not a work of comparative genocide.

13. This is not to say that class identity, at the first level of consciousness, trumps other identities. Jews were killed during the Holocaust because they were Jews, not because they were elite. Yet in Germany and beyond the figure of the Jew was constructed as elite, rich, powerful, and domineering.

14. On "eliticide," see Samuel Totten, Paul R. Bartrop, and Steven L. Jacobs, *Dictionary of Genocide*, 2 vols. (Westport, CT: Greenwood Publishing, 2009), 129–30; and Jacques Sémelin, *To Purify and Destroy. The Political Uses of Massacre and Genocides* (New York: Columbia University Press, 2007), 141, 230, 320.

15. On the notion of "class enemies," see Cheng-Chih Wang, *Words Kill: Calling for the Destruction of "Class Enemies" in China, 1949–1953* (New York: Routledge, 2002).

16. There are of course many instances in the twentieth century where the victims were not considered "elite," such as in Sudan's Darfur, massacres during decolonization, and the ethnic cleansing of the Rohingya from their homeland. Yet, it is striking that the largest, most lethal, and most brutal instances did target groups constructed as elite.

17. On Tutsis as foreign, see Nigel Eltringham, " 'Invaders who have stolen the country': The Hamitic Hypothesis, Race and the Rwandan Genocide," *Social Identities* 12, no. 4 (2006), 425–46.

18. A. Dirk Moses, "The Problems of Genocide Explained" (paper, International Association of Genocide Scholars Conference, July 2023).

19. See endnote 4 in this section.

20. Belleau, "Neighbor"; Jean-Philippe Belleau, "Hatred is Not Stronger Than Bonds: Social Relationships, Aversion to Harm, and Relational Exceptionalism," *Social Analysis* 67, no.1 (2023), 46–69.

21. Hannah Arendt, "De l'humanité dans de sombres temps," in *Vies politiques*, 11–41 (Paris: Gallimard, 1974).

22. Belleau, "Bonds."

23. Belleau, "Neighbor."

24. J. Michael Dash, *Literature and Ideology in Haïti, 1915–1961* (London: Macmillan, 1981), 171.

25. Sémelin, *Purify and Destroy*; Siniša Malešević, *The Sociology of War and Violence* (Cambridge: Cambridge University Press, 2010).

26. Sociologist Randall Collins called these types of narratives "macro-explanations of violence" predetermined by larger cultural, economic, or evolutionary forces: the idea that physical violence is caused by both symbolic and structural violence. Randall Collins, *Violence: A Micro-sociological Theory* (Princeton, NJ: Princeton University Press, 2008), 21–22, 34–35.

27. For a theoretical attempt that raises the massacre to a proper object of study, see Mark Levene, "Introduction," in *The Massacre in History*, ed. Mark Levene and Penny Roberts, 1–38 (New York: Berghahn Books, 1999); and David El Kenz, ed. *Le massacre, objet d'histoire* (Paris: Gallimard, 2005). Levene attempts to craft a working definition: "a massacre is when a group . . . of people lacking in self-defense" is killed by people with the physical means, power and technology to carry out their task; it "is complete when the targeted victims are either all dead or when the perpetrators' emotional energy is spent" (pp. 5–6). I am not sure, however, that there is (yet) a paradigm of massacre. I will also seldom use the vast literature on conflicts, for it relies on the notion of two belligerent sides, even if they are of often unequal sizes. A massacre is a one-sided event.

28. Jonathan L. Maynard recently, and convincingly, relativized ideologies' agency in mass killings. Ideological convictions vary in intensity across society while ideologies' very content is mitigated by crowds of in medias res contigencies. See Jonathan Leader Maynard, *Ideology and Mass Killing: The Radicalized Security Politics of Genocides and Deadly Atrocities* (Oxford: Oxford University Press, 2022). This book argues that convictions at all state and societal levels were negotiated with, and sometimes contradicted by, preexisting social relationships across the ideological aisle. Still, the construction and essentialization of the "mulatto" elite as hateful were very much conceptualized in an extensive intellectual corpus extending over a century and a half. They represent an inescapable context. State crimes against the elite would not make sense without the ideologies behind them, even if such ideologies were, under Duvalier, half-baked and shifted depending on context.

29. Seldom used in English, in which it has a derogative connotation, "mulatto" is a conventional endonym in Haiti, widely used in Kreyol (*milât*) and French (*mulâtre*), as well as in Spanish, and Portuguese. The U.S. ambassador who wrote the diplomatic cable mentioned at the beginning of this introduction almost certainly used the word because it was employed by his informants. Anthropology's goal to see the world through the native's point of view, as Clifford Geertz put it, compels us to use the term; the reader is to be reminded of this anthropological context throughout. See Clifford Geertz, "Thick Description: Toward an Interpretive Theory of Culture," In *The Interpretation of Cultures*, 3–30 (New York: Basic Books, 1973).

30. Philippe-Richard Marius, *The Unexceptional Case of Haiti: Race and Class Privilege in Postcolonial Bourgeois Society* (Jackson: University of Mississippi Press, 2022).

31. Mulatto elites are distinct from "middleman minorities." For Bonacich, ethnic minorities that are victimized develop strong bonds, which in turn make them efficient traders and eventually, prosperous. Zenner believed that such minorities were more likely to be genocide victims. This theory holds a kernel of truth, yet elites are not "in-between" but "above": they do not all occupy commercial occupations, far from it; and elites do not necessarily have strong bonds or constitute an ethnic group. Haitian mulattoes are not an ethnic group in any sociological context (see chapter 5). See Edna Bonacich, "A Theory of Middleman Minorities," *American Sociological Review* 38, no. 5 (1973): 583–94; Walter Zenner, "Middleman Minorities and Genocide," in *Genocide and the Modern Age: Etiology and Case Studies of Mass Death*, ed. Isidor Walliman and Michael N. Dobkowski (New York: Greenwood Press, 1987), 253–81.

32. See Fred Doura, *Mythes, paradoxes et réalités de la pigmentocratie au cours de l'histoire d'Haïti* (Boucherville, QC: Éditions DAMI, 2017); Marius, *The Unexceptional Case of Haiti*; Michèle Labelle, *Idéologies de couleur et classes sociales en Haïti* (Montreal: Presses de l'université de Montréal, 1978); Dash, *Literature and Ideology*; Léon-François Hoffmann, *Haïti. Couleurs, croyances, créole* (Montreal: CIDHICA, 1990); Trouillot, *State Against Nation*; Martin Munro, *Exile and post-1946 Literature: Alexis, Depestre, Olivier, Lafferière, Danticat* (Liverpool, UK: Liverpool University Press, 2007).

33. Justin Bouzon, *Études historiques sur la présidence de Faustin Soulouque (1847–1849)*, (Port-au-Prince: Bibliothèques Haitiennes; Paris: Gustave Guérin, 1894); Trouillot, *State Against Nation*; Michel-Rolph Trouillot, "Culture, Color, and Politics," in *Race*, ed. Steven

Gregory and Roger Sanjet, 146–74 (New Brunswick, NJ: Rutgers University Press, 1994); Alex Dupuy, *Haiti in the New World Order: The Limits of the Democratic Transition* (Boulder, CO: Westview Press, 1996); Alex Dupuy, "From François Duvalier to Jean-Bertrand Aristide: The Declining Significance of Color Politics in Haiti," in *Politics and Power in Haiti*, ed. Kate Quinn and Paul Sutton, 43–64 (New York: Palgrave Macmillan, 2013); Alex Dupuy, *From Revolutionary Slaves to Powerless Citizens: Essays on the Politics and Economics of Underdevelopment* (New York: Routledge, 2014). Trouillot adds that "terms such as *mulâtre* and *noir* do not simply mean—and sometimes do not mean at all—"mulatto" or black" in the U.S. sense." Michel-Rolph Trouillot, "Culture, Color, and Politics," 149. It must be said, however, that Trouillot's approach to race/color in *State Against Nation* was rather apophatic: recognizing that race is a construct, then proceeding to identify every single actor by race and often inferring a link between identity and political behavior. The idea that "race" would be a strangely resilient notion in the first place—and the reason why Trouillot delegitimizes such notions only then to have recourse to them—is hardly new and has been amply analyzed by Latin Americanist scholars. See for example Peter Wade, *Race and Sex in Latin America* (London: Pluto Press, 2009). Nor does it prevent scholars from finding a heuristic value in these terms—Léon-François Hoffmann uses "Blacks" and "mulattoes" as racial categories, and explicitly categorized the 1800 war between Louverture and Rigaud as a racial war. See Léon-François Hoffmann, 2008. 'L'Haïtienne fut-elle une Révolution?' in Hoffmman, Gewecke, & Fleischmann (eds.), *Haïti 1804, lumières et ténèbres: impact et résonances d'une revolution* (Madrid: Iberoamericana, 2008), 17

34. Marius, *The Unexceptional Case.*

35. On noirism, see for instance Matthew J. Smith, *Red and Black in Haiti: Radicalism, Conflict and Political Change* (Chapel Hill: University of North Carolina Press, 2009). On the intellectual fermentation in Port-au-Prince in the first half of the twentieth century, from which contemporary noirism emerged, see Rachel Beauvoir-Dominique, Jean-Luc Bonniol, Carlo Avier Célius, Rachelle Charlier-Doucet, Gaetano Ciarcia, Chantal Collard, René Despestre, et al., "Haïti et l'anthropologie." *Gradhiva* 1 (2005), https://doi .org/10.400/gradhiva.68.

36. Fatton, *Roots.*

37. Ben Kiernan, "Twentieth Century Genocides: Underlying Ideological Themes from Armenia to East Timor," in *The Specter of Genocide: Mass Murder in Historical Perspective*, ed. Robert Gellately and Ben Kiernan (Cambridge: Cambridge University Press, 2003); Ben Kiernan. *Blood and Soil. A World History of Genocide and Extermination from Sparta to Darfur* (New Haven, CT: Yale University Press, 2007).

38. Marlène Daut, *Tropics of Haiti: Race and the Literary History of the Haitian Revolution in the Atlantic World* (Liverpool, UK: Liverpool University Press, 2017).

39. Péan, *L'ensauvagement*, 49.

40. Cited in Hoffmann, *Couleurs*, 77.

41. René Depestre, "Jean Price-Mars et le mythe de l'Orphée noir ou les aventures de la négritude" *L'homme et la société* 7, no. 1 (1968): 171–81; René Depestre, "Homo Papadocus," *Europe* (September 1976).

42. Léopold Sédar Senghor, "Préface," in *Le dossier Haïti: un pays en péril*, ed. Catherine Eve di Chiara (Paris: Taillandier, 1988), vi.

43.   Péan, *L'ensauvagement*, 49.

44.   In Smith, *Red and Black*, 27.

45.   Pierre-Charles, *Radiographie*. Arthur de Gobineau was a theoretician of scientific rac-
      ism in the nineteenth century. On Léon Laleau, see Supplice, *Dictionnaire*, 449–50. On
      the position of the Haitian Communist Party on the color division, see Smith, *Red and
      Black*, 87.

46.   This point was made by Michèle Oriol, personal communications with author, Port-au-
      Prince, January 2016.

47.   These two works are: David Nicholls, *From Dessalines to Duvalier: Race, Colour and National
      Independence in Haiti* (New Brunswick, NJ: Rutgers University Press, 1996); Trouillot,
      Haiti: State Against Nation. Other works written in the course of the regime include:
      Leslie Manigat, *Haiti of the Sixties, Object of International Concern: A Tentative Global Anal-
      ysis of the Potentially Explosive Situation of a Crisis Country in the Caribbean.* (Washington,
      DC: Washington Center of Foreign Policy Research, 1964); Pierre-Charles, *Radiographie*;
      Robert Rotberg, *Haiti, the Politics of Squalor* (Boston: Houghton-Mifflin, 1971); David
      Nicholls, "On Controlling the Colonels." *Hemisphere Report* (Trinidad), (1970); David
      Nicholls, "Embryo-politics in Haiti," *Government and Opposition* 6, no. 1 (1971), 75–85;
      David Nicholls, "Biology and Politics in Haiti," *Race* 13, no. 2 (1971), 203–14; Diederich
      and Burt, *Papa Doc et les Tontons Macoutes*.

48.   For an overview of the regime, see Alex Dupuy, *The Prophet and Power: Jean-Bertrand
      Aristide, the International Community, and Haiti* (Lanham, MD: Rowman and Littlefield,
      2006), 31–42; and Dubois, *Aftershocks*, 325–49.

49.   Weibert Arthus, *Duvalier à l'ombre de la guerre froide. Les dessous de la politique étrangère
      d'Haïti (1957–1963)* (Port-au-Prince: L'Imprimeur, 2014).

50.   Diederich, *Le prix du sang*; Bernard Diederich, *Blood in the Sun: The Tyranny of Papa Doc
      Duvalier* (Port-au-Prince: Henri Deschamps, 2010); Bernard Diederich, *The Prize: Haiti's
      National Palace* (n.p: iuniverse, 2007); Bernard Diederich, *The Price of Blood. History of
      Repression and Rebellion in Haiti under Dr. François Duvalier, 1962–1971*, 2 vols. (Princeton,
      NJ: Markus Wiener, 2011).

51.   Laennec Hurbon, *Culture et dictature en Haiti: l'imaginaire sous contrôle* (Paris: L'Harmat-
      tan, 1979); Laennec Hurbon, *Comprendre Haiti: essai sur l'État, la nation, la culture* (Paris:
      Karthala, 1987); Claude Moïse, *Constitutions et luttes de pouvoir en Haïti (1815–1987)* (Mon-
      tréal: CIDIHCA, 1990); Dupuy, *New World Order*; Dupuy, "From François Duvalier";
      Dupuy, *From Revolutionary Slaves*; Robert Fatton, *Haiti's Predatory Republic: The Unending
      Transition to Democracy* (Boulder, CO: Lynne Rienner, 2002); Robert Fatton, *The Roots of
      Haitian Despotism* (Boulder, CO: Lynne Rienner, 2007); Robert Fatton, *Haiti: Trapped in
      the Outer Periphery* (Boulder, CO: Lynne Rienner, 2014); Patrick Bellegarde-Smith, *Haiti,
      the Breached Citadel* (Boulder, CO: Westview Press, 1990); Michel Hector, *Syndicalisme et
      socialisme en Haïti: 1932–1970* (Port-au-Prince: Henri Deschamps, 1989). I would also add
      the entire 2001 issue of *Chemins critiques*.

52.   After the FAD'H (Forces armées d'Haïti, or Armed Forces of Haiti) were officially dis-
      mantled in early 1995 by President Jean-Bertrand Aristide, officers and employees left
      the ministry and the military headquarters within hours. The National Archives direc-
      tor, Jean-Wilfried Bertrand rented a truck and picked up, alone, thousands of documents

that littered the floors and the nearby sidewalks. Since then, these archives have been left in the same bags. Jean-Wilfried Bertrand, personal communication with author, Port-au-Prince, January 2016.

53. U.S. Ambassador Benson E. L. Timmons had empathy for the victims. He also understood the anti-mulatto turn the regime took in the summer of 1964. Once, a colleague who endured my obsession with the Jérémie massacre asked me if, in a parallel universe, there were one actor I would like to meet, such as Duvalier—I answered I would like to meet Timmons.

54. Tad Szulc for the *New York Times*, Norman Gall and Louis Uchitelle for the *Washington Post*, and Al Burt for the *Herald Latin America*.

55. *Le Nouvelliste*, October 26, 1964, 1. See chapter 1 and Figure 18.

56. Dr. Louis Laurent, "Les vêpres de Jérémie," *Le Courrier d'Haïti*, October 20, 1976. Pastor Rocourt, in Diederich, *Prix du sang*, 330–43.

57. In-person interviews are referred to in the book as "personal communication." When communications were by phone, letter, or email, I specify so.

58. The year after an officer's name indicates his date of graduation from the military academy. When no year appears after an officer's name, it means he rose through the ranks.

59. Pierre Chérubin later became an actor of the Lavalas movement in the 1990s and followed President Jean-Bertrand Aristide into exile in 1991. He is currently writing his autobiography.

60. The archives of the Communist Party were allegedly appropriated by one of its former members and moved to Miami in the 1990s. I could not locate this report. However, having written it likely helped Jean-Claude Fignolé commit the event to memory.

1. CHRONOLOGY OF THE MASSACRE

1. On Jeune Haiti, the authoritative book is Ralph Allen, *Tombés au champ d'honneur. Les 13 de Jeune Haïti* (Port-au-Prince: Zémès, 2019). Unless otherwise specified, information about Jeune Haiti in this chapter comes from this book.

2. Wadestrandt graduated from Harvard College, Class of 1958. He lived in Lowell House. His roommate Michael Margolis described him as an outstanding person. Wadestrandt had been attending New York University School of Medicine when he joined Jeune Haiti. Michael Margolies, Email communications with author, june 2020.

3. On the April 1963 massacre, see chap 4.

4. See also Commission Internationale de Juristes (CIJ), *La situation socio-politique en Haïti* (n.p., August 5, 1963), 24.

5. Alexandra Philoctère, personal communication with author, Montréal, March 2017. Alexandra Philoctète was Geto Brierre's fiancée. This was confirmed by Mgr. Romélus (personal communication with author, Château, January 2018), who attended the same seminary.

6. See Gérard Alphonse Férère, *Massacres et autres crimes des Duvalier et des dictateurs militaires* (n.p.: Perle des Antilles, 2019), 151–64. This insurgency was also very small, with only 14 fighters, and lasted barely a few weeks.

7. See forthcoming book by Anne Fuller.

8. Pierre Biamby's wife, Kettly Ney-Pierre, was from Jérémie and likely told him about families living there.

9. Pierre Chérubin, phone communications with author, 2019–2021; William Régala, personal communication with author, Delmas, January 2016; and Abel Jérôme, personal communications with author, Lafond, 2012–2018. The Commission's composition is confirmed by the biographical vignettes in Daniel Supplice, *Dictionnaire biographique des personnalités politiques de la République d'Haïti* (Pétion-Ville, Haiti: C3 Éditions, 2014).

10. According to Abel Jérôme's account, this event took place on August 6 but this is unlikely.

11. Laurence Mombeleur was Dr. Willy Verrier's wife. Verrier was an early Duvalierist, the director of Jérémie's Saint-Antoine hospital, and a local patrician. See Eddy Cavé, *Autour des 90 ans de l'Hôpital Saint-Antoine de Jérémie* (Montréal: Papyruz, 2013), 32, 131. Verrier was Minister of Public Health under Jean-Claude Duvalier from 1976 to 1980. See Supplice, *Dictionnaire*, 717. Throughout the book, I use the term "patrician" for the French term *notable*, used by interlocutors.

12. U.S. Embtels 236–8, 241, 248, August 7, 1964.

13. U.S. Embtel 236, August 7, 1964. The U.S. Embassy received information from a variety of individuals: informers within the Haitian military and administration; priests and missionaries; employees at Pan American Airways and at the airport; and through official channels by government members, particularly André Théard (Haiti's ambassador to the United States, who was in Port-au-Prince in August 1963), René Chalmers (Haiti's Minister of Foreign Affairs), and Joseph Baguidy (Duvalier's confidant and ambassador to Switzerland, also in Port-au-Prince at the time). One of the main difficulties for the U.S. Embassy was to distinguish rumors or exaggerations from facts.

14. U.S. Embassy, Sitrep/Embtel 236, 237, 239, August 7, 1964.

15. The visit by the two peasant was mentioned in several communications with the author: Pierre Chérubin (2019), Abel Jérôme (2012), and Anonymous J-2 (2016).

16. It may have been Milou Drouin, whose home was about 150 yards from the wharf.

17. Rocourt recounted his ordeal and liberation in Bernard Diederich, *Le prix du sang*, rev. ed. (Port-au-Prince: Henri Deschamps, 2016), 330–43.

18. Trained as a pilot at the Lackland Air Force Base in San Antonio, Texas, Antoine Fénélon (1940–2006) is a minor figure here. He later served as an ambassador. See Eddy Cavé, *De mémoire de Jérémien: en pensant aux amis disparus* (Montréal: CIDIHCA; Pleine Plage, 2016), 2:98, 183. Importantly, Fénélon shared his experience and observations with the many people he had a social relationship with in Jérémie, including Jean-Claude Fignolé and Eddy Cavé.

19. According to Abel Jérôme, Dr. Fourcand pretended to have sprained his ankle while disembarking from the plane so he could be hosted by Dr. Verrier at the hospital for the duration of his visit, and thus avoid being seen in town. Abel Jérôme, personal communication with author, Lafond, January 2016.

20. The names and date of arrest are from Fr. Bruno Laroche's diary. Laurent later wrote about his ordeal but the dates he provides cannot be right (he locates the event in September). Dr. Louis Laurent, "Les vêpres de Jérémie," *Le Courrier d'Haïti*, October 20, 1976.

21. See Jean-Philippe Belleau, "Intimacy, Hostility, and State Politics: François Duvalier and His Inner-circle, 1931–1971," *History and Anthropology* 32, no. 5 (2021): 549–73.

22. Anne Fuller is preparing a book on the subject after years of ethnographic research on this event. Anne Fuller, personal and email communications with author, Port-au-Prince, 2016-2023.

23. William Régala, a second lieutenant in the Presidential Guard in the 1960s, became general in the 1980s and was an influential member of several military juntas from 1986 to 1990. William Régala, personal communication with author, Delmas, January 2016.

24. See chap. 8.

25. Both men reported the altercation to their entourage (Jean-Claude Fignolé, personal communications with author, Port-au-Prince and Jérémie 2012–17; Anariol Joseph, personal communication with author, Montréal, March 2017). According to Fignolé, Abel Jérôme anticipated that civilians were going to be executed when he saw the names of upper-class Jeremians inside the two Jeune Haiti bags seized at Prévilé.

26. Pierre Chérubin confirmed Jérôme's tactics. Pierre Chérubin, phone communication with author, 2020–2021.

27. Military telegrams were sent by the Presidential Palace or military headquarters at the Casernes Dessalines and were always encoded. Once received, they were handed to Abel Jérôme—or, between August 6 and the Commission's departure at the end of August, to Pierre Biamby—who sent them out for decoding. Once decoded, the messages were brought back and again handed to the highest military authority on site.

28. U.S. Embassy, Embtel 262, August 7, 1964.

29. Abel Jérôme, personal communication with author, Lafond, May 2012.

30. According to Jérôme, it contained hundreds of names from all over the country, not just in Jérémie. On August 19, the U.S. Embassy provides the list of these names, which confirmed Jérôme's statement. U.S. Embassy, Priority 334, August 19, 1964.

31. U.S. Embassy, Embtel 262, August 10, 1964.

32. According to Jean Alcide, these inmates were transported in two jeeps. Jean Alcide, personal communication with author, North Miami, March 2016.

33. Bossuet was in her late thirties at the time of the event, and was well known in the community.

34. According to Anariol Joseph, Dimanche's cousin, the fight was physical. He added that Dimanche was outfoxed by Jérôme, but did not know whether the altercation had taken place at the base or at Number 2. Anariol, personal communication with author, Montréal, March 2017.

35. The Commission carried out interrogations alone, probably out of concern for what the elderly Louis Drouin might reveal. This was confirmed by Jean-Claude Fignolé when he himself was arrested and interrogated in August under the suspicion that he was a communist.

36. Laurent allegedly was in the same cell as Louis Drouin and attempted to tend to his wounds. See Dr. Louis Laurent, "Les vêpres de Jérémie," *Le Courrier d'Haïti* October 20, 1976. On Jean Alcide, see chapter 7.

37. Elliott Roy, personal communication with author, Cayes-Jacmel, January 2019.

38. Elizabeth Abbott, *Haiti: A Shattered Nation* (New York: Overlook; London: Duckworth, 2011), 133; Abel Jérôme, personal communication with author, Lafond, May 2012.

39.   This truck belonged to "Boss" Weiner, a coffee trader who may have been unaware that his employee was using it. "Boss" is a Kreyol way to call an artisan or a skillful worker.

40.   A calendar from that year shows that in Haiti on August 11, 1964, the moon's waxing crescent was about one-eighth illuminated. Even if there was no cloud cover, and there likely was not any at this time of the year, it must have been rather dark, making it difficult to see the ground and difficult to recognize faces.

41.   When asked in 2016 if the "missing" names were Adeline Villedrouin and her two children, Lyssa and Frantz, Abel Jérôme refused to answer.

42.   U.S. Embassy, Embtel 287, August 14, 1964.

43.   U.S. Embassy in Haiti, Embtel 332, August 19, 1964.

44.   Priority 334, August 19, 1964.

45.   Juliette Nicolas, personal communication with author, Jérémie, January 2016.

46.   U.S. Embassy in Haiti, Embtel 351, August 22, 1964. Diederich believes that the Bajeux were arrested in July, but the arrest of a prominent family would most likely have come to the attention of the U.S. Embassy immediately. Diederich, *Prix du sang*, 66.

47.   See chap. 10.

48.   See chap. 7.

49.   There are at least four versions of what happened. In Abel Jérôme's own version, he walked to the truck, confronted Bontemps, and successfully retrieved Mona Ambroise, a Port-au-Prince native. This version is consistent with the one he told Fignolé the day after, and that Fignolé recounted to me. However, Fignolé attributed Jérôme's actions to a desire to get into Duvalier's good graces; Ambroise's father was a Duvalierist. Jérôme then drove Mona Ambroise to the home of Raymond Hilaire, a car mechanic and friend of Jérôme, whose wife, Antonine, took care of her. Antonine Hilaire, née Rousseau, was the illegitimate daughter of Guy Villedrouin, executed on August 11. Antonine was raised in the home of Chenier Villedrouin, Roger Villerouin's father. (Guiton Dorimain, personal communication with author, Port-au-Prince, January 2018; Alix Cédras, phone communication with author, 2021; Michèle Pierre-Louis, personal communication with author, Port-au-Prince, January 2019.) Mona Ambroise was exfiltrated to Port-au-Prince one to three days later. In another version given by only one secondary witness, it was Lt. William Régala, not Jérôme, who was driving the jeep. When asked about it directly, Régala evaded the question (William Régala, personal communication with author, Delmas, January 2016). That Régala would take it upon himself to confront this challenge is possible, but unlikely. In addition, to my knowledge, he did not have access to a jeep while in Jérémie. In Saintange Bontemps's version, as recounted by Pierre Chérubin, Bontemps credited himself for sparing her life and taking her to his house (Chérubin, phone conversation with author, March 2020). In Bruno Laroche's account, Mona Ambroise "was spared but left to three immoral tonton-macoutes."

50.   Efforts by Guylène Sales, head of the Fondation Devoir de Mémoire-Haïti, and myself to communicate with Mona Ambroise, who is still alive, failed.

51.   I collected no other testimony on what happened to Pierre Sansaricq. Abel Jérôme, the only person now alive who knows Sansaricq's exact fate, refused to answer questions on the subject.

52.	See Abbott, *A Shattered Nation*, 137. Cecil Valère also provided me with a full account of their ordeal. Cecil Valère, personal communication with author, Montréal, March 2017.

53.	Supplice, *Dictionnaire*,175; see also chap. 10.

54.	U.S. Embassy in Haiti, Embtel 598, September 28, 1964.

55.	U.S. Embassy in Haiti, Joint Week n.40, October 6, 1964.

56.	Albert Chassagne argued that Corinne Villedrouin, age 92 and confined to a wheelchair, was thrown from a balcony and died from the fall. Albert Chassagne, *Bain de sang en Haiti. Les macoutes opèrent à Jérémie* (New York: n.p., 1977). According to those familiar with the home, however, it was a one-story house. A few pieces of circumstantial evidence suggest that the three elderly ladies were indeed killed and their bodies disposed of at Numéro 2: according to Mgr. Willy Romélus, when a local engineer he had commissioned excavated the mass grave in 1986, the latter told him that the only pieces of cloth he had found and retrieved among the remaining bones were "a belt and *an old woman's nightgown.*" Mgr. Willy Romélus, personal communication with author, Chateau, January 2016.

57.	Some added Abel Jérôme, and others, Sony Borges, although I am not sure he was still in Jérémie at this point. One reliable resident of the Bordes neighborhood, in personal communication with me in 2020, stated that he saw Roger Villedrouin's RCA record player at Abel Jérôme's home.

58.	Willy Romélus, personal communication with author, Chateau, January 2016. Although at that time there was no shantytown in Jérémie, a poorer population lived on its outskirts.

59.	Bruno Laroche, diary, *Journal des frères de l'instruction chrétienne*, 1964. See Figure 3.

60.	Gilles Morin, personal communication with author, Pétionville, January 2016.

61.	U.S. Embassy in Haiti, Embtel 745, Oct. 24, 1964.

62.	U.S. Embassy in Haiti, Embtel 850/Deftel 338, Nov. 2, 1964.

63.	U.S. Embassy in Haiti, Embtel 745, Oct. 24, 1964. The fact that Abel Jérôme was in Port-au-Prince on the very same day that the diplomatic cable was drafted raises the possibility that Jérôme was an informant of the U.S. Embassy.

64.	U.S. Embassy in Haiti, Embtel 759, Oct. 26, 1964. The gun was probably an old Howitzer.

65.	U.S. Embassy in Haiti (signed by Ambassador Timmons), Joint Week 44, October 31, 1964.

2. CONSTRUCTING THE ENEMY

1.	François Duvalier, *Eléments d'une doctrine*, vol. 1, *Œuvres essentielles* (Port-au-Prince: Presses nationales d'Haïti, 1966), 309.

2.	The word "réfléchi" means, if taken literally, "reflects," "reflected," "think!" or "thoughtful," but probably signified "think twice before attacking." I found little historical information about this fort. It may have been built after independence since the French créole Moreau de Saint-Méry, who typically commented on every military construction, did not mention it. Moreau de Saint-Méry, *Description topographique, physique, civile, politique et historique de la partie française de l'isle Saint-Domingue* (Philadelphia, PA: n.p., 1797). The French traveler Edgar La Selve, who visited Miragoâne in 1879, made a passing reference to a "Fort Réfléchi." See Edgar La Selve, *Le pays des nègres: voyage à Haïti, ancienne* (Paris: Hachette, 1881), 280. Semextant Rouzier provides a lengthier description: "Located in Miragoâne. It played an important role in the 1869 Cacos insurgency, as well as during Boyer-Bazelais's armed actions against President Salomon [in 1883]." Semexant Rouzier, *Dictionnaire géographique et administratif universel d'Haïti illustré* (Paris: Charles Blot, 1892), 1:383. According to Price-Mars's book on the 1883 civil war, the positions on hilltops around Miragoâne were nicknamed "forts" by the besieged insurgents. See Jean Price-Mars, *Jean-Pierre Boyer-Bazelais et le drame de Miragoâne: à propos d'un lot d'autographes* (Port-au-Prince: Imprimerie d'État, 1948), 46–47. Today, the place is surrounded by urban development, as I saw when I visited it in 2016. A memorial reminds the public that Fort Réfléchi once stood there. A lesser known Fort Réfléchi, in Pestel to the west, was also built after independence to prevent the French from returning.

3.   See chapter 4.

4.   Fort Réfléchi was commanded by General Rigaud from March to June, General Sarang Jeune in June and July (Price-Mars, 1948: 68), and General Mathurin Legros in August— all of them identified in the historiography as mulattoes.

5.   I asked about this contradiction to the very interlocutors who had recounted stories about "Fort Réfléchi" (the Jeremian one). They dismissed the contradiction.

6.   Michèle Oriol, personal communications with author, Port-au-Prince and Journiac, 2010–2023.

7.   To my knowledge, the *Testament* was never formally published. The text can be found here: "Le testament des libéraux," *L'histoire des Antilles et de l'Afrique*, July 2, 2011. http://www.forumhaiti .com/t15561-le-testament-des-liberaux-important-pour-comprendre-l-actualite-du-jour.

8.   Price-Mars, *Boyer-Bazelais*, 48–50.

9.   In Price-Mars, *Boyer-Bazelais*, 50.

10. In Price-Mars *Boyer-Bazelais*, 116.

11. Both Price-Mars and Frédéric Marcelin use Desroches as their main source of information on this conflict. See Frédéric Marcelin, *Le passé: impressions haïtiennes* (Port-au-Prince: La Dodine, 2014), 37; Price-Mars, *Boyer-Bazelais*, 43

12. Gustave Vigoureux, *L'année terrible; ou 1883 à Jérémie* (Jérémie, Haiti: Imprimerie du Centenaire, 1909).

13. Gustave de Molinari, *A Panama. L'isthme de Panama, la Martinique, Haïti: lettres adressées au Journal des débats* (Paris: Guillaumin et Cie, 1887); Mark Baker Bird, *The Black Man, or Haytian Independence, Deduced from Historical Notes, and Dedicated to the Government and People of Hayti* (New York: n.p., 1869). Léon-François Hoffmann, *Haïti: couleurs, croyances, créole* (Montreal: CIDHICA, 1990). James Leyburn noted during fieldwork in 1941 that the use of explicit racial terms was usually avoided in good company. See James G. Leyburn, *The Haitian People*, 3rd ed. (Lawrence: Institute of Haitian Studies, University of Kansas Press, 1998), 3.

14. Roger Gaillard, *La guerre civile, une option dramatique (15 juillet–31 décembre 1902)*, vol. 4, *La république exterminatrice* (Port-au-Prince: Le Natal, 1993), 233.

15. In Vigoureux, *L'année terrible*, 9–11. Matthew Smith references a copy of it, which he found in the Foreign Office archives in London. Matthew J. Smith, *Liberty, Fraternity,*

Exile. Haiti and Jamaica After Emancipation (Chapel Hill: The University of North Carolina Press, 2014), 224-225.

16.   The literature on the *Protocol* is vast. See for instance Pierre-André Taguieff, *Criminaliser les Juifs: le mythe du "meurtre rituel" et ses avatars (antijudaïsme, antisémitisme, antisionisme)* (Paris: Hermann, 2020); Steven J. Zipperstein, *Pogrom: Kishinev and the Tilt of History* (New York: Liveright, 2018); and Elissa Bemporad, *Legacy of Blood: Jews, Pogroms, and Ritual Murder in the Lands of the Soviets* (New York: Oxford University Press, 2020).

17.   "Epistemic anxieties" is Ann Stoler's expression to name the entanglement of power and sentiment, of logos and pathos, in the production of colonial bureaucratic writings. See Ann Stoler, *Along the Archival Grain: Epistemic Anxieties and Colonial Common Sense* (Princeton: Princeton University Press, 2009). Nils Bubandt applies it to forgeries; see Nils Bubandt, "From the Enemy's Point of View: Violence, Empathy, and the Ethnography of Fakes," *Cultural Anthropology* 24, no. 3 (2009): 553–88.

18.   Bubandt, "From the Enemy's Point of View," 578–9.

19.   Gérard Barthélémy, *Dans la splendeur d'un après-midi d'histoire* (Port-au-Prince: Henri Deschamps, 1996).

20.   On those cultural movements, see Chelsea Stieber, "The Vocation of the *indigènes*: Cosmopolitism and Cultural Nationalism in *La revue indigène*," *Francosphères* 4, no. 1 (2015) 7–19; J. Michael Dash, *Literature and Ideology in Haiti, 1915–1961* (London: Macmillan, 1981); Hoffmann, *Couleurs*; David Nicholls, *From Dessalines to Duvalier: Race, Colour and National Independence in Haiti*, rev. ed. (New Brunswick, NJ: Rutgers University Press, 1996); Matthew J. Smith, *Red and Black in Haiti: Radicalism, Conflict, and Political Change* (Chapel Hill: University of North Carolina Press, 2009); Eddy Arnold Jean, *L'échec d'une élite: indigénisme, négritude, noirisme* (Port-au-Prince: Haïti-Demain, 1992); Martin Munro, *Exile and Post-1946 Literature: Alexis, Depestre, Ollivier, Lafferière, Danticat* (Liverpool, UK: Liverpool University Press, 2007); and Rachel Beauvoir-Dominique et al., "Haïti et l'anthropologie," *Gradhiva* 1 (2005).

21.   Léon-François Hoffmann, *Faustin Soulouque d'Haiti dans l'histoire et la littérature* (Paris: L'Harmattan, 2007), 19–20.

22.   Jean-François Sénéchal, *Le mythe révolutionnaire duvaliériste* (Montréal: CIDIHCA, 2006), 84–86.

23.   Victor Schoelcher, *Colonies étrangères et Haïti, résultats de l'émancipation anglaise*, vol. 2 (Paris: Pagnerre, 1843).

24.   Marlene Daut, *Tropics of Haiti: Race and the Literary History of the Haitian Revolution in the Atlantic World* (Liverpool, UK: University of Liverpool Press, 2017), 524–67.

25.   See Daut, *Tropics*. The European views on racial miscegenation at the time is also exemplified by this entry on *mulâtres* in a 19th century French encyclopedia: "Mulattoes and mixed-race people are known to be, in the colonies, the filth of the human species." Pierre Larousse, *Grand Dictionnaire Universel du XIXe siècle, vol. XI*, Paris: Administration du grand dictionnaire universel, 1874), 673.

26.   Schoelcher, *Colonies étrangères*, 225.

27.   Schoelcher, *Colonies étrangères*, 123–24.

28.   Schoelcher, *Colonies étrangères*, 226.

29.   Schoelcher, *Colonies étrangères*, 156.

30.   Schoelcher, *Colonies étrangères*, 240.

31.   Schoelcher, *Colonies étrangères*, 241. Schoelcher visited Haiti at a time when Boyer's long authoritarian rule and cronyism had produced an atrophied political system.

32.   Schoelcher, *Colonies étrangères*, 238–39. Schoelcher often contradicts himself. He asserts that mulattoes enable inequality, then that "blacks and mulattoes coexist on equal footing in the public arena" and share positions in the government (p. 237). The same contradiction can be seen in his discussion on education: he praised the level of education of Black figures who had in fact been educated under Boyer; then, after blaming "mulatto" control of government for the absence of schooling, he states that lack of capital is responsible for that situation (p. 274). For Jocelyne Trouillot, educational infrastructure was poor throughout the nineteenth century and everywhere in the country. Jocelyne Trouillot, *Histoire de l'éducation en Haïti* (Port-au-Prince: Éditions Université Caraïbes, 2003). For Linsey Sainte Claire, education under Pétion and Boyer was elitist; see Linsey Sainte-Claire, "Régénération et élitisme scolaire sous Alexandre Pétion et Jean-Pierre Boyer (1816–1843)," *Esprit Créateur* 56, no. 1 (2016), 116–28.

33.   Schoelcher's book is admirable in many ways. His relentless defense of racial equality between Blacks and whites went against the mainstream in the mid-nineteenth century, to say the least. His description of rural people he met in northern Haiti shows a genuine interest in and empathy for people. He was also the first Frenchman, I believe, to denounce the debt that the French banks and monarchy forced Haiti into accepting as a condition for recognition of its sovereignty: "The slaves were more entitled to an indemnity than the masters" (p. 167). Yet, Schoelcher could not emancipate himself from colonial beliefs in racial categorization, not to mention his self-righteousness and constant judging of foreign people, customs and beliefs, often lecturing locals on what to do and believe.

34.   Duvalier, *Éléments d'une doctrine*, 276, 278, 280.

35.   Duvalier, *Éléments d'une doctrine*, 265–91.

36.   Hannibal Price, *De la réhabilitation de la race noire par la République d'Haïti* (Port-au-Prince: Imprimerie J. Verrollot, 1900), 659.

37.   Alcius Charmant, *Haïti vivra-t-elle? Étude sur le préjugé de races: race noire, race jaune, race blanche, et sur la doctrine de Monroë* (Le Havre, France: F. Le Roy, 1905), 36.

38.   Charmant, *Haïti vivra-t-elle*, xii

39.   *Pensons-y toujours, n'en parlons jamais.*

40.   For an analysis of the pronouns "us" and "them" in ideologies of hatred, see Jacques Sémelin, *Purify and Destroy. The Political Uses of Massacre and Genocide*, trans. Cynthia Schoch (New York: Columbia University Press, 2007), 48–51.

41.   Léon Gambetta, *Discours de Saint-Quentin*, 16 novembre 1871. The expression became common parlance in nationalist discourse.

42.   See Michael Bilewicz, Aleksandra Cichocka, and Wictor Soral, eds., *The Psychology of Conspiracy: A Festschrift for Miroslaw Kofta* (New York: Routledge, 2015); Pierre-André Taguieff, *Court traité de complotologie, suivi de le "Complot judéo-maçonnique": fabrication d'un mythe apocalyptique modern* (Paris: Mille et une nuits, 2013).

43.   On Haitian exceptionalism, see Robert Fatton, *The Guise of Exceptionalism: Unmasking the National Narratives of Haiti and the United States* (Rutgers: Rutgers University Press, 2021).

44. Attributed in-group solidarity, whether the group is defined in ethnic, racial, or cultural term, has been a key ingredient of ideologies that otherize minorities.

45. In Hoffmann, *Couleurs*, 67; and Nicholls, *From Dessalines to Duvalier*, 110.

46. Price, *De la rehabilitation*.

47. Daniel Supplice, *Dictionnaire biographique des personnalités politiques de la République d'Haïti* (Pétionville, Haiti: C3 Éditions, 2014), 610.

48. Hoffmann, *Couleurs*, 87.

49. See Smith, *Liberty*, part 3.

50. Nicholls, *From Dessalines to Duvalier*, 110.

51. Fifteen months after this letter was published, on May 5, 1882, a massacre of fourteen elite mulattoes took place in Saint-Marc. See chapter 4.

52. See Götz Aly, *Why the Germans? Why the Jews? Envy, Race Hatred, and the Prehistory of the Holocaust* (New York: Metropolitan Books, 2014); Omer Bartov, "Defining Enemies, Making Victims: Germans, Jews, and the Holocaust," *American Historical Review* 103, no. 3 (1998): 771–816; Pierre-André Taguieff, *The Force of Prejudice: On Racism and Its Doubles* (Minneapolis: University of Minnesota Press, 2001); and Taguieff, *Criminaliser les Juifs*.

53. Alain Finkielkraut, *Discours de réception à l'Académie française* (January 26, 2016), 2. One of the most broadcasted songs by Radio Télévision Libre des Mille Collines (RTLM) in Rwanda during the genocide was titled "I Hate These Hutus," by Simon Bikindi, a popular Hutu singer, who for this song impersonates a fictive Tutsi talking about Hutus. See Alison Liebhafsky Des Forges, *"Leave None to Tell the Story": Genocide in Rwanda*, 2nd ed. (New York: Human Rights Watch, 1999), 67–68; Immaculée Immaculée Ilibagiza, *Left to Tell: Discovering God Amidst the Rwandan Holocaust* (Carlsbad, CA: Hay House, 2006).

54. Janvier, Louis Joseph, *Les affaires d'Haiti (1883–1884)* (Paris: C. Marpon et E. Flammarion, 1885), 239.

55. Duvalier, *Éléments d'une doctrine*, 244–45

56. Jean-Paul Sartre, *Critique de la raison dialectique: précédé de Question de méthode* (Paris: Gallimard, 1960), 209.

57. This is already observable in Schoelcher's 1843 book, where massacres of "mulattoes" by Toussaint's generals in 1800 and later by Christophe in 1812 are explained by mulattoes' affront to the Black majority.

58. Charmant, *Haiti vivra-t-elle*, xxxiii–xxxiv.

59. Roger Dorsinville and Maryse Condé, "Entretien avec Roger Dorsinville," *Archipelago* 3–4 (1983), 137.

60. Duvalier, *Éléments d'une doctrine*.

61. André Juste, *Nos élites et nos masses de 1685 à 1984: lettre ouverte à M. Gérard M. Laurent* (Port-au-Prince: Les Ateliers Fardin, 1984), 9.

62. Vertus Saint-Louis, "L'assassinat de Dessalines et le culte de sa mémoire," *Revista Brasileira do Caribe* 16, no. 31 (2015), 95–124; Eddy Cavé, *Haïti. Extermination des pères fondateurs et pratiques d'exclusion* (Port-au-Prince: Henri Deschamps, 2022), 234-260.

63. Duvalier would later share that opinion.

64. Hénock Trouillot, *Beaubrun Ardouin: l'homme politique et l'historien* (Port-au-Prince: n.p., 1950).

65.   David Nicholls, "Ideology and Political Protest in Haiti, 1930–46," *Journal of Contemporary History* 9, no. 4 (1974), 3–26.

66.   Péan, *L'ensauvagement macoute et ses conséquences, 1957–1990*, vol. 4, *Haïti: économie politique de la corruption* (Paris: Maisonneuve et Larose, 2007); Michèle Oriol, *Histoire et éducation Civique* (Port-au-Prince: Fondation pour la recherche iconographique et documentaire, 2001).

67.   It did not really work. Soulouque had Ardouin arrested in 1848, imprisoned, and executed a year later. The motive was conspiracy.

68.   This is a literal translation of the original title. Duvalier's syntax was not flawless.

69.   Duvalier, *Éléments d'une doctrine*, 309. This work was first published in 1948. In the 1966 edition, Lorimer Denis's name disappeared from the front cover; hence our use of Duvalier as the sole author here.

70.   Taguieff, *Court traité de complotologie*; Susan Lepselter, *The Resonance of Unseen Things: Poetics, Power, Captivity, and UFOs in the American Uncanny* (Ann Arbor: University of Michigan Press, 2016); and Bilewicz et al., *The Psychology of Conspiracy*.

71.   Taguieff, *Court traité*.

72.   Taguieff, *Court traité*, 15.

73.   The poet Jean-Richard Laforest offered an improbably Marxist variation of it: *mulâtrisme* names the ownership of capital. Jean-Richard Laforest, "Notes à propos d'un article de René Piquion." *Rencontre* 24–25 (2012): 89–94. Laforest was the nephew of two victims of the Jérémie massacre. The term was so prevalent that even Michel-Rolph Trouillot used it to characterize the behavior of "mulattoes" not only in politics (p. 148) but in general as well (p. 128). Michel-Rolph Trouillot, *Haiti, State Against Nation: The Origins and Legacy of Duvalierism* (New York: Monthly Review Press, 1990). Michèle Labelle also uses the term uncritically; see Michèle Labelle, *Idéologies de couleur et classes sociales en Haïti* (Montréal: Presses de l'Université de Montréal, 1978).

74.   Claude Lévi-Strauss, *Introduction to the Work of Marcel Mauss* (London: Routledge and Kegan Paul, 1987), 63. I believe Edward Tylor called this phenomenon "survival": when societies "cling" to opinions, beliefs, or mythological components through their own inertia even when the conditions that gave rise to them have long since disappeared. See Edward Tylor, *Primitive Culture: Researches Into the Development of Mythology, Philosophy, Religion, Art, and Custom*, (London: John Murray, 1871), 2:16.

75.   Péan, *L'ensauvagement*, 121–37

76.   Roger Dorsinville, *Lettre aux hommes clairs* (Port-au-Prince: Imprimerie de l'État, 1946).

77.   Trouillot, *Haiti, State Against Nation*, 126–28.

78.   Labelle, *Idéologies de couleur*. The ethnographic method does, however, include duly taking notes on and reporting about private discussions, intimate conversations, interviewing, and the like.

79.   A 1963 clandestine publication by the Haitian Communist Party and bearing the writing style of Gérard Pierre-Charles, called it "the most efficient weapon of Duvalier's imposture in an otherwise large demagogic arsenal." See *Duvalier mis à nu: les Macoutes mènent la danse* (Montréal: n.p., 1963?), 4–5. By 1963, the Unified Party of Haitian Communists (Parti unifié des communistes haïtiens, or PUCH) was convinced that the color question had propelled Duvalier into power by rallying the "black petty bourgeoisie looking to climb the social ladder." See *Duvalier mis à nu*, 7.

80. Duvalier, *Éléments d'une doctrine*, 268–70.

81. Duvalier, *Éléments d'une doctrine*, 271.

82. Duvalier, *Éléments d'une doctrine*, 273. The view that behaviors during the Haitian Revolution were determined by race was rather common in Duvalier's time. The Haitian historian Justin Chrysostome Dorsainvil considered that the Revolution was a racial conflict. See Justin Chrysostome Dorsainvil, *Manuel d'histoire d'Haïti* (Port-au-Prince: Procure des Frères de l'Instruction Chrétienne, 1934). For René Piquion (1906–2001), an intellectual who rose from schoolteacher to university dean under François Duvalier, Pétion and Rigaud never wanted independence, feared the "black masses," and conspired "against national sovereignty." See René Piquion, *Crépuscule de mythes* (Port-au-Prince: Imprimerie de l'État, 1962), 25. For Leslie Péan, this narrative "hijacks their history from Haitians by constructing a mythology based on noirism and identity claims." See Péan, *L'ensauvagement*, 49. For historian Laurent Dubois race was not a determinant during the Haitian Revolution. Laurent Dubois, *Avengers of the New World: The Story of the Haitian Revolution* (Cambridge, MA: Harvard University Press, 2004).

83. Duvalier, *Éléments d'une doctrine*, 275.

84. Duvalier, *Éléments d'une doctrine*, 294.

85. Dorsinville, *Lettre aux hommes clairs*.

86. Smith, *Red and Black*; Frantz Voltaire, ed, *Pouvoir noir en Haïti: l'explosion de 1946* (Montreal: CIDIHCA, 2019).

87. Smith, *Red and Black*, 71–101.

88. Pressoir Pierre, *Témoignages, 1946–1976, l'espérance déçue* (Port-au-Prince: Henri Deschamps, 1987), 58. Duvalier's daughter Simone, when asked who visited her family most often in 1956–1957, stated: "He (Dorsinville) basically lived with us." Simone Duvalier, personal communication with author, Miami, January 2018.

89. Dorsinville, *Lettre aux hommes clairs*, 5.

90. Dorsinville, *Lettre aux hommes clairs*, 12.

91. Dorsinville, *Lettre aux hommes clairs*, 11–12.

92. In mid-twentieth century parlance, *la classe* referred to the Black middle class.

93. Dorsinville, *Lettre aux hommes clairs*, 9–11.

94. Dorsinville and Condé, "Entretien," 139.

95. Dorsinville and Condé, "Entretien," 137. See also Roger Dorsinville, "Dans le fauteuil de l'histoire. Propos recueillis par Michel Adam et Edgard Gousse," *Etincelles* 1, no. 10 (1985): 18–21.

96. On this exchange of public letters, see Nicholls, *From Dessalines to Duvalier*.

97. Milo Rigaud, *Jésus ou Legba?ou les dieux se battent* (Poitiers: Amis de la poésie), 153.

98. Simon Desvarieux, *Lettre aux hommes noirs* (Port-au-Prince: Imprimerie de l'État, 1946).

99. David Norman Smith, "The Social Construction of the Enemies: Jews and Representations of Evil," *Sociological Theory* 4, no. 2 (1996), 206.

100. The term may have been coined by Frantz Fanon, in *Peau noire, masques blancs* (Paris: Seuil, 1952), 65, 110. I thank Sebastião Nascimento for his help on this matter.

101. Communism was the response of mulatto intellectuals to noirism, as Michèle Oriol stated in personal communications, Port-au-Prince and Journiac, 2010-2023. Since noirism turned mulattoes into non-Haitians, they would defend the poor and the exploited

with the most radical anti-elite ideology of the time—a doubling-down on Haitianness. On the Haitian Communist Party and its position on the color question, see Matthew Smith, *Red and Black*, 19–21, 97.

102.   Saint-Louis locates the emergence of this discourse (the notion that there is either a "mulatto" or a black version of Haitian history) in the 1920s. See Saint-Louis, "L'assassinat," 117.

103.   Hénock Trouillot, *L'intellectuel de couleur et les problèmes de discrimination raciale* (Port-au-Prince: Imprimerie de l'État, 1956), 9.

104.   Trouillot, *L'intellectuel*, 11.

105.   Trouillot, *L'intellectuel*, 34–41.

106.   Daut, *Tropics of Haiti*.

107.   Hénock Trouillot, *M. Dantès Bellegarde, un écrivain d'autrefois* (Port-au-Prince: N.A. Théodore, 1957). Bellegarde was "honorary president" of the Pan-African Congress in the early 1920s. W. E. B. Dubois called Bellegarde "the international spokesman of the Negroes of the world." Patrick Bellegarde-Smith, "Dantès Bellegarde and Pan-Africanism," *Phylon* 42, no. 3 (1981), 233. When Dubois visited Haiti, he paid a visit to Bellegarde, with whom he had a lifelong epistolary exchange.

108.   Piquion, *Crépuscule*, 24.

109.   Piquion, *Crépuscule*, 31.

110.   Supplice, *Dictionnaire*, 267.

3. OTHERING THE ELITE

1.   François Duvalier, *Eléments d'une doctrine*, vol. 1, *Œuvres essentielles* (Port-au-Prince: Presses nationales d'Haiti, 1966), 261.

2.   This was Yvon Laraque, although his name would not be known until several days later. The corpse itself had been morbidly displayed at a major crossroads of the capital since that morning, tied to a chair with a sign stating "Chief of the rebels." See *New York Times*, "Haiti Regime Braced for Rebel Attack," August 15, 1964.

3.   U.S. Embassy, Embtel 287 (August 14, 1964). The Haitian genealogical tree of the Laraque family goes back to the early eighteenth century.

4.   Embtel 287 and U.S. Embassy, Embtel 296, August 14, 1964.

5.   Elliott Roy, a lieutenant in the Presidential Guard and close to Duvalier (see chapter 9) registered his many random racial comments and admitted that "Duvalier was obsessed with the Jérémie mulattoes." Elliott Roy, personal communication with author, Cayes-Jacmel, January 2019. See also Elizabeth Abbott, *Haiti: A Shattered Nation* (New York: Overlook Duckworth, 2011); and Leslie Jean-Robert Péan, *L'ensauvagement macoute et ses conséquences, 1957–1990*, vol. 4, *Haïti: économie politique de la corruption* (Paris: Maisonneuve et Larose, 2007).

6.   Jean-François Sénéchal meticulously documented Duvalier's racialism. See Jean-François Sénéchal, *Le mythe révolutionnaire duvaliériste* (Montreal: CIDIHCA, 2006), 84–86.

7.   David Nicholls, "Biology and Politics in Haiti," *Race* 13, no. 2 (1971), 203–14.

8.   Chelsea Stieber, *Haiti's Paper War. Post-Independence Writing, Civil War, and the Making of the Republic, 1804–1954* (New York: New York University Press, 2020), 227–54; Chelsea

Stieber, "The Vocation of the *indigènes*: Cosmopolitism and Cultural Nationalism in *La revue indigene*," *Francosphères* 4, no. 1 (2015): 44–60. The notion of "integral nationalism" was Charles Maurras's master idea and project. I will discuss him more later on.

9. *Action Nationale*, January 16, 1935.

10. Duvalier, *Éléments d'une doctrine*, 247. I kept the syntactic mistakes in the quote.

11. Bob Nérée, *Duvalier. Le pouvoir sur les autres, de père en fils* (Port-au-Prince: Henri Deschamps, 1988).

12. "Third-World Leader" forms part of the title of Duvalier's 1969 book; see François Duvalier, *Mémoires d'un leader du Tiers Monde: mes négociations avec le Saint-Siège; ou, une tranche d'histoire* (Paris: Hachette, 1969).

13. For a precise description of the bombings ordered by Duvalier in 1956–1957, see Pressoir Pierre, *Témoignages, 1946–1976 : l'espérance déçue* (Port-au-Prince: Henri Deschamps, 1987); and Claude Moïse, *Constitutions et luttes de pouvoir en Haïti (1804–1987)* (Montreal: CIDIHCA, 1990).

14. The *Cagoulards* were nicknamed *Tonton Macoutes* before the bureaucratization of the National Security Volunteers (Volontaires de la Sécurité Nationale, or VSN) corps in 1962. See Bernard Diederich and Al Burt, *Papa Doc et les Tontons Macoutes: la verité sur Haïti* (Port-au-Prince: Henri Deschamps, 1986), 112.

15. Louis Joseph Janvier, *Le vieux piquet: scène de la vie haïtienne* (Jacmel, Haiti: Éditions de la Dodine, 2013).

16. Piquets did not attack or defeat Jérémie in 1883: the military did. See chapter 4.

17. A *morne* (hill) is used as the metaphor for the rural or the remote.

18. Janvier, *Le vieux piquet*, 81. Janvier's genealogical tree reveals that he is linked, through his sister's marriage, to the Dehoux, Bayard, Vaval, Laraque, and other mulatto and Black families who were already prominent in the nineteenth century. This is the same Laraque family whose member had his corpse displayed at a city crossroads in 1964. See chapter 1.

19. Interestingly, Hannibal Price expressed admiration for Janvier. See Hannibal Price, *De la réhabilitation de la race noire par la République d'Haïti* (Port-au-Prince: J. Verrollot, 1900), 686. In his demonstration that the Black race was in no way inferior in intelligence to whites, Price took Janvier as an example of intellectual achievement. Nowhere in his work did Price criticize Janvier.

20. Louis Joseph Janvier, *Les antinationaux: actes et principes* (Paris: G. Rougier, 1884); see also Janvier, *Les affaires d'Haïti (1883–1884)* (Paris: C. Marpon E. Flammarion, 1885).

21. Péan, *L'ensauvagement*, 105.

22. Laënnec Hurbon, *Esclavage, religion, et politique en Haïti* (Lyon: Presses Universitaires de Lyon, 2003).

23. Louis Herns Marcelin, "In the Name of the Nation: Ritual, Blood, and the Political Habitus of Violence in Haiti," *American Anthropologist* 114, no. 2 (2012): 253–66.

24. Ben Kiernan, "Twentieth-Century Genocides: Underlying Ideological Themes from Armenia to East Timor," in *The Specter of Genocide. Mass Murder in Historical Perspective*, ed. Robert Gellately and Ben Kiernan (Cambridge: Cambridge University Press, 2003), 29–51; Ben Kiernan. *Blood and Soil: A World History of Genocide and Extermination from Sparta to Darfur* (New Haven, CT: Yale University Press, 2007).

25. Ben Kiernan, "The First Genocide: Carthage, 146BC," *Diogenes* 51, no. 3 (2004): 30.

26. Kiernan, *Blood and Soil*, 26.

27. Kiernan suspects that Enver Pasha saw Armenians, Greeks, and Jews as "urban ethnic communities . . . capitalist parasites on the Turkish peasant body." Kiernan, "Twentieth-Century Genocides," 40.

28. See for instance Léon Lahens, *L'élite intellectuelle* (Port-au-Prince: Imprimerie de l'Abeille, 1916); Jean Price-Mars, *La vocation de l'élite* (Port-au-Prince: Presses nationales d'Haïti, 2001); Lucien Daumec, *La mission des élites: essai* (Port-au-Prince: Presses libres, 1954); Duvalier, *Éléments d'une doctrine*, vol. 1, *Œuvres essentielles* (Port-au-Prince: Presses nationales d'Haiti, 1966); Alix Lamaute, *La bourgeoisie nationale, une entité controversée* (Montreal: CIDIHCA, 1999); Jean-Jacques Honorat, *Enquête sur le développement* (Port-au-Prince: Imprimerie Centrale, 1974), 143–226; André Juste, *Nos élites et nos masses de 1685 à 1984* (Port-au-Prince: Les Ateliers Fardin, 1984); and Eddy Arnold Jean, *L'échec d'une élite: indigénisme, négritude, noirisme* (Port-au-Prince: Haïti-Demain, 1992). As the dates of publication show, the "elite question" has exceeded noirism's historical trajectory and withstood regime changes.

29. See Price-Mars, *La vocation*.

30. Price-Mars, *La vocation*, 91.

31. See Nicholls, "Biology"; see also David Nicholls, *From Dessalines to Duvalier. Race, Colour and National Independence in Haiti*, rev. ed. (New Brunswick, NJ: Rutgers University Press, 1996).

32. This situation echoes, to some extent, intellectual debates in early twentieth-century China. Even before the advent of Communist ideas, intellectual and political elites blamed traditional religion for their country's backwardness. Until then a deeply religious and spiritual society, China fell victim to the systematic destruction of its religious institutions, buildings, and practices, first by the nationalists then by the Communists. By the end of the century, traditional religion was almost entirely wiped out. See Vincent Goossaert and David A. Palmer, *The Religious Question in Modern China* (Chicago: University of Chicago Press, 2011). What I am comparing here is a diagnosis based on an ideological worldview and a three-part notion: that there is an obstacle on the road to progress; that this obstacle is societal; and that it must be eliminated to fix society.

33. All the authors mentioned in this context enjoyed a position either of power, social recognition, or socioeconomic privilege. This includes Duvalier himself who, by 1946, was a cabinet member in Dumarsais Estimé's administration and recognized as an author and a politician; his own father was a judge and for several years owned a newspaper. See Jean-Philippe Belleau, "The Stranger-King of the Caribbean: François Duvalier, State Politics, and the Othering of Brutality." *Journal of Latin American and Caribbean Anthropology* 24, no. 4 (2019): 935–57.

34. The only one to do so was Lucien Daumec, Duvalier's former ghostwriter and brother-in-law, but the definition he provided was so relative that it was epistemologically useless. See Daumec, *La mission*, 13.

35. The quotation in French is "les élites sont les nantis de l'avoir et du savoir." See Honorat, *Enquête*, 8.

36. Duvalier, *Éléments d'une doctrine*, 135–62, 261–320, 323–39.

37. See Matthew J. Smith, *Red and Black in Haiti: Radicalism, Conflict, and Political Change* (Chapel Hill: University of North Carolina Press, 2009).

38. Duvalier, *Éléments d'une doctrine*, 246.

39. Duvalier, *Éléments d'une* doctrine, 326.

40. Lucien Daumec, *La mission*, 45–46. Western racism against Haiti can be easily instrumentalized for internal political purposes rather than rejected on principles.

41. Michel-Rolph Trouillot, *Haiti, State Against Nation: The Origins and Legacy of Duvalierism* (New York: Monthly Review Press, 1990), 80–82. However, Trouillot proceeded, in apophasitic style, to reproduce this dualist sociology.

42. John Lobb, "Caste and Class in Haiti," *American Journal of Sociology* 46, no. 1 (1940): 23.

43. James G. Leyburn, *The Haitian People*, 3rd ed. (Lawrence: Institute of Haitian Studies, University of Kansas Press, 1998).

44. Eric Wolf, *Europe and the People Without History* (Los Angeles: University of California Press, 1982); Marshall Sahlins, *Islands of History* (Chicago: University of Chicago Press, 1985).

45. Leyburn, *Haitian People*, 4.

46. Leyburn, *Haitian People*, 8. Intrigued by such categoric, self-righteous assertions and the rather populist tone of an otherwise sympathetic classic, I wondered about Leyburn's own social background and life. Leyburn was born into one "of [Virginia's] noble, old, and pious Presbyterian families" and studied and worked only at elite and private institutions: Princeton, Yale, and Washington and Lee University, where he was a dean. He "was a lifelong bachelor" (email communication with Tom Camden, librarian at Washington and Lee University, September 2020.) I return to Leyburn in chapter 6.

47. This tradition is built on absolutes and a series of accumulated essentializations. In contrast, the main scientific work on the Haitian elite is built on empirical research, substantiated by evidence, and based on inductions: Philippe-Richard Marius, *The Unexceptional Case of Haiti: Race and Class Privilege in Postcolonial Bourgeois Society* (Jackson: University Press of Mississippi, 2022).

48. This structure (a societal diagnosis within a political ideology) can be found in other ideologies of hatred, such as pan-Hutu ideology and fascism. See the previous chapter.

49. On Haiti's twentieth-century intellectual history, see for example Stieber, "The Vocation of the *indigènes*"; Stieber, *Haiti's Paper War*; Smith, *Red and Black*; and J. Michael Dash, *Literature and Ideology in Haiti, 1915–1961* (London: Macmillan, 1981).

50. André Béteille, "Inequality and Equality," in *Companion Encyclopedia of Anthropology*, ed. Tim Ingold (London: Routledge, 1993), 1010.

51. Gérard Barthélémy, *Dans la splendeur d'un après-midi d'histoire* (Port-au-Prince: Henri Deschamps, 1996), 245.

52. Jean Alix René, "Le culte de l'égalité: une exploration du processus de formation de l'État et de la politique populaire en Haïti au cours de la première moitié du dix-neuvième siècle (1804–1846)" (PhD diss., Concordia University, 2014).

53. In French, *a* ("une") canaille would be translated as "scoundrel" (the indefinite article singles out a specific individual or instance); but in early nineteenth-century French *the* ("la") canaille refers to the urban lumpen, as suggested by the rest of the paragraph. Italics in this paragraph are mine.

54.   Victor Schoelcher, *Colonies étrangères et Haïti, résultats de l'émancipation anglaise*, 2 vols (Paris: Pagnerre, 1843), 301.

55.   See Florent Guénard, *La passion de l'égalité* (Paris: Seuil, 2022); Darrin McMahon, "To Write the History of Equality," *History and Theory* 58, no. 1 (2019): 112–25; Pierre Rosanvallon, *The Society of Equals*, trans. Arthur Goldhammer (Cambridge, MA: Harvard University Press, 2013); and Siep Stuurman, *François Poulain de la Barre and the Invention of Modern Equality* (Cambridge, MA: Harvard University Press, 2004). For a counterhistory of egalitarian ideas, see Aldo Schiavone, *The Pursuit of Equality in the West*, trans. Jeremy Carden (Cambridge, MA: Harvard University Press, 2022). Schiavone traces the roots of equality to Roman ideas, yet attributes to philosophers of the first modernity an essential role in how we think of equality.

56.   See also Gérald Stourzh, "Penser l'égalité. Cinq notions d'égalité chez Tocqueville," *Droits* 41, no. 1 (2005): 185–98.

57.   See for example Laurent Dubois, *Avengers of the New World: The Story of the Haitian Revolution* (Cambridge, MA: Harvard University Press, 2004).

58.   Béteille, "Inequality and Equality," 1035.

59.   Michel Forsé, *L'égalité, une passion française?* (Paris: Armand Colin, 2013).

60.   This is also Marianne Cornevin's (2002) book title: a study on this historical figure. Marianne Cornevin, *Liberté, que de crimes on commet en ton nom! Vie de Madame Roland, guillotinée le 8 novembre 1793* (Paris: Maisonneuve et Larose, 2002).

61.   See for example Alan Page Fiske and Tage Shakti Rai, *Virtuous Violence: Hurting and Killing to Create, Sustain, End, and Honor Social Relationships* (Cambridge: Cambridge University Press, 2015).

62.   François Furet, *Interpreting the French Revolution* (Cambridge: Cambridge University Press, 1981); François Furet, *The Passing of an Illusion: The Idea of Communism in the Twentieth Century* (Chicago: Chicago University Press, 1999).

63.   Timothy Tackett, *The Coming of the Terror in the French Revolution* (Cambridge, MA: Belknap Press of Harvard University Press, 2015), 2.

64.   I believe Placide David was close to make this argument; see Placide David, *L'héritage colonial en Haïti* (Madrid: Langa, 1959). A historian and politician from Les Cayes, David (1885–1967) wrote on Haiti's colonial heritage. His son, Jean Placide (1908–1987) would become a Duvalierist parliamentarian—before being exiled to Africa.

65.   Bernard Gainot, " 'Sur fond de cruelle inhumanité' ": les politiques du massacre dans la Révolution de Haïti," *Cahiers de l'Institut d'histoire de la Révolution française* 3 (2011).
        I also wonder if the drowning of civilians carried out under Dessaline's orders in 1800 and again in 1804 was not inspired by the 1794 drowning carried out in Nantes, when hundreds of families were put into galliots which were then sunk once out on the open sea—see G. Lenotre, *Les noyades de Nantes* (Paris: Perrin, 1912), exactly as would later happen in Les Cayes, Jérémie, and Aquin.

66.   Max Horkheimer and Theodore Adorno, *Dialectic of Enlightenment: Philosophical Fragments*, ed. Gunzelin Schmid Noerr, trans. Edmund Jephcott (Stanford, CA: Stanford University Press, 2002); Zygmunt Bauman, *Modernity and the Holocaust* (Ithaca, NY: Cornell University Press, 1989).

67.   Guénard, *La passion*, 3.

68. See for example Ernest Lavisse, *Histoire de France depuis les origins jusqu'à la Révolution* (Paris: Armand Colin, 1913). This idea becomes widespread throughout the nineteenth century.

69. Ran Halévi, "Hate and the Revolutionary Spirit," lecture, Marc Bloch Center, Humboldt University, October 28, 2014, Berlin, Germany, posted November 13, 2014, Bard College Berlin, YouTube, https://www.youtube.com/watch?v=dxkbb2nC4j8. Video, 1:46:54.

70. In McMahon, "To Write," 123.

71. Ran Halévi, "Les haines hexagonales," *Revue des Deux Mondes* (June 2019): 8–15.

72. Furet, *The Passing of an Illusion*, 1999. On class-based repression, the literature is particularly vast. See for instance Sheila Fitzpatrick, "Ascribing Class: The Construction of Class Identity in Soviet Russia," *Journal of Modern History* 64, no. 4 (1993): 745–70; Golfo Alexopoulos, *Stalin's Outcasts: Aliens, Citizens, and the Soviet State, 1926–1936.* (Ithaca, NY: Cornell University Press, 2003).

73. To my knowledge, neither India nor Brazil, often presented as among the most unequal societies in the world at least for the past half century according to social indicators established by the United Nations Development Program (UNDP), produced (within the fields where intellectual production encounters policies) such radical, rationalized, and widespread anti-elite ideologies—I include in this generalization the Indian states of West Bengal and Kerala, where the Communist Party, in power for almost four decades, did not punish traditional elites. These are broad generalizations for the purposes of comparison and are intended to emphasize the constructed character rather than the objectivity of anti-elite sentiments and ideology.

74. Halévi, "Les haines hexagonales"; Hannah Arendt, *The Origins of Totalitarianism* (New York: Harcourt, Brace, 1951).

75. Louis Drouin was not rich, even by local standards; neither his wooden home nor his family displayed an ostentatious wealth they did not have. The only picture of him that survived shows a rather stern face with sharp features — a face that could be from Brittany. Louis Drouin's face would not play a role against him in most circumstances, but it would if his own son was part of an insurgency aiming to overthrow the government.

76. Frantz Voltaire, ed. *Pouvoir noir en Haïti: l'explosion de 1946* (Montreal: CIDIHCA, 2019).

77. My initial intention in Moron was to "poll" oral history about possible crimes committed in the backcountry against the peasantry during the 1964 anti-insurgency operations. The research bifurcated toward representations of the elite.

78. As said by the interlocutor I identify as Anonymous J-4, *Pou nou gwen lapè, fok nou fiziyé 200 milat chak ven lané.*

79. I return to it in chapter 6. See also Diederich and Burt, *Papa Doc*, 105; Abbott, *Haiti: A Shattered Nation*, 79–80; Moïse, *Constitutions*, 381; Pierre, *Témoignages*, 134–35.

80. Rose-May Hakim-Rimpel, personal communication with author, Port-au-Prince, January 2019.

81. Pierre, *Témoignages*, 134–35.

82. In January 1958, Major Pierre Merceron was second-in-command of the Port-au-Prince police. Daniel Supplice, *Dictionnaire biographique des personnalités politiques de la République d'Haïti, 1804–2014* (Petionville, Haiti: C3 Éditions, 2014), 432. He became chief of staff the following year. He had been instrumental in Duvalier's electoral victory in 1957.

83.   Diederich's account differs slightly: it omits Elois Maître from the group of perpetrators and locates the event on January 6. Rose-May, however, remembers distinctly that the kidnapping happened on a Sunday night, which was January 5. Bernard Diederich, *Le prix du sang*, rev. ed. (Port-au-Prince: Henri Deschamps, 2016), 71–72.

84.   See Supplice, *Dictionnaire*, 364–65.

85.   See Pierre, *Témoignages*, 63; Moïse, *Constitutions*, 328, 346, 385; Supplice, *Dictionnaire*, 439; and Bernard Diederich, *Le trophée* (Port-au-Prince: Henri Deschamps, 2008), 2–3, 170–71. Fritz Cinéas denies any involvement. Fritz Cinéas, personal communication with author, Washington, D.C., October 2022.

86.   Diederich, *Le trophé*, 2–3; Moïse, *Constitutions*, 337.

87.   See Supplice, *Dictionnaire*, 439.

88.   "Haiti President Dismises Mayor," *New York Times* (May 8, 1958), 11.

89.   McMahon, "To Write," 123.

90.   Rae Yang, *Spider Eaters: A Memoir* (Los Angeles: University of California Press, 2013).

91.   Moïse, *Constitutions*, 334.

92.   David Nicholls, "Embryo-politics in Haiti," *Government and Opposition* 6, no. 1 (1971): 75–85. Duvalier's lack of intellectual curiosity about economics revealed itself during an interview with French journalist Irène Chagneau in 1961. Asked about his economic program, Duvalier cannot answer; the journalist repeats the question, and Duvalier talks about opponents' wealth, corruption, and the need for foreign experts. "Un tyran au sommet du pouvoir, 1959" (9'20" and following). https://www.youtube.com/watch?v=Y2 _OFLvFyJE

93.   On Louis Jean-Jacques Acaau, see Mimi Sheller, *Democracy After Slavery: Black Publics and Peasant Radicalism in Haiti and Jamaica* (Gainesville: University Press of Florida, 2000).

94.   Duvalier, *Eléments d'une doctrine*, 296.

95.   Duvalier, *Eléments d'une* doctrine, 240. See also Nicholls, *From Dessalines to Duvalier*, 33. It should be said emphatically that there was no land reform under Duvalier. It is a stretch to use the term "redistribution" to refer to the gang-like practice of appropriating the properties of executed or exiled opponents to (for the most part) give them away to the regime's supporters. "Redistribution" is usually employed for land reforms such as those in Mexico after 1910, Cuba after 1959, or in Guatemala in 1954. For multiple examples of false redistribution under Duvalier, see Péan, *L'ensauvagement;* Jean Alix René, *Haiti après l'esclavage: formation de l'état et culture politique populaire (1804–1846)* (Port-au-Prince: Le Natal, 2019), chap. 3.

96.   Fritz Cinéas, personal communication with author, Washington, D.C., October 2022.

97.   *Le Moniteur*, May 6, 1882. See chapter 10.

98.   Gustave de Molinari, *À Panama. L'isthme de Panama, la Martinique, Haïti: lettres adressées au Journal des débats* (Paris: Guillaumin et Cie, 1887), 213.

99.   Robert Fatton, *Haiti's Predatory Republic: The Unending Transition to Democracy* (Boulder, CO: Lynne Rienner, 2002).

100. Justin Bouzon, *Études historiques sur la présidence de Faustin Soulouque (1847–1849)* (Paris: Gustave Guérin, 1894), 92–93.

101. Marcel Gilbert, *La patrie haitienne: de Boyer-Bazelais à l'unité historique du peuple haïtien* (Port-au-Prince: Imprimerie des Antilles, 1986).

102. Michèle Oriol, *Chefs d'État en Haïti: gloire et misères* (Port-au-Prince: Fondation pour la recherche iconographique et documentaire, 2006).

103. Semexant Rouzier, *Dictionnaire géographique et administratif universel d'Haïti illustré* (Port-au-Prince: August A. Héraux, 1927), 3:81

104. Rouzier, *Dictionnaire*, 3:76.

105. Louis Joseph Janvier, *Les antinationaux: actes et principes* (Paris: G. Rougier, 1884), 30.

106. Nothing indicates that Janvier ever traveled to Jérémie, of which he thus had no personal knowledge.

107. Janvier, *Les affaires*, 236. "Liberals" was often codeword for mulattoes.

108. Nicholls, *From Dessalines to Duvalier*, 188.

109. In Albert Chassagne, *Bain de sang en Haïti. Les macoutes opèrent à Jérémie* (New York: n.p., 1977).

4. A PATTERN OF ANTI-ELITE MASSACRES, 1848–1964

1. Michel-Rolph, Trouillot, *Silencing the Past. Power and the Production of History* Boston: Beacon Press, 1995), 27.

2. According to Léon-François Hoffmann, the French consul, Maxime Reybaud, wrote under the pseudonym Gustave d'Alaux (unrelated to the eponymous architect); see Hoffman, *Haïti: couleurs, croyances, créole* (Montreal: CIDHICA, 1990).

3. Matthew J. Smith, *Liberty, Fraternity, Exile. Haiti and Jamaica After Emancipation* (Chapel Hill: The University of North Carolina Press, 2014).

4. Bouzon, *Études historiques sur la présidence de Faustin Soulouque (1847–1849)* (Paris: Gustave Guérin, 1894), 67–69.

5. Justin Chrysostome Dorsainvil, *Manuel d'histoire d'Haïti* (Port-au-Prince: Procure des Frères de l'Instruction Chrétienne, 1934).

6. Smith, *Liberty*, 82.

7. Bouzon, *Études historiques*, 70.

8. Bouzon, *Études historiques*, 70.

9. Mark Baker Bird, *The Black Man, or Haytian Independence, Deduced from Historical Notes, and Dedicated to the Government and People of Hayti* (New York: n.p., 1869), 289.

10. d'Alaux, *L'empereur Soulouque et son empire* (Paris: Michel Lévy frères, 1856), 122–23.

11. d'Alaux, *L'empereur Soulouque*, 128.

12. Dantès Bellegarde, *Histoire du peuple haïtien, 1492–1952* (Port-au-Prince: n.p., 2004), 158.

13. Bouzon, *Études historiques*, 71.

14. Smith, *Liberty*, 82.

15. d'Alaux, *L'empereur Soulouque*, 129.

16. Léon François Hoffmann, *Faustin Soulouque d'Haiti dans l'histoire et la littérature* (Paris:L'Harmattan, 2007), 50–54.

17. Bouzon, *Études historiques*, 82.

18. On Piquets, see Mimi Sheller, *Democracy After Slavery: Black Publics and Peasant Radicalism in Haiti and Jamaica* (Gainesville: University Press of Florida, 2000).

19. Peasants and urbanites may have been divided by culture and politics but were united by a shared militarism almost throughout the 19th century.

20. Hoffmann, *Soulouque*, 51.

21. Bouzon, *Études historiques*, 74.

22. Bouzon, *Études historiques*, 74.

23. Dorsainvil, *Manuel d'histoire*, 255.

24. Edgar La Selve, *Le pays des nègres: voyage à Haïti, ancienne* (Paris: Hachette, 1881), 350.

25. Bouzon, *Études historiques*, 82.

26. Bouzon, *Études historiques*, 101.

27. Bouzon, *Études historiques*, 103.

28. d'Alaux, *L'empereur Soulouque*, 147; Hoffmann, *Couleurs*, 51.

29. Bouzon, *Études historiques*, 77

30. Nicholls, *From Dessalines to Duvalier: Race, Colour and National Independence in Haiti*, rev. ed. (New Brunswick, NJ: Rutgers University Press, 1996), 389. On Salomon, see Smith, *Liberty*, 214-237.

31. His own denials are quoted in Roger Gaillard, *La république exterminatrice, première partie: une modernisation manquée (1880–1896)* (Port-au-Prince: Le Natal, 1984); and in Gustave de Molinari, *À Panama. L'isthme de Panama, la Martinique, Haïti* (Paris: Guillaumin et Compagnie, 1887).

32. Nicholls, *From Dessalines to Duvalier*, 378.

33. Bouzon credits Salomon's father with expressing the wish to "see the entire country in black" which, for Bouzon implied getting rid of all the "mulattoes." Bouzon, *Études historiques*, 91–92.

34. The primary sources I consulted do not provide the text of this public speech. What Thomas Madiou, who is usually quoted for it, actually provides are two distinct texts: a collective petition, dated June 22, 1843, to the provisional government, signed in Les Cayes by two dozen individuals, included Salomon; and a letter authored by Salomon alone to President Boyer's envoys, also dated June 22, which might include some of the key arguments of the public speech he had given earlier that day. See Thomas Madiou, *Histoire d'Haïti*, vol. 5 (Port-au-Prince: Henri Deschamps, 1988), 503–17. For the contemporary reader, Salomon's words seem rather mild and certainly not incendiary. He complains about the oppression, suffering, humiliation and discrimination (my words) endured by Blacks of Les Cayes under President Boyer (1918–1843). He also accuses the latter of favoring *jaunes* for higher offices and ignoring Blacks. It's a discourse of resentment but hardly more; it does not call for violence but argues for equality. Leslie Manigat nonetheless characterizes this moment as an "earthquake" potentially leading to "national dislocation." See Leslie Manigat, "La revolution de 1843," *Eventail d'histoire vivante: des preludes à la Révolution de Saint Domingue jusqu'à nos jours (1789–2007)* II (Port-au-Prince: CHUDAC, 2002), 59.

35. Léon Laroche, *Haïti, une page d'histoire* (Paris: Arthur Rousseau, 1885), 110–11.

36. Leslie Jean-Robert Péan, *L'état marron, 1870–1915*, vol. 2, *Haïti: économie politique de la corruption* (Paris: Maisonneuve et Larose, 2005), 203.

37. *Le Commerce*, May 27, 1882. Another of the victims was senator Destin Alexis, Jean-Jacques Dessalines's grandson, assassinated in 1806, and grandfather of novelist Jacques-Stephen Alexis, tortured to death under Duvalier.

38. See Smith, *Liberty*, 214–37; Jean Price-Mars, *Jean-Pierre Boyer Bazelais et le drame de Miragoáne: à propos d'un lot d'autographes, 1883–1884* (Port-au-Prince: Imprimerie d'État, 1948).

39. Gaillard, *La république exterminatrice*, 27.

40. Claude Moïse, *Constitutions et luttes de pouvoir en Haïti (1804–1987)* (Montréal: CIDIHCA, 1990), 216.

41. In Smith, *Liberty*, 231. Love had until then been favorable to Salomon.

42. Alfred Jean, *Il y a soixante ans, 1883–1943. Les journées des 22 et 23 septembre 1883, reportages rétrospectifs par un témoin occulaire* (Port-au-Prince: A. P. Barthelemy, 1944).

43. Bellegarde, *Histoire*, 192–93.

44. Hoffmann, *Couleurs*.

45. Bellegarde, *Histoire*, 193.

46. Smith, *Liberty*, 229.

47. Smith, *Liberty*, 229.

48. Jean, *Il y a soixante ans*, 10.

49. Adolphe Cabon, *Mgr Alexis-Jean-Marie Guilloux, deuxième archevêque de Port-au-Prince (Haïti)* (Port-au-Prince: Grand Séminaire Saint-Jacques d'Haïti, 1929), 476.

50. In Gaillard, *La république exterminatrice*, 31. Burdel was pro-Salomon because the latter was a French citizen married to a French woman, and a Francophile. See Nicholls, *From Dessalines to Duvalier*, 382.

51. Georges Corvington, *Port-au-Prince au cours des ans. La métropole haïtienne du XIXe siècle, 1804–1888* (Port-au-Prince: Henri Deschamps, 1977).

52. Cabon, *Mgr Guilloux*, 466–88, 555.

53. Jean, *Il y a soixante ans*, 20–21.

54. Gaillard, *La république exterminatrice*, 39.

55. Jean, *Il y a soixante ans*, 23.

56. Frédéric Marcelin, *Le passé: impressions haïtiennes* (Port-au-Prince: La Dodine, 2014), 44–45.

57. Gaillard, *La république exterminatrice*, 36.

58. Jean, *Il y a soixante ans*, 19.

59. Moïse, *Constitutions*, 216.

60. The names of prominent traders in early twentieth-century Port-au-Prince, as provided by Marcel Gilbert, indeed do not appear in the literature prior to 1883: "[in 1908], 'Staude, Hall, Kohler, Luders, Stempel, … Ollofson, Altieri, Gebara' … all these traders, all foreign …" Marcel Gilbert, *La patrie haitienne : de Boyer-Bazelais à l'unité historique du peuple haitien* (Haïti: Imprimerie des Antilles, 1986), 21. The last names betray German, Italian, and Lebanese origins. This was not the case in Jérémie, though, where prominent business families remain the same until 1964.

61. Cabon, *Mgr Guilloux*, 484.

62. Gaillard, *La république exterminatrice*, 39.

63. Jean, *Il y a soixante ans*, 21.

64. Georges's descendants, the Riobés, would be decimated under the Duvalier regime.

65. Péan, *L'état marron*, 200.

66. Marcelin, *Le passé*, 41.

67. Smith cites diplomatic reports; Gaillard, on the other hand, relies on Laroche's 1885 account that is supposedly based on the acts of a French parliamentary debate on December 15, 1883 and reproduced in *Le journal official*. However, I could not find any *Journal Officiel* on that date (or during that week for that matter) that contains any debate on the question. Nor does the official December 1883 *Feuilleton* of the French Parliament. See Smith, *Liberty*, 231; Gaillard, *La république exterminatrice*; Laroche, *Haïti, une page d'histoire*, 219–36).

68. de Molinari, *À Panama*, 193–94.

69. In 1888, when faced with yet another armed insurrection, government forces resorted once again to arson. Over 400 houses were burned. Smith, *Liberty*, 235.

70. Jean, *Il y a soixante ans*, 36.

71. Cabon, *Mgr Guilloux*, 478. History is written by the victors, as long as they do write—and write well. Jérémie's 1883 history is known mainly from the account left by the defeated. See Gustave Vigoureux, *L'année terrible; ou 1883 à Jérémie* (Jérémie, Haiti: Imprimerie du Centenaire, 1909), 7.

72. Philippe Zacair, "Immigrés guadeloupéens et martiniquais en Haïti dans le regard des consuls français (1848–1900)," *Bulletin de la Société d'histoire de la Guadeloupe* 154 (2009): 73–74.

73. The text is in quoted in its entirety in Vigoureux, *L'année terrible*, 9–11. Smith found an original copy in the Foreign Office archives. See Smith, *Liberty*.

74. The rank of general was liberally granted throughout the nineteenth century; this was more indicative of a militarist ethos than of the number of soldiers above whom a general is usually supposed to lead.

75. Vigoureux, *L'année terrible*, 26, 28, 37, 38.

76. Vigoureux, *L'année terrible*, 13.

77. Vigoureux, *L'année terrible*, 43.

78. Several months earlier, in late April, children and women had been evacuated during the Miragoane siege; eighty of them were brought to the capital for safety. Salomon had mandated the French consul in Port-au-Prince to do so. See Cabon, *Mgr Guilloux*, 475. Safe evacuations of women and children indicate that families were not targeted by Salomon. During this civil war, the government generally showed mercy to women and children, even if they could sometimes become collateral victims.

79. Vigoureux, *L'année terrible*, 22. Vigoureux was more interested in the military side of events than in what we today call "crimes."

80. Vigoureux, *L'année terrible*, 32–33.

81. Vigoureux, *L'année terrible*, 47–51.

82. Vigoureux, *L'année terrible*, 50.

83. Vigoureux, *L'année terrible*, 20.

84. This is in agreement with a presidential decree issued by Salomon on November 13 that granted amnesty to all insurgents and guaranteeing their properties. Cabon, *Mgr Guilloux*.

85. Gaillard, *La république exterminatrice*, 46.

86. Vigoureux, *L'année terrible*, 59.

87. Two of Laforest's granddaughters, Louise and Edith, would be executed during the 1964 Jérémie massacre.

88.   Bernard Diederich and Al Burt, *Papa Doc et les Tontons Macoutes: la verité sur Haïti* (Port-au-Prince: Henri Deschamps, 1986), 204.

89.   Guy Dallemand, personal communication with author, Port-au-Prince, January 2009.

90.   Alex Dupuy, personal communication with author, Port-au-Prince, October 2019.

91.   Diederich and Burt, *Papa Doc*, 208–9.

92.   See Francis Charles, *Haïti. Essence du pouvoir martial: la domestication de l'armée* (Port-au-Prince: Henri Deschamps, 2009), 148–52; Radio Haïti-Inter (Maître François), "Temwayaj 26 avril 1963," Radio Haïti-Inter, aired 1987, Human Rights Archive, Duke Digital Repository, https://idn.duke.edu/ark:/87924/r4sf2pn5n, audio, 23:27; and Elizabeth Abbott, *Haiti: A Shattered Nation* (New York: Overlook Duckworth, 2011), 119–21.

93.   See for instance Michel-Rolph Trouillot, *Haiti, State Against Nation: The Origins and Legacy of Duvalierism* (New York: Monthly Review Press, 1990), 168.

94.   "Oncle" is metaphoric kinship here. Clément Barbot, once an intimate of the Duvalier family who dined often with them, had been estranged for two years and imprisoned for six months; Jean-Claude Duvalier had not seen him since 1962 and had likely been warned against him.

95.   Abbott, *Haiti: A Shattered Nation*, 119.

96.   Alex Dupuy, Personal Communication, Port-au-Prince, October 2019.

97.   The distance that Sister Dallemand covered from the Sainte-Rose de Lima school to her home was slightly more than a mile.

98.   Diederich and Burt, *Papa Doc*, 206.

99.   Radio Haiti-Inter, (Maître François), "Temwayaj 26 avril 1963."

100. Devoir de Mémoire-Haïti, *Mourir pour Haïti: la résistance à la dictature en 1964* (Montreal: CIDIHCA, 2015).

101. Max Vieux, father of Didier and Paul Vieux, had been Haiti's first agronomist.

102. Yvon Guerrier, "Temwayaj sou Franck Romain avèk evènman 26 avril 1963 Lamanten yo," file 1 of 4, Radio Haïti-Inter, aired October 4, 1986, Radio Haïti-Inter Archive, Duke Digital Repository, https://idn.duke.edu/ark:/87924/r4862gb8h, MP3 audio, 16:40. I return to Yvon Guerrier's key testimony in chapter 11.

103. Smith, *Liberty*.

104. Diederich and Burt, *Papa Doc*, 204.

105. In a separate incident in 1908, the bodies of Massillon Coicou, an internationally-known poet, and of his brothers were mutilated after they had been executed by the police.

106. Adam Jones, *Gender Inclusive: Essays on Violence, Men, and Feminist International Relations* (New York: Routledge, 2008). The main exception in Haiti is the 1812 mass extermination of mulattoes in the Kingdom of Haiti ruled by King Henri Christophe. Women were systematically killed. I did not include that episode in this chapter because the anti-elite dimension of this mass killing is not documented. See Jean-Philippe Belleau, "A Misplaced Genocide. Haiti, 1812," forthcoming.

107. The documented 1986 *dechoukaj* and lynching that followed the fall of the Duvalier regime did not target elite sectors but, according to Hurbon, some VSNs and vodou priests. See Laënnec Hurbon, *Comprendre Haïti: essai sur l'État, la nation, la culture* (Paris: Karthala, 1987).

108. This pattern closely confirms Veena Das's refutation of Gustave Le Bon's "irrational mob" theory. See Veena Das, "Communities, Riots and Survivors," in *Mirrors of Violence:*

Communities, Riots and Survivors in South Asia, ed. Veena Das, 1–35 (Delhi: Oxford University Press, 1990); see also Veena Das, *Life and Words: Violence and the Descent Into the Ordinary* (Berkeley: University of California Press, 2006).

5. JÉRÉMIE'S WORLD

1. Elizabeth Abbott, *Haiti: A Shattered Nation* (New York: Overlook Duckworth, 2011), 77.
2. Daniel Supplice, personal communication with author, Port-au-Prince, January 2016.
3. Janin Léonidas, personal communication with author, Port-au-Prince, January 2016.
4. Ross Velton, *Haiti and the Dominican Republic: The Island of Hispaniola* (Chalfont St. Peter, UK: Bradt, 1999), 62.
5. Luc Pierre, *Haïti. Les origines du chaos* (Port-au-Prince: Henri Deschamps, 1997), 101.
6. Laennec Hurbon, ed., *Le phénomène religieux dans la Caraïbe: Guadeloupe, Martinique, Guyane, Haïti* (Montreal: CIDHICA, 1989), 116.
7. Leslie Jean-Robert Péan, *L'ensauvagement macoute et ses conséquences, 1957–1990*, vol. 4,*Haïti: économie politique de la corruption* (Paris: Maisonneuve et Larose, 2007), 109. Michel-Rolph Trouillot, "A Social Contract for Whom? Haitian History and Haitian Future," in *Haiti Renewed. Political and Economic Prospects*, ed. Robert Rotberg (Washington DC: Brookings Institution Press, 1997). Trouillot defines "apartheid" as "the opposite of social contract," a rather vague definition in a piece that does not explore the term or the literature on it, nor does it justify the use of the metaphor.
8. The literature on the apartheid system and on segregation is vast. On spatial segregation in a comparative perspective, see Carl H. Nightingale, *Segregation: A Global History of Divided Cities* (Chicago: Chicago University Press, 2012). On segregation in sports, see Christopher Merrett, *Sport, Space and Segregation: Politics and Society in Pietermaritzburg* (Scotsville, South Africa: University of KwaZula-Natal Press, 2009). On apartheid in education and social life, see the first three chapters of Nancy Clark and William Worger, *South Africa: The Rise and Fall of Apartheid* (Harlow, UK: Longman, 2003).
9. See for instance Douglas Massey and Nancy Denton, *American Apartheid: Segregation and the Making of the Underclass* (Cambridge, MA: Harvard University Press, 1993).
10. Here I used data collected from interlocutors and the works of two memorialists, Eddy Cavé and Jean-Pierre Alcindor. For the former, see: Eddy Cavé, *De mémoire de Jérémien: ma vie, ma ville, mon village*, vol. 1, *De mémore de Jérémien* (Pétionville, Haiti: Pleine Plage, 2011); Eddy Cavé, *Autour des 90 ans de l'Hôpital Saint-Antoine de Jérémie* (Montreal: Papyruz, 2013); Eddy Cavé, *De mémoire de Jérémien: en pensant aux amis disparus*, vol. 2 of *De mémoire de Jérémien* (Montreal: CIDIHCA; Petionville, Haiti: Pleine Plage, 2016). For the latter, see Jean-Pierre Alcindor, *Jérémie, Haiti . . . il était une fois. Une tranche de la petite histoire d'Haïti* (Port-au-Prince: Média-texte, 2011). Anthropologists and ethnologists have produced rich archives on sociality in Haiti, even if they have focused primarily on the peasantry. See Melville J. Herskovits, *Life in a Haitian Valley* (Princeton, NJ: Markus Wiener Publishers, 2007); Alfred Métraux, *L'homme et la terre dans la vallé de Marbial* (Paris: UNESCO, 1951); Rémy Bastien, *Le Paysan haïtien et sa famille. Vallée de Marbiald*, 2nd ed. (Paris: Karthala, 1985); Ira Lowenthal, " 'Marriage Is 20, Children Are 21': The Cultural Construction of Conjugality and the Family in Rural Haiti" (PhD diss., Johns Hopkins

University, 1987); Sidney W. Mintz, ed. *Working Papers in Haitian Society and Culture* (New Haven, CT: Antilles Research Program, Yale University, 1975); Sidney W. Mintz, *Three Ancient Colonies: Caribbean Themes and Variations* (Cambridge, MA: Harvard University Press, 2010); Rodrigo Bulamah, "O Lakou Haitiano e suas práticas: entre mudanças e permanências," *Temáticas* 21, no. 2 (2013); Rodrigo Bulamah, "Farming of Commons: Kinship and Social Practices in Milot, Haiti" (master's thesis, State University of Campinas, 2016); Flavia Dalmaso, "Kijan moun yo ye? As pessoas, as casas e as dinâmicas da familiaridade em Jacmel, Haiti" (PhD diss., UFRJ, Museu Nacional, Rio de Janeiro, 2014); and Louis Herns Marcelin, "La famille suburbaine à Port-au-Prince" (master's thesis, Faculté d'ethnologie, Université d'État d'Haïti, 1988). Provincial towns have not attracted much scholarly attention.

11. Cécil Valère (born 1940) is a chronological hypermnesiac interlocutor. When he recounted the day of the second wave of execution, he remembered it (while raising his eyes to the ceiling) in terms of persons he knew who performed specific actions (his mother who could not find her bag on the morning of that day, his friends who later rushed over to his place) to conclude (lowering his eyes to meet mine): "It was on the 19th, I am sure of it."

12. Marylin Strathern, *Relations: An Anthropological Account* (Durham, NC: Duke University Press, 2020).

13. This was based on scrutinizing the skin complexion of individuals in old pictures, with all the limitations this "method" entailed.

14. Jean-Claude Fignolé, personal communications with author, Port-au-Prince, Jérémie, ands Pestel, 2005–2017.

15. The above-cited memoirs by Eddy Cavé show such pictures. Other informants showed me other pictures from their own collections.

16. See Roger Lancaster, *Life Is Hard: Machismo, Danger, and the Intimacy of Power in Nicaragua* (Berkeley: University of California Press, 1992). The anthropologist Christian Geffray linked godparenthood in the Amazon region to the maintenance of oppression. See Christian Geffray, *Chroniques de la servitude en Amazonie brésilienne* (Paris: Karthala, 1996). However, he he focused on families that are both employers and employees, within an economic phenomenon framed by fictive debt. On godparenthood in the Haitian peasantry, see Bulamah, "O Lakou."

17. Alexandra Philoctète, personal communication with author, Montréal, March 2017; Ralph Allen, personal communication with author, Pétionville, January 2019.

18. Lancaster, *Life Is Hard.*

19. Erving Goffman, *Interaction Rituals: Essays on Face-to-Face Behavior* (Garden City, NY: Doubleday, 1967); Randall Collins, *Interaction Ritual Chains* (Princeton, NJ: Princeton University Press, 2004).

20. Gérard Barthélémy, *Dans la splendeur d'un après-midi d'histoire* (Port-au-Prince: Henri Deschamps, 1996).

21. On Spiralism, see the authoritative work of Kaiama Glover, *Haiti Unbound: The Spiralist Challenge to the Postcolonial Canon* (Liverpool, UK: Liverpool University Press, 2011).

22. Frédéric Marcelin's novel *Thémistocle Epaminondas Labasterre*, first published in 1901, epitomizes this phenomenon.

23.   Fignolé, personal communications with author, Port-au-Prince, Jérémie, and Pestel, 2005–2017.

24.   Rolphe Papillon, personal communications with author, Port-au-Prince, Jérémie, and Corail, 2012–2023.

25.   Société haïtienne d'histoire et de géographie, *Revue de la Société Haitienne d'Histoire et de Géographie*3, no. 8 (1932). On the very first page, Petit's inaugural words mention Lily Sansaricq's "kind generosity" (*la générosité aimable*) and her "exquisite discretion" (*tact exquis*).

26.   On community, see Robert Redfield, *The Little Community and Peasant Society and Culture* (Chicago: University of Chicago Press, 1960). On holism, see Louis Dumont, *Homo Hierarchicus. The Caste System and Its Implications*, trans. R. M. Sainsbury and Basia Gulati (Chicago: Chicago University Press, 1980). On dividuality, see McKim Marriott, "Hindu Transactions: Diversity Without Dualism, in *Transaction and Meaning: Directions in the Anthropology of Exchange and Symbolic Behavior*, ed. Bruce Kapferer (Philadelphia: Institute for the Study of Human Issues, 1976): 109–42. On partibility, see Marilyn Strathern, *The Gender of the Gift. Problems with Women and Problems with Society in Melanesia* (Berkeley: University of California Press, 1988). On repeated interactions, practices of cooperation, and their moral consequences see for instance Harold Garfinkel, *Studies in Ethnomethodology* (Englewood Cliffs, NJ: Prentice-Hall, 1967), and Randall Collins, *Interaction Ritual Chains* (Princeton, NJ: Princeton University Press, 2004), and ethnographies that show how antagonist communities keep a moral space for each other in spite of tensions, such as Torsten Kolind, *Post-War Identification: Everyday Muslim Counterdiscourse in Bosnia* (Aarhus, Denmark: Aarhus University Press, 2008); Tone Bringa, *Being Muslim the Bosnian Way: Identity and Community in a Central Bosnian Village* (Princeton, NJ: Princeton University Press, 1995); and Bhrigupati Singh, *Poverty and the Quest for Life: Spiritual and Material Striving in Rural India* (Chicago: Chicago University Press, 2015). On the notion of "world," see João de Pina-Cabral and and Joana Cabral de Oliveira, *World: An Anthropological Examination* (Chicago: HAU Books, 2017). On relatedness, see Janet Carsten, ed. *Cultures of Relatedness. New Approaches to the Study of Kinship* (New York: Cambridge University Press, 2000). On familialism, see Ernest W. Burgess and Harvey J. Locke, *The Family: From Institution to Companionship* (New York: American Book Company, 1945). On cultural intimacy, see Michael Herzfeld, *Cultural Intimacy: Social Poetics in the Nation-State*, 2nd ed. (New York: Routledge, 1997).

27.   Roberto da Matta, *Carnavais, malandros e heróis: para uma sociologia do dilema brasileiro* (Rio de Janeiro: Zahar, 1979). See also David Hess and Roberto da Matta, eds. *The Brazilian Puzzle:Culture on the Borderlands of the Western World* (New York: Columbia University Press, 1995). Personalism is unrelated to Mounier's eponymous philosophy.

28.   Guiton Dorimain, personal communication with author, Port-au-Prince, January 2016-2019.

29.   Jean-Philippe Belleau, "Intimacy, hostility, and State Politics: François Duvalier and His Inner-circle, 1931–1971," *History and Anthropology* 32, no. 5 (2021): 549–73.

30.   See for instance Georg Simmel, *The Sociology of Georg Simmel*, ed. and trans. KurtH. Wolff (Glencoe, IL: The Free Press, 1964), 320; Granovetter Mark, "The Strength of Weak Ties," *American Journal of Sociology* 78, no. 6 (1973): 1360–80; and Maxim Felder, "Strong, Weak

and Invisible Ties: A Relational Perspective on Urban Coexistence," *Sociology* 54, no. 4 (2020): 675–92.

31.   Belleau, Jean-Philippe, " 'Neighbor' Is an Empty Concept: How the Neighbourly Turn in Mass Violence Studies Has Overlooked Anthropology and Sociology," *Journal of Genocide Research* (2022).

32.   See chapter 1.

33.   Erving Goffman, *Interaction Rituals: Essays on Face-to-Face Behavior* (Garden City, NY: Doubleday, 1967).

34.   David Morgan, *Acquaintances: The Space Between Intimates and Strangers* (Maidenhead, UK: Open University Press, 2009).

35.   McKim Marriott, "Hindu Transactions"; Dumont, *Homo Hierarchicus*; Anastasia Piliavsky, *Nobody's People. Hierarchy as Hope in a Society of Thieves* (Stanford, CA: Stanford University Press, 2020).

36.   Barthélémy, *Dans la splendeur*, 39–45.

37.   Felder, "Strong, Weak, and Invisible Ties."

38.   The sociocentric logic of oral history also frames Alfred Jean's personal account of the 1883 events in Port-au-Prince, which are recounted in chapter 4. On September 22 and 23 1883, Jean, a twenty-two-year-old pharmacist, walked around the capital and witnessed its destruction. He recognized people dead, fleeing, or fighting, people he knew or knew of: 102 names are mentioned in his thirty-eight-page-long book. These 102 individuals were not all people he had a relationship with. Jean was able to identify every single person he encountered and every cadaver he saw or heard about. He identified these persons through their webs of social connections. They belonged to various social sectors, from the bourgeois to the urban poor. Interestingly, even if many are mentioned in passing, Jean demonstrates a sort of attachment to them. Just as interestingly, he does not mention people he did not know, as if only people he knew or knew of had been killed. The people he did not know became unidentifiable, unlocatable in personalistic webs— historically invisible to him. They are not *persons* in da Matta's definition of a holistic society. See Alfred Jean, *Il y a soixante ans, 1883–1943. Les journées des 22 et 23 septembre 1883, reportages rétrospectifs par un témoin occulaire* (Port-au-Prince: A. P. Barthélémy, 1944).

39.   Hannah Arendt, "De l'humanité dans de sombres temps," in *Vies politiques* (Paris: Gallimard, 1974), 11–41. See also Claude Lefort, "Hannah Arendt et la question du politique," in *Essais sur le politique: XIXe et XXe siècles* (Paris: Seuil, 1986), 59–72.

40.   On this presidential campaign and its lethality, see Claude Moïse, *Constitutions et luttes de pouvoir en Haïti (1804–1987)* (Montreal: CIDIHCA, 1990), 320–67; and Pressoir Pierre, *Témoignages, 1946–1976: l'espérance déçue* (Port-au-Prince: Henri Deschamps, 1987), 39–139.

41.   This could be either because the term I used (*amitié*, or friendship)—was too strong, or because I asked Jean Alcide about it only after he recounted the execution; he could have been embarrassed to admit having allowed Guilbaud to die in front of him. See chapter 8 for further discussion. Jean Alcide, personal communication with author, North Miami, March 2016.

42.   See chapter 7.

43.   Claude Lévi-Strauss, *Introduction to the work of Marcel Mauss* (London: Routledge and Kegan Paul, 1987), 63.

44. The elite—or, say, the top 10 to 20 percent of the socioeconomic urban segment—cut across the color line. Nevertheless, many (and possibly a majority) of its members were considered mulattos. At the time of the massacre, there were fewer than forty families identified as mulattos inside the city limits of Jérémie, which had a population of 3,000 to 5,000 inhabitants. This group of forty families was relatively porous.

6. THE EXCELSIOR

1. When I asked further questions about the exact circumstances of this incident (who said it, to whom, when, and exactly where? Were you there? Who did you hear this from? What year was this?), answers were vague, hesitant, often contradictory, and filled with "I was told that . . ." I did not encounter anyone who was a direct witness to this anecdote. The same anecdote was also mentioned about balls in Port-au-Prince.

2. The October 1932 issue of the *Revue de la Société d'histoire et de géographie d'Haïti* reported that Lily Sansaricq organized a conference there in 1931 on Défilée-La-Folle, a Haitian revolutionary figure. See chapter 5. Lily Sansaricq is one of the victims of the Jérémie Vespers.

3. Serge Picard, personal communication with author, Corail, March 2012.

4. Jean-Claude Fignolé, personal communication with author, Jérémie, January 2016.

5. Victor Schoelcher, *Colonies étrangères et Haiti, résultat de l'émancipation anglaise*, 2 vols. (Paris: Pagnerre, 1843), 2: 237.

6. François Duvalier, *Eléments d'une doctrine*, vol. 1 of *Œuvres essentielles* (Port-au-Prince: Presses Nationales d'Haiti, 1966), 267.

7. At this point and for purposes of demonstration, I will only use the term "endogamy" and conflate it with homogamy; I will distinguish between the two later on. The former refers to the practice of marrying within one's community, the latter to marrying within the same social class.

8. James G. Leyburn, *The Haitian People*, 3rd ed. (Lawrence: Institute of Haitian Studies, University of Kansas Press, 1998), 8.

9. Trouillot, Michel-Rolph, "Culture, Color, and Politics." In *Race*, ed. Steven Gregory and Roger Sanjet, 146–74 (New Brunswick, New Jersey: Rutgers University Press, 1994), 146.

10. Michel-Rolph Trouillot, *Haiti, State Against Nation. The Origins and Legacy of Duvalierism* (New York: Monthly Review Press, 1990), 118–24.

11. Trouillot's own existence disproves his assertion. He is a direct descendant (four generations above him) of a light-skinned member of the mulatto elite, Duverneau Trouillot, who was a writer, a member of the Senate in the 1840s, and a Minister of Justice in 1890. In any case, a more obvious epistemology to prove assertions of endogamy would consist in tracing family trees. Yet, none of the authors referenced here provides any. Trouillot's argument also ignores the constant influx (since Haitian independence) of isolated European men marrying into local families and Haitian men returning from Europe with European spouses. See Thorald M. Burnham, "Immigration and Marriage in the Making of Post-independence Haiti" (PhD diss., York University, 2006).

12. Jean-Richard Laforest, "Notes à propos d'un article de René Piquion," *Rencontre* 24–25 (2012):91–92. The author married a light-skin mulatto woman, Rose-Marie Gautier. This

is the same Jean-Richard Laforest whose two aunts, Louise and Edith, were executed during the Jérémie massacre.

13. See for instance Eddy Arnold Jean, *Les idées politiques haitiennes au XIXème siècle*, with Justin O. Fièvre (Port-au-Prince: Haïti-Demain, 2011); Lemoine Bonneau, "Qu'est-ce qui dans l'élite économique de ce pays est à l'origine de cette mésaventure?" *Le Nouvelliste*, September 13, 2016.

14. King's precise study examines how wealthy free women of color married poor white migrants in Saint Domingue. Stewart R. King, *Blue Coat or Powdered Wig: Free People of Color in Pre-Revolutionary Saint Domingue* (Athens: University of Georgia Press, 2001). Burnham shows the persistence of such matrimonial strategies into the nineteenth century. See Burnham, "Immigration and Marriage." There is, to my knowledge, no exhaustive study covering the contemporary period. For a study on race and endogamy in Guadeloupe, see Jean-Luc Bonniol, "La couleur des hommes, principe d'organisation sociale: le cas antillais." *Ethnologie française* 20, no. 4 (1990): 410–18. On race and sex in Latin America, see the classic study by Peter Wade, *Race and Sex in Latin America* (London: Pluto Press, 2009). My question is different: why is the supposed endogamy of a resented group conceived of as a social violation and a cause of socioeconomic inequalities?

15. Talcott Parsons may have been the first to theorize that denunciations of inequality were judgements of value. See Talcott Parsons, "Equality and Inequality in Modern Society, or Social Stratification Revisited," *Sociological Inquiry* 40, no. 2 (1970): 13–72.

16. For an exhaustive survey of the ideological roots of the view that mixing was unnatural, see Marlene Daut, *Tropics of Haiti. Race and the Literary History of the Haitian Revolution in the Atlantic World* (Liverpool: Liverpool University Press, 2017).

17. The stereotype of the mulatto woman as beautiful and eroticized is a product of the colonial era but did not die with it. See Marlene Daut, *Tropics of Haiti*, 197–207 for a study of these stereotypes. To my knowledge, there is no exhaustive study of representations of the mulatto woman in the contemporary period. Such representations are often mentioned in passing in academic studies (see the following note), but they are explored exhaustively in the literary works of Yannick Lahens, Marie Vieux-Chauvet, René Depestre, and less recently André Schwartz-Bart.

18. Leslie Péan, *L'ensauvagement macoute et ses consequences, 1957–1990*, vol. 4, *Haïti: Économie Politique de La Corruption* (Paris: Maisonneuve et Larose, 2007), 115.

19. Jean-Luc Bonniol, "Entretien avec René Despestre," *Gradhiva* 1, (2005): 11.

20. Péan, *L'ensauvagement*, 108.

21. The only print version I have read of this text was a print copy in Guy Dallemand's personal library in 2009. Dany Lafferière, "Camarade, où sont les mulâtresses?" *Haiti-Demain magazine* 13 (1986).

22. See chapters 1 and 7.

23. The combination of sexual and socioeconomic fantasies deteriorating into the stigmatization of an entire group evokes the ethnic configuration before and during the Rwandan genocide where "Tutsi women were the focal point for violent sexual fantasies. Said to be uncommonly beautiful and desirable, they were also accused of being proud and inaccessible." David Norman Smith, "The Psychological Roots of Genocide: Legitimacy

and Crisis in Rwanda," *American Psychologist* 53, no. 7 (1998): 750. Sexual envy directed at Tutsi women turned into resentment against an entire group. See also Christopher Mullins, "We Are Going to Rape You and Taste Tutsi Women: Rape During the 1994 Rwanda Genocide," *British Journal of Criminology* 49, no. 6 (2009): 719–35; and Christopher Taylor, "A Gendered Genocide: Tutsi Women and Hutu Extremists in the 1994 Rwanda Genocide," *Political and Legal Anthropology* 22, no. 1 (1999): 42–54.

24.   Marco H. D. van Leeuwen and Ineke Maas, "Endogamy and Social Class in History: An Overview," supplement to *International Review of Social History* 50 (2005): 1–23.

25.   Francis M. L. Thompson, *The Rise of Respectable Society: A Social History of Victorian Britain, 1830–1900* (London: HarperCollins, 1988), 83–113.

26.   For a survey, see the previous chapter.

27.   Guy Dallemand, personal communication with author, Port-au-Prince, January 2009.

28.   On this expression, see Jean-Philippe Belleau, "Intimacy, Hostility, and State Politics: François Duvalier and his Inner-circle, 1931–1971," *History and Anthropology* 32, no. 5 (2021): 553.

29.   Burnham, "Immigration and Marriage."

30.   This grammar, however, was turned outward—and not inward toward self-reflection. I find it amusing that some of the very critics of the elite's endogamy, past and present, almost never engaged in mésalliances themselves. That includes all members of Duvalier's inner circle, military officers, and noirist writers and scholars mentioned in this book who, to my knowledge, never married into "lower" social sectors.

31.   Philippe-Richard Marius, *The Unexceptional Case of Haiti. Race and Class Privilege in Postcolonial Bourgeois Society* (Jackson: University of Mississippi Press, 2022).

32.   This is not without evoking Sartre's statement that "the disgust for the bourgeois is bourgeois."

33.   The genealogical information in this section comes from four data banks. One was provided by the Association de Généalogie d'Haïti (Genealogical Association of Haiti) and Alix and France Cédras; another I collected using family memory; one established by Max Bissainthe; and a last one made by sociologist Michèle Oriol. I use marriage as the main form of alliance: I excluded godparenthood and illegitimate unions from relatedness but included illegitimate children.

34.   Which is not to say that color was not a determinant in matrimonial strategies, as mentioned above.

35.   Marius, *The Unexceptional Case.*

36.   See chapter 4.

37.   Jean Fouchard, *Les marrons de la liberté* (Paris: Éditions de l'École, 1972).

38.   Michèle Oriol, personal communication with author, Port-au-Prince, January 2019.

39.   Michèle Oriol, *Chefs d'État en Haïti: gloire et misères* (Port-au-Prince: Fondation pour la recherche iconographique et documentaire, 2006).

40.   See Belleau, "Intimacy."

41.   The historian Golfo Alexopoulos observed the same phenomenon among Stalin's inner circle: "Soviet leaders used kinship ties to reinforce political loyalties." See Golfo Alexopoulos, "Stalin and the Politics of Kinship: Practices of Collective Punishment, 1920s–1940s," *Comparative Studies in Society and History* 50, no. 1 (2008): 97. For

Alexopoulos, however, these ties were "engineered" from the top down to ensure party loyalty. Fritz Cinéas emotionally explained how Duvalier derailed his first marriage (by refusing to issue a visa to his bride, who did not come from a Duvalierist family, when he was living in Mexico); he eventually married another woman.

42. The Duvalierist sociopolitical group that developed its own homogamic practices interestingly seems to have continued to this day, even after it expanded to Southern Florida. For instance, François Duvalier's grandson and Claude Raymond's granddaughter are husband and wife. Claude Raymond was one of the most important actors of the regime, and the Presidential Guard's commander from 1961 to 1971. Rosalie Bousquet's daughter married the son of a Duvalierist family.

43. On the history of feminism in Haiti, see Carolle Charles's pioneering article, "Gender and Politics in Contemporary Haiti: The Duvalierist State, Transnationalism, and the Emergence of a New Feminism (1980–1990)," *Feminist Studies* 21, no.1 (1995): 137–40.

44. See Claude Moïse, *Constitutions et luttes de pouvoir en Haïti (1815–1987)* (Montreal: CIDI-HCA, 1990), 381.

45. Yvonne Hakim-Rimpel's ordeal is described in Pressoir Pierre, *Témoignages, 1946–1976 : l'espérance déçue* (Port-au-Prince: Henri Deschamps, 1987), 134–35; and succinctly in Bernard Diederich, *Le trophée* (Port-au-Prince: Henri Deschamps, 2008), 150–51. I also use the testimony of Yvonne Hakim-Rimpel's daughter, Rose-May, whom I interviewed in 2019.

46. According to Rose-May's statement, her mother told her later that as the group was leaving the scene where she was lying on the floor, one was tasked with "finishing my mother off." This man returned to the spot, shot twice, and missed Hakim-Rimpel, either intentionally or not. It was dark and the others could not see what he was doing.

47. Marie-Cécile Hakim-Rimpel, "Special Haitian Woman to Remember–Yvonne Hakim Rimpel Fought for Women to Have the Right to Vote in Haiti," television interview with Valerio Saint-Louis, Télé Image, posted April 5, 2012, 9:02, https://www.dailymotion.com/video/xpxgrh.

48. Moïse, *Constitutions*, 381; Pierre, *Témoignages*, 135–36

49. For a survey of this literature, see Jean-Philippe Belleau, "The Stranger-King of the Caribbean: François Duvalier, State Politics, and the Othering of Brutality," *Journal of Latin American and Caribbean Anthropology* 24, no. 4 (2019): 941.

50. There are many novels where the mother is not necessarily the subject but nonetheless remains ubiquitous in the background. E.g. Dany Laferrière's autobiographic masterpiece has a very present and protective mother and a father as absent as he is idealized. See Dany Laferrière, *Le cri des oiseaux fous: roman* (Paris: Zulma, 2015). Revealingly, the most common words and expressions of abuse in Haiti target the mother figure (see Belleau, "Stranger-King," 942). As Leach showed, abuses reveal social codes and moral values. See Edmund Leach, "Animal Categories and Verbal Abuse," in *New Directions for the Study of Language*, ed. Eric H. Lenneberg (Cambridge, MA: MIT Press, 1966). My observation is that adult men openly and publicly evoke their mothers, a source and object of love, in a way that conveys not their own fragility but instead filial concern—love. For this very reason, Duvalier's relationship to his own mother, whom he invisibilized, was deeply unusual. See Belleau, "The Stranger-King."

51. See Charles, "Gender and Politics," 138. Jean Price-Mars recognized women's exclusion from public roles in a visionary conference held in 1917; see Jean Price-Mars, *La femme de demain: conference prononcée en 1917* (Port-au-Prince: Presses nationales d'Haïti, 2002). Historian Mimi Sheller linked the exclusion of women from "full citizenship" after independence to militaristic traditions. See Mimi Sheller, *Citizenship from Below: Erotic agency and Caribbean Freedom* (Durham, NC: Duke University Press, 2012), 157–58.

52. William Gamson, *The Strategy of Social Protest* (Homewood, IL: Dorsey Press, 1975).

53. David Nicholls, "Review," *Hispanic American Historical Review* 71, no. 3 (1991): 651–52.

54. Trouillot, Michel-Rolph, *Haiti, State Against Nation*, 65.

55. Guy Alexandre, "Face à l'Opinion: Guy Alexandre sou rejim François Duvalier," 2 files, Radio Haïti Inter, aired September 21, 1996, Radio Haiti Archive, Duke University Digital Repository; Leslie Manigat, *Haiti of the Sixties, Object of International Concern: A Tentative Global Analysis of the Potentially Explosive Situation of a Crisis Country in the Caribbean* (Washington, DC: Washington Center of Foreign Policy Research, 1964); Gérard Pierre-Charles, *Radiographie d'une dictature: Haïti et Duvalier*, pref. Juan Bosch (Montreal: Nouvelle Optique, 1973).

56. See chapter 4.

57. Justin Bouzon, *Études historiques sur la présidence de Faustin Soulouque (1847–1849)* (Paris: Gustave Guérin, 1894).

58. See chapter 4.

59. Roger Gaillard, *La guerre civile, une option dramatique (15 juillet–31 décembre 1902)*, vol. 4, *La république exterminatrice* (Port-au-Prince: Le Natal, 1984).

60. Thomas Madiou, *Histoire d'Haïti*, vol. 5 of 7 (Port-au-Prince: Henri Deschamps, 1988), 153–75; Beaubrun Ardouin, *Études sur l'histoire d'Haïti, suivies de la vie du general J.-M. Borgella*, vol. 8 (Paris: Chez l'auteur, rue Vanneau, 1858), 1–22.

61. Belleau, "Intimacy."

62. See chapter 1.

63. Yvon Guerrier, "Temwayaj sou Franck Romain avèk evènman 26 avril 1963 Lamanten yo," file 1 of 4, aired on Radio Haiti-Inter, October 4, 1986, Radio Haiti Archive, Duke Digital Repository, MP3 audio, 16:40.

7. *KAPONAJ*

1. Beaubrun Ardouin, *Études sur l'histoire d'Haïti, suivies de la vie du general J.-M Borgella*, vol. 8 (Paris: Chez l'auteur, rue Vanneau, 1858), 7.

2. See Jean-Philippe Belleau, " 'Neighbor' is an Empty Concept: How the Neighbourly Turn in Mass Violence Studies Has Overlooked Anthropology and Sociology," *Journal of Genocide Research*, 2022. https://doi.org/10.1080/14623528.2022.2081298.

3. Belleau, "Neighbor"; and Jean-Philippe Belleau, "Hatred Is Not Stronger Than Bonds: Social Relationships, Aversion to Harm, and Relational Exceptionalism," *Social Analysis* 67, no. 1 (2023): 46–69. I return to it in chapter 9 of this book. Of course, people can harm people they know, starting with husbands who beat their wives. Violating social bonds happens, but the gravest forms of violation tend to be extremely rare—such violations are mainly committed by individuals often diagnosed as sociopathic, and do not

happen in patterns. Violating social relationships is a cognitive process analog to the incest taboo. Incest indeed happens, but it is extremely rare and, as all anthropologists would argue, its taboo is universal.

4. Louis Jabouin, personal communications with author, Port-au-Prince, January 2016; Jean-Claude Fignolé, personal communication with author, Port-au-Prince, Jérémie, and Pestel, 2005–2017; Anonymous J-2, personal communications with author, 2016–2022. The latter two had acquaintances who attended that meeting and divulged what had been said. I only give elements that coincide with those provided by Louis Jabouin, today a retired physician. Fignolé was also friend with Abel Jérôme. The latter, who attended, confirmed the existence of the two letters mentioned below but declined to name the participants in this meeting. Abel Jérôme, personal communications with author, Lafond, March 2012 and January 2018.

5. A member of parliament for the Grand'Anse commune of Roseaux since 1946, Dalvanor Etienne had a small but real personal connection to Duvalier. In June 1964, he had been one of the signatories of the new constitution that made Duvalier President-For-Life.

6. Raoul Hilberg, *Perpetrators, Victims, Bystanders: The Jewish Catastrophe, 1939–1945* (New York: HarperPerennial, 1992).

7. Robert M. Ehrenreich and Tim Cole, "The Perpetrator-Bystander-Victim Constellation: Rethinking Genocidal Relationships," *Human Organization* 64, no. 3 (2005): 213–24.

8. Lee-Ann Fuji, *Killing Neighbors: Webs of Violence in Rwanda* (Ithaca, NY: Cornell University Press, 2009); Immaculée Ilibagiza, *Left to Tell: Discovering God Amidst the Rwandan Holocaust* (Carlsbad: Hayhouse, 2006).

9. Jacques Sémelin, "The Notion of Social Reactivity: The French Case, 1942–1944," in *Probing the Limits of Categorization*, ed. Christina Morina and Krijn Thijs (New York: Berghann Books, 2019), 224–44; Jacques Sémelin, *Persécutions et entraides dans la France occupée: comment 75% des Juifs en France ont échappé la mort* (Paris: Les Arènes, 2013). Randall Collin, drawing on Goffman, also emphasizes the resilience of interaction ritual chains in inhibiting perpetrators. The personal decisions involving killing remain mentally extremely difficult to carry out. See Randall Collins, *Violence: A Micro-sociological Theory* (Princeton, NJ: Princeton University Press, 2008).

10. This moment evokes a scene described by Christopher Browning. When Major Wilhelm Trapp is ordered in July 1942 to perform the cold-blooded execution of 1,500 defenseless Jewish men, women, and children in Józefów, he convenes the entirety of his battalion and, shaken, explains the task that awaits them. He then leaves them the choice: obey and kill, or desist without disciplinary cost. Yet, instead of leaving each soldier to face alone his own conscience, as we would imagine, this choice empowered the group's micro-solidarity. The few who desisted paid a social cost (insults, ostracism, contempt). For the others, even though they were not Nazi believers, the social pressure exerted more force than their conscience. Christopher Browning, *Ordinary Men: Reserve Police Battalion 101 and the Final Solution in Poland* (New York: Harper Perennial, 2017), 55–69.

11. Belleau, "Hatred."

12. Cécil Valère Philanthrope and Anariol Joseph made clear that Jean Dimanche and his soldiers spoke freely, although with personal resentment, about the executions they had

carried out. Cécil Valère Philanthrope, personal communication with author, Montréal March 2017; Anariol Joseph, personal communication with author, Montréal, March 2017.

13. Roger Chassagne, personal communication with author, Boca Raton, September 2016.

14. Alix Cédras, phone communication with author, 2021.

15. Serge Picard, personal communication with author, Corail, May 2012. On Fort-Réfléchi, see chapter 2.

16. Pierre Bourdieu, *The Field of Cultural Production: Essays on Art and Literature* (Cambridge: Polity Press, 1993).

17. Vincent Royan (nephew of Father Barthélémy Péron), email communications with author, April 2021. See also chapter 1.

18. See chapter 1. The group fled by boat and must have secured authorization to do so from the town's military commander, who was probably happy to see them leave. Once they reached Port-au-Prince, they continued their voyage that very same day. Father Péron eventually became the priest of the Saint Vincent de Paul parish in Manhattan. Vincent Royan, email communications with author, April 2021; Marguerite Clérié (kin of Guislaine Pratt), personal communication with author, Boston, May 2022. See also Archives du diocèse de Vannes, "Liste chronologique des missionnaires arrivés en Haïti depuis 1864," *La lettre de Saint-Jacques* 95 (September–October 1989), 17.

19. See the introduction.

20. Pointed possibly at the Turgeau neighborhood, east of the intersection.

21. U.S. Embassy, Embtel 759, Oct. 28, 1964.

22. "Décret," *Le Moniteur*, October 26, 1964: 1; and *Le Nouvelliste*, October 29, 1964: 1.

23. See for instance Gérard Pierre-Charles, *Haïti: jamais, jamais plus! Les violations de droits de l'homme à l'époque des Duvalier* (Port-au-Prince: Centre de recherche et de formation économique et sociale pour le développement, 2000); Bernard Diederich and Al Burt, *Papa Doc et les Tontons Macoutes: la verité sur Haïti* (Port-au-Prince: Henri Deschamps, 1986).

24. See Claude Moïse, *Constitutions et luttes de pouvoir en Haïti (1815–1987)* (Montreal: CID-IHCA, 1990); Patrick Lemoine, *Fort-Dimanche, Fort-la-Mort* (Port-au-Prince: Éditions Regain,1996); and Organisation extérieure du Parti unifié des communistes haïtiens, *Haïti sous Duvalier: terrorisme d'État et visages de la résistance nationale* (Port-au-Prince: Parti unifié des communistes haïtiens, 1973).

25. Marvin Chochotte, "The History of Peasants, Tonton Makouts, and the Rise and Fall of the Duvalier Dictatorship in Haiti" (PhD diss., University of Michigan, 2017).

26. *Pieds poudrés* mean "with dust on their feet," a metonym for the peasant class.

27. Eddy Cavé, phone communication with author, March 2018. The "blond girl" was possibly one of the two Canadian nurses working at a local hospital that was also located on that street.

28. Guiton Dorimain, personal communication with author, Port-au-Prince, January 2019. His son Steven Brunache would become a nationally recognized musician.

29. Alix Cédras, phone communications with author, 2020–2023.

30. I could not determine when Brunache joined the VSN, although he was said to already have been a supporter of Duvalier during the 1957 elections.

31. See chapter 1.
32. Anonymous J-3, personal communication with author, 2016.
33. Albert Chassagne, *Bain de sang en Haiti. Les macoutes opèrent à Jérémie* (New York: n.p., 1977).
34. See the introduction on Chassagne and his retelling of events.
35. See the introduction.
36. Notably in the account by Elizabeth Abbott, *Haiti: A Shattered Nation* (New York: Overlook Duckworth), 130–35.
37. See Jean-Philippe Belleau, "The Stranger-King of the Caribbean: François Duvalier, State Politics, and the Othering of Brutality," *Journal of Latin American and Caribbean Anthropology* 24, no. 4 (2019): 935–57.
38. Identifying the means of communication between local Duvalierists and Duvalier is key to assessing influence. Neither Bontemps nor Balmir had access to the military communication system of coded messages that linked the military base (and Jérémie) to the Presidential Palace. This was under Abel Jérôme's control, who was hostile to both individuals. Since Duvalier refused to communicate by phone for confidentiality reasons, both Bontemps and Balmir had to travel to Port-au-Prince every time they had to convey an important information to Duvalier. Presidential Guards recall how Balmir, "an unassuming lady," visited Duvalier in his office
39. Translated literally into English, Saintange means "holy angel."
40. Pierre Chérubin, phone communication with author, March 2022.
41. Rolphe Papillon, personal communications with author, Jérémie, January 2016.
42. Catinat Sansaricq was three degrees removed from Pierre Sansaricq (a victim of the Jérémie Massacre). He was Graziela Sansaricq's uncle and father of Mgr. Guy Sansaricq, a New York bishop.
43. Personal communication from an anonymous interlocutor from the Roumer family; Alix Cédras, phone communication with author, April 2021.
44. On Bontemps during that period, see Bernard Diederich, *Le trophée* (Port-au-Prince: Henri Deschamps, 2008), 112–13.
45. See chapter 8.
46. Juliette Nicolas was Carl Nicolas's daughter and a witness to the incident. Carl Nicolas was a coffee provider. Juliette Nicolas, personal communication with author, Jérémie, January 2016.
47. Chérubin, phone communication with author, April 2021.
48. Abel Jérôme, personal communication with author, Lafond, May 2012; Fritz Cinéas, personal communications with author, Washington D.C., October 2022. Marie-Jeanne Lamartinière was a revolutionary figure who fought in battle alongside her husband. "Marie-Jeanne" therefore stressed a woman's visceral allegiance to a man in combat. On Duvalier's use of historical references, see chapters 4 and 10. See also Carolle Charles, "Gender and Politics in Contemporary Haiti: The Duvalierist State, Transnationalism, and the Emergence of a New Feminism (1980–1990)," *Feminist Studies* 21, no. 1 (1995): 140–141.
49. *Le Nouvelliste*, March 28, 1964: 1. Needless to say, the March of Gonaives was a "kangaroo" march, organized purely to legitimize Duvalier's constitutional changes.

50.   Georg Simmel, *The Sociology of Georg Simmel*, ed. and trans. KurtH. Wolff (Glencoe, IL: Free Press, 1964), 320.

51.   On a theorization of resentment (as ideology), see Helmut Schoeck, *Envy: A Theory of Social Behavior* (New York: Harcourt, Brace, and World, 1969); Marc Angenot, *Les idéologies du ressentiment* (Montréal: YXZ, 1997). Although Schoeck talks about "social" behavior, what he actually explores are beliefs, not behavior.

8. THE MILITARY COMMANDER

1.   See Gérard Alphonse Férère, *Armée d'Haïti après Magloire et hitlérisme duvaliérien (mémoire d'un officier)* (Boca Raton: Perle des Antilles, 2014).

2.   Elliott Roy, personal communication with author, Cayes-Jacmel, January 2019.

3.   Jérémie and the Grand'Anse were then part of the *Département du Sud*. It became the Département de la Grand'Anse only in 1969 with Jérémie as its administrative capital. Jérôme was thus under the authority of the commander of Les Cayes, Major Breton Claude, who would become one of the regime's most sinister figures. Breton Claude was replaced as the Les Cayes military commander by Henri Namphy in the course of the anti-insurgency operations; see chapter 1.

4.   One of Jérôme's predecessor, Second Lieutenant Prosper Maura, had courted Roseline Drouin during a six-month tenure there in 1961. (His posting is mentioned in *Haiti Sun*, December 14, 1960: 20). She rejected his insisting courtship. Humorously, she routinely shouted in the Drouin home *Maura, Maura pas* ("Maura, Maura not"), a pun on *Maura m'aura pas* ("Maura won't have me"). A year later, she married Guy Villedrouin. A Duvalierist interlocutor suspected that she rejected Maura's matrimonial ambitions because the latter was not fair-skin enough. Maura never raised above the rank of major and was described by one of his former classmates at the military academy as *falot* ("uninteresting").

5.   He had to pick up their packed meals every day from the Verrier home and deliver them to their office. See chapter 1.

6.   Albert Chassagne, *Bain de sang en Haiti. Les macoutes opèrent à Jérémie* (New York: n.p., 1977).

7.   Agrippa d'Aubigné, *Histoire universelle du sieur d'Aubigné* (Paris: Jean Mousset, 1616), chap. 9. On the life of Baron des Adret, see Gilbert Dallet, *L'étrange figure du Baron des Adrets* (Paris: Éditions de l'Aurore, 1982).

8.   See David El Kenz, "La naissance de la tolérance au 16ème siècle: l''invention' du massacre," *Sens public* (2006), http://sens-public.org/articles/340/; David El Kenz, "Le 'massacre' est-il né aux guerres de religion?" in "Les massacres aux temps des Révolutions," ed. Bruno Hervé and Pierre Serna, special issue, *La Révolution française* 3 (2011), https://doi.org/10.4000/lrf.185. The term "massacre" therefore had reactive and ethical dimensions, as the coining of "genocide" would in the twentieth century.

9.   See Edward Shils, "Primordial, Personal, Sacred and Civil Ties: Some Particular Observations on the Relationships of Sociological Research and Theory," *British Journal of Sociology* 8, no. 2 (1957): 130–45; Gitta Sereny, *Into that Darkness: An Examination of Conscience* (London: Vintage Books, 1983); Horacio Verbitsky, *El vuelo* (Buenos Aires: Planta, 1995);

Christopher Browning, *Ordinary Men: Reserve Police Battalion 101 and the Final Solution in Poland* (New York: Harper Perennial, 1998); and Hélène Dumas, *Le genocide au village: le massacre des Tutsi au Rwanda* (Paris: Seuil, 2014). See also Alette Smeulers, Maartje Weedersteijn, and Barbora Holá, eds., *Perpetrators of International Crimes: Theories, Methods, and Evidence*(Oxford: Oxford University Press, 2019).

10. Browning, *Ordinary Men*, xvi.

11. D'Aubigné, *Histoire universelle*, 154–155.

12. On violence presented as counter-violence, see chapter 2.

13. In *De Bello Gallico* the conqueror and master rhetorician justifies the massacres of the Usipetes and Tencteri tribes as just, having first prepared the reader by listing all the evils previously and supposedly committed by these tribes. See Michel Rambaud, *L'art de la déformation historique dans les Commentaires de César* (Paris: Les Belles Lettres, 1951); Kurt A Raaflaud, "Caesar and Genocide: Confronting the Dark Side of Caesar's Gallic Wars," *New England Classical Journal* 48 no. 1 (2021): 54–80.

14. Hanna Arendt, *The Origins of Totalitarianism* (New York: Harcourt, Brace, 1951).

15. See for instance Robert Debs Heinl, Nancy Gordon Heinl, and Michael Heinl, *Written in Blood: the Story of the Haitian People, 1492–1995*, 3rd ed. (Lanham, MD: University Press of America, 2005); Elizabeth Abbott, *Haiti: a Shattered Nation* (New York, London: Overlook Duckworth, 2011).

16. Prosper Avril, *Vérités et révélations*, vol. 3. *L'armée d'Haiti, bourreau ou victime?* (Port-au-Prince: Bibliothèque nationale d'Haiti, 1993).

17. Kern Delince, *Armée et politique en Haïti* (Paris: L'Harmattan, 1979); Pressoir Pierre, *Témoignages, 1946–1976 : l'espérance déçue* (Port-au-Prince: Henri Deschamps, 1987); Michel Laguerre, *The Military and Society in Haiti* (London: Palgrave Macmillan, 1993); Francis Charles, *Haïti. Essence du pouvoir martial: la domestication de l'armée* (Port-au-Prince: Henri Deschamps, 2009).

18. Daniel Supplice, *Dictionnaire biographique des personnalités politiques de la République d'Haïti* (Pétion-ville, Haiti: C3 Éditions, 2014), 782–84. The year after each name indicates their date of graduation from the military academy. Cadets typically developed strong bonds with the rest of their cohort. Since there was only one cohort at a time, students could not forge bonds with members of previous or later cohorts until after graduation. The composition of the successive military coups and juntas between 1986 and 1991 owes much to the bonds forged among members of the same cohort. Graduates also joined a social sector of their own, composed of officers, their families, and their networks. Many married within this social group: sisters, friends, or acquaintances of fellow classmates and their families, forming a social capital that would be key for their respective careers. See Jean-Philippe Belleau, "Intimacy, hostility, and state politics: François Duvalier and his Inner-circle, 1931–1971," *History and Anthropology* 32, no. 5 (2021): 567–68. This social group was also highly paradoxical, characterized, on one hand, by a strong esprit de corps, which, incidentally, proved to be a major impediment to this research. Communications and revelations stopped where unwavering loyalty to their cohort at the Military Academy started. On the other hand, it was also a world "ravaged by envy," as Francis Charles described it to me in a personal communication (Pétionville, January 2019). Competition for promotions, status, favors, and mistresses was fierce. Bonds and loyalty,

envy and betrayal were weighted, often within the immediate political context. In conversations peripheric to this research with post-1971 graduates of the Military Academy, I heard many accounts of betrayal of officers by officers. None of these betrayals was about ideologies, politics, or beliefs, but about betrayed intimacy with people who knew each other well.

19.   Contrary to a widely held belief, the VSN Rosalie Bousquet, a.k.a. Madame Adolphe, never was Fort-Dimanche's warden. See Supplice, *Dictionnaire*, 124.

20.   See chapters 1 and 11.

21.   See the previous chapter.

22.   Even Albert Chassagne's prosecutorial account admitted that Jérôme avoided attending the executions. Chassagne, *Bain de sang*, 24.

23.   Jérôme caught a military flight to travel from Jérémie urgently in order to plead for the liberation, first of Jean-Claude Fignolé, then of Gérard Noël, according to Jérôme. (That Jérôme intervened for the liberation of Noël was not confirmed by any other interlocutor). The real motives for the trips might have been different: to defend himself personally before Duvalier in the face of accusations by Saintange Bontemps that he was a *camoquin*, a subversive.

24.   See Belleau, "Intimacy." Pressoir Pierre reproduced correspondence between him and Duvalier in which the latter calls him "*mon fils*" (my son). See Pierre, *Témoignages*, 129.

25.   Max Horkeimer and Theodore Adorno, *Dialectic of Enlightenment: Philosophical Fragments*, ed. Gunzelin Schmid Noerr, trans. Edmund Jephcott (Stanford, CA: Stanford University Press, 2002); Max Horkheimer, "Authority and the Family," in *Critical Theory: Selected Essays*, 47–128 (New York: Continuum, 1975).

26.   Although never out of favor with the dictator, Jérôme was never a member of his inner circle and was always posted in provincial towns after 1962. He became the commander of Port-au-Prince only under Jean-Claude Duvalier. Of all the former high-ranking military officers I interviewed, Jérôme is the only one who still calls himself a Duvalierist; the other informants were keenly aware of the social cost of presenting themselves as such. Jérôme seemed genuinely attached to Duvalier, four decades after the latter's death.

27.   Roger Garaudy, *Perspectives de l'homme: existentialisme, pensée catholique, marxisme* (Paris: Presses Universitaires de France, 1959).

28.   In April 1961, about a dozen local young men organized a banquet at Jérémie's Versailles restaurant in honor of Second Lieutenant Elliott Roy who was on his way out. Eddy Cavé, Jean-Claude Sansaricq, and Gérard Noël were among the organizers. A few weeks earlier, following a routine redeployment, Roy, an officer at Jérémie's military base, had received a reassignment order to Petit Goave. The bonds Roy built during his eight-month tenure in the Grand'Anse would last for life. Elliott Roy, personal communication with author, Cayes-Jacmel, January 2019; Eddy Cavé, phone communication with author, February 2019.

29.   See chapter 7.

30.   Jean-Claude Fignolé did not remember the exact date but believes it was in mid-August.

31.   Pierre Clastres described it thus: "For it is often in the innocence of a half-completed gesture or an unconsciously spoken word that the fleeting singularity of meaning is hidden, the light in which everything takes shape." Pierre Clastres, *Chronicle of the Guayaki Indians* (New York: Zone Books, 2000), 2. For Geertz, the ethnographer must determine "the difference, however unphotographable, between a twitch and a wink." Clifford Geertz, "Thick description: Toward an interpretive theory of culture," in *The Interpretation of Cultures: Selected Essays*, 3–30 (New York: Basic Books, 1973), 6.

32.   "*Il ne se laisse pas marcher sur les pieds. Sauf par Duvalier.*" Fignolé, personal communication with author, Jérémie, May 2012.

33.   This last aspect alienated him further from the town's noirists such as Sanette Balmir, Saintange Bontemps, and the Fort Réfléchi VSNs such as the Desroche brothers.

34.   U.S. Embassy, Embtel 287, August 14, 1964.

35.   Action Priority 759, Timmons, Oct. 25, 1964

36.   U.S. Embassy, Embtel 745, Oct. 24, 1964; U.S. Embassy, Embtel 850/Deftel 338, November 8, 1964. These cables do not mention Jérôme being present or "dropping by."

37.   Pierre Chérubin, phone communications with author, 2019-2020.

38.   Joseph Anariol, communication with author, Montréal, March 2017.

39.   I met Anariol, Dimanche's cousin, in Montréal in 2017. He had lived with Dimanche in Port-au-Prince before and after the counterinsurgency operations:

> I knew Jeannot since I was a child, [we are] cousins on my mother's side . . . He was a turbulent child, then he went to the (Military) Academy, thanks to Adrienne, as I told you. . . . He felt he had been had. It should not have been him at Numéro 2. It should have been Abel. . . . He was a good man but he was also a brawler (*bagarreur*). He did not let anyone order him around. And he likes women, oh! yes, it often got him in trouble. . . . After '64, he drank a lot. Sometimes you knew. . . . Yes, he talked about the executions (*fusillades*), but people seldom asked him questions about it. He said he had nightmares. . . . No, he had no problem talking about the executions and what he had done . . . I do not remember him mentioning any of the soldiers, I do not remember. . . . It was Abel, he made him do it, Abel would not go there (Numéro 2) . . . I know Abel too, you know, but not well . . . no, I never met or talked to him . . . Abel was street smart (*li malin*), Jean was too honest.

> Anariol's words and those of others who knew Dimanche agree on Dimanche's "unhappy" state in the years after the massacre. I am not speculating that Dimanche's awareness of his own responsibility affected him mentally; this causality is made by those who knew him. It is not clear also if his "depression" happened immediately after the executions or later in life for other reasons.

40.   See chapter 1.

41.   Who were they? The historiography ignores them, as if the topic were irrelevant. Oral history says just as little. None of my interlocutors, even those with military networks, were able to provide information. Former military officers I interviewed seemed to consider soldiers an undifferentiated mass.

9. BONDS THAT HOLD AND BONDS TO BREAK

1.   Elliott Roy, personal communication with author, Cayes-Jacmel, January 2019.

2.   Michèle Oriol, personal communications with author, Port-au-Prince, 2012–2023. The exact day of Lucien Daumec's execution is not known.

3.   Francis Charles, personal communication with author, Pétionville, January 2019.

4.   Duvalier's regime was a world of intimacy and hostility. Its own members painted a vivid picture of the daily fear of living in it. Pierre Audain, a diplomat at the Haitian embassy in Mexico, was tasked with receiving Haitian officials traveling to Mexico for business or other reasons. He was constantly trying to angle for favors while not making himself vulnerable. His book is an incredible, if disjointed, account of intrigue and fear: the same individuals he appealed to for favors could be the ones who could fabricate a death sentence against him; some were indecipherable, others were gregarious yet also deceitful. A plot—its formation and its target—is by definition a social web. One of the main ways to advance professionally within Duvalierism was indeed through intrigue; yet intrigues could stir jealousy or insecurity in others and could therefore provoke unforeseen counter-intrigues. Pierre Audain, *Les ombres d'une politique néfaste* (Mexico: n.p., 1976). See also Jean-Philippe Belleau, "Intimacy, hostility, and state politics: François Duvalier and his Inner-circle, 1931–1971," *History and Anthropology* 32 no.5 (2021): 549–573.

5.   Daniel Goldhagen (1996), *Hitler's Willing Executioners: Ordinary Germans and the Holocaust* (New York: Vintage Books, 1997).

6.   See Christopher R. Browning, *Ordinary Men: Reserve Police Battalion 101 and the Final Solution in Poland* (New York: Harper Perennial, 1998). Siniša Malešević's entire work links fighting with sociation. See Siniša Malešević, *The Sociology of War and Violence* (Cambridge: Cambridge University Press, 2010); Siniša Malešević, *The Rise of Organised Brutality: A Historical Sociology of Violence* (Cambridge: Cambridge University Press, 2017); Siniša Malešević, "Is It Easy to Kill in War? Emotions and Violence in the Combat Zones of Croatia and Bosnia and Herzegovina (1991–1995)," *European Journal of Sociology* 62 (2020): 1–31; and Siniša Malešević, *Why Humans Fight: The Social Dynamics of Close-Range Violence* (Cambridge: Cambridge University Press, 2022).

7.   A. Dirk Moses, "Structure and Agency in the Holocaust: Daniel J. Goldhagen and His Critics," *History and Theory* 37, no. 2 (1998): 194–219.

8.   Events recapitulated in this paragraph are developed in chapters 1, 7, and 8. To be clear, this phenomenon (evasion, desistance) is distinct conceptually, empirically, and in nature from class-based resistance to oppression, as wonderfully explored in much of the social sciences of the past four decades, and in particular by James Scott, for whom cryptic resistance, noncompliance, foot-dragging, and collective withdrawal characterize the behavior of the oppressed against the rich and the powerful. See James C. Scott, *Weapons of the Weak: Everyday Forms of Peasant Resistance* (New Haven, CT: Yale University Press, 1985). It must be said, however, that this literature sometimes looks a bit like the idealization of the peasantry as explored by Ben Kiernan—see chapter 2. In any case, I am not talking here about class-based collective consciousness, material interests, or even political behavior, but individual, ethical inhibitions. Randall Collins and Siniša Malešević are more useful here than the resistance or anti-hegemony scholarship.

9.   This is when Gérard Léonidas, Antoine Apollon, Jean Alcide and possibly others argued for the release of Dr. Laurent, Sicot Gardère, and others on August 11, 1963. See chapter 1.

10. Graham Greene, *The Comedians* (London: Bodley Head, 1966).

11. Jean Florival, *Duvalier. La face cachée de Papa Doc* (Montreal: Mémoire d'encrier, 2007). Anecdotes told to me by several interlocutors, principally Frantz Desvarieux, Hervé Denis, Margaret Désinor, also emphasize performances by regime members.

12. They are named in chapter 11.

13. Social anthropologists generally refrain from making this kind of vast culturalist generalization, but I do not have enough space here to ridicule allegations, including by Haitian writers, that kinship morality collapsed under Duvalier; such allegations exoticize Haiti as a freak society. Documented cases of children denouncing parents, parents denouncing children, and spouses denouncing spouses abound in the literature on Mao Zedong's China or the Soviet Union; I did not find a single documented case in Haiti, where individuals never were "atomized." As Robert Fatton argues, Duvalierism was not (and did not have the means to be) a totalitarianism.

14. Gérard Barthélémy, *Le pays en-dehors: essai sur l'univers rural haïtien* (Port-au-Prince: Henri Deschamps, 1989). As a verb, "*marroner*" (to "marroon"), still in contemporary parlance, names the precautionary concealment of true opinion, which evokes the Persian term *taqiyya*. The use of this neologism holds an ethic dimension as it denotes frustration at dissimulation. Interestingly, during an informal conversation in 2000 Gérard Barthélémy himself expressed his frustration at the political class, particularly President René Préval, whom Barthélémy characterized as *un marron* to explain the former's lack of ingenuity.

15. Johnhenry Gonzalez, *Maroon Nation: A History of Revolutionary Haiti* (New Haven, CT: Yale University Press, 2019); Dimitri Béchacq, "Les parcours du marronnage dans l'histoire haïtienne: entre instrumentalisation politique et réinterprétation sociale," in "Haïti: face au passé/Confronting the Past," ed. Carlo A. Célius, special issue, *Ethnologies* 28, no. 1 (2006): 203–40.

16. See chapters 1 and 5.

17. Pierre Bourdieu, *Distinction: A Social Critique of the Judgement of Taste*, trans. Richard Nice (New York: Routledge, 1984). Bourdieu's ultra-deterministic concept aims to highlight an individual's behavior strictly in the context of a looming-over society. For Bourdieu, people are predominantly concerned with their social standing, worried about what other people think of them, and make choices accordingly to climb the social hierarchy.

18. Melissa M. McDonald, Andrew M. Defever, and Carlos David Navarrete, "Killing for the Greater Good: Action Aversion and the Emotional Inhibition of Harm in Moral Dilemmas," *Evolution and Human Behavior* 38, no. 6 (2017): 770–78.

19. Jean-Philippe Belleau, "Hatred Is Not Stronger Than Bonds," *Social Analysis* 67, no. 1 (2023): 49–69.

20. Max Weber, *Economy and Society: An Outline of Interpretive Sociology*, eds. Guenther Roth and Claus Wittich (Berkeley: University of California Press, 1978), 27.

21. See for instance Michael Herzfeld, *Cultural Intimacy: Social Poetics in the Nation-State*, 2nd ed. (New York: Routledge, 1997); Daniel Henig, " 'Knocking on My Neighbour's Door': On Metamorphoses of Sociality in Rural Bosnia." *Critique of Anthropology* 32, no. 1 (2012): 3–19.

22. Sherry Ortner, "Dark Anthropology and Its Others: Theory Since the Eighties." *HAU: Journal of Ethnographic Theory* 6, no. 1 (2016): 47–73; Marshall Salhins, *Apologies to Thucydides: Understanding History as Culture and Vice Versa* (Chicago: University of Chicago Press, 2004); Michael F. Brown, "On Resisting Resistance," *American Anthropologist* 98, no. 4 (1998): 729–35.

23. See Matei Candea and Giovanni da Col, eds., "The Return to Hospitality: Strangers, Guests, and Ambiguous Encounters," special issue, *Journal of the Royal Anthropological Institute* 18, no.1 (2012).

24. Carlos Fausto, "The Friend, the Enemy, and the Anthropologist: Hostility and Hospitality among the Parakanã (Amazonia, Brazil)," *Journal of the Royal Anthropological Institute* 18, no.1 (2012): 197.

25. See Randall Collins, *Violence: A Micro-sociological Theory* (Princeton, NJ: Princeton University Press, 2008); Malešević, *Sociology of War*; Malešević, *Rise of Organised Brutality*; Malešević, "Is It Easy to Kill"; and Malešević, *Why Humans Fight*.

26. Gilles Deleuze and Claire Parnet, *Dialogues* (Paris: Flammarion, 1977), 8.

27. Jérémie Foa, *Tous ceux qui tombent. Visages du massacre de la Saint-Barthélémy* (Paris: La Découverte, 2022).

28. See chapter 5.

29. Helen Fein, *Accounting for Genocide: National Responses and Jewish Victimization During the Holocaust* (New York: The Free Press, 1979). The analogy to Durkheim is mine; the book does not mention him, except once, on an unrelated subject.

30. Hannah Arendt, *Eichmann in Jerusalem: A Report on the Banality of Evil* (New York: Viking, 1964).

31. Arendt, *Eichmann*, 113.

32. Arendt, *Eichmann*, 122.

33. On these categories, see discussion in chapter 7.

34. On this opposition, see Léon-François Hoffmann, *Haïti: couleurs, croyances, créole.* (Montreal: CIDHICA, 1990).

35. Peter Berger and Thomas Luckmann, *The Social Construction of Reality. A Treatise in the Sociology of Knowledge* (New York: Anchor Books, 1966). Michèle Oriol, by showing that since Haitian independence the peasantry has relentlessly sought to acquire more and more land parcels and has done so through full acceptance and use of the terms of officialdom rather than rejecting them, refutes the *marronage* paradigm and challenges the soundness of the agency-versus-structure opposition. She examined archives of land surveyors (*arpenteurs*). It also refutes the dominant historiography, which since the late nineteenth century has been depicting the Haitian peasantry as either victims or rebels. Acquiring and transmitting land was the condition for familial reproduction, always within and by the law. Peasant heads of families—women and not just men—chose family (structure) over both rebellion (agency) or withdrawal (structure). However, such choice, which rests on relentlessness, self-empowerment, persuasion to sell, and accumulation of capital (even if in very small quantities), and always in the public space, sounds like agency pure and simple. See Michèle Oriol, *La terre et les hommes* (Montreal: CIDIHCA, forthcoming).

36. See for instance Ira Lowenthal, " 'Marriage is 20, Children are 21': the Cultural Construction of Conjugality and the Family in Rural Haiti" (PhD diss., Johns Hopkins University,

1987); Louis Herns Marcelin, "La famille suburbaine à Port-au-Prince" (master's thesis, Faculté d'ethnologie, 1988); Rodrigo Bulamah, "O Lakou Haitiano e suas práticas: entre mudanças e permanências," *Temáticas* 21, no. 2 (2013): 205-233; Rodrigo Bulamah, "Farming of Commons: Kinship and Social Practices in Milot, Haiti" (master's thesis, University of Campinas, 2016); and Sidney Mintz, *Three Ancient Colonies: Caribbean Themes and Variations* (Cambridge, MA: Harvard University Press, 2010), chap. 3.

37. Louis Herns Marcelin, "In the Name of the Nation: Ritual, Blood, and the Political Habitus of Violence in Haiti," *American Anthropologist* 114, no. 2 (2012): 253–66.

38. William Régala, perceiving my sudden interest, soon changed the subject again. I still asked: "Is this why the Villedrouin children (Lyssa, and Frantz) were added to the list on September 19?" Régala gave an improbable response: that he did not know about these children.

39. See chapter 1; see also and Ralph Allen, *Tombés au champ d'honneur. Les 13 de Jeune Haïti* (Port-au-Prince: Zémès, 2019).

40. For that reason, the notion that the targeting of entire families is a byproduct of the construction of the modern state that attempts to cut individuals from traditional allegiances and build new, impersonal ones to itself is unconvincing. Additionally, only some of the most authoritarian of "modern" states have engaged in this type of repression. Sippenhaftung, an antiquated notion of kinship or clan responsibility from the Germanic Middle Ages, reappeared under the Nazi regime. To be clear, Jewish families were systematically targeted by the Nazis because, for the Nazis, blood was race and not kinship.

41. Renaud Gagné, *Ancestral Fault in Ancient Greece* (Cambridge: Cambridge University Press, 2013).

42. Golfo Alexopoulos, "Stalin and the Politics of Kinship: Practices of Collective Punishment, 1920s–1940s," *Comparative Studies in Society and History* 50, no. 1 (2008): 94.

43. Horace Dewey quotes Genghis Khan on the matter: "Everyone who does not submit and attempts to resist shall perish, along with his wife, children, relatives and those close to him." See Horace Dewey, "Russia's Debt to the Mongols in Suretyship and Collective Responsibility," *Comparative Studies in Society and History* 30, no. 2 (1988): 251.

44. Cynthia Hooper, "Terror of Intimacy: Family Politics in the 1930s Soviet Union," in *Everyday Life in Early Soviet Russia: Taking the Revolution Inside*, ed. Christina Kiaer and Eric Naiman (Bloomington: Indiana University Press, 2006), 62.

45. See Alexopoulos, "Stalin," 92–95:

It is through the lens of kinship that the logic of Stalinist political violence reveals itself. First, we see that Bolshevik habits of terror were highly gendered. Party leaders typically constructed the political enemy as a head of household and pursued these individuals, largely men, along with their kin, mostly women and children . . . More fundamentally, the practice of collective punishment reflects a certain understanding of kinship, one in which the family and the state appear in conflict and family ties look potentially subversive.

46. Yongyi Song, "The Enduring Legacy of Blood Lineage Theory," *China Rights Forum* 4 (2004): 17. Yan Jiaqi and Gao Gao translate it as "blood relation theory." See Yan Jiaqi and Gao Gao, *Turbulent Decade: A History of the Cultural Revolution*, ed. and trans. D. W. Y. Kwok (Honolulu: University of Hawai'i Press, 1996), 102–06. Beliefs in the correlation of

lineage and politics are vividly rendered in Rae Yang, *Spider Eaters: A Memoir* (Los Angeles: University of California Press, 2013).

47.   Blaine Harden, *Escape from Camp 14: One Man's Remarkable Odyssey from North Korea to Freedom in the West* (New York: Penguin Books, 2013).

48.   The contradictions between the modern, communist ambition to create a New Man while still relying on feudal hereditary beliefs, and also between policies bent on destroying Confucianism while still relying on Confucian assumptions about hereditary abilities, were evident in the communist regimes of both China and North Korea. Confucian ethics, which proposes to model all relationships on the core relationships of the family and places the latter at the center of morality, seem to inform regimes bent on destroying it. On the relationship between Confucian ethics and the North Korean regime, see Jiyoung Son, "How Communist Is North Korea? From the Birth to the Death of Marxist Ideas of Human Rights," *Cambridge Journal of International Affairs* 23, no. 4 (2010): 561–87.

49.   John Mbiti, *African Religions and Philosophy*, 2nd ed. (Oxford: Heinemann, 1990); Roger Bastide, "Le principe d'individuation (contribution à une philosophie africaine)," in *Actes du colloque international sur la notion de personne en Afrique Noire*, Paris, 11–16 octobre 1971 (Paris: CNRS, 1973).

50.   Mbiti, *African Religions*, 106.

51.   McKim Marriott, "Hindu Transactions: Diversity Without Dualism," in *Transaction and Meaning: Directions in the Anthropology of Exchange and Symbolic Behavior*, ed. Bruce Kapferer, 109–42 (Philadelphia: Institute for the Study of Human Issues, 1976); Marilyn Strathern, *The Gender of the Gift. Problems with Women and Problems with Society in Melanesia* (Berkeley: University of California Press, 1988).

52.   Strathern, *Gender of the Gift*, 13.

53.   Marshall Sahlins, "What Kinship Is," *Journal of the Royal Anthropological Institute* 17 (2011): 11, 14.

54.   Philippe Descola has renewed perspectives on animism, breaking away from Tylorian associations by hermeneutically moving beyond the ironclad line between traditions and modernity. The advantage of using Descola here is that he does not exoticize animism; so-called modern societies retain animistic elements. Philippe Descola, *Beyond Nature and Culture*, trans. Janet Lloyd (Chicago: University of Chicago Press, 2014). At the same time, readers shocked by the repression of entire kin groups rather than of specific opponents are more modern than Latour acknowledged.

55.   Nurit Bird-David, " 'Animism' Revisited: Personhood, Environment, and Relational Epistemology," *Current Anthropology* 40, no. 1 (1999): 67–91.

56.   Marriott, "Hindu Transactions."

57.   On this difficulty, see David M. Schneider, *A Critique of the Study of Kinship* (Ann Arbor: University of Michigan Press, 1984); Janet Carsten, ed. *Cultures of Relatedness: New Approaches to the Study of Kinship* (New York: Cambridge University Press, 2000); Strathern, *Gender of the Gift*; and Sahlins, "What Kinship Is."

58.   For a recognition of these difficulties, see David Kronenfeld, "Comment: What Kinship Is *Not*—Schneider, Sahlins, and Shapiro," *Journal of the Royal Anthropological Institute* 18, no. 3 (2012): 678.

59. On social organization based on residency, see for example Meyer Fortes, *The Web of Kin-ship among the Tallensi: The Second Part of an Analysis of the Social Structure of a Trans-Volta Tribe* (New York: Oxford University Press, 1949); Pierre Bourdieu, "La maison kabyle ou le monde renversé," *Échanges et communications: mélanges offertes à Claude Lévi-Strauss à l'occasion de son 60ème anniversaire*, ed. Claude Lévi-Strauss, Pierre Maranda, and Jean Pouillon (Berlin: De Gruyter, 1970): 738–89; and Janet Carsten and Stephen Hugh-Jones, eds., *About the House: Lévi-Strauss and Beyond* (Cambridge: Cambridge University Press, 1995).

60. Claude Rosier, *Le triangle de la mort. Journal d'un prisonnier politique haïtien, 1966–1977* (Port-au-Prince: n.p., 2003), 107.

61. See chapter 4. Race was less of a factor. The first family was considered Black; the latter three, mulattoes; while the Fandal family, judging from available pictures, included both dark-skin mulattoes and Black members.

62. See Devoir de Mémoire, *Mourir pour Haïti: la résistance à la dictature en 1964* (Montreal: CIDIHCA, 2015), 51.

63. François Benoît was not there that day, and then went into exile. So did his brother-in-law, Claude Edline, also a military officer.

64. See Claude Moïse, *Constitutions et luttes de pouvoir en Haïti (1815–1987)* (Montreal: CID-IHCA, 1990), 402–05. Marie-Marguerite Clérié, personal communication, Port-au-Prince, January 2019. The officers who led the killings, Max Dominique and later Harry Tassy, both members of the 1957a graduation cohort at the military academy, knew personally, yet disliked, Claude Edeline (a 1957a cohort member) and François Benoît (a 1957b cohort member). I distinguish between the two overlapping graduation cohorts in 1957 by referring to them as 1957a and 1957b.

65. See Dewey, "Russia's Debt," 251–52.

66. Alexopoulos, "Stalin," 99–104.

67. "Invisible ties" is Maxim Felder's concept in his work on neighborly relations. See Maxim Felder, "Strong, Weak and Invisible Ties: A Relational Perspective on Urban Coexistence," *Sociology* 54, no. 4 (2020): 675–92.

68. On Émile Roumer, see Chapter 1.

69. Andrée Roumer, "Andrée Roumer, sa dernière épouse parle de Jacques-Stephen Alexis. Interview by Frantz Duval," *Le Nouvelliste*, May 16, 2022.

70. Rosier, *Le triangle*, 51.

71. See chapter 1.

72. See Eddy Cavé, *De mémoire de Jérémien: en pensant aux amis disparus*, vol. 2 of *De mémoire de Jérémien* (Montreal: CIDIHCA; Pétionville, Haiti: Pleine Plage, 2016), 397–408. Philippe Marius, personal communication, Atlanta, October 2023. Daniel Supplice, *Dictionnaire biolgraphique des personnalités politiques de la République d'Haïti, 1804-2014* (Pétionville, Haiti: C3 Éditions, 2014).

73. See Allen, *Tombés*, 217.

74. Fritz Cinéas, personal communication with author, Washington, D.C., October 2022.

75. This was the case, for instance, with Joe Gaetjens' family, who pressed Daniel Beauvoir, the Port-au-Prince police chief. Beauvoir had been Joe Gaetjens' best man at his wedding but did not intervene to save his friend. His family never forgave Beauvoir. See chapter 11;

Lesly Gaetjens, *The Shot Heard Around the World: The Joe Gaetjens Story* (Falls Church, VA: Lesly Gaetjens, 2010).

10. THE RULER'S ANXIETY

1. Fritz Cinéas, personal communication with author, Washington, D.C., October 2022. Cinéas was Duvalier's private secretary from 1962 to 1964, and knew him personally since the early 1940s; their families were immediate neighbors in the 1950s, when Duvalier lived on ruelle Roy.
2. U.S. Ambassador Benson Timmons, U.S. Embassy, Embtel, August 15, 1964.
3. On Gérard Léonidas, see chapters 1 and 7. On Jean-Claude Fignolé, see chapter 8.
4. "Dès réception de la présente, disparaissez famille Sansaricq." See chapter 1. I kept the syntactic mistake in the English version. A visual witness to the April 26, 1963 massacre also mentioned this order in a radio interview conducted in 1986. See Yvon Guerrier, "Temwayaj sou Franck Romain avèk evènman 26 avril 1963 Lamanten yo," file 1 of 4, aired on Radio Haiti-Inter October 4, 1986, Duke Digital Repository, https://idn.duke .edu/ark:/87924/r4862gb8h, 16:40.
5. See chapter 4.
6. See Justin Chrysostome Dorsainvil, *Manuel d'histoire d'Haïti* (Port-au-Pince: Procure des Frères de l'Instruction Chrétienne, 1934), 155; Dantès Bellegarde, *Histoire du peuple haïtien, 1492–1952* (Port-au-Prince: n.p., 2004), 155.
7. Justin Bouzon, *Études historiques sur la présidence de Faustin Soulouque (1847–1849)* (Paris: Gustave Guérin, 1894), 108.
8. François Duvalier, *Eléments d'une doctrine*, vol. 1 of *Œuvres essentielles* (Port-au-Prince: Presses Nationales d'Haiti, 1966), 409.
9. David Troy was a minor military figure of the Haitian Revolution; he was also from Jérémie. He is mentioned extensively by Beaubrun Ardouin. However, the historiography gives no indication of his "race."
10. Duvalier, *Éléments d'une doctrine*.
11. On these events, see chapter 4.
12. Duvalier, *Éléments d'une doctrine*, 405–421.
13. Duvalier appears captivated by the use of brute force against mulattoes beyond the historical actions of Soulouque and Salomon. Hence, Duvalier quotes Sonthonax (a French Revolutionary envoy) allegedly warning Toussaint Louverture circa 1794: "as long as you [Toussaint] will have men of color (mulattoes) among your men, you will not be free. It was then [a] question for a while, according to Madiou, to cut the throats of the mulattoes in the hills." Duvalier, *Éléments d'une doctrine*, 275. In addition, Salomon ordered the destruction of Port-au-Prince's business elite on September 22 (1883), while Duvalier was elected on the same date, September 22 (1957). He concluded that 22 was his fetish number.
14. See chapter 3.
15. Duvalier, *Éléments d'une doctrine*, 409.
16. Léon-François Hoffmann, *Faustin Soulouque d'Haiti dans l'histoire et la littérature* (Paris: L'Harmattan, 2007).

17. François Duvalier, *Mémoires d'un leader du Tiers Monde: mes négociations avec le Saint-Siège; ou, une tranche d'histoire* (Paris: Hachette, 1969), 92.

18. *Le Moniteur*, May 6, 1882, 1–2.

19. Historian Claude Moïse illustrates Salomon's megalomania with this quote from another of Salomon's speeches: "I do not accept—I do not allow under my government—men who are too important, too influential, or who think they are influential. The only influential man in the country is me, and it is me because the entire Republic is with me." See Claude Moïse, *Constitutions et luttes de pouvoir en Haïti (1804–1987)* (Montreal: CIDIHCA, 1990), 217.

20. Laurent Dubois, *Avengers of the New World: The Story of the Haitian Revolution* (Cambridge, MA: Belknap Press of Harvard University Press, 2004), 91–114.

21. Abel Hugo, *Histoire des Armées Françaises de Terre et de Mer de 1792 à 1833: ouvrage rédigé par une société de militaires et de gens de lettres*, vol. 4 (Paris: Chez Delloye, 1838), 216.

22. Hugo, *Histoire*, 216–21.

23. Eddy Cavé, *Haïti: extermination des pères fondateurs et pratiques d'exclusion*, (Port-au-Prince: Henri Deschamps, 2022), 34.

24. Linstant de Pradine, ed., *Recueil général des lois et des actes du gouvernement d'Haïti depuis la proclamation de son indépendance jusqu'à nos jours*, vol. 1, *1804–1808* (Paris: Durand & Pédone-Lauriel, 1886), 57.

25. See "Bandits or Patriots? Documents of Charlemagne Péralte, National Archives," trans. Elena and Kirill Razlogova, History Matters: The U.S. Survey Course on the Web, last updated March 22, 2018, George Mason University, http://historymatters.gmu.edu /d/4946/.

26. Eddy Cavé, phone communication with author, April 2019.

27. See Michael Herzfeld, *Cultural Intimacy. Social Poetics in the Nation-State*, 2nd ed. (New York: Routledge, 1997); Michael Herzfeld, *The Body Impolitic. Artisans and Artifice in the Global Hierarchy of Value* (Chicago: University of Chicago Press, 2003).

28. See U.S. Embassy, Embtel 759, October 26, 1964; Norman Gall, "Duvalier's Regime Keeps Haiti in Chaos", *Washington Post*, September 27, 1964, 28.

29. U.S. Embassy, Embtel 759, October 26, 1964.

30. U.S. Embassy, Embtel 759, October 26, 1964. See chapter 1.

31. Jacques Fourcand, "Discours du Dr. Jacques Fourcand," Archives of the International Committee of the Red Cross, V-S-10025-A-04, July 20, 1965, '28''10-'30-'31''45.

32. Diederich called it a "suicide mission" and "futile." Bernard Diederich, *Le trophée* (Port-au-Prince: Henri Deschamps, 2008), 194, 196.

33. See for instance Prosper Avril, *From Glory to Disgrace: The Haitian Army, 1804–1994* (Universal Publishers: n.p., 1999); Francis Charles, *Haïti. Essence du pouvoir martial: la domestication de l'armée* (Port-au-Prince: Henri Deschamps, 2009).

34. Pressoir Pierre, *Témoignages. 1946–1976: l'espérance déçue* (Port-au-Prince: Henri Deschamps, 1987), 130–31.

35. Charles, *Haïti. Essence du pouvoir*.

36. High-ranking VSNs typically visited Duvalier in his office to be debriefed, and then left.

37. The Duvalier family was composed of eight people: Duvalier, his wife Simone Ovide, their four children, and Simone Ovide's sister and aunt.

38. Visitors were first checked by on-guard officers and the Private Secretary and officers, then made to wait in the large and formal Yellow Room. It was adjacent to Duvalier's office. Duvalier had installed a secret peephole in the wall to observe people waiting in the Yellow Room. Fritz Cinéas, personal communication, October 2022, Washington, D.C.

39. See, for instance, Leslie Manigat, "Armée et politique traditionnelle dans la société traditionnelle Haïtienne," *Eventail d'histoire vivante d'Haïti: des preludes à la Révolution de Saint Domingue jusqu'à nos jours (1789–2007)*, vol. 2 (Port-au-Prince: CHUDAC, 2002): 102–20. For Hannibal Price, militarism's ubiquitous presence in society was an obstacle to progress. Hannibal Price, *De la réhabilitation de la race noire par la République d'Haïti* (Port-au-Prince: J. Verrollot, 1900), 615.

40. Pierre, *Témoignages.*

41. Gérald Férère, phone communication with author, March 2008.

42. On Merceron, see Daniel Supplice, *Dictionnaire biographique des personalités politiques de la République d'Haïti* (Port-au-Prince: n.p., 2014), 536–537.

43. See Pierre, *Témoignages.*

44. Duvalier typically sent away members of his inner circle whom he believed were too ambitious or unpredictable to undertake consular missions. General Antonio Kébreau had been sent to the Vatican; see Supplice, *Dictionnaire*, 395. Pressoir Pierre was sent to Paris; the unpredictable Windsor Laferrière was sent either to Genoa, Italy (according to Fritz Cinéas) or to Argentina (according to Diederich). Fritz Cinéas, personal communication with author, Washington, D.C., October 2022; Diederich, *Le trophée*, 170–71. Duvalier would send his son-in-law, Max Dominique, to Spain as a military attaché in 1967.

45. David Nicholls, "Embryo-politics in Haiti," *Government and Opposition* 6, no. 1 (1971): 75–85.

46. Leslie Manigat, *Haiti of the Sixties, Object of International Concern; a Tentative Global Analysis of the Potentially Explosive Situation of a Crisis Country in the Caribbean* (Washington, DC: Washington Center of Foreign Policy Research, 1964).

47. Gérard Pierre-Charles, *Radiographie d'une dictature: Haïti et Duvalier*, pref. Juan Bosch (Montreal: Nouvelle Optique, 1973).

48. Michel-Rolph Trouillot, *Haiti, State Against Nation. The Origins and Legacy of Duvalierism* (New York: Monthly Review Press, 1990).

49. David Nicholls, "Review," *The Hispanic American Historical Review* 71, no. 3 (1991): 651–52; Jean-Germain Gros, "Haiti: The Political Economy of Decay and Renewal," *Latin American Research Review* 35, no. 3 (2000): 218–19.

50. Robert Fatton, "Michel-Rolph Trouillot's *State Against Nation*: A Critique of the Totalitarian Paradigm," *Small Axe* 17, no. 3 (2013): 203–12. There were two aspects in which the Duvalier regime mirrored the totalitarian experience: racism and xenophobia. The totalitarian experiences in Germany, Italy, the USSR, Cambodia, Vietnam, and Mao's China, targeted and sometimes eliminated ethnic minorities. See Ben Kiernan, "The Pol Pot Regime's Simultaneous War Against Vietnam and Genocide of Cambodia's Ethnic Vietnamese Minority," *Critical Asian Studies* 53, no. 3 (2021): 342–58.

51. Nicolas Jallot and Émile Rabaté, dir. *Papa Doc et les Tontons Macoutes*, prod. Frédéric Tyrode Saint Louis, Paris, BCI Communication, 2019, posted on December 10, 2019, YouTube, https://www.youtube.com/watch?v=-5LBIXxamZY, 1:26:02.

52. Bernard Diederich, *Le prix du sang* (Port-au-Prince: Henri Deschamps, 2016).

53. On Gérard de Catalogne, see Chelsea Stieber, "Gérard de Catalogne, passeur transatlantique du maurassisme entre Haïti et la France," in *Doctrinaires, vulgarisateurs et passeurs des droites radicales au vingtième siècle (Europe-Amériques)*, ed. Olivier Dard (Bern, Switzerland: Peter Lang, 2012), 232–54.

54. One of the four coup plotters, Colonel Lionel Honorat,'45, was the half-brother of one of Duvalier's closest friends, Lamartinière Honorat. The two families were so close that, when Lionel's sister, Marie-Claude, married in November 1957, Duvalier brought her to the church's altar. See Bernard Diederich, *Le Trophée* (Port-au-Prince: Henri Deschamps, 2008), 143. The coup aborted in March 1963 and Lionel Honorat fled the country. *New York Times*, April 14, 1963, 14.

55. These analyses seem rather common today but were first articulated in a scholarly language, I believe, by Guglielmo Ferrero. His views on the ruler's fear and his exercise of terror (my words) appear in several of his works. Guglielmo Ferrero, *Pouvoir; les génies invisibles de la cité* (New York: Brentano's, 1942), 16 passim; Guglielmo Ferrero, *Characters and Events of Roman History, from Caesar to Nero: The Lowell Lectures of 1908*, trans. Frances Lance Ferrero (New York: Putnam, 1909), 103–42. The German historian Hans Mommsen would later develop a relatively similar "weak dictator" thesis.

56. These attempts were as follows: July 1958, by Pasquet et Perpignan; August 1959 in Les Irois by Cuban soldiers; March 1963 by Lyonel Honorat; August–September 1963, armed incursions from the Dominican Republic by General Leon Cantave; June 1964, the Fred Baptiste insurgency; August 1964, the Jeune Haïti insurgency. For sketches of these events, see Diederich, *Le prix du sang*. To categorize them as coups or insurgencies evokes Latin American traditions they largely failed to emulate.

57. Ferrero, *Pouvoir*, 22.

58. A full account of Duvalier's destruction of state institutions, violations of the Constitution, and enactment of illegal measures in 1964 can be found in Moïse, *Constitutions*, 405–13.

59. Ferrero, *Pouvoir*, 22 passim.

60. Anne Fuller, a former official of the United Nations in Haiti, is preparing a book on the subject. Anne Fuller, personal and email communications with author, Port-au-Prince, 2016–2023. Well-informed, Prosper Avril describes the peasant population as sometimes puzzled, sometimes friendly towards the Jeune Haiti guerilla in 1964—but never as hostile. Prosper Avril, *L'aventure militaire des 13 guérilleros de Jeune Haiti* (Port-au-Prince: Bibliothèque nationale d'Haïti, 2015), 133 passim. Popular support for the regime and against insurgencies appear mainly in the regime's propaganda, predictably relayed by a certain historiography.

61. An hour-per-hour analysis of the "Pasquet Coup" in 1958 invalidates the belief that Duvalierist supporters rallied right away to Duvalier's rescue. Pasquet and his six men—hardly an army, not even a faction—arrived at the Dessalines military base at 10:00 P.M. on July 28. Not encountering any resistance, they imprisoned the fifty soldiers and officers who were at the base and tied officers and noncommissioned officers to chairs. Duvalierists rallied for Duvalier over fourteen hours later, and only after sectors of the military had reacted. On the morning of July 29 they took action by placing guns in

front of the Dessalines barracks, but only once news had spread that there were only a few coup plotters. From the farthest point of Bas Peu de Choses, a neighborhood with (allegedly) the most dedicated Duvalierist supporters, it takes at most ten minutes to walk to the Presidential Palace. Given that the palace was surrounded by densely populated neighborhoods, and that the sound of gunshot must have been heard as early as 10:00 P.M. on July 28 when the mercenaries shot three guards, zeal was obviously not the order of the day.

62.   Jean Price-Mars, *Jean-Pierre Boyer-Bazelais et le drame de Miragoâne: à propos d'un lot d'autographes, 1883–1884* (Port-au-Prince: Imprimerie d'Etat, 1948), 123. Price-Mars provides also the number of casualties on the Boyer-Bazelais side during this nine-month civil war: thirty-six (twenty-one of whom died of diseases).

63.   On these events, see Laurent Dubois, *Haiti: The Aftershocks of History* (New York: Henry Holt, 2012), 167–68, 196–201; Dr. Raymond Bernardin, *Cinq siècles d'histoire politique*, 2 vols. (Port-au-Prince: n.p., 2015), 223–45.

64.   I would hypothesize also that Jean-Bertrand Aristide's astonishing choice at the beginning of his second presidential mandate in 2001 (he was a rather patriotic president), to delegate the entirety of his personal security to a U.S. company entirely composed of armed foreign agents rather than to the Haitian police he himself had created, reflected this very fear of being alone in moments of danger. Large numbers of followers, which in Aristide's case probably numbered in the millions, does not equal security.

65.   Robert Fatton talks about the absence of a "meaningful system of accountability" throughout Haiti's history. See in particular Robert Fatton, "Haiti in the Aftermath of the Earthquake: The Politics of Catastrophe," *Journal of Black Studies* 42, no. 2 (2011): 164. More largely, with different approaches, the works of Fatton and Dupuy provide evidence of this structural phenomenon. For Robert Fatton, see *Haiti's Predatory Republic: The Unending Transition to Democracy* (Boulder, CO: Lynne Rienner, 2002); *The Roots of Haitian Despotism* (Boulder, CO: Lynne Rienner, 2007); and *Haiti: Trapped in the Outer Periphery* (Boulder, CO: Lynne Rienner, 2014). For Alex Dupuy, see *Haiti in the New World Order: The Limits of the Democratic Transition* (Boulder, CO: Westview Press, 1996); *The Prophet and Power: Jean-Bertrand Aristide, the International Community, and Haiti* (Lanham, MD: Rowman and Littlefield, 2006); and *From Revolutionary Slaves to Powerless Citizens: Essays on the Politics and Economics of Underdevelopment* (London: Routledge, 2014).

66.   Diederich, *Le trophée*.

67.   See Fatton, *Haiti's Predatory Republic*; Fatton, *The Roots of Haitian Despotism*; and Fatton, *Haiti: Trapped in the Outer Periphery* (Boulder, Colorado: Lynne Rienner Publishers, 2014). See also Michèle Oriol's history of the presidency, marked by constant, brutal ruptures: Michèle Oriol, *Chefs d'Etat en Haiti: gloire et misères* (Port-au-Prince: Fondation pour la recherche iconographique et documentaire, 2006).

68.   Political instability manifested itself from inception. Eddy Cavé highlights a troubling fact: sixteen of Haiti's thirty-seven Founding Fathers were assassinated within two years after they had signed the Act of Independence; most of the others would die a violent death shortly thereafter. See Cavé, *Extermination*. Being a high-ranking officer with considerable prestige in the new, victorious country offered no guarantee of safety but rather seemed to increase the possibility of betrayal and assassination. Pierre-Étienne

also notes that the internal conflicts "for the conquest, exercise and conservation of power" occurred at inception. See Sauveur Pierre-Etienne, *L'énigme haïtienne. Échec de l'État moderne en Haïti* (Montreal: Mémoire d'Encrier, 2007), 2. Interestingly, as Cavé and Michèle Oriol noted, the emerging elite was also a small world: assassinations and conspiracies were carried out by people who knew one another. The military-political elites that survived a decade of brutal warfare shared bonds of kinship, friendship, work, neighborliness even. Betrayal was both widespread and intimate. For Cavé, "the self-extermination of the Founding Fathers" was linked to unhinged competition motivated by personal ambition rather than by competing ideological projects: "In the absence of any debate, any negotiations, any agreement on the mode of sharing wealth and the income of the new state, and in the absence of a common societal project, the Founding Fathers and the social groups they represented were condemned to face each other in the short or long term, in a frantic race for the seizure of power by force . . ." See Cavé, *Extermination*, 164.

69. See Georges Michel, "Le procès des auteurs du massacre du 27 juillet 1915," *Revue de la société haïtienne d'histoire et de géographie* 196 (1998). Michèle Oriol found copies of the death certificates of the executed opponents: their number far exceeds the usually cited number of 167 and approaches 400.

70. Scholars have similarly detected a major historical cause of political instability in Colombia in the inability to agree on basic constitutional principles, as illustrated by the indissoluble presence of guerrillas and the endemic recourse to political violence to overcome political issues. See David Bushnell, *The Making of Modern Colombia: A Nation in Spite of Itself* (Berkeley: University of California Press, 1993).

71. Fatton, *Roots of Haitian Despotism*.

72. A personal anecdote highlights this phenomenon. In the Fall of 1998, a visiting anthropologist from Brazil, Omar Ribeiro, was attending the night course I was teaching at Port-au-Prince's Faculté d'ethnologie. He was having a lively discussion with students when at some point, he matter-of-factly asked the class of about ninety undergraduates who among them was considering running at some point for the presidency. (Neither he nor I remember what led him to ask that question.) With the exception of two women students sitting on the right side, all students raised their hand. While I know for a fact that there were several individuals with the caliber for the job, the quasi-unanimity of the answer is the signifier.

73. Fatton, *Roots of Haitian Despotism*.

74. Matthew J. Smith, *Liberty, Fraternity, Exile. Haiti and Jamaica after Emancipation* (Chapel Hill: The University of North Carolina Press, 2014). As a good friend of mine and former member of the parliament puts it, "it comes with the job" (*c'est l'hypothèse de travail*).

75. See Rony Gilot, *Au gré de la mémoire: François Duvalier, le mal-aimé* (Port-au-Prince: Éditions Le Béréen, 2006); Ertha Pascal-Trouillot and Ernst Trouillot *Encyclopédie biographique d'Haïti* (Montreal: Semis, 2001), 355; and Duvalier, *Éléments d'une doctrine*.

76. Diederich, *Le prix du sang*, 41–44.

77. Trouillot, *Haiti, State Against Nation*.

78. Jonathan Leader Maynard, *Ideology and Mass Killing: The Radicalized Security Politics of Genocides and Deadly Atrocities* (Oxford: Oxford University Press, 2022), 308.

79.   It is telling that the aborted March 1963 military conspiracy, entirely composed of military officers from *la classe* (Black urban middle sectors), was thought to have been composed of mulattoes by Duvalier and his government.

80.   Oral history and some of the historiography provide two explanations for Duvalier's decision, the improbability of which testifies to the unintelligibility of the massacre. The first version goes like this: Duvalier wanted the Sansaricq family killed because of a student brawl in Mexico City in early 1964 that pitted pro- and anti-Duvalier Haitian students, all studying at UNAM (Universidad Nacional Autónoma de México, or National Autonomous University of Mexico), against each other. One of the anti-Duvalier students was Daniel Sansaricq, age twenty-five, then studying engineering. The pro-Duvalier students allegedly reported him to their consulate, which reported it to the Presidential Palace in Port-au-Prince, which five months later decided to execute all the Sansaricqs, except Daniel who was abroad. That Duvalier made the decision to exterminate a family of fourteen, infants included, because five months earlier anti-Duvalier words had been uttered during a student brawl in Mexico seems like a desperate attempt to find rationality in causality. There were many disputes involving anti-Duvalier youth in exile (in Mexico, New York, Santo Domingo, Paris, the Congo, and Montreal) and their families in Haiti were not targeted, especially months after reports were made. The second version I encountered in oral history asserts that Duvalier's ire against the Sansaricqs was ignited because Adrien Sansaricq was broadcasting an anti-Duvalier show on Radio Habana under a pseudonym. I brought this up with Lidia Guerberhof, Adrien Sansaricq's widow, who denied categorically that her husband had ever participated in any broadcast in the first place. (Lidia Guerberhof, email correspondence with author, December 2018). In any case, the writer René Depestre, who did broadcast from Radio Habana under his real name and with whom this version might mix, did not have his relatives in Jacmel threatened or harmed. Even if Adrien Sansaricq was behind such broadcasts, even if Duvalier's henchmen identified his voice (how?), it does not explain why the broadcaster's family—and not those of other broadcasters or of other opponents—was eliminated entirely. These two versions also attribute ruthless efficiency and competence in intelligence gathering and reporting to the regime, competencies it was rarely capable of in other areas. This attribution of omnipotence may well say more about the legacy of Duvalierism and its regime of terror than about actual events. Finally, these two versions move causality back toward the victims and overlook Duvalier's personality and beliefs.

81.   See chapter 1, "Oct. 22–29, 1964," and chapter 9.

82.   See chapter 4, "April 26, 1963."

11. SOCIOCENTRIC REPRESSION

1.   Robert Rotberg, *Haiti, the Politics of Squalor* (Boston: Houghton Mifflin, 1971), 344.

2.   See Jean-Philippe Belleau, "The Stranger-King of the Caribbean: François Duvalier, State Politics, and the Othering of Brutality," *Journal of Latin American and Caribbean Anthropology* 24, no. 4 (2019): 935–57; Jean-Philippe Belleau, "Intimacy, Hostility, and State Politics: François Duvalier and His Inner-circle, 1931–1971," *History and Anthropology* 32, no. 5 (2021): 549–73.

3. The "Duvalier dossier" at the Bentley Historical Library at the University of Michigan contains about a dozen items. These include official university forms that Duvalier filled out both immediately upon his arrival and later to receive his stipends. (Duvalier had a very distinct writing style, with uniquely recognizable capital Bs and capital Ds.) The last item is a report by an administrator stating that Duvalier could no longer be located and had likely dropped out, one year before finishing his degree and without notifying his adviser.

4. Neither his daughter Simone nor anyone else I collected information from had heard Duvalier talk about this period; it does not appear in his writings, either. Simone Duvalier, personal communication with author, Miami, January 2019.

5. Leslie Péan, *L'ensauvagement macoute et ses consequences, 1957–1990*, vol. 4, *Haïti: économie politique de la corruption* (Paris: Maisonneuve et Larose, 2007).

6. Siniša Malešević, *The Sociology of War and Violence* (Cambridge: Cambridge University Press, 2010), 2–3. The entirety of Malešević's work over the past fourteen years focuses on sociality in combat.

7. Francis Charles and Elliott Roy mentioned that several officers in the Presidential Guard suffered from ulcers.

8. Benson Timmons, U.S. Embassy, U.S. Action Priority Dept 310, August 15 [1964], 1:00 P.M.

9. Paul Audain, Pressoir Pierre, and Jean Florival wrote spectacular accounts of distrust, spying, and betrayal within the inner circle. See Paul Audain, *Les ombres d'une politique néfaste* (Mexico: n.p., 1976); Pressoir Pierre, *Témoignages, 1946–1976: l'espérance déçue* (Port-au-Prince: Henri Deschamps, 1987); and Jean Florival, *Duvalier. La face cachée de Papa Doc* (Montréal: Mémoire d'encrier, 2007).

10. See Michèle Oriol, "Ministres des deux Duvaliers" (unpublished manuscript, 2018).

11. Gérard Pierre-Charles, *Haïti: jamais, jamais plus! Les violations de droits de l'homme à l'époque des Duvalier* (Port-au-Prince: Centre de recherche et de formation économique et sociale pour le développement, 2000), 87–90.

12. Peter Sloterdijk, *Die schrecklichen Kinder der Neuzeit: Über das anti-genealogische Experiment der Moderne* (Berlin: Surhkamp, 2014), 179–94.

13. See chapter 8 for a detailed description.

14. See for instance Helen Fein, *Accounting for Genocide: National Responses and Jewish Victimization During the Holocaust* (New York: The Free Press, 1979); Jacques Sémelin, *Purify and Destroy. The Political Uses of Massacre and Genocide* (New York: Columbia University Press, 2007).

15. I reassessed the number of people killed by the Duvalier regime (1957–1971) in another piece. This question has looked like a "dance of numbers," with the total count sometimes posited as high as 175,000 victims, but more often stabilizing around 30,000, while some Duvalierists believe that only a few hundred opponents perished. The scholarly literature, in the absence of any study, archives, or convincing sources, tends to repeat these numbers rather than cross-check. Unless the regime responsible for mass violence is also one with a bureaucracy willing and able to keeping records, as in Chile under Pinochet, the macabre exercise of counting victims can only be tentative and, in all honesty, almost like a "finger in the air" estimation. Based on information provided by former members of the repression apparatus and by victims, I opted for a method of

estimation based on locations rather than events or types of killing. In short, outside of a few specific locations, there were few executions. I came up with a number situated between 7,200 and 49,000; below or above this range is highly improbable, with 16,500 being the most likely death toll. This represents about 0.30 percent of Haiti's population at the time, a large number for a country that was not at war or at civil war; where insurgencies were militarily and politically insignificant, if not folkloric; and where the general population was rather docile. It testifies to the brutality, if not gratuitous lethality, of the regime. Jean-Philippe Belleau, "Calculating the number of people killed by the Duvalier regime" (presentation, 33rd Annual Conference of the Haitian Studies Association, online, October 2021).

16. Hannah Arendt, *The Origins of Totalitarianism* (New York: Harcourt, Brace, 1951).

17. Daniel Supplice, *Dictionnaire biographique des personalités politiques de la République d'Haïti, 1804–2014* (Pétionville, Haiti: C3 Éditions, 2014), 690.

18. Reported in *Haiti-Sun*, April 30, 1961.

19. Aurèle Joseph and François Duvalier knew each other from medical school. See Belleau, "Intimacy, Hostility, and State Politics: François Duvalier and His Inner-circle, 1931–1971," *History and Anthropology* 32, no. 5 (2021): 555. In 1991 Jean Tassy's son married a relative of the anti-Duvalier coup plotter Philippe Dominique and of journalist Jean Dominique.

20. William Régala, personal communication with author, Delmas, January 2016.

21. Yvon Guerrier, "Temwayaj sou Franck Romain avèk evènman 26 avril 1963 Lamanten yo," first broadcast on Radio Haiti-Inter, October 4, 1986, Duke Digital Repository, file 1 of 4, MP3 audio, 16:40, https://idn.duke.edu/ark:/87924/r4862gb8h.

22. Leslie Péan gives numerous other examples. See Péan, *L'ensauvagement macoute et ses conséquences, 1957–1990*, vol. 4, *Haïti: économie politique de la corruption* (Paris: Maisonneuve et Larose, 2007). Guerrier's account, however, goes beyond corruption and correlates killing with thievery. Romain allegedly used that money to send his children to study in the United States.

23. See Claude Rosier, *Le triangle de la mort. Journal d'un prisonnier politique haïtien, 1966–1977* (Port-au-Prince: n.p., 2003); Patrick Lemoine, *Fort-Dimanche, Fort-la-Mort* (Port-au-Prince: n.p., 1996); Marc Romulus, *Les cachots des Duvalier: Marc Romulus, ex-prisonnier politique, témoigne* (Montréal: Carrefour international; Comité pour la liberation des prisonniers politiques, 1978); and Patrick Brouard-Cambronne, *Le chant des ténèbres. Morte lente au Fort-Dimanche* (Montréal: Éditions DAMI, 2009). Robert Duval and Max Bourjoly provided oral testimony in a documentary. See *Papa Doc et les Tontons Macoutes*, dir. Nicolas Jallot and Émilie Rabaté, prod. Frédéric Tyrode, posted December 10, 2019, on YouTube, https://www.youtube.com/watch?v=-5LBIXxamZY, 1:26:02.

24. Bernard Diederich, *Le prix du sang*, rev. ed. (Port-au-Prince: Henri Deschamps, 2016), 29.

25. Max Bourjoly in Jallot and Rabaté, eds., *Papa Doc*.

26. See Belleau, "Intimacy, Hostility, and State Politics." This was also true of Luc Désyr.

27. Péan alludes to this phenomenon, which deserves in-depth study. See Péan, *L'ensauvagement*.

28. Michèle Oriol, *La terre et les hommes* (Montréal: CIDIHCA, forthcoming). The only documented land redistribution concerned two islands, La Gonave and Île-à-Vache, which belonged in their entirety to the "private domain of the state." Michèle Oriol, personal

communication, Port-au-Prince, Janvier 2019. (Oriol heads Haiti's Inter-Ministerial Committee on Territorial Management, CIAT).

29.   There were four Presidential Guards bearing the last name Monestime

30.   Elizabeth Abbott, *Haiti: A Shattered Nation* (New York: Overlook Duckworth, 2011), 79–80; Pierre, *Témoignages*. Colonel Roger Villedrouin was one of the very few officers who remained impartial during the 1957 presidential campaign.

31.   See Claude Moïse, *Constitutions et lutes de pouvoir en Haïti (1804–1987)* (Montréal: CIDI-HCA, 1990), 305–60.

32.   See Lesly Gaetjens, *The Shot Heard Around the World: The Joe Gaetjens Story* (Falls Church, VA: Lesly Gaetjens, 2010); Diederich, *Le prix du sang*, 41–44;

33.   Diederich, *Le prix*, 43.

34.   Gaetjens, *The Shot Heard Around the World*, 38.

35.   Gaetjen's execution is mentioned in a declassified CIA cable sent on July 9. DB-315/00178-S4.

36.   The seminal expression "magic realism" was first coined in the 1940s by Alejo Carpentier to characterize Alexis's style.

37.   Devoir de Mémoire, *Mourir pour Haïti: la résistance à la dictature en 1964* (Montréal: CIDI-HCA, 2015), 25.

38.   Jean-Robert Sabalat, personal communications with author, Pétionville, enba tonel, February-July 2000.

39.   Serge Sabalat, personal communication with author, Port-au-Prince, January 2010.

40.   Alix Cédras told of his father's first encounter with Duvalier, which took place in Cédras's store when Duvalier was working for a vaccination campaign sponsored by the United States, prior to 1943. Alix Cédras, phone communication with author, March 2021.

41.   The lunch was narrated to me by Alix Cédras, a visual witness. The Cédras home was located a few yards from the homes of several of the victims of the Jérémie massacre; the one rented by Kesner Blain was about fifty yards away. Kesner Blain would be demoted a decade later and died in Fort-Dimanche in 1976. Dominique Blain, personal communication with author, Kenscoff, January 2019.

42.   Eddy Cavé, Phone communications with author, 2016-2024.

43.   Sometimes, even repeated information against one individual that Duvalier personally liked was not enough to tip the balance in favor of an execution. I tell one such story involving Lieutenant Elliott Roy in Belleau, "Intimacy, Hostility, and State Politics."

44.   Pierre Biamby's first experience with fame was as a member of the Haitian national soccer team in the early 1940s. See Supplice, *Dictionnaire*, 108. By 1950, at the age of thirty-three, he had become its national coach; see *Haiti Sun*, September 11, 1950, 11. In that capacity, Biamby worked with future figures of Duvalierism, such as Daniel Beauvoir, future chief of police, before becoming an executive at the public telephone company; see *Haiti Sun*, July 5, 1953, 4. Biamby was described by interlocutors as a politically savvy individual, with a reputation for discretion, sycophancy, and deception. Unlike other members of Duvalier's inner circle, he was never demoted and held the same position, "Private Executive Secretary" to the President from July 1964 until 1976, when he became Minister of Defense under Jean-Claude Duvalier. See Michèle Oriol, "Ministres," 3. In spite of such influence, Biamby almost never appears in the historiography. Still, he did

not act in the shadows of power. Every single person or group who visited Duvalier in the Presidential Palace had to go through his office (Fritz Cinéas, personal communications with author, Washington, D.C., October 2022). Official pictures I consulted from the Figaro Collection show Biamby at Duvalier's side during social events organized by the regime. When Biamby died, Jean-Claude Duvalier declared a day of national mourning (*Le Nouvelliste*, January 24, 1984). Pierre Biamby's son, Philippe Biamby (1952–2008), and Jérémie mayor's namesake son, Raoul Cédras (1949–), would be classmates at the military academy in 1971 and later, members of the same military government (1991–1994) before going into exile on the same plane on October 13, 1994 (Supplice, *Dictionnaire*, 109). In addition, René Prosper, a member of the Presidential Commission sent to Jérémie in the summer of 1964, was the director of Haiti's National Military Academy from 1971 to 1973, when Raoul Cédras fils graduated as its valedictorian. Cédras went on to marry Prosper's sister. Duvalierism was a very small world.

45.   I reconstituted Ketly Ney-Pierre's genealogical tree. Through her mother, Clorinde Lindingue, and her niece, Hélène, she was linked to the very elite Laraque family, itself linked to the Sansaricq family, although her branch of the family was poorer.

46.   Jacques Fourcand's sister, Bertha, was married to Elie Legagneur. She lived three houses down from Gérard Guilbaud and Alice Drouin, and almost in front of several individuals arrested in early August, including Gérard Degraff and Alain Rocourt. See map of Jérémie in 1964. Legagneur was appointed mayor of Jérémie by Duvalier in 1965 (after the removal of Raoul Cédras from this position), allegedly on Fourcand's recommendation.

47.   U.S. Embassy, Embtel 285, August 12, 1964.

48.   See chapter 7.

CONCLUSION

1.   See Vladimir Tismaneanu and Jordan Luber, eds., *One Hundred Years of Communist Experiments* (London: Central European University, 2021); François Furet, *The Passing of an Illusion: The Idea of Communism in the Twentieth Century* (Chicago: University of Chicago Press, 1999).

2.   Ben Kiernan. *The Pol Pot Regime: Race, Power, and Genocide in Cambodia under the Khmer Rouge, 1975–79* (New Haven, CT: Yale University Press, 2008).

3.   The literature on this subject is vast. One of the most concise and powerful studies is Marc Angenot, *Les ideologies du ressentiment* (Montreal, XYZ, 1997). See also Jacob Katz, *From Prejudice to Destruction: Anti-Semitism, 1700–1933* (Cambridge, MA.: Harvard University Press, 1980), 257–59, 324.

4.   See Claude Rivière, "Violences politiques en Afrique noire," *Anthropos* 99, no. 1 (2004): 21; Yamily Carrion-Mège, "La dictature de Francisco Macías Nguema en Guinée Équatoriale (1968–1979)" (master's thesis, Université Angers, 2013). The Macías regime is estimated to have killed over 40,000 people out of a population of three million.

5.   Elizabeth Baisly, "Genocide and Constructions of Hutu and Tutsi in Radio Propaganda," *Race & Class* 55, no. 3 (2014): 45.

6.   Léon Saur, "La frontière ethnique comme outil de conquête du pouvoir: le cas du Parmehutu,"*Journal of Eastern African Studies* 3, no. 2 (2009): 303–16.

7. Scholarly research about anti-elitism in the past decade has mainly focused on populism in democracies (mainly in Western societies or, to a lesser extent, India), and not on mass violence. See for instance Moritz Ege and Johannes Springer, eds. *The Cultural Politics of Anti-Elitism* (London: Routledge, 2023). One of the main exceptions to this academic approach is the Katyn massacre, where the targeting of Polish elites by the Soviets is indeed conceptualized as such.

8. To my knowledge, Central America was the only place where the peasantry was explicitly constructed as the figure of the enemy in the twentieth century. See for instance Aldo Lauria Santiago, *To Rise in Darkness: Revolution, Repression, and Memory in El Salvador* (Duke University Press, 2008). This would be the main outlier to Ben Kiernan's work on the idealization of the peasantry—see chapter 2.

9. Yves Benot, *Massacres coloniaux, 1944–1950: la IVe République et la mise au pas des colonies françaises* (Paris: La Découverte, 2001); Dirk Moses, ed. *Empire, Colony, Genocide: Conquest, Occupation, and Subaltern Resistance in World History* (New York: Berghahn Books, 2008); see also Ben Kiernan, *Blood and Soil. A World History of Genocide and Extermination from Sparta to Darfur* (New Haven: Yale University Press, 2007).

10. I am referring to Dostoevsky's archetypal mad revolutionary thinker in *Demons* (1871–72) whose search for justice and an ideal system makes him incapable of distinguishing good from evil—prophetically heralding intellectuals who defended mad ideas in the twentieth and twenty-first centuries.

11. A correlation, as is known, detected early by Tocqueville. For a genealogy of equality and its correlation to modernity, see Aldo Schiavone, *The Pursuit of Equality in the West* (Cambridge, MA: Harvard University Press, 2022).

12. See Schiavone, *The Pursuit of Equality*.

13. Furet, *The Passing of an Illusion*.

14. The romantic ethos and political agenda of these very ideals have been embodied for the past 200 years by the revolution as both a project and an ideal. Revolutions constructed—had to construct—a country's elite as an enemy—not simply the ruling group, but society's wider upper echelons. The revolution project itself, whether socialist, fascist, Duvalierist, even Islamic such as the Iranian revolution—all historical instances that actually explicitly used the term "revolution" in their time—cannot happen, materialize, succeed without eliminating the established elite, fundamentally change them, or drive them abroad. Even a revolution that wanted to return to an ideal past, such as the 1979 Iranian revolution, constructed contemporary elites as the enemy since the idealized past's elite was long gone.

15. See, e.g., Jonathan Leader Maynard, *Ideology and Mass Killing: The Radicalized Security Politics of Genocides and Deadly Atrocities* (Oxford: Oxford University Press, 2022).

16. For the example of Haiti, see Leslie Péan, *L'ensauvagement macoute et ses conséquences, 1957–1990*, vol. 4, *Haïti: économie politique de la corruption* (Paris: Maisonneuve et Larose, 2007). For the example of Germany, see Götz Aly, *Hitler's beneficiaries: Plunder, Racial War, and the Nazi Welfare State*, trans. Jefferson S. Chase (New York: Metropolitan Books, 2007).

17. Few social scientists would not argue that the state, at least the modern one, is not an expansion of (some) elite power. From Pareto to Engels to Mosca to Ortega y Gasset to

Norbert Elias to Foucault to Bourdieu, it is implied that the elite is the ruling class. For a more explicit correlation, see William G. Domhoff, *The Power Elite and the State: How Policy Is Made in America* (New York: Aldine de Gruyter, 1990). Some would argue that this ruling class is in dialogue with, say, commoners, the larger public, communities, or even the poor. This is certainly sometimes true, but it is more typically in dialogue with the business, religious, and intellectual elites.

18.   Two distinct steps require the involvement of intellectual elites: the construction of the enemy (as is known), and the justification of mass violence. A good example of the first is the Bahutu Manifesto, crafted in 1957 by nine Hutu intellectuals, "the ideological foundation and justification for several genocidal massacres and, ultimately, the 1994 genocide." See Samuel Totten, Paul Bartrop, and Steven Jacobs, *Dictionary of Genocide* (Westport, CT: Greenwood Publishing, 2009), 34. As chapters 2 and 3 show, the delegitimization of the mulatto elite has been an intellectual exercise for over a century in Haiti and abroad. The legitimization of the use of mass violence, and not just state violence, to achieve progress and betterment had to be intellectually crafted either for later implementation or to rationalize the crime. Intellectuals' aversion to democracy and a preference for authoritarianism are certainly as old as Socrates, Aristotle, and Plato, but a bridge was crossed with the unapologetic defense of political violence. Marx famously called violence the "midwife" of history; Sartre explicitly defended killing in the name of an ideal of justice; and Alain Badiou (allegedly the most translated French philosopher over the past decades) openly justified, apophases notwithstanding, the genocidal Khmer Rouge regime. Even a humanist such as Montaigne argued that massacres can be required for the public good. Intellectuals' fascination with and defense of political violence has been widely identified and critiqued. Historian Omer Bartov powerfully examines the role of scholars in mass violence. Both Raymond Aron and François Furet realized that twentieth-century philosophy was invaded by nihilism, a taste for brute force hidden under Hegelianism, Marxism, and a belief in history as progress. It is difficult not to see a direct link between the philosophy of history and the notion that the elite is an obstacle on the road to progress. Virility-obsessed scholars were also more likely to be seduced by violence and totalitarianisms than by democracy. Daniel Cordier, a 23-year-old SAS (Special Air Service) commando and secretary of Jean Moulin, first head of the French Resistance during the Second World War, describes an incredible encounter with Sartre circa 1943. Asked why he wanted to join the Resistance, Sartre tells Cordier that he just wants to kill Germans and requested weapons, although he had to be aware that doing so, then, would have resulted in massive reprisals and that there were many other ways to help the Resistance. Amused by the cluelessness and unreliability of the philosopher, Cordier refused. Historian François Furet argues that the 1945 Soviet victory against the ugliest of monsters, Nazism, through the use of the most brutal force (including against its own population and its own soldiers), provided an unprecedented validation of the use of mass violence. It was not just the ideals of justice, equality, and emancipation, but also the practice of extreme brutality that became seductive. See Jean-Paul Sartre, preface to *Les damnés de la terre*, by Frantz Fanon (Paris: La Découverte, 2004). For a critique of this aspect of Sartre, see Ronald E. Santoni, *Sartre on Violence: Curiously Ambivalent* (University Park: Pennsylvania State

University Press, 2003); Daniel Cordier, *La victoire en pleurant: alias Caracalla 1943–1946* (Paris: Gallimard, 2021); and Michel de Montaigne, *Les essais: edition complete*, ed. André Lanly (Paris: Gallimard, 2009), 956. For a critique of intellectuals' inclination toward mass violence and totalitarianism, see Albert Camus, *Œuvres completes*, vol. 2, ed. Jacqueline Lévy-Valensi and Raymond Gay-Crosier (Paris: Gallimard, 2006), 463; Raymond Aron, *The Opium of the Intellectuals* (New York: Routledge, 2001); Omer Bartov, "Extreme Violence and the Scholarly Community," in "Extreme Violence," ed. Jacques Sémelin, special issue, *International Social Science Journal* 54, no. 174 (2002): 509–18; Tony Judt, *Past Imperfect: French Intellectuals, 1944–1956* (New York: New York University Press, 2011); and Furet, *The Passing of an Illusion*. For one of the earliest critiques of intellectuals' "secret desire to hold the whip," see George Orwell, *The Collected Essays, Journalism, and Letters of George Orwell: "My Country Right or Left" 1940–1943*, vol. 2 (London: Secker & Warburg, 1968).

19. Tatjana Thelen, Larissa Vetters, and Keebet von Benda-Beckmann, eds, *Stategraphy: Toward a Relational Anthropology of the State* (New York: Berghahn, 2018).

20. *To court* implies an asymmetrical relationship in a field of political power: an intent on the part of those below to make connections with the powerful at the top. As its etymology betrays, a ruler's *court* is a space, where favors can be obtained solely by forging social bonds.

21. Matthew J. Smith, *Liberty, Fraternity, Exile. Haiti and Jamaica after Emancipation* (Chapel Hill: The University of North Carolina Press, 2014).

22. "The government against the nation" is Edmond Paul's expression. Edmond Paul, *Les causes de nos malheurs. Appel au peuple* (Kingston, Jamaica: G. Henderson, 1882). Michel-Rolph Trouillot, *Haiti, State Against Nation. The Origins and Legacy of Duvalierism* (New York: Monthly Review Press, 1990). Both Edmond Paul (1837–1893), a prolific author, and Michel-Rolph Trouillot (1949–2012) went into exile almost a century apart.

23. Faustin Soulouque exiled Joseph Courtois (1785–1877), after having failed to execute him. Courtois was an exceptional man: a polymath, a teacher, an intellectual with an expansive mind, founder of an important newspaper and of a school opened to children of all backgrounds. He had been recognized in his childhood as a prodigy by Toussaint Louverture who sent him to an elite school in Paris. Courtois's brother, Sévère, was an admiral in Simon Bolivar's fleet. See Vanessa Mongey, "A Tale of Two Brothers: Haiti's Other Revolutions," *Americas* 69, no. 1 (2012): 37–60.

24. Michèle Oriol, personal communication with author, Port-au-Prince, January 2016.

25. Philippe Girard, *Haiti: The Tumultuous History from Pearl of the Caribbean to Broken Nation* (New York: St. Martin's Griffin, 2010), 112. Girard gives the highly symbolic example of ONEC, the *Office national d'alphabétisation et d'action communautaire* (Office of National Literacy and Community Action), which carried out literacy campaigns and was dismantled by Duvalier.

26. Sidney Mintz, "Papa Doc is Dead but the "Mystery" Lingers on," *New York Times*, April 25, 1971.

27. In Nicolas Jallot and Émile Rabaté, dir., *Papa Doc et les Tontons Macoutes*, prod. Frédéric Tyrode Saint Louis, Paris: BCI Communication, 2019, posted to YouTube December 10, 2019, https://www.youtube.com/watch?v=-5LBIXxamZY.

28.   Jallot and Rabaté, dir., *Papa Doc.*
29.   Haiti never recovered from the systematic lack of investments in infrastructure during that period, contrary to what occurred in the Dominican Republic, where even the brutal and kleptomaniac dictatorship of Rafael Trujillo continuously invested in national infrastructures. Robert Fatton, "The Unending Political Crisis" (paper, 34th Annual Haitian Studies Association conference, Washington DC, October 2022).

Bibliography

Abbott, Elizabeth. *Haiti: A Shattered Nation.* New York: Overlook Duckworth, 2011.

Akhavan, Payan. *Reducing Genocide to Law: Definition, Meaning, and the Ultimate Crime.* Cambridge: Cambridge University Press, 2012.

Alaux, Gustave d'. *L'empereur Soulouque et son empire.* Paris: Michel Lévy frères, 1856.

Alcindor, Jean-Pierre. *Jérémie, Haïti . . . il était une fois. Une tranche de la petite histoire d'Haïti.* Port-au-Prince: Média-texte, 2011.

Alexandre, Guy. "Face à l'Opinion: Guy Alexandre sou rejim François Duvalier 1." File 1 of 2. Aired on Radio Haïti-Inter, September 21, 1996. Radio Haiti Archive, Duke University Digital Repository. https://idn.duke.edu/ark:/87924/r4833r432. Audio, 44:37.

——. "Face à l'Opinion: Guy Alexandre sou rejim François Duvalier 1." File 2 of 2. Aired on Radio Haïti-Inter, September 21, 1996. Radio Haiti Archive, Duke University Digital Repository. https://idn.duke.edu/ark:/87924/r4pz54r7q. Audio, 24:38.

Alexopoulos, Golfo. "Stalin and the Politics of Kinship: Practices of Collective Punishment, 1920s–1940s." *Comparative Studies in Society and History* 50, no. 1 (2008): 91–117.

——. *Stalin's Outcasts: Aliens, Citizens, and the Soviet State, 1926–1936.* Ithaca, NY: Cornell University Press, 2003.

Allen, Ralph. *Tombés au champ d'honneur. Les 13 de Jeune Haïti,* Port-au-Prince: Zémès, 2019.

Aly, Götz. *Why the Germans? Why the Jews? Envy, Race Hatred, and the Prehistory of the Holocaust.* New York: Metropolitan Books, 2014.

Angenot, Marc. *Les idéologies du ressentiment.* Montréal: XYZ, 1997.

Ans, André Marcel d'. *Haïti: paysage et société.* Paris: Karthala, 1987.

——. "Haïti, Paysage et Societé." Interview by Jean L. Dominique, Radio Haiti-Inter, September 16, 1989. Radio Haiti Archive, Duke Digital Repository. https://repository.duke.edu/dc/radiohaiti/RL10059-RR-0659_01

Arcelin, Paul. *Cercueil sous le bras.* Queens Village, NY: Atlas Premium Management, 1999.

Archives du diocèse de Vannes. "Liste chronologique des missionnaires arrivés en Haïti depuis 1864." *La lettre de Saint-Jacques* 95 (September–October 1989).

Ardant du Picq, Charles. *Études sur le combat: combat antique et combat moderne.* Paris: Champ libre, 1978. First published 1880 by Hachette et cie (Paris).

Arendt, Hannah. "De l'humanité dans de sombres temps." In *Vies politiques,* 11–41. Paris: Gallimard, 1974.

——. *Eichmann in Jerusalem: A Report on the Banality of Evil.* New York: Viking, 1964.

——. *The Origins of Totalitarianism.* New York: Harcourt, Brace, 1951.

Aron, Raymond. *The Opium of the Intellectuals.* New York: Routledge, 2001.

Arthus, Weibert. *Duvalier à l'ombre de la guerre froide. Les dessous de la politique étrangère d'Haïti (1957–1963).* Port-au-Prince: L'Imprimeur, 2014.

Aubigné, Agrippa d'. *Histoire universelle du sieur d'Aubigné.* Paris: Jean Mousset, 1616.

Audain, Paul. *Les ombres d'une politique néfaste.* Mexico: n.p., 1976.

Avril, Prosper. *From Glory to Disgrace: The Haitian Army, 1804–1994.* N.p.: Universal Publishers, 1999.

——. *L'aventure militaire des 13 guérilleros de Jeune Haiti.* Port-au-Prince: Bibliothèque nationale d'Haïti, 2015.

——. *Vérités et révélations* vol. 3, *L'armée d'Haiti, bourreau ou victime?* Port-au-Prince: Bibliothèque nationale d'Haïti, 1993.

Barthélémy, Gérard. *Créoles, bossales: conflit en Haïti.* Petit-Bourg, Guadeloupe: Ibis Rouge, 2000.

——. *Dans la splendeur d'un après-midi d'histoire.* Port-au-Prince: Henri Deschamps, 1996.

——. *Le pays en-dehors: essai sur l'univers rural haïtien.* Port-au-Prince: Henri Deschamps, 1989.

Bartov, Omer. "Defining Enemies, Making Victims: Germans, Jews, and the Holocaust." *American Historical Review* 103, no. 3 (1998): 771–816.

——. "Extreme Violence and the Scholarly Community." In "Extreme Violence," edited by Jacques Sémelin. Special issue, *International Social Science Journal* 54, no. 174 (2002): 509–18.

Bastide, Roger. "Le principe d'individuation (contribution à une philosophie africaine)." In *Actes du colloque international sur la notion de personne en Afrique Noire,* Paris, 11–16 octobre 1971, 33–43. Paris: CNRS, 1973.

Bastien, Rémy. *Le paysan haïtien et sa famille. Vallée de Marbial.* 2nd ed. Paris: Karthala, 1985.

Bauman, Zygmunt. *Modernity and the Holocaust.* Ithaca, NY: Cornell University Press, 1989.

Beauvoir-Dominique, Rachel, Jean-Luc Bonniol, Carlo Avier Célius, Rachelle Charlier-Doucet, Gaetano Ciarcia, Chantal Collard, René Despestre, et al. "Haïti et l'anthropologie." *Gradhiva* 1 (2005). https://doi.org/10.400/gradhiva.68.

Béchacq, Dimitri. "Les parcours du marronnage dans l'histoire haïtienne: entre instrumentalisation politique et réinterprétation sociale." In "Haïti: face au passé/Confronting the Past," edited by Carlo A. Célius. Special issue, *Ethnologies* 28, no. 1 (2006): 203–40.

Belleau, Jean-Philippe. "A Misplaced Genocide. Haiti, 1812," forthcoming.

——. "Calculating the Number of People Killed by the Duvalier Regime." Paper presented at the 33rd Annual Conference of the Haitian Studies Association, online, October 2021.

——. "For an Anthropological Approach to Denial: Social Bonds, Pathophobia, and the Duvalier Regime in Haiti." 45–61. In *Denial: The Final Stage of Genocide,* edited by John Cox, Amal Khoury, and Sarah Minslow. New York: Routledge, 2021.

——. "Hatred Is Not Stronger Than Bonds: Social Relationships, Aversion to Harm, and Relational Exceptionalism." *Social Analysis* 67, no.1 (2023): 46–69.

——. "Intimacy, Hostility, and State Politics: François Duvalier and His Inner-circle, 1931–1971." *History and Anthropology* 32, no. 5 (2021): 549–73.

——. " 'Neighbor' is an Empty Concept: How the Neighbourly Turn in Mass Violence Studies Has Overlooked Anthropology and Sociology." *Journal of Genocide Research,* 2022. https://doi.org/10.1080/14623528.2022.2081298

——. "The Stranger-King of the Caribbean: François Duvalier, State Politics, and the Othering of Brutality." *Journal of Latin American and Caribbean Anthropology* 24, no. 4 (2019): 935–57.

Bellegarde, Dantès. *Histoire du peuple haïtien, 1492–1952.* Port-au-Prince: n.p., 2004. First published 1953 by Held (Port-au-Prince).

Bellegarde-Smith, Patrick. "Dantès Bellegarde and Pan-Africanism." *Phylon* 42, no. 3 (1981): 233–44.

——. *Haiti: The Breached Citadel.* Boulder: Westview Press, 1990.

Bemporad, Elissa. *Legacy of Blood: Jews, Pogroms, and Ritual Murder in the Lands of the Soviets.* New York: Oxford University Press, 2020.

Benoît, François. *François Benoît rakonte konman Duvalier te masakre tout fanmil 26 avril 1963.* Documentary interview with additional participation by Claude Edeline, Jean-Marie Benoît, and Josie Benoît. Boston: Louverture Media, 2021. Posted October 31, 2021, YouTube, https://www.youtube.com/watch?v=SL9n-8OEtAc. Video, 30:21.

Benoît, Geri. "Harnessing History to Development: The Story of Cazale." *Haiti Papers* 6, Washington, DC; Trinity College, 2006.

Berger, Peter and Thomas Luckmann. *The Social Construction of Reality: A Treatise in the Sociology of Knowledge.* New York: Anchor Books, 1966.

Bernardin, Raymond. *Cinq siècles d'histoire politique.* 2 vols. Port-au-Prince: n.p., 2015.

Béteille, André. "Inequality and Equality." In *Companion Encyclopedia of Anthropology*, edited by Tim Ingold, 1010–40. London: Routledge, 1993.

Bilewicz, Michal, Aleksandra Cichocka and Wictor Soral, eds. *The Psychology of Conspiracy: A Festschrift for Miroslaw Kofta.* New York: Routledge, 2015

Bird, Mark Baker. *The Black Man, or Haytian Independence, Deduced from Historical Notes, and Dedicated to the Government and People of Hayti.* New York: n.p., 1869.

Bird-David, Nurit. " 'Animism' Revisited: Personhood, Environment, and Relational Epistemology." *Current Anthropology* 40, no. 1 (1999): 67–91.

Bonneau, Lemoine. "En quoi l'élite économique du pays est-elle à l'origine de cette mésaventure?" *Le Nouvelliste*, September 13, 2016.

Bonniol, Jean-Luc. "La couleur des hommes, principe d'organisation sociale: le cas antillais." *Ethnologie française* 20, no. 4 (1990): 410–18.

——. "Entretien avec René Depestre." *Gradhiva* 1 (2005): 31–45.

Bourdieu, Pierre. *Distinction: A Social Critique of the Judgement of Taste.* Translated by Richard Nice. New York: Routledge, 1984.

——. *The Field of Cultural Production: Essays on Art and Literature.* Translated by Randal Johnson. Cambridge: Polity Press, 1993.

——. "La maison kabyle ou le monde renversé." *Échanges et communications: mélanges offertes à Claude Lévi-Strauss à l'occasion de son 60ème anniversaire*, edited by Claude Lévi-Strauss, Pierre Maranda, and Jean Pouillon, 738–89. Berlin: De Gruyter, 1970.

Bouzon, Justin. *Études historiques sur la présidence de Faustin Soulouque (1847–1849).* Paris: Gustave Guérin, 1894.

Bringa, Tone. *Being Muslim the Bosnian Way: Identity and Community in a Central Bosnian Village.* Princeton, NJ: Princeton University Press, 1995.

Brouard-Cambronne, Jean-Claude. *Le chant des ténèbres. Mort lente au Fort-Dimanche.* Montreal: Éditions DAMI, 2009.

——. *Haïti: chroniques d'un massacre annoncé.* Montreal: Éditions DAMI, 2009.

Brown, Michael F. "On Resisting Resistance." *American Anthropologist* 98, no. 4 (1998): 729–35.

Browning, Christopher. *Ordinary Men: Reserve Police Battalion 101and the Final Solution in Poland.* New York: Harper Perennial, 1998.

Brutus, Edner. *Instruction publique en Haïti, 1492–1945.* Port-au-Prince: Éditions Panorama, 1979.

Bubandt, Nils. "From the Enemy's Point of View: Violence, Empathy, and the Ethnography of Fakes." *Cultural Anthropology* 24, no. 3 (2009): 553–88.

Bulamah, Rodrigo. "Farming of Commons: Kinship and Social Practices in Milot, Haiti." MA thesis, State University of Campinas, 2016.

——. "O Lakou Haitiano e suas práticas: entre mudanças e permanéncias." *Temáticas* 21, no. 2 (2013): 205-233.

Burgess, Ernest W., and Harvey J. Locke. *The Family: From Institution to Companionship.* New York: American Book Company, 1945.

Burnham, Thorald M. " 'Everything They Hate': Michèle, Mildred, and Elite Haitian Marrying Strategies in Historical Perspective." *Journal of Family History* 31, no. 1 (2006): 83–109.

——. "Immigration and Marriage in the Making of Post-independence Haiti." PhD diss., York University, 2006.

Bushnell, David. *The Making of Modern Colombia: A Nation in Spite of Itself.* Berkeley: University of California Press, 1993.

Cabon, Adolphe. *Mgr Alexis-Jean-Marie Guilloux, deuxième archevêque de Port-au-Prince (Haiti).* Port-au-Prince: Grand Séminaire Saint-Jacques d'Haïti, 1929.

Cambronne, Jean-Claude. *Le chant des ténèbres. Morte lente au Fort-Dimanche: récits.* Montréal: Éditions DAMI, 2009.

Candea, Matei, and Giovanni da Col, eds. *The Return to Hospitality: Strangers, Guests, and Ambiguous Encounters.* Special issue, *Journal of the Royal Anthropological Institute* 18, no.1 (2012).

Carsten, Janet, ed. *Cultures of Relatedness: New Approaches to the Study of Kinship.* New York: Cambridge University Press, 2000.

Carsten, Janet, and Stephen Hugh-Jones, eds. *About the House: Lévi-Strauss and Beyond.* Cambridge: Cambridge University Press, 1995.

Cavé, Eddy. *Autour des 90 ans de l'Hôpital Saint-Antoine de Jérémie.* Montréal: Papyruz, 2013.

——. *De mémoire de Jérémien: en pensant aux amis disparus.* Vol. 2 of *De mémoire de Jérémien.* Montreal: CIDIHCA; Pétionville, Haiti: Pleine Plage, 2016.

——. *De mémoire de Jérémien: ma vie, ma ville, mon village.* Vol. 1 of *De mémoire de Jérémien.* Pétionville, Haiti: Pleine Plage, 2011.

——. *Haïti. Extermination des pères fondateurs et pratiques d'exclusion.* N.p., 2022.

Charles, Carolle. "Gender and Politics in Contemporary Haiti: The Duvalierist State, Transnationalism, and the Emergence of a New Feminism (1980–1990)." *Feminist Studies* 21, no. 1 (1995): 137–40.

Charles, Francis. *Haïti. Essence du pouvoir martial: la domestication de l'armée.* Port-au-Prince: Henri Deschamps, 2009.

Charmant, Alcius. *Haiti vivra-t-elle? Etude sur le préjugé de races: race noire, race jaune, race blanche, et sur la doctrine de Monroë.* Le Havre, France: F. Le Roy, 1905.

Chassagne, Albert. *Bain de sang en Haiti. Les macoutes opèrent à Jérémie,* New York: n.p., 1977.

Chochotte, Marvin. "The History of Peasants, Tonton Makouts, and the Rise and Fall of the Duvalier Dictatorship in Haiti." PhD diss., University of Michigan, 2017.

Clark, Nancy, and William Worger. *South Africa: The Rise and Fall of Apartheid*. Harlow, England: Longman, 2003.

Clastres, Pierre. *Chronicle of the Guayaki Indians*. New York: Zone Books, 2000 [1972].

Collectif Paroles. *1946–1976: trente ans de pouvoir noir en Haïti. L'explosion de 1946. Bilan et perspectives*, Lasalle, ON: Collectif Paroles, 1976.

Collins, Randall. *Interaction Ritual Chains*. Princeton, NJ: Princeton University Press, 2004.

——. *Violence: A Micro-sociological Theory*. Princeton, NJ: Princeton University Press, 2008.

Commission Internationale de Juristes (CIJ). *La situation socio-politique en Haïti*. In La situation politique et sociale en Haïti – aoÛt 1963, 5–21. Lawrence: Institute of Haitian Studies, University of Kansas, 2000.

Cordier, Daniel. *La victoire en pleurant: alias Caracalla 1943–1946*. Paris: Gallimard, 2021.

Cornevin, Marianne. *Liberté, que de crimes on commet en ton nom! Vie de Madame Roland, guillotinée le 8 novembre 1793*. Paris: Maisonneuve & Larose, 2002.

Corvington, Georges. *Port-au-Prince au cours des ans. La métropole haïtienne du XIXe siècle, 1804–1888*. Port-au-Prince: Henri Deschamps, 1977.

Corvington, Serge. "A l'auteur de la 'Lettre aux hommes clairs.'" *La Forge* 7 (1946).

Dahomay, Jacky. "La tentation tyrannique haïtienne." *Chemins critiques* 5, no. 1 (2001): 11–36.

Dallet, Gilbert. *L'étrange figure du Baron des Adrets*. Paris: Éditions de l'Aurore, 1982.

Dalmaso, Flavia, "Kijan moun yo ye? As pessoas, as casas e as dinâmicas da familiaridade em Jacmel, Haiti." PhD diss., UFRJ, Museu Nacional, Rio de Janeiro, 2014.

Das, Veena. "Communities, Riots and Survivors." In *Mirrors of Violence: Communities, Riots and Survivors in South Asia*, edited by Veena Das, 1–35. Delhi: Oxford University Press, 1990.

——. *Life and Words: Violence and the Descent Into the Ordinary*. Berkeley: University of California Press, 2006.

Dash, J. Michael. *Literature and Ideology in Haiti, 1915–1961*. London: Macmillan, 1981.

Daumec, Lucien. *La mission des élites: essai*. Port-au-Prince: Presses libres, 1954.

David, Placide. *Figures historiques*. Pétion-Ville, Haiti: C3 Éditions, 2013.

——. *L'héritage colonial en Haïti*. Madrid: Langa, 1959.

——. *Sur les rives du passé: choses de Saint-Domingue*. Montréal: Léméac, 1972.

Daut, Marlène. *Baron de Vastey and the Origins of Black Atlantic Humanism*. New York: Palgrave Macmillan, 2017.

——. *Tropics of Haiti: Race and the Literary History of the Haitian Revolution in the Atlantic World*. Liverpool, UK: Liverpool University Press, 2017.

Deleuze, Gilles, and Claire Parnet, *Dialogues*. Paris: Flammarion, 1977.

Delince, Kern. *Armée et politique en Haïti*. Paris: L'Harmattan, 1979.

Denis, Lorimer, and François Duvalier. *Problèmes des classes sociales à travers l'histoire d'Haïti*. Port-au-Prince: n.p., 1958.

Depestre, René. "Homo Papadocus." *Europe*, September 1976.

——. "Jean Price-Mars et le mythe de l'Orphée noir ou les aventures de la négritude." *L'homme et la société* 7, no. 1 (1968): 171–81.

Des Forges, Alison Liebhafsky. *"Leave None to Tell the Story": Genocide in Rwanda*. 2nd ed. New York: Human Rights Watch, 1999.

Descola, Philippe. *Beyond Nature and Culture*. Translated by Janet Lloyd. Chicago: University of Chicago Press, 2014.

Desvarieux, Simon. *Lettre aux hommes noirs*. Port-au-Prince: Imprimerie de l'État, 1946.

Devoir de Mémoire. *Mourir pour Haïti: la résistance à la dictature en 1964*. Montréal: Les éditions du CIDIHCA, 2015.

Dewey, Horace. "Russia's Debt to the Mongols in Suretyship and Collective Responsibility." *Comparative Studies in Society and History* 30, no. 2 (1988): 249–70.

Dhormoys, Paul. *Une visite chez Soulouque: souvenirs d'un voyage dans l'île d'Haïti*. Delmas, Haiti: C3 Éditions, 2015.

Diederich, Bernard. *Blood in the Sun: The Tyranny of Papa Doc Duvalier*. Port-au-Prince: Henri Deschamps, 2010.

——. *The Price of Blood. History of Repression and Rebellion in Haiti under Dr. François Duvalier, 1962–1971*. Companion volume to *The Price of Blood: History of Repression and Rebellion in Haiti under Dr. François Duvalier, 1957–1961*. Princeton, NJ: Markus Wiener, 2011.

——. *Le prix du sang*. Port-au-Prince: Henri Deschamps, 2005.

——. *Le prix du sang*. Rev. ed. Port-au-Prince: Henri Deschamps, 2016.

——. *The Prize: Haiti's National Palace*. New York: iUniverse, 2007.

——. *Le trophée*. Port-au-Prince: Henri Deschamps, 2008.

Diedrich, Bernard, and Al Burt. *Papa Doc: The Truth about Haiti Today*. New York: Avon, 1969.

——. *Papa Doc et les Tontons Macoutes: la verité sur Haïti*. Port-au-Prince: Henri Deschamps, 1986.

Domhoff, William G. *The Power Elite and the State: How Policy Is Made in America*. New York: Aldine de Gruyter, 1990.

Dorsainvil, Justin Chrysostome. *Manuel d'histoire d'Haïti*. Port-au-Prince: Procure des Frères de l'Instruction Chrétienne, 1934.

Dorsinville, Roger. "Dans le fauteuil de l'histoire. Propos recueillis par Michel Adam et Edgard Gousse." *Etincelles* 1, no. 10 (1985): 18–21

——. *Lettre à mon ami Serge Corvington*. Port-au-Prince: Imprimerie de l'État, 1946.

——. *Lettre aux hommes clairs*. Port-au-Prince: Imprimerie de l'Etat, 1946.

——. "1946 ou le délire opportuniste." *Nouvelle Optique* 6–7 (1972): 117–40.

Dorsinville, Roger, and Maryse Condé. "Entretien avec Roger Dorsinville." *Archipelago* 3–4 (1983): 134–40.

Doura, Fred. *Mythes, paradoxes et réalités de la pigmentocratie au cours de l'histoire d'Haïti*. Boucherville, QC: Éditions DAMI, 2017.

Dubois, Laurent. *Avengers of the New World: The Story of the Haitian Revolution*. Cambridge, MA: Belknap Press of Harvard University Press, 2004.

——. *Haiti: The Aftershocks of History*. New York: Henry Holt, 2012.

Dumas, Hélène. *Le génocide au village: le massacre des Tutsi au Rwanda*. Paris: Seuil, 2014.

Dumont, Louis. *Homo Hierarchicus. The Caste System and Its Implications*. Translated by R. M. Sainsbury and Basia Gulati. Chicago: Chicago University Press, 1980.

Dunlap, David. "A French Church Near its End." *New York Times*, April 5, 2012.

Dupuy, Alex. "Class, Race, and Nation: Unresolved Contradictions of the Haitian Revolution." *Journal of Haitian Studies* 10, no. 1 (2004): 6–21.

——. "Conceptualizing the Duvalier Dictatorship." *Latin American Perspectives* 15, no. 4 (1988): 105–14.

——. "From François Duvalier to Jean-Bertrand Aristide: The Declining Significance of Color Politics in Haiti." *Politics and Power in Haiti*. Edited by Kate Quinn and Paul Sutton, 43–64. New York: Palgrave Macmillan, 2013.

——. *From Revolutionary Slaves to Powerless Citizens: Essays on the Politics and Economics of Underdevelopment.* London: Routledge, 2014.

——. *Haiti in the New World Order: The Limits of the Democratic Transition.* Boulder, CO: Westview Press, 1996.

——. *The Prophet and Power: Jean-Bertrand Aristide, the International Community, and Haiti.* Lanham, MD: Rowman and Littlefield, 2006.

Duvalier mis à nu: les Macoutes mènent la danse. Montreal: n.p., 1963?

Duvalier, François. *Mémoires d'un leader du Tiers Monde: mes négociations avec le Saint-Siège; ou, une tranche d'histoire.* Paris: Hachette, 1969.

——. *Eléments d'une doctrine.* Vol. 1 of *Œuvres essentielles.* Port-au-Prince: Presses Nationales d'Haiti, 1966.

——. *La marche à la présidence.* Vol. 2 of *Œuvres Essentielles.* Port-au-Prince: Presses Nationales d'Haiti, 1966.

——. Interview by Irène Chagneau, Irène, *Voyage sans passeport*, d.u. Posted on June 16, 2019, https://www.youtube.com/watch?v=Y2_OFLvFyJE

Ehrenreich, Robert M., and Tim Cole. "The Perpetrator-Bystander-Victim Constellation: Rethinking Genocidal Relationships." *Human Organization* 64, no. 3 (2005): 213–24.

El Kenz, David. "Le 'massacre' est-il né aux guerres de religion?" in "Les massacres aux temps des Révolutions," edited by Bruno Hervé and Pierre Serna. Special issue, *La Révolution française* (2011). https://doi.org/10.4000/lrf.185.

——, ed. *Le massacre, objet d'histoire.* Paris: Gallimard, 2005.

——. "La naissance de la tolérance au 16ème siècle: l' 'invention' du massacre." *Sens public* (2006). http://sens-public.org/articles/340/

Eltringham, Nigel. " 'Invaders who have stolen the country': The Hamitic Hypothesis, Race and the Rwandan Genocide." *Social Identities* 12, no. 4 (2006): 425–46.

Esses, Victoria M., and Richard Vernon, eds. *Explaining the Breakdown of Ethnic Relations: Why Neighbors Kill.* Malden, MA: Blackwell, 2006.

Fanon, Frantz. *Peau noire, masques blancs.* Paris: Seuil, 1952.

Fatton, Robert. *The Guise of Exceptionalism: Unmasking the National Narratives of Haiti and the United States.* Rutgers, NJ: Rutgers University Press, 2021.

——. "Haiti in the Aftermath of the Earthquake: The Politics of Catastrophe." *Journal of Black Studies* 42, no. 2 (2011): 158–85.

——. "Haiti: The Saturnalia of Emancipation and the Vicissitudes of Predatory Rule." *Third World Quarterly* 27, no. 1 (2006): 115–33.

——. *Haiti: Trapped in the Outer Periphery.* Boulder, CO: Lynne Rienner, 2014.

——. "The Haitian Authoritarian Habitus and the Contradictory Legacy of 1804." *Journal of Haitian Studies* 10, no. 1 (2004): 22–43.

——. *Haiti's Predatory Republic: The Unending Transition to Democracy.* Boulder, CO: Lynne Rienner, 2002.

——. "Michel-Rolph Trouillot's *State Against Nation*: A Critique of the Totalitarian Paradigm." *Small Axe* 17, no. 3 (2013): 203–12.

——. *The Roots of Haitian Despotism.* Boulder, CO: Lynne Rienner, 2007.

——. "The Unending Political Crisis." Paper presented at the 34th Annual Haitian Studies Association conference, Washington, DC, October 2022.

Fausto, Carlos. "The Friend, the Enemy, and the Anthropologist: Hostility and Hospitality Among the Parakanã (Amazonia, Brazil)." *Journal of the Royal Anthropological Institute* 18, no.1 (2012): 196–219.

Fein, Helen. *Accounting for Genocide: National Responses and Jewish Victimization During the Holocaust.* New York: The Free Press, 1979.

Felder, Maxime. "Strong, Weak and Invisible Ties: A Relational Perspective on Urban Coexistence." *Sociology* 54, no. 4 (2020): 675–92.

Férère, Gérard Alphonse. *Armée d'Haïti après Magloire et hitlérisme duvaliérien (mémoire d'un officier).* Port-au-Prince: Perle des Antilles, 2014.

——. *Massacres des Duvaliers et des dictateurs militaires.* Port-au-Prince: Perle des Antilles, 2019.

Ferrero, Guglielmo. *Characters and Events of Roman History, from Caesar to Nero: The Lowell Lectures of 1908.* Translated by Frances Lance Ferrero. New York: Putnam, 1909.

——. *Pouvoir; les génies invisibles de la cité.* New York: Brentano's, 1942.

——. *The Ruin of the Ancient Civilization and the Triumph of Christianity, With Some Consideration of Conditions in the Europe of Today.* Translated by Marian Cecilia Broderick Whitehead. New York: G. P. Putnam's Sons, 1921.

Firmin, Anténor. *M. Roosevelt, président des États-Unis et la République d'Haïti.* New York: Hamilton Bank Note Engraving and Printing, 1905.

Finkielkraut, Alain. *Discours de réception à l'Académie française* (January 26, 2016). Posted January 28, 2016, https://www.academie-francaise.fr/discours-de-reception-de-m-alain-finkielkraut

Fiske, Alan Page and Tage Shakti Rai. Foreword by Steven Pinker. *Virtuous Violence: Hurting and Killing to Create, Sustain, End, and Honor Social Relationships.* Cambridge: Cambridge University Press, 2015.

Fitzpatrick, Sheila. "Ascribing Class: The Construction of Class Identity in Soviet Russia." *Journal of Modern History* 64, no. 4 (1993): 745–70.

Florival, Jean. *Duvalier. La face cachée de Papa Doc.* Montréal: Mémoire d'encrier, 2007.

Foa, Jérémie. *Tous ceux qui tombent. Visages du massacre de la Saint-Barthélémy.* Paris: La Découverte, 2021.

Forsé, Michel. *L'égalité, une passion française?* Paris: Armand Collin, 2013.

Fortes, Meyer. *The Web of Kinship among the Tallensi: The Second Part of an Analysis of the Social Structure of a Trans-Volta Tribe.* London: Oxford University Press, 1949.

Fouchard, Jean. *Les marrons de la liberté.* Paris: Éditions de l'École, 1972.

Fourcand, Jacques. "Discours du Dr. Jacques Fourcand," July 20, 1965, Archives of the International Committee of the Red Cross, V-S-10025-A-04. Audio recording. https://avarchives.icrc.org/Sound/6359

Fuji, Lee Ann. *Killing Neighbors: Webs of Violence in Rwanda.* Ithaca, NY: Cornell University Press, 2009.

Furet, François. *Interpreting the French Revolution.* Cambridge: Cambridge University Press, 1981.

——. *The Passing of an Illusion: The Idea of Communism in the Twentieth Century.* Chicago: Chicago University Press, 1999.

Furet, François and Ernst Nolte. *Fascism and Communism.* Lincoln: University of Nebraska Press, 2001.

Gaillard, Roger. *Les cent jours de Rosalvo Bobo ou une mise à mort politique (1914–1915).* Vol. 1 of *Les blancs débarquent.* Port-au-Prince: Presses Nationales, 1974.

——. *La déroute de l'intelligence (mai–juillet 1902)*. Vol. 3 of *La république exterminatrice*. Port-au-Prince: Le Natal, 1993.

——. *La guerre civile, une option dramatique (15 juillet–31 décembre 1902)*. Vol. 4 of *La république exterminatrice*. Port-au-Prince: Le Natal, 1984.

——. *La république autoritaire (1916–1917)*. Vol. 3 of *Les blancs débarquent*. Port-au-Prince: Le Natal, 1981.

——. *La république exterminatrice, première partie: une modernisation manquée (1880–1896)*. Port-au-Prince: Le Natal, 1984.

Gainot, Bernard. " 'Sur fond de cruelle inhumanité' ": les politiques du massacre dans la Révolution de Haïti." *Cahiers de l'Institut d'histoire de la Révolution française* 3 (2011). http://journals.openedition.org/lrf/239 ; DOI : https://doi.org/10.4000/lrf.239

Gaetjens, Lesly. *The Shot Heard Around the World: The Joe Gaetjens Story*. Falls Church, VA: Lesly Gaetjens, 2010.

Gall, Norman, "Duvalier's Regime Keeps Haiti in Chaos." *Washington Post*, September 27, 1964.

——. "Hopes of Haitians Rise as Revolt Is Stepped Up." *Washington Post*, September 26, 1964.

Gagné, Renaud. *Ancestral Fault in Ancient Greece*. Cambridge: Cambridge University Press, 2013.

Gamson, William. *The Strategy of Social Protest*. Homewood, IL: Dorsey Press, 1975.

Garaudy, Roger. *Perspectives de l'homme: existentialisme, pensée catholique, marxisme*. Paris: Presses Universitaires de France, 1959.

Garfinkel, Harold. *Studies in Ethnomethodology*. Englewood Cliffs, NJ: Prentice-Hall, 1967.

Garrigus, John D. *Before Haiti: Race and Citizenship in French Saint-Domingue*. New York: Palgrave Macmillan, 2006.

Geertz, Clifford. "Thick Description: Toward an Interpretive Theory of Culture." In *The Interpretation of Cultures: Selected Essays*, 3–30. New York: Basic Books, 1973.

Geffray, Christian. *Chroniques de la servitude en Amazonie brésilienne*. Paris: Karthala, 1996.

Gilbert, Marcel. *La patrie haïtienne: de Boyer-Bazelais à l'unité historique du peuple haïtien*. Haïti: Imprimerie des Antilles, 1986.

Gilot, Rony. *Au gré de la mémoire: François Duvalier, le mal-aimé*. Port-au-Prince: Éditions Le Béréen, 2006.

Girard, Philippe R. "Caribbean Genocide: Racial War in Haiti, 1802–1804." *Pattern of Prejudice* 39, no. 2 (2005): 138–61.

——. *Haiti: The Tumultuous History from Pearl of the Caribbean to Broken Nation*. New York: St. Martin's Griffin, 2010.

Glover, Kaiama. *Haiti Unbound: The Spiralist Challenge to the Postcolonial Canon*. Liverpool, UK: Liverpool University Press, 2011.

Goffman, Erving. *Interaction Rituals: Essays on Face-to-Face Behavior*. Garden City, NY: Doubleday, 1967.

Goldhagen, Daniel. *Hitler's Willing Executioners: Ordinary Germans and the Holocaust*. New York: Vintage Books, 1997.

Gonzalez, Johnhenry. *Maroon Nation: A History of Revolutionary Haiti*. New Haven, CT: Yale University Press, 2019.

Goossaert, Vincent, and David A. Palmer. *The Religious Question in Modern China*. Chicago: University of Chicago Press, 2011.

Granovetter Mark. "The Strength of Weak Ties." *American Journal of Sociology* 78, no. 6 (1973): 1360–80.

Greene, Graham. *The Comedians*. London: Bodley Head, 1966.

Gros, Jean-Germain. "Haiti: The Political Economy of Decay and Renewal." *Latin American Research Review* 35, no. 3 (2000): 211–26.

Gross, Jan T. *Neighbors: The Destruction of the Jewish Community in Jedwabne, Poland*. New York: Penguin Books, 2002.

Guénard, Florent. *La passion de l'égalité*. Paris: Seuil, 2022.

Guerrier, Yvon. "Temwayaj sou Franck Romain avèk evènman 26 avril 1963 Lamanten yo." File 1 of 4. Aired on Radio Haiti-Inter, October 4, 1986. Duke Digital Repository. Permalink https://idn.duke.edu/ark:/87924/r4862gb8h. MP3 audio, 16:40.

Hakim-Rimpel, Marie-Cécile. "Special Haitian Woman to Remember–Yvonne Hakim Rimpel Fought for Women to Have the Right to Vote in Haiti." Interview by Valerio Saint-Louis, Télé Image, 2012. Posted April 5, 2012, https://www.dailymotion.com/video/xpxgrh. Video, 9:02.

Halévi, Ran. "Les haines hexagonales." *Revue des deux mondes* (June 2019): 8–15.

——. "Hate and the Revolutionary Spirit," lecture, Marc Bloch Center, Humboldt University, October 28, 2014, Berlin, Germany, posted November 13, 2014, Bard College Berlin, You-Tube, https://www.youtube.com/watch?v=dxkbb2nC4j8. Video, 1:46:54.

Harden, Blaine. *Escape from Camp 14: One Man's Remarkable Odyssey from North Korea to Freedom in the West*. New York: Penguin Books, 2013.

Haïti, 1919-1920: livre bleu d'Haïti, blue book of Hayti: revue illustrée de la république d'Haïti, contenant des articles spéciaux concernant l'histoire. New York: Klebeld Press, 1919.

Hector, Cary, and Hérard Jadotte, eds. *Haïti et l'après-Duvalier: continuités et ruptures*. Montreal: CIDIHCA, 1991.

Hector, Michel. *Syndicalisme et socialisme en Haïti: 1932–1970*. Port-au-Prince: Henri Deschamps, 1989.

Heinl, Robert Debs, Nancy Gordon Heinl, and Michael Heinl. *Written in Blood: The Story of the Haitian People, 1492–1995*, 3rd ed. Lanham, MD: University Press of America, 2005.

Henig, David. " 'Knocking on My Neighbour's Door': On Metamorphoses of Sociality in Rural Bosnia." *Critique of Anthropology* 32, no. 1 (2012): 3–19.

Herskovits, Melville J. *Life in a Haitian Valley*. Introduction by Sidney W. Mintz. Princeton: Markus Wiener, 2007. First published 1937 by A. A. Knopf (New York).

Herzfeld, Michael. *Cultural Intimacy: Social Poetics in the Nation-State*. 2nd ed. New York: Routledge, 1997.

Hess, David J., and Roberto da Matta, eds. *The Brazilian Puzzle: Culture on the Borderlands of the Western World*. New York: Columbia University Press, 1995.

Hilberg, Raul. *Perpetrators, Victims, Bystanders: The Jewish Catastrophe, 1939–1945*. New York: HarperPerennial, 1992.

Hinton, Alexander Laban, ed. *Annihilating Differences. The Anthropology of Genocide*. Foreword by Kenneth Roth, Human Rights Watch. Berkeley: University of California Press, 2002.

Hoffmann, Léon-François. 'L''Haïtienne fut-elle une Révolution?' in Hoffmman, Gewecke, & Fleischmann (eds.), *Haïti 1804, lumières et ténèbres: impact et résonances d'une revolution*. Madrid: Iberoamericana, 2008.

Hoffmann, Léon-François. *Faustin Soulouque d'Haiti dans l'histoire et la literature*. Paris: L'Harmattan, 2007.

——. *Haïti: couleurs, croyances, créole*. Montreal: CIDHICA, 1990.

Honorat, Jean-Jacques. *Enquête sur le développement*. Port-au-Prince: Imprimerie Centrale, 1974.

Hooper, Cynthia. "Terror of Intimacy: Family Politics in the 1930s Soviet Union." In *Everyday Life in Early Soviet Russia: Taking the Revolution Inside*, edited by Christina Kiaer and Eric Naiman, 61–91. Bloomington: Indiana University Press, 2006.

Horkheimer, Max. "Authority and the Family." In *Critical Theory: Selected Essays*, 47–128. Translated by Matthew J. O'Connell. New York: Continuum, 1975.

Horkeimer, Max and Theodore Adorno. *Dialectic of Enlightenment: Philosophical Fragments*. Edited by Gunzelin Schmid Noerr, translated by Edmund Jephcott. Stanford, CA: Stanford University Press, 2002.

Hugo, Abel. *Histoire des Armées Françaises de Terre et de Mer de 1792 à 1833: ouvrage rédigé par une société de militaires et de gens de lettres*. Vol. 4. Paris: Chez Delloye, 1838.

Hurbon, Laënnec. *Comprendre Haiti: essai sur l'État, la nation, la culture*. Paris: Karthala, 1987.

——. *Culture et dictature en Haiti: l'imaginaire sous contrôle*. Paris: L'Harmattan, 1979.

——. *Esclavage, religions, et politique en Haïti*. Lyon, France: Presses Universitaires de Lyon, 2003.

——. ed. *Le phénomène religieux dans la Caraïbe: Guadeloupe, Martinique, Guyane, Haïti*. Montréal: CIDHICA, 1989.

Ilibagiza, Immaculée. *Left to Tell: Discovering God Amidst the Rwandan Holocaust*. With Steve Erwin, foreword by Wayne W. Dyer. Carlsbad, CA: Hay House, 2006.

Inter-American Commission on Human Rights. *Report on the Situation of Human Rights in Haiti*. OEA/Ser.L/V/II.46. Washington, DC: OAS, 1979.

Jallot, Nicolas, and Émile Rabaté, directors. *Papa Doc et les Tontons Macoutes*. Documentary produced by Frédéric Tyrode Saint Louis. Paris: BCI Communication, 2019. Posted December 10, 2019, YouTube, https://www.youtube.com/watch?v=-5LBIXxamZY. Video, 1:26:02.

Janvier, Louis Joseph. *Les affaires d'Haïti (1883–1884)*. Paris: C. Marpon et E. Flammarion, 1885.

——. *Les antinationaux: actes et principes*. Paris: G. Rougier, 1884.

——. *Haïti aux Haïtiens*. Paris: A. Parent et A. Davy, 1884.

——. *La république d'Haïti et ses visiteurs (1840–1882). Réponse à M. Victor Cochinat (de la Petite Presse) et à quelques autres écrivains*. Paris: Marpon et Flammarion, 1883.

——. *Le vieux piquet: scène de la vie haïtienne*. Jacmel, Haiti: Éditions de la dodine, 2013. First published 1884 by A. Parent (Paris).

Jean, Alfred. *Il y a soixante ans, 1883–1943. Les journées des 22 et 23 septembre 1883, reportages rétrospectifs par un témoin oculaire*. Port-au-Prince: A. P. Barthelemy, 1944.

Jean, Eddy Arnold. *L'échec d'une élite: indigénisme, négritude, noirisme*. Port-au-Prince: Haïti-Demain, 1992.

——. *Les idées politiques au XIXème siècle*. Collaboration by Justin O. Fièvre. Port-au-Prince: Haïti-Demain, 2011.

Jiaqi, Yan, and Gao Gao. *Turbulent Decade: A History of the Cultural Revolution*. Edited and translated by D. W. Y. Kwok. Honolulu: University of Hawai'i Press, 1996.

Joachim, Benoît. "La bourgeoisie d'affaires en Haïti de l'Indépendance à l'Occupation américaine." *Nouvelle Optique* 1 (1971).

Johnson, Ian. *The Souls of China: The Return of Religion After Mao*. New York: Pantheon Books, 2017.

Jones, Adam. *Gender Inclusive: Essays on Violence, Men, and Feminist International Relations.* New York: Routledge, 2008.

——. *Sites of Genocide.* London: Routledge, 2022.

Judt, Tony. *Past Imperfect: French Intellectuals, 1944–1956.* New York: New York University Press, 2011.

Juste, André. *Nos élites et nos masses de 1685 à 1984: lettre ouverte à M. Gérard M. Laurent.* Port-au-Prince: Les Ateliers Fardin, 1984.

Katz, Jacob. *From Prejudice to Destruction: Anti-Semitism, 1700–1933.* Cambridge, MA: Harvard University Press, 1980.

Kay, Alex J. *The Making of an SS Killer: The Life of Colonel Alfred Filbert, 1905–1990.* Cambridge: Cambridge University Press, 2016.

Keegan, John. *The Face of Battle.* New York: Penguin Books, 1983.

Kiernan Ben. *Blood and Soil: A World History of Genocide and Extermination from Sparta to Darfur.* New Haven, CT: Yale University Press, 2007.

——. "The First Genocide: Carthage, 146 BC," *Diogenes* 51, no.3 (2004): 27–39.

——. *The Pol Pot Regime: Race, Power, and Genocide in Cambodia under the Khmer Rouge, 1975–79.* 3rd ed. New Haven, CT: Yale University Press, 2008.

——. "The Pol Pot Regime's Simultaneous War Against Vietnam and Genocide of Cambodia's Ethnic Vietnamese Minority," *Critical Asian Studies* 53, no.3 (2021): 342–58.

——. "Twentieth Century Genocides: Underlying Ideological Themes from Armenia to East Timor." In *The Specter of Genocide: Mass Murder in Historical Perspective,* edited by Robert Gellately and Ben Kiernan, 29–51. Cambridge: Cambridge University Press, 2003.

Klang, Gary, and Anthony Phelps. *Le massacre de Jérémie—operation vengeance: roman.* Montreal: Dialogue Nord-Sud, 2015.

Khlevniuk, Oleg. *Master of the House: Stalin and His Inner Circle.* Translated by Nora Seligman Favorov. New Haven: Yale University Press, 2008.

King, Stewart R. *Blue Coat or Powdered Wig: Free People of Color in Pre-Revolutionary Saint Domingue.* Athens: University of Georgia Press, 2001.

Kolind, Torsten. *Post-War Identification: Everyday Muslim Counterdiscourse in Bosnia.* Aarhus, Denmark: Aarhus University Press, 2008.

Kopstein, Jeffrey S., and Jason Wittenberg. *Intimate Violence: Anti-Jewish Pogroms on the Eve of the Holocaust.* Ithaca, NY: Cornell University Press, 2018.

Kronenfeld, David. "Comment: What Kinship Is *Not*—Schneider, Sahlins, and Shapiro." *Journal of the Royal Anthropological Institute* 18, no. 3 (2012): 678–80.

Labelle, Michèle. *Idéologie de couleur et classes sociales en Haïti.* Montréal: Presses de l'Université de Montréal, 1978.

Laferrière, Dany. "Camarade, où sont les mulâtresses?" *Haïti Demain* 13 (1986).

——. *Le cri des oiseaux fous: roman.* Paris: Zulma, 2015.

Laforest, Jean-Richard. "Notes à propos d'un article de René Piquion." *Rencontre* 24–25 (2012): 89–94.

Laforest, Pierre. *A la mémoire du chanoine Barthélémy Péron.* Jérémie, Haiti: n.p., 1989.

Laguerre, Michel. *The Military and Society in Haiti.* London: Palgrave Macmillan, 1993.

Lahens, Léon. *L'élite intellectuelle.* Port-au-Prince: Imprimerie de l'Abeille, 1916.

Lamaute, Alix. *La bourgeoisie nationale, une entité controversée.* Montreal: CIDIHCA, 1999.

de Lame, Danielle. "Anthropology and Genocide." *Mass Violence and Resistance*, 2007. https://www.sciencespo.fr/mass-violence-war-massacre-resistance/fr/document/anthropology-and-genocide.html

Lamour, Sabine. "L'héritage politique de Marie Saint-Dédée Bazile, dite Défilée." *Recherches féministes* 34, no. 2 (2021): 107–22.

Lancaster, Roger N. *Life is Hard: Machismo, Danger, and the Intimacy of Power in Nicaragua.* Berkeley: University of California Press, 1992.

Laraque, Franck, and Paul Laraque. *Haïti: la lutte et l'espoir.* Montral: CIDIHCA, 2003.

Laroche, Bruno. *Journal des frères de l'instruction chrétienne.* Unpublished diary, 1964.

Laroche, Léon. *Haïti, une page d'histoire.* Paris: A. Rousseau, 1885.

Larousse, Pierre, *Grand Dictionnaire Universel du XIXe siècle, vol. XI*, Paris: Administration du grand dictionnaire universel, 1874.

La Selve, Edgar. *Le pays des nègres: voyage à Haïti.* Paris: Hachette, 1881.

Laurent, Dr. Louis. "Les vêpres de Jérémie." *Le Courrier d'Haïti*, October 20, 1976.

Lauria Santiago, Aldo. *To Rise in Darkness: Revolution, Repression, and Memory in El Salvador, 1920–1932.* Durham, NC: Duke University Press, 2008.

Lavisse, Ernest. *Histoire de France depuis les origines jusqu'à la Révolution.* Paris: Hachette, 1913.

Leach, Edmund. "Animal Categories and Verbal Abuse." In *New Directions in the Study of Language*, edited by Eric H. Lenneberg. Cambridge, MA: The MIT Press, 1966.

Leconte, Frantz-Antoine, ed. *En grandissant sous Duvalier: l'agonie d'un État-nation.* Paris: L'Harmattan, 1999.

Van Leeuwen, Marco H. D., and Ineke Maas. "Endogamy and Social Class in History: An Overview." Supplement to *International Review of Social History* 50 (2005): 1–23.

Lefort, Claude. "Hannah Arendt et la question du politique." In *Essais sur le politique: XIXe et XXe siècles*, 59–72. Paris: Seuil, 1986.

Lemoine, Patrick. *Fort-Dimanche, Fort-la-Mort.* Port-au-Prince: n.p., 1996.

Lenotre, G. *Les noyades de Nantes.* Paris: Perrin, 1912.

Lepselter, Susan. *The Resonance of Unseen Things: Poetics, Power, Captivity, and UFOs in the American Uncanny.* Ann Arbor: University of Michigan Press, 2016.

Lestage, J. Elie. *Mémoire d'un jérémien.* Port-au-Prince: Imprimerie Centrale, 1987.

Levene, Mark. "Introduction." In *The Massacre in History*, edited by Mark Levene and Penny Roberts, 1–38. New York: Berghahn Books, 1999.

Lévi-Strauss, Claude. *Introduction to the work of Marcel Mauss.* London: Routledge and Kegan Paul, 1987 [1950].

——. *Structural Anthropology, Volume 2.* Translated by Monique Layton. New York: Basic Books, 1976.

Leyburn, James Graham. *The Haitian People.* 3rd ed. Lawrence: Institute of Haitian Studies, University of Kansas Press, 1998.

Linstant, S., *Essai sur les moyens d'extirper les préjugés des Blancs contre la couleur des Africains et des Sang-Mélés*, Paris: Pagnerre, 1841.

Lobb, John. "Caste and Class in Haiti." *American Journal of Sociology* 46, no. 1 (1940): 23–34.

Lowenthal, Ira. " 'Marriage Is 20, Children Are 21': The Cultural Construction of Conjugality and the Family in Rural Haiti." PhD diss., Johns Hopkins University, 1987.

Madiou, Thomas. *Histoire d'Haïti.* 7 vols. Port-au-Prince: Deschamps, 1988–1989. First published 1847 by J. Courtois (Port-au-Prince).

Malešević, Siniša. "Is It Easy to Kill in War? Emotions and Violence in the Combat Zones of Croatia and Bosnia and Herzegovina (1991–1995)." *European Journal of Sociology* 62 (2020): 1–31.

——. *The Rise of Organised Brutality: A Historical Sociology of Violence*. Cambridge: Cambridge University Press, 2017.

——. *The Sociology of War and Violence*. Cambridge: Cambridge University Press, 2010.

——. *Why Humans Fight: The Social Dynamics of Close-Range Violence*. Cambridge: Cambridge University Press, 2022.

Manigat, Leslie. "Armée et politique traditionnelle dans la société traditionnelle haïtienne," Éventail d'histoire vivante II. Port-au-Prince: CHUDAC, 2002.

——. *Haiti of the Sixties, Object of International Concern: A Tentative Global Analysis of the Potentially Explosive Situation of a Crisis Country in the Caribbean*. Washington, DC: Washington Center of Foreign Policy Research, 1964.

Marcelin, Frédéric. *Le Passé. Impressions Haïtiennes*. Port-au-Prince: La Dodine, 2014. First published 1902 by P. Taillefer (Paris).

Marcelin, Louis Herns. "La famille suburbaine à Port-au-Prince." MA thesis, Faculté d'ethnologie, 1988.

——. "In the Name of the Nation: Ritual, Blood, and the Political Habitus of Violence in Haiti." *American Anthropologist* 114, no. 2 (2012): 253–66.

Marriott, McKim. "Hindu Transactions: Diversity Without Dualism." In *Transaction and Meaning: Directions in the Anthropology of Exchange and Symbolic Behavior*, edited by Bruce Kapferer, 109–142. Philadelphia: Institute for the Study of Human Issues, 1976.

Marius, Philippe-Richard. *The Unexceptional Case of Haiti: Race and Class Privilege in Postcolonial Bourgeois Society*. Jackson: University Press of Mississippi, 2022.

Massey, Douglas, and Nancy Denton. *American Apartheid: Segregation and the Making of the Underclass*. Cambridge, MA: Harvard University Press, 1993.

Matta, Roberto da. *Carnavais, malandros e heróis: para uma sociologia do dilema brasileiro*. Rio de Janeiro: Zahar, 1979.

Maynard, Jonathan Leader. *Ideology and Mass Killing: The Radicalized Security Politics of Genocides and Deadly Atrocities*. Oxford: Oxford University Press, 2022.

Mbiti, John. *African Religions and Philosophy*. 2nd ed. Oxford: Heinemann, 1990.

McDonald, Melissa M., Andrew M. Defever, and Carlos David Navarrete. "Killing for the Greater Good: Action Aversion and the Emotional Inhibition of Harm in Moral Dilemmas." *Evolution and Human Behavior* 38, no. 6 (2017): 770–78.

McMahon, Darrin. "To Write the History of Equality." *History and Theory* 58, no. 1 (2019): 112–25.

Merrett, Christopher. *Sport, Space and Segregation: Politics and Society in Pietermaritzburg*. Scotsville, South Africa: University of KwaZula-Natal Press, 2009.

Métraux, Alfred. *L'homme et la terre dans la vallé de Marbial*. Paris: UNESCO, 1951.

Michel, Georges. "Le procès des auteurs du massacre du 27 juillet 1915." *Revue de la société haïtienne d'histoire et de géographie* 196 (1998).

Mintz, Sidney W. *Caribbean Transformations*. Chicago: Aldine Publishing, 1974.

——. "Groups, Group Boundaries and the Perception of Race." *Comparative Studies in Society and History* 13, no. 4 (1971): 437–50.

——. "Papa Doc Is Dead But the 'Mystery' Lingers On." *New York Times*, April 25, 1971.

——. *Three Ancient Colonies: Caribbean Themes and Variations.* Cambridge, MA: Harvard University Press, 2010.

Mintz, Sidney W., ed. *Working papers in Haitian Society and Culture.* New Haven, CT: Antilles Research Program, Yale University, 1975.

Moïse, Claude. *Constitutions et luttes de pouvoir en Haïti (1804–1987).* Montreal: CIDIHCA, 1990.

Molinari, Gustave de. *A Panama. L'isthme de Panama, la Martinique, Haïti: lettres adressées au Journal des débats.* Paris: Guillaumin et Cie, 1887.

Mongey, Vanessa. "A Tale of Two Brothers: Haiti's Other Revolutions." *Americas* 69, no. 1 (2012): 37–60.

Montaigne, Michel de. *Les essais: édition complète.* Edited by André Lanly. Paris: Gallimard, 2009.

Morgan, David. *Acquaintances: The Space Between Intimates and Strangers.* Maidenhead, UK: Open University Press, 2009.

Moses, A. Dirk. "Structure and Agency in the Holocaust: Daniel J. Goldhagen and His Critics." *History and Theory* 37, no. 2 (1998): 194–219.

Moses, A. Dirk, ed. *Empire, Colony, Genocide: Conquest, Occupation, and Subaltern Resistance in World History.* New York: Berghahn Books, 2008.

Mullins, Christopher. "We Are Going to Rape You and Taste Tutsi Women: Rape During the 1994 Rwanda Genocide." *British Journal of Criminology* 49, no. 6 (2009): 719–35.

Munro, Martin. *Exile and Post-1946 Haitian Literature: Alexis, Depestre, Ollivier, Laffèrière, Danticat.* Liverpool, UK: Liverpool University Press, 2007.

Nérée, Bob, *Duvalier. Le pouvoir sur les autres, de père en fils.* Port-au-Prince: Henri Deschamps, 1988.

Nicholls, David. "Biology and Politics in Haiti." *Race* 13, no. 2 (1971): 203–14.

——. "The Duvalier Regime in Haiti." In *Sultanistic Regimes,* edited by H. E. Chehabi and Juan J. Linz, 153–81. Baltimore, MD: Johns Hopkins University Press, 1998.

——. "Embryo-politics in Haiti." *Government and Opposition* 6, no. 1 (1971): 75–85.

——. *From Dessalines to Duvalier: Race, Colour and National Independence in Haiti.* Rev. ed. New Brunswick, NJ: Rutgers University Press, 1996.

——. "Ideology and Political Protest in Haiti, 1930–46." *Journal of Contemporary History* 9, no. 4 (1974): 3–26.

——. "On Controlling the Colonels." *Hemisphere Report* (Trinidad), 1970.

——. "Review." *The Hispanic American Historical Review* 71 no. 3 (1991): 650–52.

——. "The Wisdom of Salomon: Myth or Reality?" *Journal of Interamerican Studies and World Affairs* 20, no. 4 (1978): 377–92.

Nightingale, Carl H. *Segregation: A Global History of Divided Cities.* Chicago: Chicago University Press, 2012.

Organisation extérieure du Parti unifié des communistes haïtiens. *Haïti sous Duvalier: terrorisme d'État et visages de la résistance nationale.* Port-au-Prince: Parti unifié des communistes haïtiens, 1973.

Oriol, Michèle. *Chefs d'Etat en Haïti: gloire et misères.* Port-au-Prince: Fondation pour la recherche iconographique et documentaire, 2006.

——. *Chronologie de l'histoire d'Haïti.* Port-au-Prince: Éditions de l'Université d'État d'Haïti, 2013.

——. *Histoire et éducation civique.* Port-au-Prince: Fondation pour la recherche iconographique et documentaire, 2001.

——. "Ministres des deux Duvaliers." Unpublished manuscript, 2018.

——. *La terre et les hommes*, Montreal: CIDIHCA, forthcoming.

Ortner, Sherry. "Dark Anthropology and Its Others: Theory Since the Eighties." *HAU: Journal of Ethnographic Theory* 6, no. 1 (2016): 47–73.

Orwell, George. *The Collected Essays, Journalism, and Letters of George Orwell: "My Country Right or Left" 1940–1943*. Vol. 2. London: Secker & Warburg, 1968.

Parsons, Talcott. "Equality and Inequality in Modern Society, or Social Stratification Revisited." *Sociological Inquiry* 40, no. 2 (1970): 13–72.

Parti unifié des communistes haïtiens. *Haiti sous Duvalier: terrorisme d'État et visages de la résistance nationale*. N.p., Organisation extérieure du Parti unifié des communistes haïtiens, 1972.

Pascal-Trouillot, Ertha, and Ernst Trouillot. *Encyclopédie Biographique d'Haïti*. Montreal: Semis, 2001.

Paul, Edmond. *Les causes de nos malheurs. Appel au peuple*. Kingston, Jamaica: G. Henderson, 1882.

Péan, Leslie Jean-Robert. *Aux origines de l'état marron en Haïti*. Port-au-Prince: Presses de l'Université d'État d'Haïti, 2009.

——. *L'ensauvagement macoute et ses conséquences, 1957–1990*. Vol. 4 of *Haïti: économie politique de la corruption*. Paris: Maisonneuve et Larose, 2007.

——. *L'état marron, 1870–1915*. Vol. 2 of *Haïti: économie politique de la corruption*. Paris: Maisonneuve et Larose, 2004.

——. "Haiti/1915-100 ans. L'occupation américaine et les larmes de sang prédites par Hannibal Price." First installment. *AlterPresse*, July 24, 2015.

——. "La semaine Dessalines: le mauvais chemin pris par Haïti dans l'histoire." 7 installments. *AlterPresse*, October 13–19, 2015.

Péralte, Charlemagne. "Bandits or Patriots? Documents of Charlemagne Péralte, National Archives." Translated. by Elena and Kirill Razlogova. History Matters: The U.S. Survey Course on the Web, last updated March 22, 2018, George Mason University, http://historymatters.gmu.edu/d/4946/.

Pierre-Etienne, Sauveur. *L'énigme haïtienne. Échec de l'État moderne en Haïti*. Montréal: Mémoire d'Encrier, 2007.

Pierre, Luc. *Haïti. Les origines du chaos*. Port-au-Prince: Henri Deschamps, 1997.

Pierre, Pressoir. *Témoignages, 1946–1976: l'espérance déçue*. Port-au-Prince: Henri Deschamps, 1987.

Pierre-Audin, Julio J. *Les ombres d'une politique néfaste*. Mexico City: n.p., 1976.

Pierre-Charles, Gérard. *Radiographie d'une dictature: Haïti et Duvalier*. Preface by Juan Bosch. Montreal: Nouvelle Optique, 1973.

——. "Un entretien avec Gérard Pierre-Charles. La problématique du Duvaliérisme." *Le Nouvelliste*, August 16, 15, 17, 1986.

Pierre-Charles, Gérard, ed. *Haïti, jamais, jamais plus! Les violations de droits de l'homme à l'époque des Duvalier*. Port-au-Prince: Centre de recherche et de formation économique et sociale pour le développement, 2000.

Piliavsky, Anastasia. *Nobody's People. Hierarchy as Hope in a Society of Thieves*. Stanford, CA: Stanford University Press, 2020.

Pina-Cabral, João de. *World: An Anthropological Examination*. Chicago: HAU Books, 2017.

Piquion, René. *Crépuscule de mythes*. Port-au-Prince: Imprimerie de l'État, 1962.

——. *Manuel de négritude*. Port-au-Prince: Henri Deschamps, 1966.

——. *Masques et portraits (réponse à une lettre du Dr Jean Price Mars sur la 'question sociale et politique en Haïti').* Port-au-Prince: Presses nationales d'Haïti, 1967.

Plummer, Brenda Gayle. *Haiti and the Great Powers, 1902–1915.* Baton Rouge: Louisiana State University Press, 1988.

——. "The Metropolitan Connection: Foreign and Semiforeign Elites in Haiti, 1900–1915." *Latin American Research Review* 19, no. 2 (1984): 119–42.

Pradine, Linstant, ed. *Recueil général des lois et des actes du gouvernement d'Haïti depuis la proclamation de son indépendance jusqu'à nos jours.* Vol. 1, *1804–1808.* Paris: A. Durand et Pédone-Lauriel, 1886.

Price, Hannibal. *De la réhabilitation de la race noire par la République d'Haïti.* Port-au-Prince: J. Verrollot, 1900.

Price-Mars, Jean. *Jean-Pierre Boyer Bazelais et le drame de Miragoâne: à propos d'un lot d'autographes, 1883–1884.* Port-au-Prince: Imprimerie d'État, 1948.

——. *Lettre ouverte au Dr. René Piquion, directeur de l'École normale supérieure, sur son "Manuel de la négritude": Le préjugé de couleur est-il la question sociale?* 2nd ed. Port-au-Prince: Éditions des Antilles, 1967.

——. *La vocation de l'élite.* Port-au-Prince: E. Chenet, 1919

Raaflaud, Kurt A. "Caesar and Genocide: Confronting the Dark Side of Caesar's Gallic Wars," *New England Classical Journal* 48, no. 1 (2021): 54–80.

Radio Haïti-Inter. "Temwayaj 26 avril 1963." Aired on Radio Haïti-Inter in 1987. Human Rights Archive, Duke Digital Repository. Permalink: https://idn.duke.edu/ark:/87924/r4sf2pn5n

Radio Kiskeya, "Le poète et journaliste haïtien Jacques Roche kidnappé et exécuté à Port-au-Prince." Aired on Radio Kiskeya, July 14, 2005.

Rambaud, Michel. *L'art de la déformation historique dans les Commentaires de César.* Paris: Les Belles Lettres, 2011.

Redfield, Robert. *The Little Community and Peasant Society and Culture.* Chicago: University of Chicago Press, 1960.

René, Jean Alix. "Le culte de l'égalité: une exploration du processus de formation de l'État et de la politique dministr en Haïti au cours de la première moitié du dix-neuvième siècle (1804–1846)." PhD diss., Concordia University, 2014.

——, *Haïti après l'esclavage: formation de l'État et culture politique dministr, 1804–1846.* Port-au-Prince: Le Natal, 2019.

Ribeiro Thomaz, Omar. "Haitian Elites and Their Perception of Poverty and Inequality." In *Elite Perceptions of Poverty and Inequality,* edited by Elisa Pereira Reis and Mick Moore, 127–55. London and New York: Zed Books, 2005.

Rigaud, Milo. *Lettre aux Haïtiens de toutes couleurs.* Port-au-Prince, February 9, 1946.

Rigaud, Milo. *Jésus ou Legba? ou, les dieux se battent.* Poitiers: Amis de la poésie, 1933.

Robben, Antonius C. G. M., and Alexander Laban Hinton. *Perpetrators: Encountering Humanity's Dark Side.* Stanford, CA: Stanford University Press, 2023.

Romulus, Marc. *Les cachots des Duvalier: Marc Romulus, ex-prisonnier politique, témoigne.* Montreal: Carrefour international, 1978.

Rosanvallon, Pierre. *The Society of Equals.* Cambridge, MA: Harvard University Press, 2013.

Rosier, Claude. *Le triangle de la mort. Journal d'un prisonnier politique haïtien, 1966–1977.* Port-au-Prince: n.p., 2003.

Rosso, Corrado. *Mythe de l'égalité et rayonnement des lumières.* Pisa: Goliardica, 1980.

Rotberg, Robert. *Haiti, the Politics of Squalor.* Boston: Houghton Mifflin, 1971.

Roumer, Andrée. "Andrée Roumer, sa dernière épouse parle de Jacques-Stephen Alexis." Interview by Frantz Duval. *Le Nouvelliste,* May 16, 2022.

Rouzier, Arthur. *Les belles figures de l'intelligentsia jérémienne: du temps passé—et du present.* Port-au-Prince: n.p., 1986.

Rouzier, Semexant. *Dictionnaire géographique et administratif universel d'Haïti illustré.* Vol. 1. Paris: Charles Blot, 1892.

——. *Dictionnaire géographique et adminsitratif universel d'Haïti illustré.* Vol. 3. Port-au-Prince: August A. Héraux, 1927.

Sahlins, Marshall. *Apologies to Thucydides: Understanding History as Culture and Vice Versa* Chicago: University of Chicago Press, 2004.

——. *Islands of History.* Chicago: University of Chicago Press, 1985.

——. "What Kinship Is." *Journal of the Royal Anthropological Institute* 17, no. (2011): 2–19.

Saint-Louis, Vertus. "L'assassinat de Dessalines et le culte de sa mémoire." *Revista Brasileira do Caribe* 16, no. 31 (2015): 95–124.

Saint-Méry, Moreau de. *Description topographique, physique, civile, politique et historique de la partie francaise de l'isle Saint-Domingue.* Philadelphia: n.p., 1797.

Sainte-Claire, Linsey. "Régénération et élitisme scolaire sous Alexandre Pétion et Jean-Pierre Boyer (1816–1843)." *Esprit créateur* 56, no. 1 (2016): 116–28.

Salomon, Lysius Félicité. "Discours du 23 avril 1882." *Le Moniteur,* May 6, 1882.

Sansaricq, Lidia. *Traición multiple.* Montral: CIDIHCA, 2015.

Santoni, Ronald E. *Sartre on Violence: Curiously Ambivalent.* University Park: Pennsylvania State University Press, 2003.

Sartre, Jean-Paul. *Critique de la raison dialectique: précédé de Question de méthode.* Paris: Gallimard, 1960.

——. Preface to *Les damnés de la terre,* by Frantz Fanon. Paris: La Découverte, 2004.

Schiavone, Aldo. *The Pursuit of Equality in the West.* Translated by Jeremy Carden. Cambridge. MA: Harvard University Press, 2022.

Schneider, David M. *A Critique of the Study of Kinship.* Ann Arbor: University of Michigan Press, 1984.

Schoeck, Helmut. *Envy: A Theory of Social Behavior.* New York: Harcourt, Brace and World, 1969.

Schoelcher, Victor. *Colonies étrangères et Haïti, résultats de l'émancipation anglaise.* 2 vols. Paris: Pagnerre, 1843.

Scott, James C. *Weapons of the Weak: Everyday Forms of Peasant Resistance.* New Haven, CT: Yale University Press, 1985.

Sémelin, Jacques. "The Notion of Social Reactivity: The French Case, 1942–1944." In *Probing the Limits of Categorization: The Bystander in Holocaust History,* edited by Christina Morina and Krijn Thijs, 224–44. New York: Berghahn Books, 2019.

——. *Persécutions et entraides dans la France occupée: comment 75% des Juifs en France ont échappé la mort.* Paris: Les Arènes, 2013.

——. *Purify and Destroy: The Political Uses of Massacre and Genocide.* New York: Columbia University Press, 2007.

Sénéchal, Jean-François. *Le mythe révolutionnaire duvaliériste.* Montral: CIDIHCA, 2006.

Senghor, Léopold Sédar. "Préface." In *Le dossier Haïti: un pays en péril*, Catherine Eve di Chiara, Paris: Tallandier, 1988.

Sereny, Gitta. *Into that Darkness: An Examination of Conscience*. London: Vintage Books, 1983.

Sheller, Mimi. *Citizenship from Below: Erotic Agency and Caribbean Freedom*. Durham, NC: Duke University Press, 2012.

——. *Democracy After Slavery: Black Publics and Peasant Radicalism in Haiti and Jamaica*. Gainesville: University Press of Florida, 2000.

Shils, Edward. "Primordial, Personal, Sacred and Civil Ties: Some Particular Observations on the Relationships of Sociological Research and Theory." *British Journal of Sociology* 8, no. 2 (1957): 130–45.

Simmel, Georg. *The Sociology of Georg Simmel*. Edited and translated by Kurt H. Wolff. Glencoe, IL: Free Press, 1964.

Singh, Bhrigupati. *Poverty and the Quest for Life: Spiritual and Material Striving in Rural India*. Chicago: Chicago University Press, 2015.

Sloterdijk, Peter. *Die schrecklichen Kinder der Neuzeit: Über das anti-genealogische Experiment der Moderne*. Berlin: Suhrkamp, 2014.

Smeulers, Alette, Maartje Weerdesteijn, and Barbora Holá, eds. *Perpetrators of International Crimes: Theories, Methods, and Evidence*. Oxford: Oxford University Press, 2019.

Smith, David Norman. "The Psychological Roots of Genocide: Legitimacy and Crisis in Rwanda." *American Psychologist* 53, no. 7 (1998): 743–53.

——. "The Social Construction of the Enemies: Jews and Representations of Evil." *Sociological Theory* 4, no. 2 (1996): 203–40.

Smith, Matthew J. *Liberty, Fraternity, Exile. Haiti and Jamaica after Emancipation*. Chapel Hill: The University of North Carolina Press, 2014.

——. *Red and Black in Haiti: Radicalism, Conflict, and Political Change*. University of North Carolina Press, 2009.

Smith, Pierre Michel. "Jérémie demande des comptes sur le genocide de 1964." *Haiti Connexion Culture*, October 29, 2014. http://haiticonnexion-culture.blogspot.com/2014/10/.

Société haïtienne d'histoire et de géographie. *Revue de la Société d'histoire et de géographie d'Haïti* 3, no. 8 (1932).

Son, Jiyoung. "How Communist Is North Korea? From the Birth to the Death of Marxist Ideas of Human Rights." *Cambridge Journal of International Affairs* 23, no. 4 (2010): 561–87.

Song, Yongyi, "The Enduring Legacy of Blood Lineage Theory." *China Rights Forum* 4 (2004): 13–23.

Steflja, Izabela and Jessica Trisko Darden. *Women as War Criminals: Gender, Agency, and Justice*. Stanford, CA: Stanford University Press, 2020.

Stieber, Chelsea. "Gérard de Catalogne, passeur transatlantique du maurrassisme entre Haïti et la France." In *Doctrinaires, vulgarisateurs et passeurs des droites radicales au vingtième siècle (Europe-Amériques)*, edited by Olivier Dard, 232–254. Bern, Switzerland: Peter Lang, 2012.

——. *Haiti's Paper War: Post-Independence Writing, Civil War, and the Making of the Republic, 1804–1954*. New York: New York University Press, 2020.

——. "The Northern *récit paysan*: Regional Variations of the Modern Peasant Novel in Haiti." *French Studies* 70, no. 1 (2016): 44–60.

——. "The Vocation of the *indigènes*: Cosmopolitism and Cultural Nationalism in *La revue indigène.*" *Francosphères* 4, no. 1 (2015): 7–19.

Stoler, Ann. *Along the Archival Grain: Epistemic Anxieties and Colonial Common Sense.* Princeton: Princeton University Press, 2009.

Stourzh, Gérald. "Penser l'égalité. Cinq notions d'égalité chez Tocqueville." *Droits* 41, no. 1 (2005): 185–98.

Strathern, Marilyn. *The Gender of the Gift: Problems with Women and Problems with Society in Melanesia.* Berkeley: University of California Press, 1988.

——. *Relations: An Anthropological Account.* Durham, NC: Duke University Press, 2020.

Stuurman, Siep. *François Poulain de la Barre and the Invention of Modern Equality.* Cambridge, MA: Harvard University Press, 2004.

Supplice, Daniel. *Dictionnaire biographique des personnalités politiques de la République d'Haïti, 1804–2014.* Pétionville, Haiti: C3 Éditions, 2014.

Szulc, Tad. "Wave of Killings in Haiti Reported." *New York Times,* August 23, 1964.

Tackett, Timothy. *The Coming of the Terror in the French Revolution.* Cambridge, MA: Belknap. Press of Harvard University Press, 2015.

Taguieff, Pierre-André. *L'antisémitisme.* Paris: Presses universitaires de France, 2015.

——. *Court traité de complotologie, suivi de le "Complot judéo-maçonnique": fabrication d'un mythe apocalyptique moderne.* Paris: Mille et une nuits, 2013

——. *Criminaliser les Juifs: le mythe du "meurtre rituel" et ses avatars (antijudaïsme, antisémitisme, antisionisme).* Paris: Hermann, 2020.

——. *The Force of Prejudice: On Racism and Its Doubles.* Minneapolis: University of Minnesota Press, 2001.

Taylor, Christopher. "A Gendered Genocide: Tutsi Women and Hutu Extremists in the 1994 Rwanda Genocide." *Political and Legal Anthropology* 22, no. 1 (1999): 42–54.

Thelen, Tatjana, Larissa Vetters, and Keebet von Benda-Beckmann, eds. *Stategraphy: Toward a Relational Anthropology of the State.* New York: Berghahn, 2018.

Thompson, Allan, ed. *The Media and the Rwanda Genocide.* London: Pluto Press, 1999.

Thompson, Francis M.L. *The Rise of Respectable Society: A Social History of Victorian Britain, 1830–1900.* London: HarperCollins, 1988.

Thomson, Ian, *Bonjour Blanc: A Journey Through Haiti.* New York: Vintage, 2004.

Tocqueville, Alexis de. *The Ancien Regime and the Revolution.* Translated by Gerald Bevan. New York: Penguin Classics, 2008.

Totten, Samuel, Paul R. Bartrop, and Steven L. Jacobs. *Dictionary of Genocide.* 2 vols. Westport, CT: Greenwood Publishing, 2009.

Trouillot, Hénock. *Beaubrun Ardouin: l'homme politique et l'historien.* Port-au-Prince, n.p., 1950.

——. *L'intellectuel de couleur et les problèmes de la discrimination raciale.* Port-au-Prince: Imprimerie de l'État, 1956.

——. *M. Dantes Bellegarde, un écrivain d'autrefois.* Port-au-Prince: Imprimerie N.A. Théodore, 1957.

Trouillot, Jocelyne. *Histoire de l'éducation en Haïti.* Port-au-Prince: Éditions Université Caraïbes, 2003.

Trouillot, Michel-Rolph. "Culture, Color, and Politics." In *Race,* edited by Steven Gregory and Roger Sanjet, 146–74. New Brunswick, NJ: Rutgers University Press, 1994.

——. *Haiti, State Against Nation. The Origins and Legacy of Duvalierism.* New York: Monthly Review Press, 1990.

——. *Silencing the Past: Power and the Production of History.* Boston: Beacon Press, 1995.

——. "A Social Contract for Whom? Haitian History and Haitian Future." In *Haiti Renewed. Political and Economic Prospects,* edited by Robert Rotberg, 47–59. Washington, DC: Brookings Institution Press, 1997.

Tylor, Edward Burnett. *Primitive Culture: Researches Into the Development of Mythology, Philosophy, Religion, Art, and Custom.* Vol. 2. London: John Murray, 1871.

Velton, Ross. *Haiti and the Dominican Republic: The Island of Hispaniola* (Chalfont St. Peter, UK: Bradt, 1999).

Verbitsky, Horacio. *El vuelo.* Buenos Aires: Planta, 1995.

Vigoureux, Gustave. *L'année terrible; ou 1883 à Jérémie.* Jeremie, Haiti: Imprimerie du Centenaire, 1909.

——. *Brice et Salnave.* Jeremie, Haiti: Imprimerie du Centenaire, 1922.

Voltaire, Franz, dir. *Au nom du père . . . Duvalier.* Co-produced by Didier Berry. Montreal: CIDI-HCA and MBETV TV, 2004. 52 min.

Voltaire, Franz, ed. *Pouvoir noir en Haiti: l'explosion de 1946.* Montreal: CIDIHCA, 2019.

Wade, Peter. *Race and Sex in Latin America.* London: Pluto Press, 2009.

Washington Office on Haiti. *Report to Congress One Year After Duvalier.* Washington, DC: Washington Office on Haiti, 1987.

Wang, Cheng-Chih. *Words Kill: Calling for the Destruction of "Class Enemies" in China, 1949–1953.* New York: Routledge, 2002.

Weber, Max. *Economy and Society: An Outline of Interpretive Sociology.* Edited by Guenther Roth and Claus Wittich. Berkeley: University of California Press, 1978.

Wèche, Mérès. *Le songe d'une nuit de carnage: une évocation des vêpres de Jérémie, 1964.* Port-au-Prince: Collection-Antilles, 2011.

Wolf, Eric. *Europe and the People Without History.* Los Angeles: University of California Press, 1982.

Yang, Rae. *Spider Eaters: A Memoir.* Los Angeles: University of California Press, 2013.

Zacair, Philippe. "Immigrés guadeloupéens et martiniquais en Haiti dans le regard des consuls français (1848–1900)." *Bulletin de la Société d'histoire de la Guadeloupe* 154 (2009): 59–77.

Zipperstein, Steven J. *Pogrom: Kishinev and the Tilt of History.* New York: Liveright, 2018.

Index

Cover Captions

Top row, left to right:
Louise Sansaricq and three of her children, circa 1945. Source: *Devoir de Mémoire*; Jean-Philippe Vil-Lubin. Source: *Schomburg Center for Research in Black Culture*; Jean-Claude and Graziela Sansaricq. Source: Guy Drouin, *Devoir de Mémoire*; Joe Gaetjens after scoring the winning goal for the United States, 1950. Source: *Public Domain*.

Second row, left to right:
Lionel Bance. Source: Bance family, *Devoir de Mémoire*; Gérard and Aline Guilbaud. Source: Guy Drouin, *Devoir de Mémoire*; Broussais Brice. Source: *Fondation pour la recherche iconographique et documentaire*; Oreste Zamor. Source: *Public Domain*; René Péan. Source: Péan family, *Devoir de Mémoire*; Horace Coicou. Source: Collection Jean-Claude Bruffaerts.

Third row, left to right:
Ghislaine Edline Duchatelier. Source: *Devoir de Mémoire*; Albert Poitevin. Source: *Devoir de Mémoire*; Jacques-Stephen Alexis. Source: *Public domain*; Edith Laforest, Pierre Sansaricq, and Louise Laforest. Source: May Sansaricq; Col. Edouard Roy. Source: Ed Thébaud.

Fourth row, left to right:
Eric Tippenhauer. Source: *Devoir de Mémoire*; Graziela Sansaricq and her three children. Source: Guy Drouin, *Devoir de Mémoire*.

Fifth row, left to right:
Jean Bouchereau. Source: *Devoir de Mémoire*; Jean-Jacques Dessalines Ambroise. Source: *Public Domain*; Ducasse Jumelle. Source: *Devoir de Mémoire*; Guy Drouin.

Source: Guy Drouin (self-portrait), *Devoir de Mémoire*; Jean Chenet. Source: *Rockefeller Foundation Archives*.

Bottom row, left to right:

Antonio Vieux, circa 1948. Source: *Centre International de Documentation et d'Information Haitienne, Caribéenne et Afro-Canadienne (CIDIHCA)*; Adrien Sansaricq. Source: Eddy Cavé; Pierre and Louise Sansaricq. Source: *Devoir de Mémoire*.

GPSR Authorized Representative: Easy Access System Europe, Mustamäe tee
50, 10621 Tallinn, Estonia, gpsr.requests@easproject.com

www.ingramcontent.com/pod-product-compliance
Lightning Source LLC
LaVergne TN
LVHW091807170425
808934LV00008B/170